# INTIMATIONS
## *of* LOVE
## DIVINE

**ROBERT ALEXANDER ANDERSON**

ISBN 0 9529488 0 X


British Library Cataloguing in Publication Data.
A catalogue record of this book is available from the British Library.



Published by

Leaping Salmon Trust
PO Box 12750
Musselburgh
EH21 8YZ
Scotland

*"So do not be afraid of people.*
*Whatever is now covered up will be uncovered,*
*and every secret will be made known.*
*What I am telling you in the dark*
*you must repeat in broad daylight,*
*and what you have heard in private,*
*you must announce from the housetops.*

*Do not be afraid of those who kill the body*
*but cannot kill the soul;*
*rather be afraid of God,*
*who can destroy both body and soul in hell.*

*For only a penny you can buy two sparrows,*
*yet not one sparrow falls to the ground*
*without your Father's consent.*

*As for you, even the hairs of your head*
*have all been counted.*
*So do not be afraid;*
*you are worth much more than many sparrows"*

*(Matthew 10: 26-31)*

for the seeking - encouragement

for the believing - strengthening

for the doubting - evidence

for the dismissive - warning

# Acknowledgements

I wish to acknowledge the prayers, friendship, encouragement and personal kindness of many people throughout my life.

I am grateful to Dr Hugh Montgomery and Christine Main for helpful suggestions on presentation.

# CONTENTS

# *Introduction*

The claims of Christianity are true. It is possible to know God in and through Jesus Christ. Personal destiny is to be found in relationship to God and the life eternal beyond this physical existence. All human achievement finds its proper context in comparison with this discovered truth. This is not a matter of private psychology as Calvary was not. There is possible a dynamic and historical relationship of love between each human being and our Maker. This is at once the best and highest and deepest of relationships. Confirmations and verifications are possible within the logic of our Maker's revelation to persons. It is possible to meet and to know Jesus Christ and to receive the realities of His spiritual promises. It is even possible to actually glimpse the life to follow in all its blessedness and joy.

The events of the twentieth century, likely to be continued in the twenty-first which mark the decline and dissolution of Christianised Europe are historically similar to those which accompanied the downfall of the Roman Empire in the fifth and sixth centuries. Today's political constructs are as likely to fail as other such attempts have failed in the past. Religious wars and economic grievances will breach the walls of fortress Europe. St Augustine mentally struggled with the complex issues of the political and military fragmentation of the once great Roman Empire. Likewise the downfall of Israel between the eighth and sixth centuries before Christ was accompanied by the same kinds of actions and reactions. Israel's classical prophets attempted to explain the causes of that nation's eclipse. They sought to interpret human history in relation to God. They attempted to defend God against human criticism and to explain the best reasons why human beings should continue to relate to God in personal devotion, collective faith and neighbourly action.

Reconciling belief in God's election with actual providence was not easy for Israel's prophets. They laid the blame for Israel's demise by and large on the spiritual apostasy of the chosen people, on elective personal immorality, on social injustice, on religious syncretism and on the unwillingness and failure of most people to respond with love and joy to their Maker's love for them. Loss of their distinct and spiritual vocation mean that the raison d'être of the chosen people had been extinguished.

For Augustine, history had a beginning, a middle and an end. The earthly city, Rome, which had been defeated, represented the lust of power and possession, the will to dominate, exploit and inflict suffering, personal choices of hedonism and self-indulgence and many other proud frailties of human character. The political and economic order was wrecked. These were not permanent entities. The heavenly city of eternal salvation, light, truth and faith in Christ would remain, said Augustine, long after the earthly city had collapsed. He was right.

Equal factors are present in contemporary Europe. Nations with Christian histories cannot repudiate such history with impunity. The secular is not the equal of the spiritual. Counter forces of destructive effect take the place of the saving system that Christianity represents within human consciousness and community. There are no neutralities. Scientific rationalism negates the supernatural, yet the power and influence of the supernatural does not abate. It just takes different forms, less coherent, less noble, less good, less effective, less saving than Christianity. The vacuum thus created is then filled with many alternatives, creating fragmentations of competing interpretations instead of adherence to one living Maker revealed in Jesus Christ. To each and all of these every individual human life is vulnerable. Societies which are organised on false premises sow seeds of self-destruction. Nations which exalt and divinise themselves create monsters for future generations to deal with as the history of Germany in the nineteenth and twentieth century shows. World agencies which try to limit the inherent capacity of the human community to damage and obliterate itself will be under greater pressure to continue to do so. This will lead to oppressive new systems of law enforcement. The spirit of humanity will be in chains. Christianity will erupt from within this enclosed system. Remnant representatives of the prodigal human race, conscious of a better sense of purpose and destiny will return to their Maker in acknowledgement. The age old struggles will continue. Israel, Rome, Europe - the world!

At such a time as this, in and during the life given to me on earth, I have found myself wrestling with God and struggling with my fellow human beings. This book describes some of the wrestling and some of the struggling. The central issue is relationship with our Maker. You must recognise the higher purpose of this book. It is to corroborate the claims of Christianity. This is not subjective retreat from reality though doubtless some critics will think so. Indeed, the relationship between truth and history is what matters throughout.

For me there is not likely to be peace. I do not seek recognition nor acceptance. I seek to be of service. It is necessary for me to share the vision in order to declare the reality of God. Easier it would be to remain in blissful anonymity. Scotland is an excellent place for such a condition. Sacrificial indeed to put my failing sinful life under future scrutiny, to be expected to live up to the greatness of God which I as a human can never do and to be an agent of renewal of the minds and lives of others. Never fear. Scots and Scotland will not let me rise above much. Yet - into such an inhibiting and unrewarding climate the true vision may fall and seed may grow in time, thereafter to wind its way into the hearts of any who seek their own Maker and follow the inner spiritual imperative which has commanded me all my days. And if it is only in the heart of the single one, here and there, that this book finds use and value, then it will have served its purpose. However, God among us is a reviving, vivifying, stimulating, imaginative and revolutionary personal power and agency. So was Jesus. The Spirit will blow where the Spirit wills. No area of human consciousness or community can be untouched.

This book is not an autobiography. It is an attempt to relate the results and consequences of my search for God. I might say - of God's calling of me - but I will let readers form their own conclusions. God will have the last evaluation of my life. This book is written to share the things that have happened to me which so many of the thinkers of our time tell us cannot happen. I have found God and been found by God. But the opening of God's life to me has been amidst turmoil and crisis.

I have not fought and struggled with the world as such. My battles have been with people claiming to be Christians in the visible churches. I did not go looking for trouble. Rather, I was thrown into successive troubled circumstances and in becoming involved and then in extricating myself I found God to be present for me. Especially and supremely so. I am surprised that I am still alive and that I have been given the grace to write this book.

No doubt the struggle will now intensify. It would be foolish and naive to think otherwise. The issues however of the reality of God in Jesus Christ in our midst are far too great for me to keep what has happened to me in my life silent and to myself. I wish I could believe that those who name Jesus Christ in churches might respond with understanding. The contrary is as much likely.

Life and death are risked in publishing such a book as this. Here is no fiction, no faction, no allegory, no extended parable. For our Maker is part of our personal history, human social evolution, national destiny and global future ever since the Incarnation in Jesus Christ. Many have lived close to God. Even today, in what may appear to be an apostate society, many men, women and children talk of deep personal experience of God. I myself am no perfect specimen of Christianity. I am however making the claim that on occasions, God has spoken and acted for and through me in a redemptive way.

My concern is that we may all be taken up out of ourselves and into our Maker's friendship and that this truest purpose of human living may be known to as many as can receive such knowledge with a welcoming heart and mind. Given the knowledge of God in the Judaeo-Christian tradition, we would not expect in a struggling time for Christianity, to be left without such a witness.

I have a commitment to the Providence of God in Scotland. To live and die here. A prophet is not without honour except in his own country. I will not go away. I do not seek conflict but the renewal and revival of Christianity. How strange that the churches in Scotland representing so many good things in the history of Christianity on earth, consumed as they are by theological division, greed and power seeking miniatures of Christian character should fail to see the causes of their collective demise.

I have risked much and all throughout my calling. I have tried to find in the outcoming of disagreements, struggles and battles the truth of God. I have sought to give God space to order events. Mine has been the way of negation and of self-surrender. I have been prepared before God to say 'I was wrong'. I have known loss and restoration and death and life. To go 'public' is a great risk but I am bidden not to bury this talent in the ground for ever.

Above all personal and human considerations, collective, global whatever, this book tells of the kind of Being our Maker is. The manner in which God will speak to us and deal with us in and through Jesus Christ. The lovely Person God is. The beautiful things God does. The gift of eternal life and friendship with God. The highest aspirations of the human spirit concluded. The finitude of earthly life answered. The promise of the continuation of a good purpose in creation, understood eternally. Jesus Christ as the only Mediator of all of this. To these the very best and highest of human hopes, I am a witness.

Robert Anderson

Edinburgh

October 1996

On The Thirtieth Anniversary Of My Call To The Ministry

# *1 : The Spirit Within*

## A Childhood Memory

When I was six years old, I was taken to Seafield Hospital in Ayr to have my tonsils removed. As I lay recovering from the operation, a boy in the bed next to me began to cry. He was about the same age as myself. He became more and more upset. I asked him where he came from and he said "Saltcoats." He continued to cry and no-one came to comfort him. I felt that I should try to help him. I stretched out my arm and asked him to hold my hand. I was vividly aware of a force of spiritual energy, light, power, strength and love passing through me to the boy. Within seconds he was at peace. Then he fell asleep. The next day we said "Bye" to each other, smiling, each in his own way blessed.

## Normality

I was born on 3rd April 1947, at home, Garnock Bank, in Kilwinning, Ayrshire, Scotland, the second child and first son of Alexander and Jessie Anderson. I was given the names of my maternal grandfather and father. 'Robert' in folk lore means 'bright in fame', Alexander is 'a helper of men' and Anderson derives from Andrew which in turn derives from the Greek 'aner andros 'o' meaning ' a male person of full age and stature'.

We were far from rich but my parents were dedicated to Shona, myself and Alex jnr. and we wanted for nothing good. I was fortunate to have my own world play area behind our house, a field, a market garden, a private road, trees, stables. People were always coming and going. I used to 'help' old Mr Sloan with his vegetables. Later I 'helped' Davy Muir with his horse and cart and later still in my early teens I helped Alex McKie with his pleasure boats and his brother Tom with his garage in the centre of the town. To the front and below our house lay the main road between Irvine and Ardrossan. Beyond it the River Garnock wound its way to meet the River Irvine at its estuary. Cars, buses, lorries, motor-cycles all passed by and I learned the names of every one of them, taking down thousands of registration numbers - for what purpose I cannot now remember. At school I was usually fairly near the top of my primary school classes but I did not excel in anything. I neither disliked nor particularly enjoyed school. Summer holidays, on the other hand, were much anticipated from one year to the next. I enjoyed playing with my Dinky toys and they were my consolation after school. My friend of many years was Lucky, our pet terrier. Lucky lived a long life to bark at and chase many postmen.

Teen-age years for me were as for so many, a strange mixture of seeking and growing and changing and of confusion and rejoicing. At school my progress was satisfactory but not brilliant. I was learning to play the piano but finding the severity of my teacher difficult to bear. I found myself playing a drum for a school band and persuaded my parents to buy me a second-hand drum kit. Later four of us formed a Beatles style pop group called 'The Arrows' and that kept me out of mischief for a while. Then I played piano in a Glasgow based quartet for a brief period before gladly giving it up for more spiritual things.

I think I was under-occupied and under-stimulated in childhood but otherwise was blessed with a sane and healthy environment. I remember following my father round Bogside Golf Course before rheumatoid arthritis forced him to give up his sport. As far as I can remember there was always a reasonable balance between discipline and freedom. I did not have any goals throughout my teenage years. There was nothing to drive me on. I did not know what I wanted to do. I reacted to the normal rites of school passage. I did not transfer from Kilwinning High School to Irvine Royal Academy at the end of my second year and later to my enormous surprise became Kilwinning's School Captain. When I did go to Irvine Academy for my fifth and sixth year it was not enjoyable for me. The Head teacher Macmillan informed me that I would never go to university. And at that point in time I believed him.

I took week-end jobs to make pocket money for myself. And in the summer when I was sixteen, I ventured upon a building labourer's job. The first bag of cement which descended from the lorry on to my back split open and I assumed a uniform greyish colour. At Christmas time that same year I was employed by the local post office to deliver Christmas mail. I found myself delivering mail to my own home. I, of course, offered a personal service at this address and took the mail round to the back door. When I entered the kitchen with the letters, my father, for a joke, shouted "Post!" But Lucky the terrier had a canine aversion to postmen. Waking from his slumber beside the fire in the living room, he careered through to the kitchen, snarling and barking. Not waiting to properly identify the postman who had invaded his territory, he launched himself through the air towards me and fastened his teeth into my right leg below the knee. He tugged and moved his head from side to side. "It's me, you idiot," I shouted. And he looked up without relaxing his grip. And his eyes softened. And his expression became apologetic and 'sheepish' as in a Tom and Jerry cartoon. He slowly began to wag his tail while refusing to ease his jaws from my leg. Then I shook him off, turned him on his back and placed my foot on his neck and gave a slight press just to remind him who was boss. Then, of course, we were pals again. Bitten by my own dog - it caused me some existential anxiety for a time - some questioning about the meaning of the universe and much hilarity the story gave to everyone who heard about it.

There were jobs for all of us when we left school in 1965. I began a traineeship in hospital administration with the Western Regional Hospital Board as it then was. I disliked the train journey to and from Glasgow each day and generally felt under-occupied and under-challenged.

## Eternal Life

On the 8th of May 1966, on a Sunday morning at 9 30am my father died suddenly of a coronary thrombosis. As I looked on his body I was convinced (as many are convinced) that physical death is not the end of human existence. I could not believe that the body which lay still was the whole person I had known as my father.

My task that day was to visit relatives and friends and inform them about my father's death. In the evening, our Minister, the Reverend Colin MacKenzie came to see us. He brought with him a reassuring and consoling presence. His prayers gave peace to our home and to my mother, sister, brother and myself. I felt that this was meant to be, that there was a higher purpose involved and that everything would be all right in spite of the brutal grief which had overtaken us. When Mr MacKenzie left, I wept for the first time that day.

More people than I had expected attended my father's funeral. I considered that my father had lived unnoticed and unregarded. My parents were not wealthy, prominent in community or visibly successful in anything. I was deeply affected by the good things people said they had seen in my father's life. Perhaps this was because I myself had not recognised them. Eternal Life seemed to have a quality, distinctive from anything I had perceived as important.

During the summer of that year, I thought deeply and prayerfully about what I had learned from my father's death. In this I was no different from other mortals who experience sudden bereavement. But I did not give up this mental struggle. I wanted to resolve the issues and values involved in life, death and Eternal Life. I could not do so. I therefore prayed even more, asking God to do so for me.

## The Call

Throughout the summer of 1966 I awakened to the reality of God. I was working in a Glasgow hospital at the time and travelling daily by train from my home in Ayrshire. Each lunchtime I would spend in solitary prayer, usually outside in the relative warmth. Sometimes I ate no food. A change was taking place within me. My feeble human ambitions were being supplanted by spiritual longing.

On Tuesday 25th October at 9 30am, in a kind of voluntary exhalation of seeking I cried:

**"O God, what have I to do with my life?"**

To my lasting surprise and astonishment there came an immediate, unexpected and unwanted answer:

**"You will be a Minister."**

I heard no voice in any physically audible sense. I believed with great surprise that this was the still small voice of the Living God speaking within my soul and it brought both relief and peace.

I had been brought up in one of the local Church Of Scotland congregations, Erskine (later with Fergushill). I had gone through Sunday School, Bible Class and Youth Fellowship. Since 1960 I had been firstly a Sunday School teacher and then a Bible Class leader. I had enjoyed these commitments which were not without their humours. Yet the image of the dog collar, dark clothes and unusual role in society made me reluctant to accept such a remarkable and instantaneous call. It occurred to me that I'd lose my friends.

During the following weeks, the call was intimated again on two occasions. I decided to attend Sunday worship to find out if the call could in any way be corroborated. Colin MacKenzie preached on the text, "And He must needs go through Samaria." His theme was that there are things in life we may not want or choose to do but we have to do them.

I told my mother that I "wanted to be a Minister." She, still grieving for my father was surprised and a little uncertain about me. She did not discourage me. My girlfriend was pleased. Mr MacKenzie's response was helpful and positive. He set about making practical inquiries.

My own assessment of the call was that I would at least try to find out if it was genuine. Thus I embarked on an experiment to prove or disprove the nature of my call to the ministry. I have throughout my life maintained an experimental basis to my spiritual calling. I have asked God to corroborate my call at all stages and I have looked to events and personal history to provide me with evidence of the continuing true nature of the original call.

## Devotions

For private devotional purposes I began to read 'The Sermon On The Mount." It surely matters what Scripture influences the initial stages of spiritual life and calling. Ever since those early days, I have been formed and informed by the beauty and radical completeness of this part of Jesus' teaching. I continued to attend morning worship in Erskine Church. In the summer of 1967 I had gone along as usual though Mr MacKenzie was on annual holiday for a few weeks. On one occasion, the pulpit supply preacher failed to appear. With only two or three minutes to the appointed hour, the service was about to be cancelled when I volunteered to conduct the worship. I had never been in a pulpit and had never conducted all or part of a service, nor had I preached anywhere. I was able to speak for a little while on "The Sermon On The Mount." Even if this did not amount to a formal sermon, along with hymns, prayers, children's address and, of course, the intimations, it was enough to suggest that a service of worship had taken place.

## Glasgow University

In the spring of 1967 I began studying to repeat higher French and Latin to add to the English and History which I had already passed at school. Success would gain me entrance to Glasgow University. I also attended the Church of Scotland selection school for prospective candidates for the ministry. Professor James Blackie took me aside and said, "It is refreshing to meet someone without any preconceived opinions." I did not pass. Neither did I fail. Instead I received a letter from Dr Henry Sefton who informed me that they were giving me "time to adjust to the relatively new situation in which I now found myself." Some explanation of the reasons for this decision would have been helpful. None were given.

In July the highers results appeared. I passed the French but to my dismay, I found that I had been awarded a compensatory 'O' level in Latin which meant that I had failed by a few marks. My mother, on her own initiative, wrote to ask if there had been a mistake. There had. The examiner had failed to add the marks correctly. I had actually passed the Latin and could now go to Glasgow University in the autumn. Hanging by a thread, by the skin of my teeth, or by whatever other metaphor may be appropriate, wonderfully, frail like a new birth, my call to the Ministry was being confirmed.

## Discipleship

I took everything very seriously. The deep spiritual seeking continued. I discovered three books, each of which had a profound bearing upon my life. 'The Forgotten Talent' by Cameron Peddie, a Church Of Scotland Minister told the story of his discovery and practice of the healing ministry. Peddie's example of keeping an 'hour of watch' each night challenged me to do the same. I loved the last hour of the day when I would sit or lie still, meditate and wait, silent in the presence of God. I enjoyed being with God. But I did not entirely know what I was doing. I did not know what effect this pattern of devotion was having on me in other ways. I did not know where it was taking me. I hoped to exercise a healing ministry as part of my future calling and I was sure that God would honour this discipleship.

The second book was 'Training In Christianity' by Søren Kierkegaard. He had taken Christian discipleship seriously and had contrasted the real demands of Jesus Christ with the comfortable civil religion of bourgeoise nineteenth century Denmark. More than that, he had broken off his engagement to Regina Olsen because he thought that marriage and domesticity were incompatible with true allegiance to Jesus Christ.

Like many others I found Thomas à Kempis's 'Imitation Of Christ' helpful and nourishing. He distinguished fellowship with God from fellowship with people. The former was higher and better, the latter was a distraction to the former. I was beginning to understand what he meant.

## Down To Earth

During the long summer holidays from university studies, I took various forms of employment. I did many humble jobs throughout my student years. I shovelled hamburger meat into a machine which tinned hamburgers. I attended an apparatus which sliced and wrapped bread. Sometimes it did not work very well throwing slices all over the place. I got the sack from this job because I did not want to work on a Sunday. I cleaned out boilers in a glass-making factory. I also laboured for various building firms. I took up my hod daily. I liked the company of the men and women I met on these jobs. They had a wonderful sense of humour and a continual appreciation of the absurd in life.

One summer I had just begun labouring for a well-known house-building conglomerate. My hands had not yet hardened to the pick and shovel. I was sent as part of a squad to dig a trench across an asphalt road because pipes had not been led into the already built houses. I was given an old pick and a shovel with no T-piece handle. By four o' clock I had twelve blisters, six on each hand. The inner skin had also burst and most of the blisters were bleeding. I was very tired in the unusually warm late afternoon sunshine. I began to feel nauseous and faint. I thought I'd soon be going home, but we were told we would have to work until six-thirty. I did not think I could make it. I could barely hold the pick and shovel. But I would not give in. I would not admit that I could not do this work. I did not want to lose the job either. It was four-thirty. I felt weak and exhausted. I looked up at the pitilessly blue clear sky and prayed to God to help me. Within minutes clouds appeared and with them a sudden and unexpected shower of rain. It was heavy enough for us to be allowed to stop work and take shelter. After half-an-hour the rain stopped and the sun reappeared in the once again cloudless sky. I recovered sufficient strength to continue until we all went home. My hands required bandages but I was able to work the following day and thereafter throughout the summer. Even allowing for Scotland's variable climatic conditions I do not believe the meteorological change was simply a coincidence.

On another summer I was employed preparing a site for residential caravans. In the squad there was a young man with a reputation for violence. One day I was working in a trench and he shouted over to me from some distance asking me for a loan of my shovel. I pretended that I had not heard him, put my hand to my ear, and mimed "What?" He repeated his request and I made the same reply. He then bellowed, "Gi'e me yer ———— shovel, ya ————!" Again I feigned hard of hearing. He then cast about himself and found an empty lemonade bottle. He held it by the neck and smashed the end against a brick, breaking the bottle. He now held a very dangerous weapon in his hand and he turned and marched menacingly towards me. Men came running and begged him not to do anything. He was incensed and swore that he was going to slash my face. He stopped two feet from me and held up the broken bottle ready to injure and disfigure me. I was possessed of an extreme calm and prayed silently to my God. My adversary cursed and swore. The men pleaded with him but he became more and more angry. The men became quiet. I stood still and looked him in the eye. I said nothing. If I had moved he would have struck. After what seemed a very long time, he lowered his arm. I remained still. A little while longer and he turned and walked away. I breathed a huge sigh of relief. The men said they could not understand why he had not followed through with his threat. I believe My Lord came between him and me. I also repented my risky humours.

Many are the laughs I shared with the characters I met during holiday work. They usually found out what I was doing with my life and subjected me to much good-humoured banter. "Do you smoke?" "No." "Do you drink?" "No." "Are you fond of your ruff?" "No." "Not worth your while living, is it?" "No." One summer I worked on the building of a huge concrete cooling tower for a nylon plant. Subsequently the whole thing fell down in a gale! For part of the time I hauled heavy bundles of wooden slats thirty to forty feet up inside the cooling tower. On a particular day I was actually at the top level where the slats were in place. There were concrete steps on the outside of the tower. The general foreman told me to go and bring up a heavy metal ceiling support. To make the other men laugh, he shouted, "Bring two." One only can be carried comfortably. I decided to try for the last laugh by bringing two. I struggled up the outside steps of the tower with two of these heavy implements. I tottered in and dropped them at his feet. "I was only kidding," said he. "So was I," said I.

In another place on another occasion the bacon in someone's lunchtime sandwich was replaced with a piece of damp-course. More hilariously a sheep was then let loose in the canteen just before a tea break and feasted generously on everyone's sandwiches. Men quite often addressed me piously, saying, "I believe in heaven - I do - there must be a heaven, because this is hell." Some tried to be polite. "Good morning Robert, how are we this morning?" To which I replied "We are fine - how are youse?" On another job one of the wits informed us that our next contract was to rebuild Hadrian's Wall.

Even after graduating with a Doctor of Philosophy degree from Oxford University, I spent several weeks in the summer labouring with a firm who were renovating council houses close to where I had been brought up. A certain foreman walked into our canteen one day and shouted, "Robert, get a pick and shovel, we are going to Kilwinning." "Are we going to knock it down?" I asked, to the merriment of the squad. It was easy enough for me. These men had to work during the winter months. I knew I was privileged. Waiting at the canteen one evening for the clocking off siren, I was challenged by a fellow worker, "That's you - first oot the door." "At least when I'm here - I hing aboot," I replied, disarming the complainer. So many characters abounded in these places. Each building site was like a Shakespeare play. Without, I hope being patronising, I have always maintained a sympathy for what are known as 'working class people'. I regret that they seem often to be marginalised as far as church life is concerned. But their lack of pretence was always refreshing to me.

## Rugby

I also played rugby. I had gained my school colours while playing as a wing-threequarter for Irvine Academy. As a teen-ager I had found that I possessed a turn of sprint speed and this had helped me also to become a school and later an Ayshire county champion long jumper. While I was a divinity student, I continued to play for Irvine Former Pupils XV. Here again I received some good-natured banter. It was course rugby although I did score tries over the years and Saturday afternoons provided a contrast to my studies and devotional life during the week. I remember that during one game I was standing close to our own line. We had been awarded a scrum. Our scrum-half always liked to make cutting remarks about my calling. I used simply to ignore them. He gathered the ball and, for fun, sent me what is known as a hospital pass, that is, one that is so slow and high that the opposing players will reach you before the ball does. I managed to collect the ball but was immediately flattened by three opposing players. As I struggled to the surface, he shouted to me, "Waken up!" I replied, "I am awake - I had to wait for the —— —— thing to come back to earth!" After that altercation, he did not bother me again.

I played rugby for nine years. I would have played longer but at a game in Lanark I sustained a depressed fracture of the left maxilla arch. I completed the game but remember feeling rather weak on the return journey. I seemed not to be able to move my jaw. I went straight to Kilmarnock Infirmary where I was X-rayed and admitted. The ward was noisy on a

Saturday evening. There was I in the midst of various local worthies who had been carted in during the evening with various problems resulting from falls and fights while under the influence of alcohol. At 8 30pm a dear little nurse came to my bed and asked me if I had had any food. I shook my head. She appeared fifteen minutes later with a plate of fish and chips. All I could do was to suck one chip which I'd spiked on to a fork.

The next morning I was awakened by another young nurse. "Time for your pre-med," said she, in the conspiratorial way that nurses talk, using terms lay people do not understand. "Just turn over for a moment." I had not completed this turn when I was hit in the backside with what seemed to me to be a harpoon. I shot into the air and thumped back down on to the bed. "That's fine," quoth she and tripped merrily away.

I was then told that the surgeon, Mr Kennedy, had arrived from Glasgow to perform the operation on my face. I was duly wheeled to theatre. He was a charming man and treated me with grace and kindness. He told me that they would have to open up the left side of my head and pull the bone back into place. "Does that mean the sideburns have to go?" I inquired, wholly in jest. He took a look and then said, "No, we'll cut you behind the ear and work down to where the problem is." I had a full anaesthetic. The operation was successful.

I had a date with the girl I'd just met to go to the University Christmas Ball on the following Wednesday. I made it, but I was rather exhausted by the end of the evening. A few weeks later I sustained another head injury and landed in Kilmarnock Infirmary again. I decided not to risk further chance of injury. I wondered why I was being exposed in this way and thought that there must be a spiritual reason for it. I always regretted stopping playing and I missed the fitness and the tingle after a game on a cold winter's day. However I became an enthusiastic spectator until the mid-nineties when money and politics seemed to take the innocence and joy from the game itself.

## Music

Taking a Sunday School class when I was thirteen years of age seems eminently presumptuous looking back. I also had an occasional week-end job in a local garage. Tom McKie, the young owner and I had some lively discussions about all sorts of things. One day he said to me, "You know Robert son, you'll be killed someday for doing the right thing." Time was to prove him nearly right. I led the Bible Class in Erskine Church for a few years until 1971. It was a great privilege to have young people coming at 9 30am each Sunday to study Christianity in some depth. I know that some of those who came along found a living faith and remained within the church. I also formed a music group with seven attractive girls and five nutty guys. Brian and Dorothy Allison have remained friends to this day. We practised in my home each Sunday afternoon or evening and sang in churches and halls throughout Ayrshire. One day I received an invitation for the group to sing at a Woman's Guild Daffodil Tea in the village of Ochiltree. I was very doubtful about persuading one of the guitarists, a long haired youth, to attend such an occasion, so I did not actually tell the group where we were going. But when we met to go in cars to Ochiltree, he said to me, "Where are we going?" I replied, "Wait and see." "No - I have to know," said he. "It's a Daffodil Tea," I confessed. "Oh that's good - I like daffodils," he enjoined, jumping into his battered mini.

The hall was bedecked with enormous daffodils. Hundreds of them. It was a beautiful sight. We sang and shared supper. I told the ladies that I was glad to have so many of the group present since this was not our usual kind of event. Then in a moment of nonsense, I added, "One of our members has told me how much he likes daffodils - so - (picking out the largest one I could see on the platform) - I thought we might ask him to taste one." The bold chap strode forward, bowed, accepted the daffodil, took a bite or two and then munched the entire flower down to the last inch of stem. Everyone dissolved into paroxysms of laughter. Unfortunately, the poor fellow lost his sight for two days and was ill for a week. Chagrined, I went round to his house to apologise to his parents. They were forgiving.

## Renouncing Self

I was studying for the degree of Bachelor of Divinity. Once I learned how to cope with academic strategy I began to do quite well. In 1969 I was awarded a scholarship to attend a study conference with the World Council Of Churches at Bossey, Switzerland, along with theological students from all over the world. When I returned, everything and everyone seemed parochial in comparison.

My studies progressed but within myself, I was torn in three directions. The higher criticism which reduced the status and truth content of the Bible without offering anything positive in its place forced me to depend on my experience of God for continuation of faith. We were told that certain things in the Bible did not actually happen. Yet my own life's testimony was that if living spiritual things could happen to me, how much more could they have happened in and around Jesus of Nazareth.

The deep seeking of God continued and the hour of watch was central to this way of life. My girlfriend had become my fiancée. However, she did not seem able to share my sense of journey and of spiritual pilgrimage. She was a good church person, happy in her faith and without complication. We both 'went forward' together at the Tent Hall in Glasgow on 4th July 1970 in response to a particularly gracious invitation at the end of the evangelistic rally. Mr and Mrs Moore dealt kindly with us. We knelt in prayer and I heard the words, "Give them the strength to do what they must do." At that moment I knew that the pathways forward for my fiancée and I would lead us to travel in different directions.

I still have the little card I signed that evening. It reads:

**"Acknowledging myself as a sinner before God, I do here and now**
**accept Jesus Christ, the Son of God, as my Saviour and Lord,**
**promising by His grace to confess and serve Him, fully depending**
**on the indwelling Holy Spirit for strength and guidance."**

I knew that this was right for me and I found much peace of spirit. I would not call it a conversion, but rather a dedication. It was a step forward but it was not the first or the last of such steps of faith. I received more than I expected. This was a meeting with the Risen Jesus Christ which was of a qualitatively different nature from the assimilation of knowledge about Jesus from the Gospels. 'Going forward' is treated suspiciously in church circles and many are the protestations that 'it is not for me'. However, if we, like Naaman the Syrian General, humble ourselves, we may open up the possibilities of unthought of blessings. Even Our Lord submitted to public baptism as the prelude to His public ministry. Beyond the occasion and the people involved is God. If the intention of the individual is right then the spiritual meeting occurs. Human pride often prevents the simple way to realised faith. Many who live and work in churches deny themselves the blessings and assurances that come from 'going forward'. They then may spend many years trying to compensate in other ways. Worse, they may oppose and persecute those who have taken this step of faith.

## The Vision

It took me until February of 1971 to finally break our engagement. I simply said what I knew to be the truth, "I cannot marry you." I was overwhelmed by sadness and guilt and misery. I retreated into a shell-like depression. After I began to recover I found distance and space which made the intolerable burden easier to bear. The Reverend Eric Alexander chided me. He was concerned for my fiancée but in the midst of my own struggle and agony told me that I had 'an unteachable spirit.' His attitude caused me to be wary of conservative evangelicals. The Reverend Peter G Thomson, on the other hand met me while we were both watching a rugby match. "I hear you've been a bad boy," he said, exacerbating my conscience, but then he kindly put his arm around me and gave me an understanding hug. That was one of those spontaneous touches of compassion which one never forgets.

Some of our friends were very upset. One decided that he would make every effort to bring my ex-fiancée and I together again. I shrank from this. One Wednesday at lunchtime I was walking slowly back to the flat where I stayed in Glasgow. No-one was there when I arrived. I lay down and was still. I shared with God the problem of the well-intentioned friend. I sought God's presence and guidance. Something happened to me for the first time. I was granted a vision. My inner spiritual eye viewed a mass of purple colour. Then a door was carved in silver against this purple background. Through the door I could see the most beautiful silver-green-gold colour like a meadow in summer. I looked out and seemed to step through. Minutes lapsed while this vision impressed on my external memory. This vision was cleansing and reassuring and brought me peace, but I had no idea what it meant. However my inner torment was healed by this mystical experience. I had been attending Rev Alan Boyd Robson's Services Of Healing on Wednesday evenings in Kelvinside Botanical Gardens Church as part of the supporting congregation. He had been an associate of Cameron Peddie. I always enjoyed the special peace of the service.

That same Wednesday of the vision I went along as usual. Alan Robson read the text for his talk. It was Revelation 3:8:

**"I know thy works; behold I have set before thee an open door,**
**and no man can shut it; for thou hast a little strength,**
**and hast kept my word, and hast not denied my name."**

I rejoiced all the way home. The meaning of the beautiful vision had been made clear in a congregation of the Church to which I belonged and through an ordained Minister of the Word and Sacraments. The sense of God's concern for me was strong and I was at peace. I never took my call for granted and felt that I was being confirmed and sustained in my vocation. I was a happy person again. My ex-fiancée was not left comfortless. She told me she had been "held by God in His arms." The following year, she married someone else.

## Taizé

I completed that academic year and went off to Taizé, the Protestant monastic community in central France. I did not intend joining but like many, wanted to share in the Taizé experience. I was much impressed by the worship. I also enjoyed the company of Frère Thomas (a fellow Scot who had been a Minister of the Church of Scotland), Frère Didier in the pottery and the organ-playing of Jean-Luc. I think I wept quite a bit during those five weeks. I talked with Thomas about generalities. Spiritual youthfulness shone on the faces of the brothers. I thought there was another side to Taizé which we did not see. Much healed within, I took my leave as Thomas said, "There is unfinished business in Scotland."

## Being Alone

I was still suffering the reactions in my body and emotions from breaking our engagement. I realised that one takes for granted the energies and confidence that a relationship brings until these are taken away. Part of one's life dies. It is a partial bereavement. I learned what those who live alone endure. I have felt sympathy for single people ever since. Man-woman companionship is natural and good and for many it is not easy to continue alone. Perhaps spiritual compatibility is very difficult to find. Certainly Jesus of Nazareth disrupted relationships. However, I believe He has cemented many more over the centuries than have ever been broken by zeal for Himself and His Kingdom.

## Psychical Studies

At Glasgow University Professor John McDonald taught us Hebrew and Old Testament. He appeared as a relaxed, informal and friendly man who took a pastoral interest in students. As early as 1968 I came under his influence. He was approachable and seemed to be the only person who wanted to talk about spiritual things rather than just academic things. He disguised his real interest in the name of academic research and it was this which confused me. I did not know the Bible well enough to recognise the dangers behind his seemingly pastoral language. I later learned that he was involved in psychical research. I knew absolutely nothing about any of this. He invited me to join a small group of experimenters in the paranormal. Other ordained clergy shared in this group although not uncritically, and I suppose that was what made me think it might be all right to participate. We hoped to produce 'scientific' papers on our research and findings. However, from my point of view, some of the developments were sinister. From meditation sessions we moved to hypnotism and then to experiments in regression to the pre-natal state. I recalled playing in the sunshine as a small child in our back garden with my sister, brother and our pet dogs. They tried pre-life regression but got nowhere. I myself was conscious under hypnosis of no previous existence, identity or personality. However, I was aware that there was a depth in me which countered the suggestions I was receiving under hypnosis. My subconscious state was altered. The emotional, mental and spiritual chaos that the implantation of this inner battle created in me when I came out of the hypnotic state was real. Max Magee, who was Chaplain to Strathclyde University at that time often conducted these experiments. He contrasted my outward appearance of weakness and diffidence with the discovery of my internal spiritual strength under hypnosis. At a certain level, the Holy Spirit within started to testify. John McDonald seemed perplexed and uneasy about this and said on more than one occasion, "There is a tertiary personality, there is a tertiary personality." On one occasion he urged me "Seek the gold, seek the gold." I did not know what he meant at the time. He was not talking about money, nor academic achievement. It was a vague insight into God's provenance over me - as if he himself prophesied without knowing what he was saying. Max Magee used to say of his perception of my internal existence "Robert is like a puppy playing in the sun."

I myself did not know what I was doing. McDonald and Magee were spiritualists. In taking part in their experiments, I opened myself up to harmful influences. I learned from this experience about the reality of the unseen world of spiritual forces which are in contrast to and in tension with the Kingdom of God in Jesus Christ. It is a dangerous world. Scripture forbids these kinds of contacts to those who would follow God's way. Academia justifies much in terms of the pursuit of knowledge. I was damaged quite seriously by my involvement. Even Max Magee seemed to recognise that I was being damaged because he said on one occasion, "Robert is a sensitive intrument - not to be abused." Sometimes messages received from 'outside' seemed hostile to me. Although I continued with the group, I began to discriminate. My spiritual health had begun to suffer and this had affected my behaviour. The rebellious aspect of my personality seemed to be activated. I was greatly tempted to sexual immorality. I seemed to be protected from within. On one occasion I instructed myself, "I cannot forget God." However I also remember being spiritually ill for two days and feeling like the prodigal son far away from his Father's home. Shortly after this occurrence, I made an inner resolution to get out of psychical research. I attended a few more meetings but prepared myself spiritually before going. During one unofficial 'seance' type of meeting, a 'message' was being communicated which I interpreted as negation of myself, my calling and salvation in Jesus Christ. I never went back. I have never taken part in any such experimentation since. There have been however, throughout my life, remaining memories of the trauma caused by my brief introduction to the non-Christian powers of the universe.

## Human Love

Coincidentally with this psychical experimentation, I had a brief love affair with a fellow student. She was not a Christian and seemed to have an interest in astrology. Although there was a fondness at the human level, there was complete incompatibility at the spiritual level. There were together pleasure and pain for both of us. We belonged to different kingdoms. When we said, "Good-bye" on Gilmorehill, I felt a return of God's presence to myself and that relief that a man feels when he is once again free. Extricating myself from the psychical research and a doomed relationship allowed me to resume my spiritual journey. I learned a great deal in that abyss. It was also I believe the cause of my exposure to physical injury in sport. Thereafter I was scarred and a sadder and wiser man. I have often wondered if it was necessary for me to have travelled that particular path. Perhaps it was an expression of residual human sinfulness. Through it, however, I discovered the existence of what I have called ever since, 'The Objective Kingdom Of Evil.' This was first hand experience and not an abstract doctrine. I realised that the world is surrounded and permeated by powerful energies and forces and some of these seem to have a personal nature. Spiritualism deals with this twilight area. I found it harmful and set in opposition both to the Christianity of the Church and to the relationship with God which blessed and governed my life.

## Canada

In the summer months of 1972 and 1973 I held missionary posts with the Presbyterian Church of Canada. Both were in remote places, Wabush in Labrador and Flin Flon in north Manitoba. These temporary appointments were rewarding and enjoyable. In each case, seemingly dying congregations sprung to life and attendances rose steadily throughout my short ministries. I liked Canada and found a measure of personal freedom although I learned too about the rootlessness of the culture in such a vast and sparsely populated country. While at Wabush I took advantage of free company plane trips out to Sept-Iles and then on to Montreal. I visited the shrine dedicated to Brother Andrew where healings had taken place. I also visited Quebec City where, as an English speaker (English accented French speaker) I did not feel particularly welcome. In a restaurant the waiter dropped my plate of chicken salad from a foot high on to the table. I went to the museum which I found disappointing. There was a large display of General Montcalm dying. I looked for Wolfe and found a small case with the terse inscription 'The English General Wolfe.' It occurred to me that neither Montcalm nor Wolfe could have been the brightest of military leaders. It took Wolfe a long time to realise that there was a back entrance to Quebec City and when he did, Montcalm had not protected it. I loved trips on to the tundra in north

Labrador and northern Quebec. The black flies were merciless, however and made the 'midgies' of my native land seem like a blessing. Pierre Trudeau visited Wabush while I was there and I shook hands with him.

Manitoba is a land of lakes, lakes lakes. Winnepeg has 'wall to wall blue' as the locals say, so describing the horizons of sky which meet the flat plains on all sides. I loved canoeing on the lakes and also visited northern Saskatchewan. Canada has many Scots expatriates and I met them wherever I went. I found Rangers and Celtic fans in most places too. I asked one Rangers devotee whether God had not made a mistake in making all the grass so green. "Naw," he replied, "Ye can walk a' ower it."

Most Scots had an enviable lifestyle with much taken for granted that was still classed as luxury in the old country. Scots were well regarded as hard workers and capable people in skills and professions, somewhat like British regard Germans and Europeans regard Japanese. So many 'ethnic' groups make up Canada's population that there is no unifying allegiance other than in trying to maintain a distinction from the overwhelming influence of America. Canada is a young person's country and if you want to stay, you need to do so for a long time. I myself missed the history and culture of Europe and the spiritual depth of its Christian tradition. Yet I could understand that the personal freedoms which drew people there unburdened lives of conventions and expectations. On the other hand, there were no restraints of family or society such as in the villages and towns back home.

## Assisting

I left Erskine Church in 1971 and in 1972 I became a student assistant in Kelvinside Botanical Gardens Church. I remember the humours more than anything else. Alan Boyd Robson and I used to have some heated discussions. One Sunday morning, just before the service was about to begin, we were arguing about a miners' strike which was taking place at the time. He said he was appalled that he had had to change his meal times because of power cuts. I contrasted his self-interest with the plight of miners' families. He argued back. Eventually I said, "All right, keep your hair on." Then I looked quizzically at his very bald pate and added, "Perhaps I should change the metaphor." At that point he leapt up from his desk and began to run across his vestry towards me, intent on doing me some physical harm by the look of him. I took to my heels and, running past parishioners entering for the service, did not stop until I was safely out in Great Western Road.

On one occasion I informed Alan Boyd Robson with a certain amount of naive self-righteousness that there were four brothels in his parish. "Goodness me," he replied, "Only four!" He was the only person I ever heard include a commercial for political conservatism in a Good Friday sermon. He mentioned "Peter, with his very successful fishing business, there in Galilee." Alan enjoyed baiting me. He once prayed for "..our brave soldiers in Northern Ireland, standing to their duty." I rebuked him with the words, "It's 1972 not 1872!" After that, he bought a book of modern prayers. At one Boys Brigade Parade he took the salute, resplendent in his single Second World War 'Huts And Canteens' medal. He marched down Byres Road, head held high. I followed with my head lowered. I saw the enormous pile of dog excrement. He did not. To my delight all of his manufactured pomposity was wrecked in a single unfortunate step. At another service attended by the Boys Brigade, I read the lesson from John chapter fifteen. As I stepped up to the lectern, I noticed that one member of the Brigade had extremely long hair. I then pronounced, "I am the true vine and my Father is the hairdresser."

I encountered polite insincerity, something which permeates church circles throughout the world. I decided that I would not participate in polite insincerity and I never have. But then, I have not advanced in the church. After morning service one Sunday, I was standing at the door greeting the people as they left. A large county type lady appeared, stuck out an arm and boomed, "Are you enjoying yourself with us, Mr Anderson?" "Not all that much," I replied. "Good," said she and marched on.

Eventually, Alan Robson allowed me to preach a sermon, but only at the evening service. I asked for the lights not to be dimmed just before the sermon as was the custom so that those who attended might, if they wished, follow the exposition of Psalm one hundred and thirty-nine in their own Bibles. I began by apologising to members of the (paid) choir whose habit it was to sleep during the sermon. Afterwards Alan Robson congratulated me and gave me a book with the inscription, "On learning that you have a mind." I thanked him with the rejoinder, "I've still to discover whether you have one." Before I left, I presented him with a book on one of his interests which was art. It was called, 'The World Through Blunted Sight.' His relatives thought I was being cheeky.

## Academia

I enjoyed Glasgow University. Having felt under-employed throughout my childhood and adolescence it was good to have the range of stimuli which university life offered. I responded enthusiastically. The lecturers varied from poor to excellent. William Barclay was stimulating although I was sceptical about some of his rationalist explanations of New Testament miracles. The suggestion that the story of the Feeding of Five Thousand was really about people sharing their sandwich lunch-packs seemed particularly unconvincing. He was subjected to much professional jealousy because at that time he was arguably the most popular Christian communicator in Scotland, having his own television series. I found him to be a warm and caring person. Once on passing me in Trinity College common room he put his arm round me and in a fatherly way enquired, "How are you today, Robert?" You don't forget these unsought kindnesses. I thoroughly enjoyed lunchtime banter with fellow students although I also kept a personal distance apart not through strategy but simply because it was natural for me to do so. That essential 'space' has always mattered and still does. It was necessary because I was always trying to live my life out in relation to God, learning, discovering where I was going, finding out how God relates to us, absorbing Christianity. I took an interest in Systematic Theology because it was intellectually demanding and stretched and developed my under-utilised thinking processes.

My brother Alex was studying medicine and we shared a flat in Windsor Terrace, Glasgow owned by our great uncle Dr Thomas Reid.

He was an extraordinary character. He had been a medical officer in the trenches in France during the First World War. In 1921 he began work as a general practioner in Windsor Terrace. By the nineteen-seventies he was still fit and healthy. He had decided not to retire and continued to drive fast cars in from his castle-house overlooking the River Clyde at Cardross for surgeries in the flat in which my brother and I shared a room. He was wealthy having successfully played the stock market for many years. He took a no-nonsense approach to patients and was certainly what is now called 'politically incorrect'. "I may not be popular - but I'm pleased with myself." he used to boast. "The finest tonic there is - a rise in your shares," he would happily quip on a good day, "Some people collect butterflies; some people collect stamps; I collect money." was another of his witticisms. "Never help anyone - they won't forgive you." was the least attractive of his aphorisms. Like many wealthy people he was extremely mean. Had he been a ghost I doubt if he would have given anyone a fright! He finally retired after practising medicine in that one place for more than fifty years. He died in his nineties.

I was not involved in theological politics at Glasgow University and I did not join any party or group or society with its own agenda. I was primarily concerned to complete my course. The 'Power Without Glory' debate broke and then Ian Henderson met a premature death. Ronald Gregor Smith was reputed to begin his first year classes with the pronouncement "The bones of the man Jesus are rotting somewhere in Palestine." I was spared this because he too died suddenly in middle age. And Alan Galloway became Regius Professor of Divinity, much to his and everyone else's surprise.

I had taken an arts degree before undertaking an extra year of study to convert my divinity degree to honours. I paid for this final year from my own meagre savings. I had specialised in Systematic Theology in which I already had been awarded the Cleland and Rae Wilson Gold Medal. For the last three months of study I moved to comfortable accommodation in a hall of residence. Nothing and no-one interrupted my preparations for these examinations. I was awarded a First Class Honours. To have begun so humbly and to have finished at Glasgow so well was indeed gratifying. I was already looking forward to undertaking doctoral studies at Oxford University. On leaving Glasgow, I felt that my call had been confirmed once again. I was also deeply moved by the generosity of God's providence over me in the academic arena. I liked the academic environment. Yet education was never an end in itself. It was the spiritual journey which mattered.

## Friends

I may have lost a few friends in following my call to the ministry but I gained lasting friends in their place. John Campbell and Ross Mitchell have remained so ever since. With fellow students we formed a gospel band called "Impact" and toured Scotland, leading worship and speaking to young people about Jesus Christ. We even appeared on Scottish Television's

"Late Call." On the Friday evening we were due to be on just before the late night horror movie. The continuity girl got mixed up. She announced, "Now, for your weekly date with horror." and then we appeared playing "When the saints go marching in." This faux-pas in turn gave us more publicity by way of a photograph and an article in one of the Sunday newspapers with the title "Holy Terrors."

## Edinburgh

On leaving Glasgow I took up a position as assistant Minister in Greenbank Church, Edinburgh. My relationship with the Minister, Donald Mackay was strained and without humour. He did not glow with spiritual fire and he did not seem convinced by the great spiritual truths of our Faith. He was the type of minister Edinburgh congregations normally call. He left me in charge as he took his annual summer holiday in Arran. There was a worthwhile practice of having the sermon typed, copied and distributed to house-bound members. However, I had to announce that my sermon was not to be typed in this way. I added, "It might be the best sermon I'll ever preach." (laughter from congregation) "It might be the best sermon, you'll ever hear." (silence from congregation) "But it is not to be." A Morningside lady came to me afterwards and said, "Thet seemed to impley, thet Mr Mackay might not preach a better sermon." "You don't say," I responded.

I was given charge of the junior youth fellowship. Gordon Kennedy who later became a television presenter and comedian attended. I remember in my peroration one Sunday morning trying to distinguish existential guilt from other forms and found myself saying to the teenagers, "Guilt is not just bad feelings about sex." Then spying Gordon in the front row, I added, "Or - in Gordon's case - good feelings about sex." He ruefully acknowledged the direction of his thoughts at the moment in question. I thoroughly enjoyed the company of these young people and we had, I think, a successful year. I found the senior youth fellowship snobbish and clannish. I reacted against the presumptions of superiority fostered by the fee-paying school culture in which they were being educated. The Assistant Minister was expected to share in the fun of their annual review. I decided not to take part. It was because I thought them worthy of more serious consideration and ministry. I really wanted them to think more deeply about Christianity before I would make a fool of myself for them. I also knew that Edinburgh congregations enjoy humiliating their ministers. I thought I would not allow them their spectacle. However, Mr Mackay criticised me in public.

The annual general meeting of the congregation took place in March. It was the third week in Lent. As the business drew to a close, one of the elders said, "Now let us have our sing-song. What shall we sing?" Someone suggested "By The Light Of The Silvery Moon," which was duly sung with great gusto. The following Sunday I was scheduled to preach at the morning service. At one point I said, "It is the third week in Lent, Christ is already hanging on his cross and people here are singing 'By The Light Of The Silvery Moon' - Oh dear, Oh dear!" When I finished my sermon, unprecedented scenes followed. An old man struggled to his unsteady feet and shouted out, "Amen" and then fell back into his pew (uninjured). At the end of the service, enraged worshippers divided into two groups, the women verbally attacked the old man and the men verbally attacked, surrounded and jostled me. Donald Mackay never mentioned the sermon or the fracas. I left in April. My probationary term was sustained. I had also worked hard and visited very many of the parishioners. The only gift I received was a book by George Mackay Brown from a family of three gorgeous little blonde girls along with a painting each of them had done for me. An elder, John Sutherland, encouraged me all the way, kept in touch over the years and still is a friend. One lady said, "You are like David Read. He picked out the best from the rest." David Read had been Minister of Greenbank Church for only two or three years. He then left Scotland to become the famous Minister of a congregation in New York.

The congregation was rich in people, gifts, talents and reasonable but not extravagant wealth. Yet their Christianity seemed to me to be shallow and not of the same standard as their success and achievements in their professions. Somehow, the deeper truths of Christianity were hidden from them and they reacted with great arrogance when challenged by the pulpit. Edinburgh congregations are pampered and spoilt, I deduced, perhaps more so than in the middle class areas of the rest of Scotland.

## Ministry Of Deliverance

I have always had an inner life, existing alongside the external social person. I have kept this inner counsel silent. It would have seemed unbearable to articulate every inner thought. It would have been impossible to live other than as a hermit unless one ministered objective truths of Christian expectation rather than one's own subjective understanding. Perhaps this is what all successful ministers do. However, I had learned in personal experience that this subjective understanding and inner life was more real and true than anything exterior. It was a journey that I was on - to the interior of my own life and consciousness - to where God wanted to meet me - not on the outside - but deep within my soul.

Within weeks of arriving in Edinburgh, I had noticed an advertisement for a conference on the healing ministry. I decided to go along. There were various speakers but the last of them, an Anglican priest called Donald Baker spoke about the wrongs, harmfulness and sinfulness of dabbling in spiritualism and the occult. I sought his advice. He referred me to the Scriptural passage Deuteronomy 18:9-13 which warned against involvement with the unseen spiritual world. Donald Baker offered to give me the ministry of deliverance.

I accepted this offer and submitted myself to his ministry. A blessing followed. I had extricated myself from earlier participation in psychical research by my inner leading and spiritual instincts but, on accepting the need for repentance and ministry I discovered the Objective Kingdom Of Grace, as an actual reality and not just as a doctrine to be believed. Donald Baker also attempted an analysis of my own psyche which was flawed. He coupled this with a diminution of my theological heritage and tradition. He seemed to overdramatise everything. In the midst of his ministry to me, my gentle internal witness reassured me with words which, had I addressed them to him, would have said, "You would not understand." However, at the level of meeting the unseen spiritual world, I believe he was correct in his understanding and in the teaching and advice he gave me. My own Lord, who knew me better than Donald Baker, opened my eyes to his own Kingdom of Grace as an Objective Reality in this moment of submission. Like Naaman and like Jesus, it is in dying to self that we are healed and born again to eternal life.

I had applied for admission to Oxford University to study for a doctoral degree. I sought the blue ribbon of theology. It was a dream, but I was on my way. Little did I know what I would find there. I could never have expected what was in store, both in personal suffering, and in God's breathtaking confirmation of my call in His service.

# 2 : The Ministry Of Angels

## Oxford

In October 1975 I arrived in Oxford to take up studies which I hoped would lead to the degree of Doctor of Philosophy. Having had no knowledge of Oxford Colleges, I simply left the choice of College to the University Admissions Office. But, while praying over the application form some months before I had consciously prayed, "I will go where I am most needed."

I was glad to accept the offer of a place at Hertford College. When I arrived there I found the spiritual atmosphere anything but beautiful. I had wanted some spiritual privacy but I wanted also to experience Anglican church life and worship. I received conflicting reports about what went on in the College Chapel. I was aware of carrying golden treasure within my being, aware too of being in a hostile environment, and this made me guarded. I did not answer the forward personal questions that were asked of me at meal-times. I played the archetype dour Scot for safety and for survival.

It seemed good to me to accept the discipline of attending College Holy Communion at 8 30am Sunday by Sunday because I have always loved services of Holy Communion. I intended to dedicate myself for each week's work at that particular time. And so I did. Sadly, however, there was no spiritual peace or joy to be found at these services for me. The personality of the Chaplain obtruded. It was the custom for students to comment on the sermon and pray in an extemporary manner. This then was some kind of evangelicalism. During prayers of intercession, only one congregation was ever mentioned, St Aldate's, evangelical by reputation whose Rector was Michael Green. This seemed a far cry from the image of Oxford. It was religious introversion and it did not seem healthy to me. Although I continued to attend, I always breathed a huge sigh of relief when it was over. As the weeks went on, I found that my spiritual person and internal peace were being affected.

I met the Chaplain Michael Chantry on several occasions and the best that I could say for him at the beginning was that he seemed to be under personal stress. He probably needed help but I was doubtful if he realised how much this may have been so. The Senior Student denounced his 'tactless introspective meddling.' An academic described him as 'dull.' He was a bully though without the sensitivies required to properly minister to students. He interpreted differing opinions as personal rejection and even as spiritual contumacy. But he had gathered a clique of immature students around him. Were these props which supported him? I thought so. He once mentioned having financial problems. That was not unusual for a clergyman with children and in itself was no shame. But was his employment at Hertford motivated by the love of God and the care of students or by the need of money? I began to feel that my spiritual life was being subjected to spiritual coercion. There are groups of evangelicals who pray intensely for individuals without telling them that they are doing so. I have never liked this practice. I felt that that was happening to me. It began to affect my concentration and therefore affected my work. For some reason I kept attending these services of Holy Communion. A wiser person would have ceased to do so. The usual service was often shortened with necessary sentences left out. The appearance was one of hurry and lack of real spiritual concern. The Chaplain seemed to be paranoid about real or imagined criticism. His reference to everyone's sexual needs seemed inappropriate and unhealthy in the context of early morning Holy Communion.

Significantly, every week of term I went on to attend the University Sermon and Parish Communion in the University Church of St Mary The Virgin. The sermons usually provided something to disagree with. The services of Holy Communion were however spiritual, beautiful and meaningful and I was blessed in taking Holy Communion for the second time. The contrast was great. Here was peace and privacy and gentleness of worship - what I was looking for in church attendance as a post-graduate student from Scotland. I was surprised by the anti-establishment tone of the vicar's sermons. It was no surprise to me to read some years later that Peter Cornwell had 'gone over' to the Roman Catholic Church - one of a number of married Anglican priests accepted by that Church.

## Troubled Times

Hilary Term of 1976 began in January. Communion services at Hertford College became even more unpredictable and unpleasant. It seemed strange in university to hear repeated denunciations of the place and importance of the mind. It was not Biblical either if Our Lord's teaching in St Luke 10:27 was to be taken seriously. The celebrant's conduct was erratic and a number of his pronouncements were troubled and confused. On Sunday morning February 23rd 1976, he exclaimed in the middle of his homily, "I have enemies in this College." That may have been true but I did not think that an early service of Communion was the time or place to be saying so. I began to feel that I should begin to make some contribution to the free prayers during the service. I had never done so, wanting to worship in peace and anonymity.

That week, a post-graduate student suffered some personal abuse. He had attended the Chapel but had become disenchanted. The Chaplain invited him to a 'reconciliatory' talk at which he called the student 'arrogant.' This was far from true. I felt that I should address this Chaplain in the context of worship at the time for sharing and commenting which was always part of the service. However, I felt that there was some kind of spiritual struggle involved and that there was more happening than I understood. I did not think from personal experience that the Chaplain would listen to reasonable conversation. Bullies generally need just a little of their own medicine for them to find the pathway to change.

On Thursday 5th March 1976, I entered a discipline of prayer and fasting which lasted until the service of Holy Communion on the 8th. During that time, I realised for the first time just how seriously my own spiritual health had been affected. My capacity to 'think spiritually' had been impaired. My 'God consciousness' had been damaged. The three day spiritual discipline restored my soul. Towards the end of the time of preparation, a message was formulated in my mind which, I believed, I was to deliver during the service of Holy Communion. There was a healing and saving intention in this 'Word' for the Chaplain. It was meant for the health and welfare of students in Hertford College. It was to be communicated quietly but firmly during the time for free discussion and prayer.

On Sunday 8th March, I set out at 8 00am to attend Communion. I sought God's blessing on my life and intended action. The sky was overcast. I asked for the 'sun of righteousness' described in Malachi 4:2 to shine upon me. As I walked towards the College, the clouds above and in front of me parted and on my head and breast shone the light and warmth of the sun. I was given strength and peace. It occurred to me that I might have to suffer for what was about to happen. I even thought that my post-graduate career could be damaged or even terminated. I expected to surrender a measure of privacy. However, I remembered that Jesus had accepted the necessity of the Cross of Calvary. What was asked of me was much easier. It had been my long-standing ambition to become a Doctor of Philosophy of Oxford University. I was, however, prepared to risk its fulfilment.

## A Saving Word

During the time of open discussion and comment I delivered the 'Word' in a quiet voice of petition to the Chaplain.

> *"I have a Word for you Michael: it has come as a result of three days of fasting and prayer; In the Name of God Almighty, and under the protection of the Cross of Jesus Christ, His Son our Lord, and with the instruction of the Holy Spirit.*
> *You continue to place yourself and your own opinions between me and the mouths of my children, says the Lord*
> *You have injured and scattered more of my children than you will ever know, says the Lord*
> *As for those who remain, you cover their souls with your own darkness and uncleanness*
> *This is known in heaven.*
> *You are called to resign this Chaplaincy and to seek the deliverance of the Lord Jesus Christ for your troubles, and the peace of God Almighty for the rest of your life on earth.*
> *And you will ignore this warning at your eternal peril."*

The reaction was not unexpected. It was not receptive. "Yes, well, it's nice to criticise, it's nice to criticise," said the Chaplain. I said that it was not and added "It has broken my heart to have had to do this." He said he did not believe that. I asked if I should repeat the Word. He said "If you want to." I did. Word for Word. Exactly. I looked sadly at him and said "There's no repentance." He said in a derogatory way "How do you know there's no repentance? How do you know there's no repentance?" During prayer I asked the Father of our souls to take 'the hireling' from our midst and in His own time and circumstance send a true pastor for His children in Hertford College. However, there was no commotion - rather an atmosphere of passivity and resignation. At breakfast the Chaplain said, "Well Robert I see that Oxford got beaten again yesterday," referring to the local football team which he supported.

The Word was a direct, saving and living Word which nevertheless exposed the organised and external formalities of some evangelical religion. Evangelicals deal in the certainties of past history and in the certainty of a distant God but many are not at all redeemed in living fact. Therefore formal adherence to doctrine and a harshness towards others take the place of a truly realised and inspired relationship with God in Jesus Christ. Add personal problems, anxieties and false dichotomies and you get an unstable and unattractive picture. If this becomes oppressive over vulnerable people's lives, it can assume an objectively demonic character. Therefore what is portrayed as spiritual light is in fact spiritual darkness. It was that darkness which the living Word recognised and addressed in Oxford - that great place of learning and high temple of Anglicanism, and it was given by a Presbyterian and a Scot. The same Oxford where few people took Christianity seriously and believed much or anything. Where theologians desecrated Christian truth with their prejudices and ignorance.

I spent the remainder of that Sunday attending Parish Communion at St Mary's, having lunch with a friend (to whom I said nothing about what had just happened) at St Edmund Hall and listening to a performance of the St Matthew Passion at the City Hall. When I returned to my lodgings that evening, a postcard awaited me inviting me to meet a certain tutor and the Chaplain the following day. I declined to go to this meeting. The tutor wrote to me expressing his regret that I had not attended. He also asked me to do nothing to 'disrupt' public worship and this suggested that what had happened had been misrepresented.

On March 17th I received a note summoning me to appear before the Principal of Hertford College. He was Geoffrey Warnock, philosopher, agnostic and husband of Mary Warnock. He was an approachable and decent enough man and was held responsible for having revived Hertford College by admitting able pupils from comprehensive schools. An entirely spiritual matter had become one of discipline. I was annoyed that my first personal meeting with the Principal was to be in this context. The questions which the Principal asked indicated to me that further misrepresentation had taken place. I was disappointed that the Principal seemed to have believed what he had been told and had not waited to make a proper and balanced judgement. I was rebuked for being 'impolite' at Communion. The Principal gave me sufficient tacit indication to conclude that he knew that all was not well. Yet he was prepared to do nothing. He asked me why I had not just gone away like the rest. I was warned as to my future conduct and dismissed with some grace.

## Conflict

At the beginning of Trinity term, I began to attend services of Communion though not every week as had been the case since arriving in Oxford. The celebrant did not welcome my appearance. He spoke of being afraid and of "a man taking on a College single handed and then taking on the world." The time of open discussion and prayer had been stopped. The atmosphere was not such as one would expect from and in a service of Holy Communion. It was as if a struggle was taking place in the unseen realms. One week-end I visited my sister Shona, her husband Ian and children Kenneth and Ruth who lived near London. On the way back I noticed a poster in Oxford Railway station. It read, 'Be not afraid, but speak and hold not thy peace, for I am with thee.' This was a quotation from Acts 18:9-10, referring to one of Paul's visits to Corinth.

I attended Communion on May 9th. Discussion time had returned. I contributed. There was no problem. I attended communal breakfast afterwards. On May 12th, as I walked to the University Parks, the sky was overcast. I again sought the 'sun of righteousness' to shine. It did, enveloping my soul, head and breast. I felt close to God.

On May 16th I attended Holy Communion. It was a disturbing experience. Non-sequiturs permeated the unprepared homily. The Chaplain spoke in a mocking way of "a man in College trying to follow Jesus." His voice became faster and louder suggesting inner turmoil, stress and spiritual pressure. The lack of coherence, form or structure was not untypical of his sermons but that morning it was greater than usual. Twice he exclaimed as if something was being pushed out from deep within him almost against his own wishes "It didn't have to be a physical resurrection. It didn't have to be a physical resurrection." During the time of prayer, I prayed a prayer using words of deliverance with great strength. When I was doing so I thought the Holy Spirit was sweeping through me to the Chaplain. Others prayed too for different things. Breakfast followed. That afternoon, I felt exhausted. I attended Evensong at one of the city churches and found comfort. On Tuesday 18th I was approached by one of the students who belonged to the Chaplain's group. I was asked how long I would be at Hertford and if I intended coming to Communion services in future. I affirmed my intention to complete my Doctorate and to continue to attend Communion Services. The following day (May 19th), I took myself to the University Parks to pray. If Sunday had been my own Mount Carmel experience, this was my Horeb. There was sadness in my soul and I was troubled and burdened. I sought the 'sun of righteousness.' I was dressed in a shirt and slacks. It began to rain. This became a downpour. Thunder roared and forked lightning streaked from the sky, crackling around me with frightening ferocity. I stood under the trees. The rain dripped off the boughs on to my head and shoulders. I looked upward and prayed, "O God, I ask you to take away my life just now, if I am in the wrong, lest I should ever, any more, harm your church or your people." I waited.

After a few minutes the thunder rolled away and lightening ceased. I could see both move in the distance towards the south. The sky brightened. I walked slowly to my lodgings. I changed clothes and lay down to sleep. In the evening I took up my Bible. I had been reading from the Book of Revelation, a chapter each day. Today was chapter four. My mind was arrested by verse five which reads, "Flashes of lightening were coming from the throne and the sound of peals of thunder, and in front of the throne there were seven flaming lamps burning, the seven spirits of God." (Jerusalem Bible)

This to me described my afternoon experience. I felt cared for. I continued to read in chapter five. The words "Because you were sacrificed" impressed upon my mind. Much as I pondered these words, I could not connect them with my immediate experience. That night, I slept more soundly than for some time.

When I arrived at College the next day, Thursday May 20th a note awaited me. It summoned me to appear before the Principal that afternoon at 4 00pm. I attended.

| | |
|---|---|
| Principal : | *"Don't go back to Communion."* |
| Robert : | *"You can't tell me not to go to Communion."* |
| Principal : | *"Well if you must go, don't pray."* |
| Robert : | *"You can't tell me not to pray.* |
| | *It is my life to pray."* |
| Principal : | *"Well if you can't keep silent, don't go back."* |

The Principal left his room without grace and closed his door. I was left to make my own exit. That evening, the meaning of the words, "You were sacrificed" struck me. I had been blamed for a disturbance in Chapel. It became clear to me that I could accomplish nothing more by continuing to attend Communion Services in Hertford College. From that day I never returned. I continued to take Holy Communion at St Mary's.

On 29th May I wrote a letter of formal complaint to the Principal offering evidences for the problems in the Chaplaincy. I listed three areas of concern, College, Treatment of Individual Students and Conduct of Holy Communion. I recognised the dangers in forming a clique of immature students around the chapel which in turn excluded other students, some of whom were of more mature and deeper Christian Faith. There was continual breach of pastoral trust and, as is the practice in evangelical circles, individual lives were discussed when they are not present. Conduct of Holy Communion did not conform to accepted practice in the Church of England. Geoffrey Warnock acknowledged the complaint but seemed not prepared to do anything about it. His reply said "I believe you are mistaken in your basic complaint and I must add that I am rather astonished by the assurance with which you feel called upon to make it."

I then wrote to the Bishop of Oxford, Kenneth Woollcombe. I received a two-sentence reply saying that 'my problem' had been referred to my tutor. My tutor was not unkind but did not take the issue seriously. I received another summons to meet the Principal. He asked me why I'd written to the Bishop.

| | |
|---|---|
| Principal : | *"You're mad."* |
| Robert : | *"No, I'm not."* |
| Principal : | *"It sounds cracked to me.* |

|            | *Will you not go and see a psychiatrist?"* |
| Robert :   | *"Yes, I'll go and see a psychiatrist* |
|            | *on one condition, if the Chaplain* |
|            | *goes to see a psychiatrist."* |
| Principal : | *"That means no."* |
| Robert :   | *"No it doesn't. I'm willing* |
|            | *to be investigated."* |
| Principal : | *"You're mad."* |
| Robert :   | *"It's not true."* |
| Principal : | *"Will you not go and see a psychiatrist?"* |
| Robert :   | *"It's quite unnecessary."* |

I told the Principal "I hold you morally responsible that that man continues as Chaplain of this College." He agreed that he was. It would have been a social revolution if the Principal had taken me seriously. The authority structures of the College and the conventions of English society would have been stood on their head. Oxford had survived for centuries on the silence of those abused by its questionable preferences. No issue of justice or right or truth mattered more than expediency and self-defensiveness. The old pals act. Straightforward corruption. The principle is not admitted. Academics bind together and wait. Students come, students go. The overall strategy is not to take much seriously. Not God. Not a humble Scot. Not a Living Word of God.

On a beautiful evening the following week, I entered the University Parks. The sun, although setting, was glorious, crimson in its aspect, flooding the whole pastoral scene with light and warmth. There were few people around. I lay down near two bushes. I wept. Later I returned home, feeling demeaned and destitute.

## Aiona

I enjoyed the summer months of 1976. My mother had left Kilwinning after twenty-nine years to live in the village of Dundonald where she had gone to school as a girl. I suggested to her that she call the her little house 'Aiona' which I interpreted as 'Ages To Come.' The move had taken place at the very end of 1975. I spent my holiday laying out the gardens of her new home. It was a fabulous summer. I thoroughly enjoyed the fresh air, the outdoor work and the beauty of that particular part of Ayrshire. By September, I was ready to return to Oxford for whatever was in store. I was grateful still to be a post-graduate there and I was determined to complete my studies.

## Further Trouble

On arriving back at Hertford, I learned that a post-graduate student whom I'd known had suffered from association with the Chapel group. He had attended Chapel regularly but had expressed serious reservations about what went on there. He had often complained that in his view the Chaplain reduced Christianity to nothing. His most frequent grievance was "There is a contradiction in that that man is a priest." The Chaplain had invited him for a meal. The student had repeatedly asked the Chaplain "Are you a Christian?" The only answer he had received was "What do you mean?" After having had spiritual coercion visited on him, he had taken a form of nervous breakdown. He was committed to hospital and put on drugs. The student eventually had to leave Oxford and return home without completing his degree course. Another student who had attended Chapel had also decided to worship elsewhere. The Chaplain then expressed doubts about his mental health to his tutor. The tutor rejected these representations. The student took a 'First' in physics and went on to doctoral studies. Thus the students who suffered during my time at Hertford College were post-graduates, committed Christians with sensitivities and intelligence. They expressed doubts about the conduct of the Chaplaincy and they suffered for so doing.

I did not attend Chapel but I felt that I was still subject to 'spiritual coercion'. On 7th November 1976 Lord Hailsham preached the University Sermon in St Mary's. The church was full. The Principal of Hertford attended. I could not remember that happening before. I rejoiced to hear, ringing from that famous pulpit, among other things, the following words:

"....A modern university is concerned with truth...we are surely under an obligation to provide an intellectual justification for our faith in a place of learning and a climate of scepticism......The discharge of this duty is no easy option even as compared with those who live a more practical form of Christian life.............It requires indispensably a life of spiritual peril and suffering....It is only Christian men who may save even pagan things..They must not permit themselves to be driven back into the catacombs, or made to occupy some obscure intellectual ghetto..."

I think that the Principal recognised the joy on my face at the end of the service. He seemed most anxious not to meet me on leaving the church. I returned to my lodgings and began to consider how I might continue my particular struggle. Within the hour I'd formulated an idea for a public debate on Christianity in Hertford College. I invited the Chaplain to meet me and informed the leaders of student groups. He never replied. The Principal told me in another letter that he would advise the Chaplain not to take part in any debate. How strange, I thought, in famous Oxford, not to have a debate on Christianity! Why? I wrote to the Principal and questioned his competence and impartiality to decide on a spiritual matter. I ended up before him once again. The discussion was frank. I distinguished cultural Christianity and its spiritual forms. I was advised to let the matter drop. Recalling his previous suggestions, I said, "I thought it was only in Russia that dissidents were reduced to the status of psychiatric cases." He did not reply. I named the other students who had suffered. He did not respond. He accused me of arrogance. I asked for an independent investigation of my complaints. There was no reply.

The Principal said I could attend Communion as long as I did not pray. I replied, "You cannot tell me not to pray." I was ordered not to take the matter outside the College. I said, "You wouldn't like that would you?" He said "No." I said, "Neither would I." The meeting ended with me saying how disappointed I was at receiving this kind of treatment at Oxford.

I was still being subjected to spiritual coercion. I sent three notes indicating that I was aware of this spiritual coercion. Eventually it stopped. About the same time a temporary tutor for graduates summoned me to meet him. He was a kind of academic hit-man who bullied people who would not conform. He labled my original interjection on May 8th as 'disruption'. "We can't have two chaplains," said he. I made the reasonable point that I had made a formal complaint which had not been taken seriously. Since this matter affected student welfare, I had expected it to be referred to the College Governing Body. "It would not come before us in that form," he replied. He said that only the Bishop could ask the Governing Body to intervene. I told him that the Bishop had referred my complaint to my tutor. "Standard procedure," he said. He suggested I organise a College petition, but I thought he was merely setting me up for expulsion. I said "Classical prophecy is an individual voice." I lamented the lack of interest in the truth. The tutor told me that I had made my point and then used words such as "have him put away," "expelled," and "sent down," describing possible fates for me if I did not cease my struggle. I refused to be browbeaten into submission. The tutor said that I had challenged "the authority and dignity of the Principal." I said that I would engage in no organised student activity but I added words which hung on the ensuing silence, "I cannot sit still among the dead and be silent." The matter of the Chaplaincy was one of conscience. I absolved the tutor from responsibility for what might happen to me since he had clearly stated where I stood in relation to those who could have me expelled. Oxford bullying. USSR style. Chinese style. Tyranny. Injustice. Godlessness.

On November 24th I received another letter from the Principal requiring me not to attend Chapel on the 28th and inviting me to come and discuss this if I would like to. I replied by saying that I had had no intention of attending Chapel on the 28th, and that I was unaware of any service since I had received no term syllabus. I also suggested that he consider what had made him write this letter if not false representation. Finally, I was covertly informed by a fellow post-graduate student that I had been declared "persona non grata" in Oxford. This intelligence did not cause me to lose any sleep.

About this time I was being interviewed for a post as a part-time tutor in a College of Education near Oxford. I was given the job verbally. Then - I received a letter telling me that I would not, in fact, be getting the job. I asked for an explanation but none came. The friend who had recommended me for the job told me that tales of what had been going on at Hertford had passed through the grapevine to my detriment.

In the first months of 1977, I continued to make representations from time to time on the subject of the Chaplaincy at Hertford College. My theologocal tutor, Professor John Macquarrie, a Scot, former Presbyterian and convert to Anglo-Catholicism was appalled by what I had said and done. He begged me to desist. He suggested having a chat with Don Cuppitt, who, he told me, was interested in my case. Cuppitt of the extreme reductionism and liberalism and nothingness and denial of Christianity? I said "No thanks."

## Studies

My studies had progressed in spite of these distractions which seemed to be the spiritual price I had to pay for the academic qualification which I sought. I gained doctoral status after my first academic year and continued with the hard work of research into John McLeod Campbell's life and thought. It was always a comfort and inspiration to be working on a person who had suffered at the hands of his fellow clergy. To my surprise, I began to see the theological difficulties his views had presented to the Church of Scotland between 1825 and 1831. I was not convinced by his theology of the atonement which seemed to depend more on Christ's confession in Gethsemane than His death on Calvary. The story of John McLeod Cambell's partial vindication, however, encouraged me in my own spiritual battles.

I enjoyed the academic work and the friendship of post-graduates. I used to look forward to seminars in Campion Hall. I met Roman Catholic priests from various places throughout the world. Some seemed incredibly sophisticated and yet I found them unconvincing as human beings. I argued with one about his interpretation of the altercation between Jesus and the Syrophoenician woman (Matthew 15:21-28). He said Jesus was driving the woman to deep humility. I said I thought he was having a laugh with her. Probably the truth was half-way between our respective points of view. Edward Yarnold and Kallistos Ware were well respected. I discussed some of what was going on at Hertford only with Billy Abraham who later became an academic and published books on theology. I thought his young son Timothy would surely, one day, follow him into the ministry.

I had little respect for the theology of Maurice Wiles and his 'Myth Of God Incarnate' cronies. If my own life was anything to go by, they were mistaken indeed not only in denying the supernatural dimension of Biblical revelation, but in being so cocksure that nothing similar could happen today. John Macquarrie left me to myself. I appreciated that even though the work I produced was not of as high a standard as I would have wished. The diversions in Hertford reduced the effectiveness of my academic training. However, they brought a spiritual deepening and awakening which gave the highest significance to the remainder of my life.

An American post-graduate researching Kierkegaard with Macquarrie met me after one of his tutorial sessions. He told me that Macquarrie had been angry with conclusions which had differed from his own. He had taken the essay in question, rolled it up, and had begun to eat it. Oxbridge is, of course, famous for its eccentrics. It later amused me to think that this suggested a new style of assessing academic work. Instead of giving marks out of one hundred per cent, it might be possible to grade essays as follows: delicious, tasty, bland, undercooked, inedible and offal!

I had many laughs in Hertford with other post-graduates. On one occasion another American who was from a wealthy Californian background, entered the middle common room. He looked ghastly. I exclaimed, "And here, gentlemen, is proof that there is life after death." His older brother once sent him a greetings card for his birthday - it was a get-well-card. He bought a Morgan sports car to take back home after his one year Master's degree course.

I met Kenneth Woollcombe, the Bishop of Oxford. I was not impressed. John Robinson came to speak. I asked him a question. He replied, "Oh - I wouldn't go to the stake for much." Cardinal Suenens of Belgium led a mission which was less than challenging and more concerned with ecclesiastical diplomacy. Geoffrey Lampe gave the Bampton Lectures. I was dismayed by the assurance with which he took the reductionist path. Such lack of personal, spiritual and intellectual humility typified Oxbridge. The question of God was no more important than the question of which wine to have at an evening meal. The Christianity of choir-boys who had never become spiritual men was what I saw.

John R Gray, Moderator of the General Assembly of the Church of Scotland visited and I attended a reception for him in John Macquarrie's house at Christ Church. John Gray put a fatherly arm around me and wished me well. It was a helpful thing to do. I wrote to him years later when it was announced that he had terminal cancer. He replied briefly, saying, "It is much easier to die as a Christian than to live as one." He had his detractors in the Church of Scotland but proved himself a man of substance in his last days on earth.

I loved walking beyond Oxford to the countryside and neighbouring villages. I found the Cotswolds enchanting. Oxford itself stank in mid-winter. It was an unhealthy place with the strongest influenza germs I'd ever known. I took good advantage of whatever better weather came later in each year.

## Oxford And Westminster

On occasions I visited London and particularly enjoyed wandering around Westminster. I liked attending Strangers' Gallery. I remember listening to Harold Lever and Michael Hezeltine debating. Harold Lever suggested that the Honorable Gentleman's speech would be most acceptable to maiden ladies in Cheltenham. Tony Benn sat with his feet up on the table. What impressed me was the concurrence between the childish behaviour of the Oxford Union and the conduct of government. I attended Union debates on occasions. Benazir Bhutto and Colin Moynihan were there are at that time. I was amused by the immature pretensions of the speakers. One rather pathetic creature attempted seriously to model his rhetorical style on that of Winston Churchill though, unfortunately for him, there was no national crisis on which to depend for recognition. Rowan Atkinson appeared. I had enjoyed seeing him at the Edinburgh Festival Fringe.

Oxford taught me much. I learned about Britain, how it was governed, its conventions, its unwritten constitution which meant that a post-graduate had little means of redressing wrong other than to take a private law-suit. I saw how the establishment ruled by manipulating the ghastly English class system. Because there was no British Constitution each person who achieved a position with power over others was free to exercise such power without much restraint. The conventions of public school bred supine acceptance of the system and the perverted use of privilege. If you had suffered as a child at school you might want the chance to get your own back later in life. Was that why Margaret Thatcher disdained establishment people and values?

I realised that Scotland was a different country. I thought Scotland had democratic sensitivities not represented in the south and I considered that our general appreciation of life made us more sensible and humane. I suffered no inferiority complex. On the contrary, I felt grateful for the spiritual privileges of my tradition and I understood for the first time how distinct they were. I thought that spiritual privileges bred political privileges. It occurred to me that England lacked both in comparative measure.

There was one uproarious moment. I was watching the 1977 England versus Scotland football international on television in the company of about forty students packed into the television room at College. David Coleman was commentating in his usual biased fashion. At one point he exclaimed, "And there is Ray Clemence, the best goal-keeper in the world." I guffawed. One minute later, Kenny Dalglish received a pass, advanced on the English goal-keeper and placed the ball through his legs and into the net. I shouted out, "Oh yes, the best goal-keeper in the world." There was total silence in the room. Coleman did not say a word for more than a minute - the famous 'Coleman silence'. Scotland won. The fans invaded the pitch after the match and took pieces of turf as souvenirs. One student complained about this to me. I was amused and laughed much. One Anglican post-graduate student often baited me and mimicked a Scots accent. "Are you feeling dour today?" he would ask for a wheeze. I took this for some time and then once only quietly replied in front of others "While I realise that it is good for my soul to suffer your insults, if you do it again, I will break your nose." I was left in peace. I had my spiritual struggles in Hertford, but the entire experience of Oxford was seminal. I would not have missed it for anything. And if I had suffered much in Hertford College, the God who had led me there was about to reward me far beyond what my mental horizons could have ever imagined.

## Angels

On the first Sunday of Trinity Term 1977, I attended College Chapel Evensong. The Bishop of Norwich had been due to preach but had cancelled. The Chaplain's sermon was theologically and spiritually suspect. I had produced a report and sent a copy to the Bishop of Oxford. I wrote also to the Professor of Moral and Pastoral Theology on May 26th.

I then received a letter, dated 27th May 1977 from Geoffrey Warnock. "The College" had considered my case. I was not to communicate with the Chaplain. I was not to communicate about the Chaplain to anyone else. I was to cease to attend all services in the College Chapel. The letter informed me that if I breached these rules, I would be sent out of residence or expelled. Some of the Principal's colleagues had felt that I should be committed for psychiatric treatment. They had decided not to require this but to suggest its desirability.

I replied the following day saying that I understood "the factors underlying the resolution and opinion expressed" in his letter. "I feel myself to be in a position like that of a naval rating aboard a sinking ship, who, as he is about to be thrown into the sea, shouts, "We've been torpedoed," and is later court-martialled for speaking out of turn....For your own part, Principal, the letter is evidence of a continual cynicism toward Christianity. If all this 'God-business' is true (and it is) I'm sure you will not expect to be exempted from the necessity to give an account of your life. Therein, too, lies the source of my own peace, in this atrocious affair regarding the Chaplain of the College."

My health had deriorated. Above all, I now considered that I had been presumptuous and wrong, both in the original word spoken in Chapel at Communion and in my struggle to shed light on what I thought were oppressive and unhealthy goings-on around the Chapel group and actual harm to several students. I had been defeated in visible terms. Everyone had ignored my complaint and no-one had taken anything I said seriously. All that had happened was that I was thought to be in need of psychiatric care. I did not think that. What did bother me, however, was whether I had spoken falsely or presumptuously. If I was wrong, then I had to admit that my life was wrong and my call was at least suspect and at worst false.

The life experiment seemed to have ground to a halt. I had lost my way. I could see no way forward. Neither did it seem possible for me to carry on with my studies. The second year had gone reasonably well, but my relationship with God was more important to me than study for its own sake. Here was I, 'a lad o' pairts' in Oxford, England, in trouble, out on a limb. It looked as if I had confirmed all the worst prejudices about Scots and Presbyterians. The high culture of Oxford was seemingly too much for me. Like many before me over the centuries, I had been broken by Oxford.

I remembered that Donald Baker had told me about Crowhurst. It is an Anglican Healing Centre in Sussex. I had read the book 'Miracle At Crowhurst' by George Bennett and I had promised myself a visit there sometime. As I looked bleakly at my own personal future, now seemed like the right time to go. Even so, I was not enthusiastic about going to a 'Healing Centre' to admit my need of help.

There was no alternative however and I set off on 9th June 1977 to travel by train to Battle and then to go by taxi to Crowhurst. Rev Paul Peters was the Warden. He was a kindly man. I had taken my written account of the main problems I thought existed in Hertford. I handed it over ruefully, thinking that this man would not be sympathetic to a renegade from the north. However, he was really not much concerned with events in Oxford. He put aside time for a service of healing. I submitted myself to this out of great personal need. I asked forgiveness for my life and all that was wrong with it. I asked God to help me find the way forward.

Paul Peters' ministry to me was quiet and effective. I felt taken up into a clean spiritual environment. I just drifted and allowed whatever was to happen to happen. I think I took no food that evening. I was given a lovely room on the front of the house, upstairs, overlooking gardens. I lay in bed, propped up against the pillows and read my Bible. I would say that I was at peace. It was 9 30pm. In time I would have drifted off to sleep.

Suddenly the room was filled with a rushing kind of air. It was refreshing and stimulated and energised me. The room was bathed in light too. Five angels appeared before me, three on my left side and two on the right. An angel greater than the others came forward to me, and touched my mouth with what looked like a live coal from an altar. The angels remained for some time and then departed. I felt supremely blessed and extraordinarily peaceful. Later, I fell asleep and rested well.

Next morning I began to realise the significance of what had happened. I read Isaiah chapter six, verses six and seven.

**"One of the seraphim flew to me, carrying in his hand a glowing coal which he had take from the altar with a pair of tongs. He touched my mouth with it and said, "This has touched your lips; now your iniquity is removed and your sin is wiped out."**

The beauty and significance of what had happened slowly dawned on me. I read on:

**"Go, tell this people, However hard you listen, you will never understand. However hard you look, you will never perceive. This people's wits are dulled; they have stopped their ears and shut their eyes, so that they may not see with their eyes, nor listen with their ears, nor understand with their wits, and then turn and be healed."**

All the pain and trauma of the last twenty months evaporated. I was not simply healed. I was elevated. Could it be possible that I was being given a calling within the New Covenant comparable to that of Isaiah of Jerusalem under the Old Covenant? It was surely a vindication of the Word spoken at Chapel in Hertford on March 8th 1976, fifteen months before. I now felt that my original call to the ministry was genuine after having had months of anguish and doubt. When I looked back on my childhood and adult life, it all seemed to make sense although I was filled with regret for the sins I had committed in my life which were not worthy of this great and high calling. Yet God had blessed and vindicated me. God still watched over me, had time for me, knew me and loved me. All of this was so wonderful that I could not express it. I thought of myself as being privileged among human beings who have lived this earthly life. This was not a subjective 'vision'. It was an objective occurrence in the spiritual realm. These angels came to me. They were real beings. Angels exist. So does God!

I told Paul Peters what had happened and he said nothing but he nodded his head affirmatively. I decided to tell no-one at Oxford. This beautiful thing from God was too lovely, too precious to be cheapened in the telling. Who, in any case, would believe me? No-one. Isaiah himself had written, "Who could have believed what we have heard?" I also read Isaiah chapter fifty-three. I accepted that there was another aspect to this calling. It may mean that I would in some ways be a suffering servant for the rest of my life. The prospect did not fill me with encouragement. However, there was only one way forward. It was God who had all the words of eternal life. Thus I was kept humble from the outset of this new and exciting chapter in my life. Crowhurst was a watershed. God raised me up. I wished I could have stayed there. If that was a mount of transfiguration, a deep valley awaited me. But no-one can take way the joy of being so especially blessed by God. I keep it in trust for eternity.

## A Large Space

June until August of 1977 was a blessed time for me. I had decided to remain in Oxford and work throughout the summer on my doctoral thesis. I would take long walks into the surrounding countryside during which I felt closer to God than at any time in my life. I thought of many things. It seemed to me that much of the theology that had been written over the last two hundred years was mistaken. People wrote about their doubts as to the truth of the Bible, in negation of spiritual and supernatural dimensions to life and about the closed universe of matter and the human mind. They may have achieved recognition while simply testifying to their own poverty of understanding. Theological conclusion without spiritual seeking and finding must be a dangerous game. Yet European university faculties of theology and divinity had been dominated by agnostics, atheists, reductionists, scoffers and sceptics for a very long time.

The Church itself was corrupted, I concluded. People there are in holy orders who actually do not know anything with certainty about what the Church has professed for centuries. The decline of Christianity in Britain is accompanied by expressions of doubt about the basic tenets of faith. The spiritual claims of Christianity do not seem to fit the scientifically ordered society. Yet, that society was fragmenting. The influence of Marxist thought still permeated much of academia. Freud too, had turned many away from faith by offering psychologically based explanations for happenings and human conduct. Darwin still ruled in most biological research. The infinite dimensions of space corresponded to the longevity of the planet earth and the solar system. It was hard to make a case for God through words and arguments alone.

I considered the possibility that in later times, perhaps two hundred years or so, Oxford might be over-run and destroyed in war, and the rest of Britain with it. It was possible if not likely that there would be some kind of nuclear holocaust in the future life of the human community. Being an ordinary human concerned with self-preservation, I thought that this might not happen in my own lifetime, and I was relieved. Yet I also thought with much humility that a society which cannot treat a poor man like myself justly does not deserve the sustaining protection of our Maker. Oxford and Cambridge, the twin cultural mammals on which Englishmen had for centuries been breast-fed but never weaned, were such grotesque examples of class division, privilege, misuse of position, outright social snobbery, chaotic deceitful presentation, false worship, false teaching and personal sycophancy that they did not deserve in a just God's eyes to persist. I had not expected this of Oxford. I did not voluntarily form such a view. It was the logical inference of the ministry of angels. Foolish it would be for the proud of heart to dismiss the possibility that God's divine will extends into human history. Justice and truth come in time to light. Christ's resurrection is clearly seen with hindsight. The world can accommodate the possibility of His resurrection. It does make sense to some.

This interaction of God and human history was contrary to the theology of the myth peddled in Oxford at the very moment when it happened. How apposite. How precise. How fearful. How just. People have an obligation to act fairly to one another. The deliberate denial of justice and the crushing of a quest for truth is not tolerable to our Maker. If a poor man cannot worship God freely then the society which will not allow him to do so must perish. Yet there is an offer of forgiveness upon repentance. Were these sodden cultures willing to re-embrace a truthful and dynamic Christianity, they may avoid for future generations the consequence of present actions. Indeed, God is gracious. Here is a correction to the mistaken, sight to the blind and a way forward for the lost. But will they take it - riven with their theological prejudices and shallow humanisms? And the scoffing agnostics and atheists - will they sigh with wonder to learn of the reality of the Living God in their midst in judgement such as is recognisable as just. Reverse the political correctness! Believe in Jesus Christ for His own sake, fully, profoundly. You will be saved. Christianity is meant to save the world not to destroy it. But the rejection of Christianity is self-destruction.

I thought of the purpose and influence of the writings of the classical prophets of Judaism. They had articulated a wider knowledge of God than had been the case in the earlier period of Israel's history. They made an intellectual case for believing in One Maker of the universe. They corresponded historical events to human disbelief in and refusal to relate in personal and social terms to this One Creator. They looked forward to new revelations of God to come.

I viewed the spiritual decay of 'the west' with a broad sweep. If the institutional church continued to die, what would take its place? Would Islam once again spread west? Would secularism triumph? I concluded that Christianity would only be reborn in the world through a dying of the old Christianity of the corrupted church and the awakening of everyone to a new and more immediate knowledge of God in and through Jesus Christ, His Son.

It occurred to me now that the supernatural happenings associated with the life of Christ were probably true. If something as beautiful could have happened to me, then surely what was recorded as having happened in Jesus Christ must have happened. I could see that the virgin birth might have happened as it is stated in the Gospels of Matthew and Luke. The miracles too, were probably reliable accounts of actual supernatural occurrences. The physical resurrection of Jesus I had always thought was without comparison and without deniability. But now I felt that I knew that it must have taken place as the Gospels of Matthew, Mark, Luke and John testified, notwithstanding the minor deviations that anyone would accept from different sets of eyes and ears. So many miserable man-made 'theologies' of our time denied any direct historical connection between God and our life and society. This undermined the main purpose of creation and of human life which is to live in loving personal relationship to God. The society which had despised this purpose had forfeited its right to continue in existence. God's providential ordering and sustaining would henceforth be unobtainable. History sooner or later would mark this truth out. Though many would not have eyes to see. Yet if there was collective repentance, a theological re-ordering of the prevailing agnosticism and a sincere return to the honouring of Jesus Christ in public and private life in this country, then mitigation and possibly even avoidance of the consequences of current behaviour could result.

All of this knowledge enthralled me and I felt greatly privileged to be party to it. I never thought of telling anyone. What delighted me was to know that my relationship with God was restored and indeed, set on a new plane. I hoped to complete my degree and return to Scotland. Any feelings of triumphalism were tempered by the remembering of the suffering servant, of Christ's own dying, and in recalling a tradition which held that Isaiah had been sawn in half during Manasseh's reign. I had been through enough suffering in the previous twenty months to understand that whatever was in store for me would not be a pathway of peace and ease nor a bed of roses. Indeed, I wondered if and how I could function in the church which was corrupted if I was called to be its minister and critic under the Lordship of its Head, Jesus Christ. The very serious question had to be considered "Does God repeat Himself?" Most Christian thinkers would say "No." And yet I could not deny the visitation of the angels or the specific ministry given to me. It had happened. What did it mean for me? I would learn as life went on.

## Dying

I had had no girlfriends for years. I was happy and content and my relationship with God filled me with peace and happiness. My academic work was on schedule for a spring 1978 submission and June graduation. My scholarship expired at the end of three years and I was under financial pressure to complete my doctorate within that time. However, in the weeks of 1977's high summer, I rarely missed an opportunity for a long walk each afternoon.

An American post-graduate (male) theology student had moved into the section of the graduate flats where I lived. I had been uncomfortable with his presence. I began to feel some of the coercion which had marked earlier times in Oxford. It became more difficult to pray in peace. Spiritual hostility visited me from time to time. There was nothing I could do. He had as much right to be there as I had.

One afternoon in late August I returned from a wonderful walk. I'd never felt as healthy or as happy. I lived in 'a high place' spiritually and rejoiced in relationship to my Saviour Jesus Christ. Our section of the building had rooms and a communal kitchen, bathroom and separate toilet. I went in to pass water. As I breathed my first breath inside the small, windowless, closed and restricted room, I felt unwell. There was a ghastly smell - an unclean atmosphere. Had someone been masturbating there before I myself had entered? The coincidence of this action and the presence which had been hostile to me resulted in my taking in a disease of some kind. It affected my breathing instantly. Over the next weeks that followed I felt progressively and slowly weaker. The spiritual coercion continued. I could not breathe properly and my sleeping pattern became more and more erratic and disturbed. I did not go to see any doctor and the reason was that I felt that whatever was wrong had had a spiritual and supernatural cause and would require a spiritual and supernatural solution. None came.

Throughout September and October my condition deteriorated. I had never been subject to any disease in my adult life and had never had to take medicine for any ongoing problem. I had always been blessed with rude peasant health. I was not asthmatic. I was not claustrophobic and I had been living in my room in the post-graduate building since the previous September without experiencing any health difficulties. I was working hard, typing chapters of my thesis for the penultimate draft. I worked late but sometimes had a short rest in the late afternoon. My diet was not wonderful but I was eating well enough. I did not have psychological problems since all that mattered to me by way of reassurance in relationship to God had been given to me.

By November I felt that something was wrong. Yet I trusted God for my life. I actually began to think I was dying. I thought that perhaps having been given such a beautiful gift from God, that my life was to end. I accepted this with equanimity. I did not fight. I did not weep. I did write to my mother to tell her I was ill. She told me later she was not surprised to learn this from me. She had felt me 'slipping away' for some time.

By December I was no longer able to study and my work had ground to a halt. It is not uncommon to 'dry up' in research, but this was more serious. I had no strength left. I spent a lot of time each day lying on my bed. I did not sleep at all at night. On the afternoon of December 10th 1977 about 4 30pm, I felt that I was about to leave this life. I was still and cold. I was inert, but conscious. My eyes closed. Whether I 'died' or not I do not know.

Suddenly, there appeared before me a vision of a golden crown and this was placed in my hand. I woke up. I sat upright. I leapt out of bed and wrote a note, 'I have the golden crown of victory.' Then I returned to bed and fell asleep. Later, I awoke and began to feel that the worst was over. I started to eat and thought that I had enough strength to go home to Dundonald for a three week holiday to see if my recovery could be completed.

I decided that I'd go via Edinburgh and I arranged an appointment with Reverend Clarence Finlayson, who had earlier in life been one of Cameron Peddie's associates in the healing ministry. I think I told him something of what I thought had been wrong with me but I was too weak to remember the details. He ministered to me and anointed me with oil in the name of Jesus. This 'anointing with oil' was exactly right for me. I felt the 'balm' penetrate my soul, where, I thought, the invasion had occurred. I felt a healing process take place. The 'unclean' thing was dealt with and I felt grace take over. Wholesomeness and wholeness began to take the place of whatever diminishing and destructive thing had resided within me. I was left, however, with a slight breathing weakness of which I was conscious on very rare occasions. It eventually disappeared completely in a place where there was much warmth and sunshine.

I arrived at Dundonald. Warmth and comfort awaited. The village in the countryside was beautiful in mid-winter. Fresh air and relaxation restored me. After three weeks of care and rest I felt fit and well and ready to resume my studies. I also felt ready to counteract and countermand anything that I might find in and around the halls of residence where I stayed in Oxford.

I set about completing my research and worked non-stop for three months. I have always been grateful that, notwithstanding the hindrance of that time of illness, I completed my doctoral thesis on time, in April 1978, two and a half years after arriving in Oxford. My 'viva' was in June and that evening I telephoned John Macquarrie to enquire about the result. To my lifelong joy he congratulated me on becoming a Doctor of Philosophy.

## The Holy City

One afternoon, in early 1978 as I was praying and meditating, a vision of a golden house appeared before me. I did not know what this meant. Some time afterwards a vision of the Holy City of Jerusalem appeared before me. It was beautiful, shining in gold and of huge expanse. The purpose of this vision was to give me assurance about my eternal place in God's Kingdom. Resulting from this vision I took a greater interest in the Book of Revelation. I thought of John Bunyan and 'Pilgrim's Progress.' The circumstances of his life and others to whom this particular vision have been given corroborate its objective truth. I learned what Jesus and all the great saints have said consistently through the ages. It is by way of negation that we find God. It is in dying that we are born to eternal life. It was so remarkable to me that I should experience these things in an age and culture in which doubt and scepticism rule. The safest thing seemed to me to keep as quiet as I could. I never thought anyone would believe me anyway. You cannot testify for yourself. Others must do so for you. The Vision of the Holy City has remained with me ever since and is part of my inner spiritual consciousness.

In addition to the vision of the Holy City of Jerusalem I received what is described in Revelation chapter three verse twelve:

**"He who overcomes, I will make him a pillar**
**in the temple of my God,**
**and he shall go out no more.**
**And I will write on him**
**the name of my God**
**and the name of the city of my God,**
**the new Jerusalem,**
**which comes down out of heaven**
**from my God.**
**and I will write on him my new name."**

I recognised that something was written on my soul in gold letters, the Names of God and of Jesus Christ and the name of the Holy City. I saw the initials of these names written on my forehead. These are often intimated to me as reminders of God's Grace and Faithfulness. The first visions of the Holy City appeared concidentally with the seventh anniversary of the time I received the vision of the opening door (Revelation 3:8) and its interpretation in church the same evening. Moreover, the texts form part of a unity in Revelation chapter three, verses seven to thirteen. I could never have manufactured such a coincidence. I receive these as a mental vision. Different was the visitation of the angels. Angels have bodies. Angels occupy space and time. Angels exist. So does God.

Visions are real too, dramatically so, and they are part of subjective consciousness as well as entries into an objective reality. They reveal the inner soul and confirm who one truly is in God's perfect sight. In Revelation chapter twenty-one there is a description of the Holy City appearing to the writer, whose name was John. Verse two reads:

**"Then I, John, saw the holy city,**
**new Jerusalem,**
**coming down out of heaven from God."**

Verse three reads:

**"Now God's home is with mankind!**
**He will live with them and they shall be his people.**
**God himself will be with them and he will be their God."**

This existential understanding of the eschatological vision is important. Distance between human beings and God is eradicated. There is both union and communion. Occasionally in Christian history individual lives remind us of the extent of the possibility of relationship with our Maker in and through Jesus Christ. I have never thought that those who look for the Second Coming of Jesus and the cessation of the world community were properly motivated.

I believe the vision of the Holy City given to me (and since it continues as a present reality) is a testimony to the incarnation of God and man in Jesus Christ. The union and communion of God and a human life is incarnational in principle and reality. The desire of God is personal inter-relationship with human beings. This is a higher truth than that of the end of the world. It more truly demonstrates the nature of our Maker and His faithfulness to the human race. I believe that the world will continue. It will get better and it will get worse. It may self-destruct. It may succumb to the processes of the expanding universe. I believe it is our Maker's intent to relate to each of us personally while we live this human life and to continue that relationship after physical death.

These intimations did not make me a perfect human being. Neither did I choose the cloister. I thought I'd take my chances in the world. I feared nothing and no-one on earth or anywhere else. Neither did I wish to move from one church or denomination to another. I presumed God knew what he was doing in having had me brought up a Protestant, in the Church of Scotland, of which I was a Minister. I sympathised with John Henry Newman but I had no sense of the necessity to make a linear journey across denominational boundaries. I intended to live naturally as a child of God in the world and keep the personality I was given and not become a product of any ecclesiastical mould. I thought it unwise to tell people my spiritual story until I felt the time was right. The climate of the late seventies was not favourable for any such intimation. As we approach the millenium, spiritual issues are informing debate and discussion about the nature of society. This does not surprise me.

## John McLeod Campbell

I was sustained throughout my spiritual struggle in Oxford by researching John McLeod Campbell. He was in some ways a kindred spirit. I identified with his impatience with the church of his day, with his zeal, with the misunderstandings which had broken him and with the marginalisation which characterised most of his life. I found solace in his distinction between spiritual things and ecclesiastical institutions and with his sensitivity to the sufferings of Jesus Christ as a spiritual person on earth. I parted company with McLeod Campbell in his emphasis on the atoning value of Christ's prayer in Gethsemane over against His actual death on Calvary. I concluded that he was not a thinker solely in the Reformed tradition and that he had invited reaction implicitly in his early ministry and explicitly in his later published theology. However, he was also a Christian romantic who struggled for a better life for his parishioners than perhaps they were able to understand was available to and for them in Christ. Today he is regarded as something of a saint. Spiritual truth is usually vindicated, given time.

## Graduation

I graduated on schedule in July. My mother came down to stay with my sister Shona and both attended. We had a lovely visit to Blenheim Palace on a beautiful afternoon. My doctoral thesis was not of the standard I would have wanted. But, given all else that had happened, I had achieved my goal. I had paid a terrible price in my spiritual life which God alone had repaid not only in full but with outrageous generosity. My academic training had ended. Here was I single, available for Christ's service, committed, well educated and ready. Would anyone want me as a minister? Could I work within the church? What price would I pay for doing so? How long would my life last? I felt that my own salvation was assured to me and that I should give back to the church whatever I could. I thought that God would hold the beautiful intimations of June 1977, December 1977 and early 1978 for me, whatever happened and although I thought it possible that I could so reject God that I could forfeit salvation, I did not see that ever happening. God had given me too much for me ever to turn away.

## Taking Leave

Before leaving Oxford, I asked to see Maurice Wiles. I appreciated the fact that when he met students he sat on a low chair at the same level as the student. I recalled to him John Wesley's ostracism from Oxford for preaching an immediate Christian Gospel. I also recalled John Henry Newman's rejection of Oxford Anglicanism in the nineteenth century. I then read some verses from Isaiah chapter six to him. I did not explain why I was doing so and told him nothing of what had happened to me over the past year. He looked at me quizically and gave me a typical Oxford reply. He said, "Have you any hobbies?" I left.

# 3 : Call To Africa

## Wandering In The Wilderness

I left Oxford in July 1978. I had twenty pounds in my pocket and no other money of any kind. I spent the summer months working as a builder's labourer. It was something of a change after the spiritual and intellectual heights of recent years. However, I was glad to be alive and summers in Ayrshire can be most pleasant.

I was most uncertain about what to do. I thought of not being a minister at all. It seemed to me that the church was so corrupt that I'd always find it difficult to live and work in. I wondered if I might not just get a job in industry and live a hidden spiritual life. One Sunday in September 1978 I conducted Morning Service in my home church at the invitation of David Ness, Minister of Dundonald Parish. For the one and only time in any public place I described the visitation of the angels at Crowhurst. I also stated that I had received a vision of the Heavenly City with the interpretation that it was meant to be to me an assurance of eternal life and salvation in and through Jesus Christ. I'm sure no-one could possibly have understood what I was saying. Now writing in 1996, I am glad that I made that public statement since anyone who might wish to suggest that I have invented such a spiritual call in the light of and to suit later circumstances may be refuted. I mentioned the visitation of the angels to my friend John Campbell not long afterwards and he asked "What do angels look like?" On 14th April 1989 during a visit to George Fox I also testified to and described the intimations of the divine given to me in 1977 and 1978. Otherwise I have never revealed these secrets of God's living providence. During the winter months I took a job helping a transport firm to set-up their business in Irvine. However, I was not cut out for that and by early 1979 I was thinking of going to America.

## New York New York

I set off in May of that year for NewYork. I was offered a job as a locum pastor in a Presbyterian church in a rough area. I thought that I would have to stay for ten years if I wanted to do anything worthwhile. I also considered the physical danger and did not feel convinced that I would survive. I travelled upstate but did not find the scenery particularly wonderful. I was interested by the names of towns in Jersey such as Tenafly and Paramus!

In New York a quite extraordinary supernatural occurrence took place which I can remember as if it was yesterday. My hosts, the Reformed Church of America had booked me into a hotel near Times Square. I was there only for a couple of days. One afternoon I went out for a walk. I found myself in a street with booths and film shows which seemed to be part of the New York sex industry. I got lost and could not find my way back to the hotel. A 'young man' appeared by my side and led me along a sidewalk, across a road and along to a bus stop. He never spoke to me nor I to him. He was gracious and caring and smiled, but never said a word. He was dressed in a grey suit, pink shirt and striped tie. How did he know I was lost? How did he know where I stayed? How did he know what number of bus I required to get back to the hotel? He knew all of these things it seemed. He then disappeared without saying anything. People say that they have had such saving angelic experiences. It was supernatural, I am sure. In Mark 16:5 there is a reference to a 'young man' whose presence seems angelic rather than human. I was being looked after. I have always thought so and I was suitably grateful. I requested a move from Times Square and went to live for three weeks with a family in New Jersey. I have never returned to New York.

## Canada Again

After three weeks I departed for Canada where my previous work in 1972 and in 1973 was still remembered. I was given a temporary summer position as an assistant minister in Windsor Ontario. There was no church there, but there were Scots. I worked hard combing through the new estate looking for possible new members. The weather was warm. I liked being out in the fresh air. On one occasion I knocked on the door of a house. To my consternation the man who answered confessed to being a Jehovah's Witness. I realised I was in for a long and unproductive interlude. I looked him in the eye, measured the distance from the door to the garden-gate, turned round, took to my heels and ran. To my chagrin, he saw my calculation and also ran. Not having to turn he reached the gate before me and barred my exit. It took more than one hour before I could extricate myself and carry on with my search for possible new members.

The congregation met in a school. The minister was a devotee of possibility thinking! He was aggressive and ambitious and wanted to model his church on a crystal cathedral in California. He actually treated me quite badly. I was amazed by his arrogance. When he returned from annual holiday he learned the nature of my preaching in his absence and decided to get rid of me. Some of his congregation were disappointed in seeing a side to him they had not recognised.

I was given another position in British Columbia. I'd always wanted to go there and I was delighted with the chance to live just south of Vancouver. St Andrew's Church congregation was not what I expected. I did not last long. In Canada there is much moving between denominations. Community churches gather malcontents and disaffected members from other congregations. A man of Dutch extraction took exception to my humours and reported me to Presbytery. I was charged by him with bringing the Bible into disrepute. A 'lynching' committee was set up without any proper representation or due process. The charge was not found but I was dismissed from my temporary position. There was no appeal. I had to return home to Scotland. I might have been ordained a few weeks later though I did not see myself staying in British Columbia for a long time. I felt like Jonah - as if I had been travelling in the wrong direction.

I was not desperately sorry. I found the churches in America and Canada in 1979 to be societies of people from complex and difficult family backgrounds. Britain in the nineties also shows such symptoms of social confusion. They seemed to be indulged and spoilt. If I was expected to accept the congregational norms and status quo then I could not minister with integrity. I remember meeting a Scottish minister who had retired and lived in a wooden house in British

Columbia. He had been in Canada for twenty years. He had had several heart operations and both his daughters' marriages had ended in divorce. He told me he had kept a suitcase in his vestry and when difficult people came to abuse him, he pointed to it and said he was leaving. This strange practice had mitigated the personal onslaughts which were, I am afraid, all too typical of the non-sophisticated forms of church life in the wilder regions of Canada.

I missed the sense of history and the respect for ministry which I thought could still be found in Scotland. A fine couple allowed me to stay with them in their home until I left. I stopped off in Toronto where my friends at church headquarters advised me to think about how I related to others. I really had done nothing wrong in Windsor or Surrey B C. What happened was that just by being there, by preaching, reactions occurred in those who listened. One is paid to keep the peace, to 'moderate,' not to stir people up, not to enthuse them or convict them or expose them to themselves.

I made friends in both Ontario and British Columbia and still keep in touch. The summer of 1979 had been enjoyable. I was carefree, absurdly so, naively so. I visited Ohio and Michigan. I travelled into the beautiful interior of British Columbia, up the western coast and also across to Victoria. The weather was wonderful and in late summer the colours were spectacular. However, I considered the scenes to be not as awesome as those in the west highlands of Scotland. The scale was larger but lacking in drama like a water colour. Scotland's lochs and hills and islands and trees and fields and rivers and skies seemed to me to be a nature painting in oils, rich in colour and intensity, unsurpassed in conception and beauty.

## Edinburgh In Spring

I returned once again to Dundonald. I applied for vacant charges but got nowhere. Deep within me there was an idea which I had always cherished. Africa. I had always wanted to go there. My grandfather had visited Africa and worked there and my father had been stationed there during the Second World War. I applied to the Board Of World Mission And Unity of the Church of Scotland to be considered for a posting as a missionary. I was accepted.

In April 1980 I returned to Edinburgh to attend a short preparatory course for 'missionaries' at St Colm's College. There was merit in being in limbo and turning thoughts from 'home' to 'abroad.' Edinburgh was beautiful in the early summer months. The study was not arduous, not even taxing. George and Audrey Sangster were going out to Nairobi. Malcolm and Olwen McNeil were going to Chogoria.

I had asked to go to Africa. In return I was asked if I'd go to India. I said no and added "If I go to India, I will still have to go to Africa - I feel called to go to Africa." Africa it was! I had not stipulated any particular job that I might do, nor did I specify which country I wanted to go to. I thought I'd leave God and the Board Of World Mission And Unity to place me where I might be needed and where I might be of most use.

As part of my training I was given a 'placement' at the Chaplaincy in Edinburgh University and I dutifully turned up every Wednesday at lunch time for the mid-week service. Fergus Smith the Assistant Chaplain prophesied that one day I'd be Chaplain to Edinburgh University. I doubted it myself. There was a lovely Irish girl at St Colm's called Christine. She had a serious boyfriend and they eventually married. However, I thought of her as a friend and enjoyed a few laughs with her. Once she poured a jug of water over me and I reciprocated by pouring a pint of milk over her. I called her 'little Irish friend.' During a dreadfully boring lecture on what was supposed to be theology (George Sangster, master of the understatement, had once asked, "Is there anything we can do to turn this into theology?") I sent a note round the circle of about thirty students to 'little Irish friend.' It read, "Give us a kiss!" Back came the note with the question, "Where?"

I used to have convulsions of suppressed laughter during these 'lectures.' Someone called Victor Pogue (I had asked someone if he was the old man who played the piano and cracked jokes) was droning on about something or other when suddenly he offered an illustration, "Suppose your daughter comes home and informs you she is going to marry a Pakistani." My eye caught one of the deaconess trainees called Heather in contortions of suppressed hilarity. I imploded. I thought I'd burst. I laughed for hours and hours.

Another student called Elaine was having a year out between school and university. Her Bible teacher had given her a puzzle which was to find where Diotrephes appears in the New Testament (in the Third Epistle of John, actually). She asked me at lunch, "Have you heard of Diotrephes?" "Yes," I responded, "He's a striker for Panathinaikos." "Oh," said she seriously, "I didn't know they played football in the Bible."

## Invergarry

By the end of my course in mid-June, there was no actual posting. I asked for a summer locum job and was sent to Invergarry and then to Unst in Shetland to relieve ministers taking annual leave. I had actually visited Invergarry Church years before in January 1974 as a pulpit supply while a student. I had borrowed my brother's Volkswagen and left on the Saturday morning. When I was locking the car in a Fort William car park during a stop for lunch, I realised I'd left my suit in Glasgow. I was wearing checked trousers, a black polo necked shirt, suede shoes and a leather style jacket. I wondered what I'd do. I could not preach dressed as I was. I resolved to try to borrow a suit from someone whenever I arrived at my overnight bed and breakfast place.

The Sinclairs were from Orkney. After my evening meal the lady asked me if everything was all right. I said that in fact I had a problem in that I'd left my suit in Glasgow. "Could I borrow one of your husband's, perhaps?" She said "Yes, you are about the same height." She disappeared and produced a grey suit with wide trouser bottoms and a jacket with a double breast and huge pointed lapels. As I tried it on, I put my hand in one of the pockets. I found a small card, took it out and read the inspiring words, "Please take cord number 7." I decided that this suit was not for me. "Have you anything else?" "No - oh - wait a minute - there is his kilt and jacket." "Splendid," said I, "I have never worn the kilt - I have always wanted to." She produced a magnificent set of kilt, choice of two jackets, shoes, socks, tie and Skean Dhu. I tried it on. It felt magnificent, masculine, marvellous. I duly preached in the kilt. Parishioners remarked on this while leaving after the service. "So nice of you to wear the kilt for us." "I wouldn't have worn anything else."

I thoroughly enjoyed my few weeks in Invergarry during the summer of 1980 and stayed with Ian and Isobel Henderson, members of the congregation. Isobel's mother, Mrs Stewart is a great lady, full of vitality and humour. She was an ardent royalist and I enjoyed disagreeing with her. I later christened her 'The Queen Mother of Invergarry' and practised royal waves whenever we met. I remember arriving in the Henderson's house at about 4 30pm. Ian immediately switched off the television out of courtesy for his guest. After a few minutes awkward silence I asked him if he would not mind me learning what the football results were. He leapt forward and switched the television back on. We were usually entertained by "Callum the Grousebeater," "Tickles" or Ronald. I still visit the Hendersons and Mrs Stewart and never fail to enjoy a laugh with them. I discovered the extraordinary wilderness beauty of Kintail with its breathtaking passage between the brooding sentinel mountains. I found the south side of Loch Ness to be a paradise. Loch Hourn seemed to have no right to be so far inland. Eilean Donan was as magical as every calendar suggests.

A great character called Alistair Grant owned a small holding called Faichemard outside Invergarry village with a camping, caravaning and chalet site for tourists. He was an elder, a poet and inventor and a man of spiritual sensitivity. He was not young in years but he had persona which reflected a youthful spirit. He also enjoyed a joke. He told me of how he had once placed the empty bark of a tree trunk in front of a certain Mrs Campbell's door. He had then rung the doorbell, got inside the bark and holding a branch in each hand had waved them up and down when she appeared at the door. Marvellous eccentricity! For my children's address on one occasion, I drew a tractor with a contraption emitting sheep being towed behind it and smoke belching from the back. I told the children this was the 'Grant patented sheep spreader" which ensured that the sheep got their exercise and ate good grass. On another occasion I drew a tractor towing a huge open hand and I called this the 'Grant patented camping money collecting, thanking and hand-shaking machine." Alistair asked me if I would send him tea plants from Africa when I eventually got there so that he could test his theory that he could grow tea in Invergarry! The experiment failed because the soil and not the climate was unsuitable.

I think the parishioners liked having the guitar in church for the Sunday School children's songs. Mr McCallum, owner of the Invergarry Castle Hotel where Isobel and Mrs Stewart and other members of the family worked is a gentleman. I visited a lot and was made welcome everywhere. Three people walked out of one of my sermons at Spean Bridge - but I can't remember why. I took my leave and flew from Inverness to Shetland, driving on to Unst and my first visit to these northern islands.

## Unst

You walk at a permanent angle of forty-five degrees. If there is a sudden lull - you fall down. The fog comes to visit and stays for days. But when the sun shines the cleanliness of the air enthralls you. The wild life is fascinating though you can get lost on the large bird sanctuary at the northernmost tip. Great Skuas and one hundred and twenty foot high waves breaking on Muckle Flugga. Norse place names abound and Christianity seemed a foreign influence. The air smelt pagan, the place unconverted. But the church in which I preached at Baltasound was alive. In fact there was lightness in the air - in the spiritual atmosphere - associated with simplicty and lack of industrialism - a 'thin' place as people say Iona is a thin place. There was joy in worship and excellent singing. I had beautiful times of prayer in the fields overlooking the wicks. I felt near to God and blessed. I rejoiced but with an accompanying sadness which those of spiritual inclination will understand. On August 24th I preached on the subject of death. On the 25th an eleven year old boy, the son of an RAF family fell off the cliffs and died. I also preached at Fetlar, Mid-Yell, Cullivoe and elsewhere. The Gospel and the elements in contention - sometimes in concord.

Saxa Vord Air Force Base was interesting. In 1980, Russian warplanes made sorties everyday towards the British coast, testing out radar and air defences. Scramblings of fighters resulted and everyone was kept on their toes. The military people there seemed to need and want a moral justification for their lives and vocations. But their lifestyle was ordered, protected and seemingly youthful always, inured against the hash and bash of civilian life. I made a trip by helicopter to the Ninian Central and South oil platforms. The helicopter seemed flimsy - like a silver paper toy inside - I enjoyed the trip and the view from the jump-seat. What an odd contrast of eerie silence and mechanical noise so many miles from land. And the amazing presence of the grey North Sea prowling around the platform legs like a monster patiently waiting for its next meal.

I remember visiting a husband and wife in their cottage on Unst. Much out-of-date furniture and strange artefacts cluttered the dwelling. "Will ye take a cup of tea aff me?" said the lady, much surprised to have me sitting in her home. "Yes," I replied. "Will ye?" she asked again, disbelieving. She encircled me and stretched out her arm full length when delivering the said refreshment. It was as if I was another species, someone odd and awful, or much to be respected and recognised as holy and from God. It was an uncomfortable deference and I did my best to be at peace for her sake. Still, in 1980 there were cottages with herrings strung across the living rooms drying. A patch of potatoes complemented the diet. Humble living indeed. And down the road, women were now getting five thousand pounds a year to change beds in the oil workers' hostel. What a contrast of times and seasons and of cultures and economics. One afternoon as I walked around visiting folks in their homes I saw an elderly woman dressed in black, with a sickle in her hand, cutting corn in her croft of half-an-acre. This was my entrée to Africa whither I was bound.

The environs of Inverness airport - that luscious easter side of the great glen - seemed like the garden of Eden in comparison with the barrenness and remoteness of Shetland. For I was on my way at last. I had been given one week to get to St Paul's United Theological College, Limuru in Kenya for the start of term in September. I was surprised to be asked to teach and was apprehensive about my ability to do so well. However, I was assured that there was great need for the College was short-staffed. I felt a pang of guilt at landing a job in Kenya which I thought to be a peaceful and pleasant place. I would have preferred South Africa with its struggles and risks and problems and spiritual earthquakes. I was also relieved. I thought I was meant to enjoy my time in Africa. I intended doing so.

## Kenya

I arrived in Kenya on Sunday 7th September 1980, just in time to start the term. I'd never seen such a blue sky. The blue of Britain's skies is grey in comparison. This was the real thing. The soil is red! How strange - ours is dirty browny black. You felt you'd never need to wash your hands, that you could play in it all day and not get mucky and that its warm colour suggested a fertility unknown in cold northern climes. My face was white - conspicuously so! I was a member of a minority tribe of whites, looked at with special interest wherever we went. The road signs were in green. Exactly the same design as those at home. How unexpected! How colonial!

Limuru, thirty-four kilometres north west of Nairobi was seven thousand feet above sea level, cooler than Nairobi and pleasing to the white man's skin. The college was small and unpretentious but seemed idyllic and peaceful. The ubiquitous Volkswagen parked at a house assured me that I was still in the same world. Everyone is so polite. Each person takes time to say 'Hello'. In fact, much time is spent on greetings and news exchanging, some would say to the detriment of commitment and work-rate. A matatu is a pick-up truck with a minibus body perched on top into which up to twenty passengers crush on hair-raising journeys at breath-taking speeds - this was to my basic means of transport.

## St Paul's United Theological College, Limuru

I was happy. I felt my years of seeking and struggle and academic achievement made sense. I was putting my vocation into practice at last. I hoped that I might even recover the closeness to God which I'd lost over the wandering two years. You don't have to sin to lose touch with God. It happens to everyone. Ask some of Christendom's great saints if you ever chance upon them! And, for me, having been on high mountains as well as deep valleys, there was no expectation of continuing revelations but an expectation of that straightforward knowledge of God's close presence which I'd been blessed with throughout most of my life.

Anyone who has ever lectured knows that producing lectures for four different courses from scratch is hard work. However I was determined to give the students the best I could. I was not an African. I brought my European learning with me. However, I felt that the juxtaposition of that learning with their African reception and perception would surely enable them to understand the Christianity they had received and were later to communicate and would allow them a base from which to embark on their own theological journeys of exploration. I found the standard of education to be patronising and requiring upgrading both in style of teaching and content of courses. I wanted students to know what the great thinkers thought and why. Only then could their own theology develop with the sort of credibility that is required in a literate culture. Kenya was not short of intellectuals, but its churches had few. Most students aspired to post-graduate study in the west one day and this seemed further reason for me to lay bare the false trails of much European theological scepticism and academic hand-wringing. However I also shared with my fellow-learners the thoughts of those who had devoted their lives to seeking and finding the truth of the Revelation of God in Jesus Christ and I took the view that whatever anyone had found out was of help to those who followed, wherever that person may have lived. Augustine, I reminded them, was an African!

Spiritually and inwardly I felt that I was on my own. I did not doubt God's continuing love for me but I was not aware of any special intimations which at that moment might have verified this assurance. I knew I could not live on the mountain-tops for ever. In any case wonderful and life-changing as they had been for me, they had been followed by visits to the deepest valleys. Perhaps a more stable pattern of spiritual life was to be my share of divine Grace. Worship in College Chapel was less boisterous than one might have expected, given African Christianity's reputation for enthusiastic and rhythmical alternatives to four-four European musical order. However some of the songs were wonderful and the charismatic extempore preaching of the students put the manuscript addicts of Britain's churches to shame. Local churches were full. Go late and there's no seat for you. The services take long. Sometimes there are three collections and perhaps an auction of 'kind' offerings such as sugar-cane, chickens or vegetables. I never thought I'd sit in church for two-and-a-half hours! On one occasion I and a student were presented with a single baton of sugar-cane each. I immediately challenged the student to a 'kung-fu' sparring session after the service was over.

St Thomas Aquinas Seminary in Nairobi was a palace compared with our humble Protestant college. Not for the first time I was impressed by the fact that even if they have no wives, Roman Catholic priests have more home comforts than most other followers of the Lord Jesus. Life long security too - that seemed bliss to me in the uncertainties and precariousness of my own existence on earth and even within the Body Of Christ.

## The Church Corrupt

We Europeans expect too much. After all, it took us thousands of years to reach the levels of incompetence, deceit and corruption which typify government in our part of the world. Why should we imagine that Africans could do better within three generations? Ah - but the Church of Jesus did not begin corruptly. It began of the best life that ever lived and throughout its earliest years was led well and at great cost to those who were caught up in this great spiritual movement which swept the ancient world.

Europe's mediaeval church was full of licence, nepotism, military warfare, exploitation, politicking, witch-hunting, persecution and much else. At least, that's what's gone down in history. Tabloid journalism was never an invention of the twentieth century. There were great heroic spiritual movements as well. The freedoms enjoyed and indulged by all of us today were born of the European Reformation. In time Africa will have its spiritual greats and some have already emerged. But that does not excuse the dishonesty which is so prevalent. Coming from a Presbyterian background and from a humble people, it occurred to me that perhaps one of the unsung and unrecognised gifts of the Holy Spirit is scrupulous management of church finances. It grieved me that in a poor country the givings of the poor as well as those of the comfortable were in part misused. I could not see why Anglican bishops had to drive Mercedes and large Peugots even if the poor themselves derived vicarious satisfaction from the eminence of their pastoral heads. It was the scale of differentials that pained me. A bishop could drive a car which cost the equivalent of one hundred years of a skilled person's gross salary.

The Presbyterian Church Of East Africa received me coolly. John Gatu, the Moderator - an executive position unlike in Scotland - was type-cast as wanting no more whites to work in Kenya. He was a great man and in the Anglican Church would have been an Archbishop. However, I cannot say that his Christianity was transparent. I had one or two brushes with him and paid the price later in time. The grudging nature of the 'welcome' spoke volumes. Days after arriving, I was already on borrowed time. I sympathised with the principle of *moratorium* which advocated a halt to white 'missionaries' going to Africa. I believed that I was there to help students reach a sufficient level of education which would allow them to do the work I was doing. I intended staying for two terms of three years each and then returning home.

Bureaucracy rules in Africa - not O K! Interminably long meetings without much decision-reaching typify church life, and, I suspected, government life too. Traditional African organisation depended on chiefs and elders. Presbyterianism was a natural form of church institution for Kikuyus. The pace was agonisingly slow. I'd never sat in four hour meetings before. The internal politics were no better and no worse than those of the churches at home. However accountability was less visible. And the 'bwana kubwa' (big man) usually got his way.

I attended my first 'harambee' at The Church Of The Torch, Thogoto. President Daniel arap Moi was Guest of Honour. I disliked the system whereby government leaders made donations to church projects. They accrued popularity based on size of donation. Much of the money was development money from overseas. It was channelled for personal political advantage by heads of government departments.

I thought the churches should be self-dependent and thus free to criticise if necessary the policies and practices of government. African Christianity has had its martyrs in the past. But I did not see many heroes in my six years in Kenya. There was an idolisation of the political leadership - a personality cult - and church leaders enjoyed the reflected glory of their closeness to the political centre. They rarely spoke out for much and Kenya paid the price in the late eighties and early nineties.

## Real Poverty

Africa changes you. Africa changes your values. For ever. A plastic bag is a possession to be treasured. Many have no shoes on their feet. There is no social security. Millions do not even earn a wage. Sure, the warm weather makes life tolerable, more so than in colder regions, but the scale and originality of the material poverty is mind-shattering. Some 'whites' chose to insulate themselves from their surroundings. So, of course, do wealthy Africans. I could not. My students thought I was rich. One said, "His father is rich." How true, I thought of my Heavenly Father but not of my earthly circumstances. Rich I was though in comparison to those who called at my door everyday. Great were the legends I listened to from those who wanted money from me and some were true. I could not harden my heart. I did my best for some and made friends with as many as I could, not patronising them I hope but out of a common sense of contingency, even although I always knew where my next meal was coming from. I did not challenge the structure of payments since I was paid a modest allowance as a single person. I felt I could and should use what I had in proportion to help those who needed help. I never found Africans to be inveterate socialists. They wanted to improve and better themselves and though they shared their resources with 'the extended family,' they required resources in the first place to be able to do that.

## Rest And Recreation

I enjoyed my days in Nairobi too, swimming at the YMCA and having a snack in a cafe. I played football with the students and was able to claim the role of a striker without much objection. I managed to score goals too. I jogged to Nairobi once - all twenty miles downhill. The thin air makes you able to perform physical miracles. It is no mystery why Kenya consistently produces the greatest distance and middle distance runners in the world.

I lived modestly and enjoyed a holiday each year, either at the wonderful Indian Ocean or in Masai Mara, or in some other part of glorious Kenya. It would have seemed foolish not to have taken advantage of such beautiful sights. I took a dinghy out at the coast, got into a little difficulty through inexperience and rejoiced when a manoeuvre worked, the sail filled, and I sped across the bay to shore. The marine life in the Indian Ocean reflected paradise. Turquoises and reds and silvers and yellows swimming past your face as you snorkelled around for hours on end, never getting cold. Driving a Land Rover in the Mara with a friend and his wife and children on board, I tried to race an ostrich. She treated me with contempt. As we bumped and swayed across the bush, the ostrich regally looked round and increased her pace by the exact amount necessary to keep a hundred yards or so ahead. Eventually, I gave up the futile chase. Later I saw a lioness cuff her badly behaved cubs just as humans used to do. So close to hippos, giraffes, cheetahs, lion prides, elephants, gazelles and even rhinoceros - Kenya offers a northern life like mine the unparalleled joy of seeing part of creation in its original form.

## The Distant God

African religion is spiritualistic. Clean conversions to Christianity were few. People held on to the old beliefs while adopting the new creed from the west. If a problem occurred and the church seemed not to be able to offer a solution, Africans returned to the local medicine man or seer and tried to find a way forward through the explanations of traditional religion. Kikuyu society impressed me as being subtle. If white missionaries had discounted local culture on arriving in Kenya, that seemed to me to have been a great mistake. Local chroniclers contrasted the attitudes of English settlers with those of Scottish. The latter, unsurprisingly, showed a more egalitarian appreciation of the people in whose country they had come to live. The basic form of natural religion throughout the world is spiritualistic. Continuation of life after death is guaranteed and communication is possible through mediums thus providing a solution system for problems in this life. Africans shared this spiritualistic communality. But they recognised the way out of it also and flocked to Christianity in unparalleled numbers. Africa remains one of the great growth areas for Christianity in the world. It would be naive however, to assume that all interest and conversion was not motivated by the need for and possibility of education and a better standard of life. I met no African who enjoyed being poor! I met no-one who justified poverty spiritually, morally, philosophically or theologically.

Africa rubs off on you. You can't avoid it. You can't fight it either. You have to immerse yourself in the African experience and see what happens and where you go. You get lost. You hang on in there. You find a light - a way forward. You travel on. You reach the end of your African journey. The God you brought with you leaves you to find out what its like without Him. Though He does not abandon your heart, you have to work it out for yourself, route, compass, supplies, obstacles, days, weeks, months and years. And if you get into trouble - God will find a path for you.

Single, alone, unmarried - a social offence in a culture in which marriage is all, you remain a 'kijana' (young man) inexperienced and not qualified to give a credible opinion on the great issues of village or tribal life. So too church life. And without all the culture props of the country from which you have come, there is a hollowness around you and your voice echoes from it. You give of your best and express whatever humanity you have been graced with. You are stepping only a few feet inside the forest. You have moved only a little way on the long, long journey.

## African Wedding

Africans are great. They know how to celebrate. I was invited to preach at the wedding of one of my students called Geoffrey Gathairu about a year after I had arrived in Kenya. This took place in the village of his future wife, Jane, a teacher. Geoffrey told me he was paying the 'bride price' and would be doing so for a long time to come. When a female of working age left to marry, the family was entitled by custom to receive compensation. Since Jane was an educated professional, she was worth much. I joked with Geoffrey that he had got his wife on 'H P' (hire purchase or finance as it is now known.)

No invitations are sent out. Everyone goes anyway. The whole village attended. I could not count the bridesmaids. Quantity is the unit of value in Africa though that, fortunately is now changing slowly by slowly. It was an open air service, of course, in beautiful sunshine. The reception followed. There was a set table for the bridal couple and their families. Everyone else sat down on the clean green grass and food was distributed. Children got a large helping of maize on a banana leaf for a plate. What a contrast to our tortured rituals here. Who can we exclude? Where are they to sit? Disco only! African society is communal and egalitarian still though these qualities are fast disappearing as class and wealth divide. Your life belongs to everyone not to yourself. A marriage is primarily a social not a personal event. The self-destructive individualism of the west is making its inroads and eventually will succeed in destroying this sense of social wholeness. What a pity!

## Attempted Coup

At 3am on 1st August 1982 members of the Kenya Air Force attempted to overthrow President Moi and his government. Such an event creates fear and uncertainty everywhere, not least in the expatriate community whose guilt surfaces as the prospect of an arbitrary and unaccountable regime is suddenly presented. The causes were not immediate. People generally feel that those in government enrich themselves at the expense of the poorer members of society. Tribal favouritism and tribal exclusion are common factors in African post-colonial history. Artificial nation states were created by Europeans and tribes without mutual sympathy were forced together into new 'political' units which were imposed from outside the environment in which they were supposed to work. Kenya had declined since the heady days of Independence. Kenyatta had been respected and feared. Moi was never anyone's fool, but he was a keeper of an inherited uneasy peace rather than the father figure of a nation. Luos thought that too many Kikuyus still held prominent positions. Kikuyus resented not having one of their own tribe as President any more.

The Army had also planned a coup and it was due to be attempted the following week. The Air Force jumped the gun. Had the two armed forces combined their efforts, then undoubtedly Kenya's President and government would have fallen. Moi survived, not for the last time. He was humble in victory but was able to strengthen his *de facto* dictatorship in the aftermath of the failed coup. Years later, he was forced by the west to hold general elections. Opposition parties could not unite around one leader and Moi won the day again. Moi has not been an extreme African political leader. He may have blood on his hands but not very much in comparison with other political heads of African states. Yet in the nineties, Kenya continues to suffer from extreme poverty and lack of overall progress and development.

With one of the highest birth rates in the world, the infrastructure cannot cope with a projected trebling of population in twenty-five years. The unit of value for the uneducated is still number. Education and development tend to reduce the birth rate. But in the meantime Kenya suffers from the worst consequences of transition. There is a low child mortality rate and still far too many children are being born. Unlike in China or India, it would be politically impossible to limit the size of families by governmental decree. Africans have a deep cosmic sense of the imperative to reproduce. Nothing and no-one except themselves someday seeing with their own eyes will stop the geometric expansion of population. And for all the money that primary western donating agencies supply to family planning work, the results are pitifully inadequate.

## Unbalanced Economies

Kenya is not rich in mineral wealth. Its currency earners have been the export of tea and coffee and the organisation of tourism. The price of tea and coffee is not set in Nairobi, it is set in London and in other western market-places. There are other countries in the world producing these commodities. Kenya cannot name its price. Therefore produce is sold at prices favourable to the western consumer and this means that the return to workers is very small. Tea-pickers on the estates near the College in which I worked for six years earned as little as twelve to fourteen pounds per month.

I used to take students to conduct Sunday worship at a farm nearby. It had been built up by a white settler family and 'compulsorily' purchased by a relative of Jomo Kenyatta. It was very productive and successful. We were given a pig-sty in which to hold our services of worship. It was a clean pig-sty, but a pig-sty nonetheless. The owner thought he was humane since he took his workers in his pick-up to hospital when they were sick. There was no facility for mothers to leave their children. For nine hours in the blazing sunshine, they would work, carrying small children on their backs. There was no school either and the houses in which the workers lived were decrepit. The African owner drove a large Mercedes-Benz.

The churches did not speak out against such scales of inequality. The leaders were quiescent participants in the system. And if they needed something for their churches, these rich men were willing to fork out as long as they were left in peace to continue to exploit their fellow Kenyans. The students used to say that they had exchanged a white master for a black one and that their lot was no better.

## Healings

I retained a residual interest in healing but did not practice a healing ministry. However, there were three occasions when I was called upon to exercise such a ministry. One evening I returned late and found a Malawian student walking on the road while carrying his child. I stopped and asked what the problem was and he told me that the child had been unable to sleep for some time and he was taking him to hospital. A few days later I called to see how the little boy was and his parents said that although he was with them at home he was no better. The little boy came forward to me, bowed in the custom of Malawi and climbed up on to my knee. This was unusual. African children are not used to being cuddled and no African child would without permission climb up on to a white person. After a few minutes, the little boy fell asleep and after half-an-hour he was in a deep sleep. We put him to bed. To my astonishment, his parents told me a few days later that his problem had disappeared.

There was a great young student called David Githii, a Kikuyu and a leader of his people. His father had been condemned to death at the time of Mau-Mau but he had escaped from prison in Nairobi. His death notice had appeared in a newspaper and his wife thought her husband was dead. David's father went to hide in the bush (the forrest) for months before returning to his family. Young David aged four years had walked sixty miles with his baby brother on his back as the family sought safety in the region of Nakuru. David had been a successful, nay charismatic school teacher. As a student minister he was conscientious and determined to do as well as he could at College. I heard that he had become ill. I went to see him and found that he had been playing football and something had happened to him. He had broken no limb but something had taken his strength away and he had become unable to read or study. He had an essay to complete and examinations to prepare for. He was struggling with self-reproach at being so foolish as to expose himself to whatever virus or bug had infected him. I said to him, "David, you played football because the others asked you to; you played football to help them." He seemed to change and lay back on his bed in peace. We prayed together and then I left. Within a few hours he was up and about, fit and well and carrying on with his academic programme. When I was ordained in The Church Of The Torch in 1984, I asked that he should read a lesson from Scripture. Before he did so, and in front of that church packed with dignitaries he said, "I was ill. Dr Anderson prayed for me and I became well again."

I loved African children and they were frequent visitors to my house. I loved the children of my European colleagues as well and they too were always welcome. One of the little African boys who came around was the son of Principal Isaiah Muita. His name was Stephen. He used to punch me in the stomach. He seemed to be extraordinarily strong and his punches were quite powerful. In late 1984 I began to think that his punches had grown much weaker. I think I attributed that to his concern for me. One day he seemed to be a little distant as if he was lacking in normal robustness. I asked his father if he was all right and learned that in fact there was something wrong with him and they were trying to find out what it was.

Eventually he had to go to hospital in Nairobi for tests. It was with terrible shock that we learned that he had leukaemia. He was operated on to remove certain tissues. However, he did not respond to this treatment and was kept on a ventilator. One evening his father happened to be in my home on academic business and as we concluded I asked how Stephen was. He shook his head sadly and said, "Probably - he is not going to make it." I felt that I could not just let him go with the usual pious expressions of concern and prayerfulness. I mentioned that I had been used before by the Lord in healing ministry. Would he agree to us going together to have a special service of healing with Stephen? I invited him as a partner lest I would appear as some kind of white 'saviour.' He said he'd talk to his wife. She agreed.

We went down the following evening. As I looked at Stephen's mother, she looked at me and said, "I have faith." Stephen's father and I went in and found the little boy lying on his side, still on the ventilator. He was semi-conscious. I held a twenty minute service of healing and Stephen's father and I laid hands on Stephen in Jesus' Name. At one point, I gasped, "The angels - the angels!" For indeed I saw angels above us and with the sight of them I was filled with hope. We left in peace. Stephen's father and I covenanted to go together at 11 00am the next morning to see Stephen. I was nervous and apprehensive all the way to Nairobi. We entered the ward.

Stephen was out of bed and sitting up in a chair. The nurse proudly told us, "He has had an egg for his breakfast this morning." Stephen's parents and I were filled with joy. We knew he had a struggle ahead but the change was so quick and significant that we felt he was going to recover.

Stephen remained in hospital to recuperate. I visited him once or twice. On Sunday the 18th of November I preached in St Andrew's Church, Nairobi and prayed for Stephen's life. I had arranged with Stephen's parents that I'd go to the hospital after the service and ask the doctors to let me take Stephen home for at least an afternoon and if possible for a day. This I did. I remember Stephen looking out the window of his father's car (which I had borrowed) all the way to Limuru. He was taking in all the sights he'd missed as we all do when illness deprives us of the natural joys of daily life. I was not emotionally prepared for what happened when we arrived home. When Stephen entered his home, seated in a large circle round the lounge were twenty-five children. School-friends and St Paul's playmates, they had been invited to welcome him. As he went in, led by the lovely ten year old Beatrice, they began to sing, "Jesus never fails." I was overcome by the moment. As long as I live I will consider it one of the most beautiful things I have ever seen or heard. Stephen continued to recover and I never heard of any relapse.

## Henry And Others

Education is prized in Africa. Children actually enjoy school and look forward to their lessons. None of the cynicism and laziness and alienation which typifies some schools in the West can be found in Africa. Schools represent the social side of life since it is a collective undertaking. It is also the route to literacy and therefore to prosperity. Primary education in Kenya is ostensibly free but parents still require funds to provide uniforms, books and other necessary items. Secondary education is not free. Many young people are prevented from continuing in secondary education because of lack of funds. Appeals for education sponsorship have been part of charitable outreach in the West for many years. In Kenya there are state bursaries and there are local 'harambee' schools with low fees, but it is virtually impossible for a young person to go through secondary education without paying either for basic fees plus additional expenses or at least all additional expenses. Many secondary schools are boarding schools and so the cost is disproportionate to the earning capacity of so many. Throughout my years in Kenya I was able to help young people through their schooling. Friends in Scotland provided funds for pupils in the knowledge that there was a genuine need which they could meet. One hundred or two hundred pounds would normally suffice to keep a pupil in secondary education for a year. Henry was a typical case.

I employed a part-time gardener called Geoffrey and a part-time housekeeper called Dorine. It was considered the correct thing to do since it allowed local people to earn much needed cash. In practice, if you employed people you took on further responsibilities for them and their families and thus shared your income with them. One day I returned from teaching and found a young man cleaning my kitchen. I asked him what he was doing and he told me his aunt Dorine was unwell and had sent him to do the housework. I asked him why he was not in school and he told me that although he had left primary education with good grades and had been given a place at a state school, he had had to leave because his parents had no money. I asked him to bring his school certificates to let me see. He did this next day and I saw that he had passed his state examinations well. I asked him if he wanted to go back to school and he said yes. I then found the necessary money to send him. Henry said that he did not want to take an academic course. Instead he wanted to train to be a joiner and then to have his own furniture-making business.

I found out that there was a Christian Technical College in Nairobi and after some negotiations, Henry began his training there. Eventually he graduated and set up his own one man business. He succeeded and is still working at the vocation of his choice. He married and now has a family. Henry was one of thousands of young people whose talents and skills can be lost through lack of opportunity brought about by poverty. There surely can be no lovlier thing than to help someone like Henry find the means to earn a living. Alice, Eunice, David, Leah, Paul, Peter, Karau, Tom and others were helped in the same way. Over the years the privilege of helping has continued and there are always new requests. I believe in helping individuals. Only they know what it means to receive an education which otherwise would have been beyond their means. The politics of charities in the West often stress community projects rather than individual benefits. As a 'lad o' pairts' myself, I rejoiced in seeing a young person succeeding at school and going on to a better life.

## Feeding The Hungry

Kenya suffered the tail-end of the 1984 famine which devastated the north east of Africa. UNICEF had organised a food distribution in the stricken parts of Kenya. I had gone to Chogoria to spend Christmas with my friends Malcolm and Olwen McNeil. They were distributing food at the clinics in the surrounding countryside and I went along to help. Thus I was privileged to spend Christmas Eve 1984 distributing food to mothers and children who had nothing. I was a dilettante; others made this their life's work. But I was glad that I had been there and had seen what we see on our televisions at first hand. It is hard for us westerners to realise what it is like to depend on rainfall for food. If rains fail, no maize grows. People have no other staple food and no cash to buy food. They starve. Seventy-five per cent of the people we screened that day were underweight - some seriously so. But they were also fortunate. They were alive and were receiving food supplies.

It must also be said that where great famines have occurred, there have been political factors involved. Africa grows enough food for everyone under normal circumstances. Where large numbers of people are found to be starving there is usually a war of some kind going on in which one side controls the food supply to the other. This was true of the major starvation situations in the sixties, seventies, eighties and nineties throughout Africa, in places like Biafra, the Karamajong, Eritrea, the Sudan, Mozambique and Rwanda. Kenya in 1984 had no such political or military problems. Food could be transported from Mombasa to those in need. Some people did die in the north west of Kenya at that time but mercifully few. I will always remember mixing the maize meal and presenting it in basins to children that Christmas Eve. It was a Christmas gift to me to be there at that time.

## Teaching And Learning

I enjoyed my fellow students and so I enjoyed teaching. Sometimes it was exhausting. In Africa you are not allowed the luxury of concentrating on your own specialised subjects. Therefore I taught Systematic Theology and in addition, History Of Philosophy, New Testament, Old Testament, Homiletics and other subjects from time to time as need arose.

It was good to introduce students to the great minds of the past, including Thales, Socrates, Plato, Aristotle, Augustine, Aquinas, Duns Scotus, Descartes, Locke, Hume, Marx, Luther, Calvin and Barth. Torrance was also treated along with others. Contemporary African thinkers like Mbiti, Ngugi and others were included in the syllabi. I explained that many had tried to express their understanding of the world without recourse to revelation. There were therefore interesting parallels and possibilities for those who wanted to set the Christian revelation aside and begin an 'African Theology' from scratch.

Throughout my time at St Paul's the issue which generated heat and light in equal quantities was African Theology. Some wanted to develop an African theology independent of Christian revelation and felt that they had a right to do so in order to free themselves from colonialism in its religious forms. African Christian Theology, on the other hand would seek to explain Jesus Christ to African people. It would build on the tradition inherited while adapting its strengths to the African context. African Theology is equivalent in style and purpose to some European liberal theology. I thought that there would be as much a continuing discussion and divergence between African Theology and African Christian Theology in Africa in future years as there had been between liberal and orthodox theology in Europe for centuries. It was because of my understanding of who Jesus Christ is that I took the orthodox view myself. Of course, I was not an African. But I was not a liberal theologian either.

I was made Dean Of Studies in 1981 in succession to David Philpot. I thoroughly enjoyed this role and it allowed me to attend all sorts of meetings throughout Kenya and in Tanzania and Uganda. As Dean I could play the advocate for students to greater effect. However 'Africanisation' was always an issue and I suffered internal politics throughout my years at St Paul's. I was made Dean again in 1983 and then handed over to a Kenya colleague in 1985. I was also Head of the Department of Theology and Philosophy from 1983 until 1986. We did a lot of planning and formulating of new courses and syllabi. St Paul's was to become a University College in time and a Masters Programme had to be developed. Whites are only allowed to do so much. Hard it is to strike a balance between sane silence and protestation at theological suicide. Most of the students were devout in their Christian life. Many were even more devout Africans. It was always a confused situation made bearable by the expanding churches and the need to train ministers and pastors for the many who wanted to know about Jesus Christ. The problems were those of expansion not of contraction as in the West.

## Humours A Plenty

Humour did not desert me in Africa. I risked some nonsense on occasions, sometimes for example when sending out timetables and circulars to members of staff. There was a wonderful Kenyan colleague called Imunde. He was a proponent of African Theology. He had a clever and subtle mind and he was the father of six children with Agnes his long-suffering wife. He enjoyed a laugh. I used to send him notes with various classical allusions such as 'Lux Imunde,' 'Imunde Sensibile,' 'Imunde Invisibile' and eventually 'Imunde in Tenebris.' He once met me when I was carrying a ladder. I explained, "This is the original ladder which Jacob saw at Bethel." and on another occasion I informed him that the large stone jar in one of the classrooms was the original jar which the woman of Samaria had carried to the well when she met Jesus. "Was it filled with McEwan's Beer?" asked Imunde (for he had been a post-graduate at Aberdeen University!)

I used to send spoof term timetables to the Hungarian member of staff who was blessed with an outrageous sense of humour himself. Monday - 8 00 Theology 9 00 Mending Clutch On Volkswagen 10 00 Christian Doctrine 11 00 Arguing With Wife 12 00 Ethics. Tuesday - 8 00 Theology 9 00 Making Sausages 10 00 Philosophy 11 00 Counting Money In Bank Account 12 00 Counting Money In Bank Account. The same tutor used to teach something called 'The Vestiges Of The Trinity' in which he pointed out how many things in the natural order happen in threes. I loved mocking this by saying that I'd seen yet another vestige - a car with a flat tyre! At Limuru market, the women used to place three potatoes together for sale for one Kenya Shilling. I instanced that practice as another vestige and he replied, "But I saw a woman with four potatoes for sale - that is heresy."

Two of the Kenyan tutors, myself and another 'white' imagined setting up a musical group called 'The Zebras,' however it never got off the ground. A lady member of staff asked at coffee one morning, "What is the African equivalent to the British symbol of an owl for wisdom?" "It is a Meru Minister," I replied.

The Roman Catholic priests were funds of stories and jokes. One Holy Ghost Father told me a famous joke. The Pope was talking to God and asked to have three questions answered. "Will the churches ever be united?" God answered "Not in your life time." "Will women become priests?" "Not in your life time." "After me, will there be another Polish Pope?" God answered, "Not in my life time."

Albert Juffer, a Dutch colleague and I shared many a laugh. He used to wear clogs when off duty. When visiting me he would leave them at the door. On one occasion as I looked down at them I asked, "Is it Ascension Day?" Albert burst into a great bellow. It brought Principal John Nyesi over from his house to see what was going on. Another Dutch tutor was a radio ham. He had a habit of prowling around on the roof of his house in order the better to pick up various contacts throughout the world. We imagined him teaching his classes up there. Patrick was a male nurse at Chogoria who loved bananas. I witnessed him eating fourteen bananas while paying a brief visit to my friends Malcolm and Olwen. The same Patrick had acted as interpreter for a nursing sister from New York who was giving lectures to Chogoria nurses. He translated her New York 'English' into Kenyan English!

Cross-cultural humour is risky but I always found Africans witty and humorous themselves. They had the same sense of irony and of the absurd which we have and were clever enough to see the funny side of life. Even anti-white students of a political nature could laugh at themselves in our company. Hence I learned why Africans have flat noses. One such student told me it was because when they were small they were carried in a shawl on their mothers' backs. They kept banging their noses against their mothers' backs and so ended up having flat noses, all of them!

## Matatus, Mosquitoes And Bullets

It was never a dull life in Africa. For most of my time in Kenya I travelled in matatus, overcrowded, unfit for the road, uninsured and unhindered by such niceties as speed limits. One of these was called 'The Heaven Express.' I asked why this was and was told, "Because there is as much chance of you ending up in heaven as in getting to Nairobi." Encouraged by this intelligence, I travelled on this sublime vehicle. Once, having journeyed from Nyeri to Nairobi I was shocked to see that a similar matatu had crashed into a train at a level crossing on the same journey leaving seven people dead and others injured. The driver fled to the forest to escape arrest. I remembered that level crossing. It transpired that the matatu driver had seen the train coming and decided to race it to the level crossing.

On another occasion I was hurtling down the hill to Nairobi in the back seat of a Peugeot estate car matatu. There were ten other passengers and I was on the left in one of the back seats next to the door. At sixty miles per hour the door suddenly flew open and I fell half-way out, clinging to the sleeve of the person who had been sitting next to me until the matatu finally slowed down and stopped so that I could get in again. On a short trip to Limuru market the driver of a matatu suddenly decided to take short cut through a field with eighteen of us on board. Up and down we went. Women were screaming. But - he achieved his objective. We got to the next stop ahead of a rival matatu and he collected one more fare.

Last century the white man died of malaria in numbers as he made his way up from the coast. Even today many Africans suffer from malaria and it still kills. Mosquitoes apparently are becoming resistant to quinine based medicines and have become stronger in order to compete with the antidote. I think I contracted malaria after a visit to Uganda in 1981. I'd gone there for an academic conference. I remember being delirious with a fire in my mind that I'd never known. At the same time my body shook and quivered and I collapsed at home several times. I vomited frequently and also had diarrhoea. For some reason I told no-one and as I lived alone, no-one knew I had been ill. I thought I'd trust the healing power of nature, 'vis medicatrix naturae' as my old uncle used to say when he dismissed malingerers from his surgery in Windsor Terrace in Glasgow. I recovered on the fourth day. I did not take quinine tablets except when going to Uganda or to the coast. I suppose therefore I was not resistant to the possibilities of contraction of the disease. Even now I sometimes think that mild symptoms of malaria make themselves felt within me although I have suffered no lasting damage as far as I know.

The bullets were another story. On each of my three visits to Uganda on academic business in 1981, 1983 and in 1985, I found myself in the middle of some shoot-up. In 1981 I had to lie down in the back of a pick-up truck to avoid stopping a bullet or two on my way through the streets of Kampala to Makerere University. In 1983 soldiers and police staged a pitched battle at Mukono where I and colleagues were staying. We dived for cover as tracer bullets lit up the sky above us.

The last occasion was the most dramatic. I'd stayed on in Kampala on Saturday 27th July 1985 to visit Makerere University to try to obtain diplomas for students. With exceptional timing I found myself outside the main post office in Kampala just as Tito Okello's soldiers entered the capital to oust Milton Obote as President and take over the government. Everyone scattered. I was conspicuously white and alone. I made my way on foot to the University and came I think, as close to being killed as I would ever do without it happening. Someone took a pot shot at me in my whiteness. The bullet struck a wooden post inches from me at chest height. Shooting and explosions began. A young officer commandeered a car and began driving up and down Kampala Road waving his hat and gun in the air. I avoided further cross-fire and reached Makerere. There I found a member of the staff at Mukono and we travelled back together in a pick-up truck. It was interesting watching thousands of Obote's soldiers retreating from the capital going towards Jinja. At Mukono we listened to the B B C world service for news. I had to remain in Uganda until Wednesday 31st July when the United Nations organised a British Army escorted convoy to evacuate those who wished to leave the very unstable situation. Kampala city centre was wrecked in four days. I was relieved and happy to return to Kenya and to St Paul's College. My passport was stamped with a debt of twelve hundred Kenya Shillings, the cost of my evacuation from Uganda!

Still, I survived everything. I often mused that God did not want to see me very much. If God had, there were plenty of opportunities for me to have left this earthly life. Any one of them would have done. It never bothered me. I had no ties on earth. I often thought about the words of St Paul, "For me to live is Christ and to die is gain." But I never thought then that I'd justified my calling, nor had I seen sufficient harvest of my own suffering, nor had God entrusted me with that much on earth, even if I was blessed spiritually and possibly even in terms of heaven. I lived an anonymous life and never shared my inner experiences or convictions with anyone. It made no sense to do so. If you make claims for yourself, people reject you. At best, you can hope to make a helpful contribution which will stand independently of yourself. You wonder why God went to the bother of opening up the Kingdom to you. You were glad that this had happened but frustrated that it had brought little here on earth, in the church or out of it. But if complacency ever visited, it did not stay long. Eventful was life in Africa, and the last year was more eventful than the others.

# 4 : Christian God : African God

## Skirmishing

I never thought that I should be a cipher in Africa, a pleasant fellow of no opinion. On the contrary, I wished to fulfil the spiritual calling given to me. I took on 'issues' in sermons in St Paul's College and elsewhere if and when I was invited to preach or speak. Dr Timothy Njoya was willing to risk my presence in the pulpit of St Andrew's Church, Nairobi. It was always a great occasion for a westerner to preach to such a very large congregation, overflowing into the grounds around the church building and ministered to via a public address system. However, two sermons I preached there landed me in hot water, and, later, when I needed help and protection from the Presbyterian Church of East Africa, I did not get it.

John Gatu, now an ex-Moderator of the Presbyterian Church of East Africa visited St Paul's College from time to time in his capacity as a member of the College Council which was its governing body. On one of these occasions I happened to find myself sitting next to him, on his left, at a meeting with staff and students. He wore fashionable 'Kaunda' safari style suits which were sleeveless. I noticed that he was wearing a very expensive watch. I took a closer look. It was a solid gold Rolex chronometer. I was shocked. Such a watch would cost a great deal of money in a country like Kenya with its heavy import taxes on luxury goods. Afterwards I began to calculate that an ordinary worker would need to work for thirty years to save enough money to buy such a watch, provided he did not eat and had no other payments to make. If he were to marry and have children, then no matter how long he lived, he would never ever save enough money to buy such a watch.

I wondered what kind of message this was conveying. Many people in the P. C. E. A. as in every other church, did not have any shoes on their feet. They struggled year by year to avoid illness and malnutrition at worst and at best to feed and clothe and educate their children. Here was an extravagant and even vulgar symbol of western concupiscence and of conspicuous consumption. I did not think that it was right for a church leader to display such an obvious sign of personal affluence among people themselves so poor.

In a sermon at St Andrew's Church, where the same person was one of the ministry team, though he was not present on this occasion, I mentioned the issue of the gold watch as an illustration of the lack of credibility which attached to Africans who continued to blame westerners for the state of their country. The P. C. E. A. had been independent since 1956, seven years ahead of Kenya's political independence. Continuing to use the colonialists as 'whipping boys' was doing no good at all, I was saying. I did not name the ex-Moderator but everyone knew who I was talking about.

The sermon was well received at the point of delivery and I heard nothing other than thanks. However, some weeks later, I received a letter through the post from the Executive Committee of the P. C. E. A. rebuking me and disciplining me for my remarks about an individual.

This gave me further ammunition. This was misuse and abuse of the due processes of Presbyterianism. I had heard of no complaint about the sermon and none had been intimated to me.

Dr Timothy Njoya invited me to preach again in St Andrew's Church a few weeks later. In my sermon I spoke about abuse of power in all walks of life and then mentioned the church. I took out of my pocket the letter of rebuke and discipline and informed the congregation of its contents. I did this not out of malice, nor bravura, nor piquancy nor inadequacy. I did it because in Africa any person in power can misuse the organisation to which he or she belongs for his or her own ends. To be sure, this also happens everywhere else in the world, but that is no reason to keep silent when in Africa as long as one is consistent in other places at other times. I wanted to expose abuse of a position of privilege and service in the Church of which I was both a member and a Minister.

It was sometime later that I heard that the Kirk Session of St Andrew's Church had taken great exception to my being reprimanded by the Executive Committee of the P. C. E. A. The point at issue is that only the Kirk Session of St Andrew's Church could take forward any complaint concerning a sermon preached in their church. Further, any complaint would require to be investigated as to substance and defence. It would then be referred to the relevant Presbytery and so on through the courts of the church until the matter would be resolved.

Dr Njoya had witnessed the interrogation of the ex-Moderator by his elders and he reported what had happened to me. They asked him if he possessed such a watch as had been described and he admitted that he did. Apparently, he was driven so far on the defensive, that at one point it looked to Dr Njoya that the ex-Moderator might have to tender his resignation as a Minister of St Andrew's Church, not for wearing a watch but for misusing his position in the Church. However, skilful, wily and able man that he was, he apologised, agreed not to wear the watch and undertook not to abuse his position in such a way again.

The democracies of Presbyterianism are significant. Lay people have actual spiritual power. They can make decisions and these can be effected. I rejoiced not in any personal sense but in the example of people having a proper say in the organisation and management of part of the Body of Christ on earth. However a 'white' does not take on an African 'chief' in his own country with impunity. The person concerned would not forget a bearding in his own den!

## The Adversary

Everywhere I have been in the service of Jesus Christ there has been an adversary for me. There has been a certain person who has taken a great dislike to me, who has made it his or her business to frustrate, hinder, injure and even destroy me. I am not alone in this. Much of life is adversarial. Politics, the law and sport are great examples. The problem is that the Church of Jesus is not meant to be like that. But it more than is.

Even this should not actually be surprising. The Bible is the history of adversaries. Jesus had His Judas and he did his worst. Both the Old Testament and the ensuing history of the

Christian Church are replete with adversarial issues, situations and conflicts. Those who dream of peace on earth, dream in vain. Those who advocate peace in the church, do so out of naive idealism and wishful thinking.

An adversary arrived in St Paul's College, a new member of the teaching staff. He was an Episcopalian priest called Sipo Mzimela who had been a refugee from South Africa and had lived in America for some time. He took an existential - nay a cosmic - dislike to me. It was a hatred. He was appalled that someone like me, a white man with orthodox Christian views, was teaching in St Paul's College. A political animal, he resolved immediately to undermine me, turn the Principal of the College against me, complain about me outside the College, frustrate me in my work, teach me a lesson, and, if possible, get rid of me back to where I belonged.

Had he been a person of great spiritual stature, integrity, learning and example, I would have perhaps have felt utterly discouraged. One is also known by the quality of one's enemies (or the lack thereof). At first the students treated him as a hero, a freedom fighter, a blood brother, a slayer of white demons and as an advocate of the complete decolonisation of Africa. It was not easy for those of us with white faces after his arrival and I seemed to be picked out for special treatment. At one point I thought I would simply have to leave the College in order that the atmosphere might alleviate. St Paul's had always been an unstable place, but in 1985, it was hot for the 'mzungu.' (white)

As the weeks and months went by, stories about the lifestyle of my adversary began to circulate. There was a history of alcoholism and of psychological imbalance, added to which were visible evidences of the same plus continuing actual adultery and recklessness in living. It was hard for the students to realise that their hero was a rotter. It was hard for them to sympathise with the white man against their own self-appointed guerrilla warrior. They did not do so either, until I left St Paul's College. When he was chased late at night by a mob from Kabuku village after having shouted and shrieked outside the home of a divorced woman who would not let him in and was rescued only by the College askaris (security guards) from fists, 'pangas' and dogs mad enough to tear him in pieces, when his wife sued for divorce, when he left at least one young unmarried village woman pregnant and when his life disintegrated, then they sadly ceased to follow him. But I had gone. And the College Principal had taken his part against me - he over whose son we had prayed together whom God had healed.

## Publications

I entered into public debate on a number of issues while in Kenya through the media of the newspapers and magazines. 'Christians and the State' appeared in 'The Weekly Review' in August 1984. 'The Eucharistic Congress- An Evaluation' was published in the 'Daily Nation' in September 1985. 'Christian Leadership In Second Corinthians' appeared in 'Beyond' magazine in November 1985. I also wrote an article called 'Family Planning And The Church' which was published in 'The Weekly Review' in November 1985 and I wrote an article on 'Christmas' for 'The Standard' newspaper which was published in December 1985.

In the first of these articles, I expressed the view that Christians have a dual loyalty, firstly to God and secondly to the state. I explained the origin and nature of the Church's prophetic ministry and I discussed the issue of free speech. "The Christian preacher stretches the tolerance of the law, thus exposing how the law is being used at any given time." I also reminded readers that Christians are supposed to love their enemies, ".....an exceedingly difficult principle to practise in the political sphere." I distinguished the eternal dimension of life from the social. "The Christian preacher must give voice to the purposes of God." but I also expressed the view that true preaching could discomfit national governments from time to time and was not limited in is references to the private life of individuals.

On 'Family Planning' I began somewhat provocatively, "God practised birth control. He had only one Son." and then argued that "The Divine Will understood from the Bible does not advocate uncontrolled reproduction of the species." I also argued from common sense that human capacity for reproduction outweighs necessity. Therefore we are expected to practise birth control. I pointed out that St Paul did not legislate in matters of intimacy and contrasted his attitude with that of the celibate hierarchy of the Roman Catholic Church. "Christianity calls those who want to love and serve God within the married state to do so with responsibility and with wisdom, following His example and using the benefits of scientific discovery for the bettering of the human condition."

I enjoyed amateur journalism. It was an excellent way of reaching a wider audience and of making public issues of the Christian Gospel. However, I did not choose easy subjects and would probably merit the journalese description of 'controversial.' I never thought Jesus was anything but controversial. No Christian preacher worth much ever avoided controversy. Where Christianity falls asleep or seems to die, there you will find moderate and pleasant opinion, usually of a superficial nature which is proved in later history to be wrong.

## Sikuku*

It was a *great day for St Paul's College on 30th November 1985 when His Excellency President Daniel T. arap Moi visited the College to attend graduation and conduct a fund-raising 'harambee.' He shook hands with all of us and was personally gracious. The Vice-President, Mwai Kibaki and other Ministers of the Government also attended. Moi was dignified, gentle, slow of speech. His eyes suggested medication. As a Christian himself, he expressed care and concern for the church. He thought that people should tithe and that clergy salaries should be such as to prevent them from being tempted to corruption. Extraordinary naiveté there! Or just good politics! The children's choir stole the show. African children sing with such complete energy and enthusiasm that everyone is bowled over.

As a culture contrast the same evening I gave the toast 'To The Kirk' at the St Andrew's Dinner of the Caledonian Society in Nairobi. That's where I had my first taste of Atholl Brose! However, I suggested to my fellow Scots that they could and should reform the Caledonian Society of Kenya into a pro-active educational charity concerned "for the people you pass in your cars every day." There was a division among the people. However, a youngish member took the message and its challenge to heart and promised to see what could be done.

## The Closing Net

By early 1986, relationships among the staff had deteriorated. The role of 'Iago' had been played to great effect by my adversary. The Academic Board of 21st January which met to discuss academic development degenerated into verbal violence. My adversary's ideas failed to take into account much previous planning. He informed the meeting that my own paper on future development had been put in the waste paper basket. To defend himself, he added that he had done this because I had submitted my paper late. An outright lie! Staff Minute 62/85/v asked for papers on academic development to be submitted by November 22nd. I had taken mine to his house on the 21st. The African members of staff were silent. A Minister of the P. C. E. A. tried to counter my adversary's non-theological, non-Christian ramblings. The entire meeting was a shambles.

It was not easy to 'wind down' after such trauma. I was fortunate in that I could go to my Dutch colleague Albert Juffer for a chat. Invariably we'd manage to have a laugh. On this occasion, I remember taking a 'Beano' book and a T-shirt for one of Albert's son's birthday. We decided that young Anne-Wym looked very like Denis The Menace and then found resemblances between all the 'Beano' characters and people we knew at St Paul's College. It was welcome anarchy and fantasy.

The staff met on an evening from time to time for a joint study and discussion session. Usually, someone prepared a paper on a topic of personal interest which served as the basis for interaction. It so happened that I was due to give this kind of talk on Thursday 30th January 1986. I had chosen the sensitive subject "Christianity, The Church And Money" and had prepared a paper which I had circulated in time for staff members to read before coming to the meeting.

At 5pm on Thursday 30th January a Kenyan member of staff arrived with a sealed letter for me. It was from the Principal and the letter asked if I had given any copies of my paper to anyone outside the College since its contents were seriously prejudicial to the College. I replied immediately that I had not done so. My Kenyan colleague also informed me that the staff study meeting scheduled for that evening had been cancelled because five members of staff were unwilling to attend. He added that if the C. I. D. got hold of the paper I would be in trouble. He then said that certain members of staff who did not like me could use the paper to get rid of me. It was not a comfortable evening.

The substance of the paper in question concerned the churches' acceptance of 'harambee' money from politicians and government ministers including the President. I suggested that this practice compromised the churches and left them unable to speak prophetically to the government about justice and truth and right and indeed the spiritual claims of Christianity on the lives of all of us. The paper said what many thought and a few dared to talk about privately. Kenyan members of staff in particular felt unable to share in such a conversation. I understood their point of view.

They were family men. It would be very easy for them to be considered subversives. Even free discussion of the theological principles involved was dangerous for them. I also thought them lacking in courage. I was disappointed in their reaction because I felt that they of all people should be thinking about these things and teaching future pastors the issues that mattered.

I had a few sleepless nights. I began to wish that I could be at home. I was scheduled to leave in the summer of 1986 at the end of my second three-year contract. I had already informed my employer in Edinburgh that I would not be returning to Kenya. Although I still enjoyed teaching students and got on well with them I thought that my life had become intolerable for other reasons. I also considered that a number of large issues were coming together. The paper "Christianity, The Church And Money" was the last of these.

Throughout 1985 in particular, I had publicly challenged the misuse and abuse of position and power within the P. C. E. A. I had published articles on "Christians And The State" and "Family Planning And the Church" among others. These were controversial. Within St Paul's there was a struggle as to whether the College academic syllabus would depart from its foundations in European Christianity and represent only African theology. I clearly stood for the Centrality, Uniqueness and Lordship of Jesus Christ to be applied in the African context. I advocated free speech in Christian pulpits and exhorted students to distinguish the spiritual claims of Christianity from politics and society.

I felt my words and actions returning to me. I was not unhappy about this. I regarded it as a sign of continuing vocation. However, I became apprehensive as to my personal safety. Living in an arbitrary political environment teaches you much. I had had nearly six years of this, and I had witnessed an attempted coup in Kenya and a successful coup at first hand in Uganda. I knew that a white face is not first in line for justice and fair treatment. I was a member of a minority culture which had a past many Kenyans wished to negate. I knew the P. C. E. A. would not support or help me. The only ones who would were the students and my colleague Albert Juffer. I had a conversation with the Principal of St Paul's, Isaiah Muita. You will note the anti-coincidence of his given name.

Principal:    *"You regard yourself as a prophet."*
Robert:    *"I am not self-regarding."*
Principal:    *"You are a prophet."*
Robert:    *"If God speaks through me in a prophetic way - then you will appreciate that it is a greatburden to bear."*
Principal:    *"The greatest burden - prophecy must also be connected with love."*

We prayed and shook hands. There was another issue. The single man - the radical - the risk-taker - the unsocialised and unearthed as married men are socialised and earthed, the outsider, the non-conformist, the dissenter. The struggler for truth, Christian truth, Christ's truth. In Africa. Anywhere. I was teaching Kierkegaard to the third year Bachelor of Divinity class at this very time. I taught him as an example of the rejection of comfortable Christianity. Peter Cheboiywo, a bright and good student asked if anyone had taken Kierkegaard seriously. I said "No." Peter said that if the Christian missionaries had been like Kierkegaard, today's problems would not have occurred. I said "No" again, explaining that no-one in Africa would have wanted Kierkegaard either. "You must apply his thought to yourself first - and only then to others."

On a pleasant day out I climbed the extinct volcano called Longonot in the Rift Valley with Albert and the children. Continuing personal prayer kept me together. I became introspective, or rather, I exercised the introspective side of my nature. I reflected on my adulthood and my life as a Minister of Jesus Christ. I was not impressed. It seemed I had achieved little. I was without a home of my own, without security both in the short and long terms, I had neither wife nor children and I had made no name for myself such that would act as a springboard for service or even future employment. I had let God down time and time again. I seemed unable to compromise on relationships and therefore caused problems for myself and others. There was a dying in the midst of life.

## Quick Exit

At 4pm on Tuesday 18th February 1986 I received a message telling me that the College Council Chairman wanted me to attend the meeting of the College Council Executive Committee in Nairobi the following day at 1 pm to answer for my paper "Christianity, The Church And Money." They never talked directly with members of staff - so I was in trouble. I was grateful however that I was to get a hearing. I asked some senior students to pray for me.

I had lunch with the College Council Executive Committee. Their meeting began. I sat outside like a schoolboy outside the Head Teacher's room, waiting to be summoned. At 2 50pm I was called in. The Presiding Bishop of the Methodist Church in Kenya Lawi Imathiu chaired the meeting. The Moderator of the P. C. E. A. George Wanjau and other Presbyterian Ministers were there. The Anglican Archbishop Manasses Kuria was present along with other bishops, including a former colleague. Representatives of the Reformed Church Of East Africa were also present.

I was asked about my intentions in writing the paper. Politeness gave way to heat on the part of my examiners. To my surprise, all those present denied any connection between political 'harambee' money and corruption. Although I had been in Kenya for nearly six years, I still found this astonishing. I was accused of being a paternalist and a colonialist and of having a 'saviour' complex. I replied, "I was six years old when I heard about Mau-Mau on the radio - I was with you - I was on your side." They laughed.

I made familiar general points. All governments are corrupt. Church and state should be separate. The churches of Kenya are closely associated with acquisitive wealth-gathering in the post-colonial era. I had lived at St Paul's College when during a financially tough time the children of students cried because they had no food to eat. This was a direct challenge to continuing underfunding of St Paul's College by the churches.

The Chairman said "We are not going to let you be a martyr if that's what you want - we are going to let you go in peace." I replied that I had been praying that I might be allowed to leave in peace since I was due to return home for good in a few months time. The Anglican Archbishop recommended that I leave on schedule at the end of June. I left the meeting discouraged and returned to St Paul's.

I was scarcely in the door of my house when my adversary telephoned and asked to if he could come over for a chat. He showed remorse. Not a lot, but some. He stayed for two hours. I questioned him on his treatment of me and others and on his theology. He told me that he rejected St Paul and Trinitarian theology, St John's Gospel, Acts, the Creeds and all the theological history of the West. His Jesus was a revolutionary and a human being. He despised the evangelical vocabulary of ninety per cent of St Paul's students. He called them liars, false and crazy. The Trinitarian blessings His Anglo-Catholicism required of him were, he said, only ritual. He admitted that he had taken my paper out of the College. He apologised for getting me into trouble. He said he'd been involved with the African National Congress for thirty-three years. He execrated the Kenyan members of staff, including the Principal. I challenged him about hypocrisy.

I never thought to go into deeper spiritual matters. On the reasons why I adhered to the centrality of Christ I said nothing. To have tried to share some instances from my own spiritual journey would have been futile. The minute you 'step up' a gear and speak with authority, you are in dead trouble all over the place. Neither can you expect people to believe personal testimony which cannot be directly corroborated. Consistency of conduct may convince over a period of time, with some evidence of the possibility of truth, but only to those who like St Peter are given insight and recognition, not by 'flesh and blood' or ordinary human deduction. So you argue the substance of whatever case with which you are involved on its merit and you present an angle which someone else may not have thought of. If you speak with assurance, you are thought to be arrogant. If you speak with authority then you may be respected but you are also feared or envied. You are associated with forms of fundamentalism whereas in your life you have deduced from divine intimation what you conclude on earth. There is a living source of your understanding, but you cannot share it. You may be proved right in time, but that will not help the present. And so it was. My adversary left St Paul's not long after me in disgrace. I left, to be sure, but not in disgrace. My adversary's causes were diminished by his conduct and student sympathy was with me. The Principal feared a student strike. Christianity survived at St Paul's.

On Friday 21st February 1986 I planned to go to the P. C. E. A. headquarters in Nairobi to ask about the non-payment of a student's salary while he had been a Minister (for ordained clergy often returned to take a higher course of studies.) I left the house at 8 10am. Before I left the College grounds however, I was given a letter by hand. It was headed "Termination Of Services" and its text gave me one week to pack and return to Scotland. I was very surprised and excited, but I was not depressed or anxious. I discussed the matter with two colleagues and then left for Nairobi to book a flight home for Tuesday 25th February.

I will always be grateful to Alan and Kaye Ross, friends whom I had met through the

McNeils. Alan is a Minister of the Church of Scotland and also a Chartered Accountant and was working in Nairobi. Kaye is Australian and they have a daughter and son, Morag and Callum. I did not know them well, but they offered to sell what possessions I wanted to leave behind and pack my books and ship them home. This they did over the following weeks and their help allowed me to enjoy my last three days in Africa without worrying about post, and customs, and advertisements, and selling things and all the hassles of a quick relocation.

I telephoned the Board of World Mission and Unity in Edinburgh and the late Tom Kiltie treated me with care and sympathy. This was most helpful since, by the nature of things, I was in an invidious position. I was not feeling too clever and I was apprehensive, both about leaving and about the future in general.

Students came round to see me and we prayed together. They said that my adversary "was not an African." By this they meant that he was not a real African. It was a significant testimony against the self-made freedom fighter. Another student simply said, "You are a man." I was expelled. The issues which I'd articulated throughout my time in Kenya came to a head in the manner of my enforced departure. Teaching and life situation came together. I was at peace within. I thought my vocation was validated.

Jackson who with his wife Dorine had helped me in the house came round to visit and began weeping. "This is Kenya," he cried, "This is Kenya." I explained how good it was for me to go since the issues I'd struggled for would come to light. He was a poor man but he had wisdom and grace that morning. I was deeply touched by his tears for me.

On Sunday 23rd I had a last visit to Nairobi National Park and later a lovely meal with the Rosses and McNeils. Back at the College, a steady stream of workers and students came to say how sorry they were. I wrote a letter of appeal to send to the P. C. E. A. This was for the record. I did not expect them to do anything about an absent European. Yet it would have been in their own interests to have made some serious enquiries. I also wrote to Bedan Mbugua, Editor of the Christian magazine 'Beyond,' letting him know what had happened from my point of view and enclosing some relevant documents. I wrote also to Dr Njoya. A few weeks later, the manner of my going became a public issue.

In Chapel on my last morning in Kenya, Albert Juffer preached a sermon on the passage from Second Chronicles 18: 1-27. This concerned the prophet Micaiah who was distinguished from the court prophets by his being a genuinely called mouthpiece of God. At 4 00pm the College held a farewell party, organised by the students. It was both serious and moving. I was given a clock. Some tutors were also present. The Dean of Studies Moses Motuiri explained some of the immediate causes of my sudden departure. He added that my life was in danger and that I had to go.

I said a few words and compared myself with the students, saying that I had come from a poor background and from a rural area. I saw myself in each student face. I recalled my ordination. The first children I baptised were African children. The first people to whom I administered Holy Communion were Africans. I mentioned the 'theology outside of Jesus Christ' issue and warned that some people only see Jesus of Nazareth with a machine gun in his hands. I explained my reluctance to discuss things with someone before writing or speaking and simply said, "What the Lord would give me, I would give." I continued by saying that the real reason why I was going was to save the churches from having an issue with the Government of Kenya. I exhorted everyone to be steadfast in Christian Faith. Peter Cheboiywo called for a reformation "Because we don't want to be taught this way." He was applauded. We concluded by praying together. Students lined up to shake hands. It was what a Christian farewell should be. There was no cant and no hypocrisy.

Members of the P. C. E. A. Executive visited to say "Kwaheri" (Good-bye). They gave me a little sword and shield. I said my goodbyes to the Juffer children. Anne-Wym gave me a painting of a leopard which he had made. My house was empty. I had one case and one bag to carry. I left St Paul's College at 7 10pm. Albert and his wife and two students took me to the airport via a delicious meal in Nairobi. At 9 45pm we arrived at the airport. The Rosses came to say "Good-bye." The great Dr Timothy Njoya arrived (unexpectedly from my point of view). Others arrived. Timothy led us all in prayer. He also spoke. He said "You have been crucified" and he said he could smell the blood. He told us that he had been asked to take my place at St Paul's College and had replied that he would think about it in order "to carry on the struggle of Dr Anderson." He said missionaries had been puppets for too long but now a new direction would be taken. Dr Njoya handed me a beautiful cross made of two nails. It was a powerful symbol and remains one of my most treasured possessions.

I shook hands with everyone and departed. I left Kenya on Tuesday 25th February, taking an overnight flight to Schipol Airport in Holland. When the aircraft left the runway and lifted into the night sky, I began to breathe huge sighs of relief and gladness which lasted for some time. I was so thankful to be alive. I was so glad to have been able to make a clean exit. Thirty five thousand feet above Africa I was safe. I was going home. It would be cold, I thought.

The Amsterdam morning was a resurrection from the dead of night. There was no cloud. The enormous sun - a blinding fiery ball rose slowly drenching everything in its golden light. I had no regrets. The issues had been well worth fighting for. I enumerated them:

*The unchanging revelation in Jesus Christ*
*Freedom of speech, of academic research, thought and discussion*
*The negation of an African theology without Jesus Christ*
*Misuse and abuse of position in the Presbyterian Church of East Africa*
*Financial corruption in the churches*
*Churches' acceptance of 'political' money for Christian purposes*
*The subservience of church to state*
*The idolisation of political leaders*
*The catastrophic distinction between poor and rich*
*The identification of Church leaders' lifestyles with the latter of these*

*The cost of Christian vocation*

*The difference between Christianity and non-Christianity*

*Neo-colonialism*

*How to live as a Christian*

It seemed to be a privilege to have been associated with these great issues. I was much aware of the guiding and sustaining Presence of God in the hours between 4 00pm and 10 00pm on the 25th of February 1986. At Schipol I felt gloriously happy, free and at peace. When I left, I held the teaching record for students achieving first class grades in external examinations. Yet I felt that I had been encompassed too much and that I had not achieved what I might have. I parodied a text of Scripture, "He could do no mighty works there - because he was white." On arrival I had gone to the Chapel at Schipol Airport. There I prayed with a thankful heart. I wrote in the book, "Out of the fowler's snare...Thanks to the Living God in Jesus' Name."

I waited a few hours for the connection to Glasgow. As I reached Scotland I saw the fields covered with frost and some snow. The air was clear and fresh. I rejoiced. David Ness, Minister of Dundonald met me and drove me home. It was all so beautiful. The seasons, the colours, the fresh sharp air, the hills and the Firth of Clyde nearby amazed me. I had not seen Scotland in winter since 1979. But within me there is a small and pleasant fire. It burns perhaps in many who have been privileged to work in Africa. No matter how cold or bitter the northern chill may be, in my being there is a warmth that will never leave. For a Scot to live and work in Africa is a lifetime treat. Though I'd never go back to work there, my life was changed. My values were stood on their head. I learned. I came back a wiser man. Nothing that we spoilt Europeans think is important is necessarily so. For five and a half years I lived with those who struggled to stay alive each day. Everything else is negotiable. The indomitable spirit of the African remains in my mind as a symbol of providence. If God should be good to them spiritually, no-one should begrudge them such blessing. Our churches may be empty and often too so are our hearts. In Africa, churches are full. Christianity grows. And the light of Christ carries forward those who will respond to His eternal Grace.

## Public Issue In Kenya

In April 1986 'Beyond' magazine published an article entitled, "P. C. E. A. Deports Missionary." "The question that is being asked by some of the church leaders after the fact is whether the P. C. E. A. church exhausted all her legal machinery before kicking out Dr Anderson. Did the fact that he was a foreigner mean that he could be dispensed with without the normal constitutional procedure?" The article focused on the relationship between church and state with respect to harambee fund-raising. "Whether privately or publicly, these same questions have been voiced by many a concerned citizen." 'Beyond' quoted the ex-Moderator whom I had brushed with in the pulpit of St Andrew's Church as having once said, "Democracy can be Demo-crazy." The article inferred that I had been the victim of a personal grudge which caused the constitution of the P. C. E. A. to be ignored. The writers, Bedan Mbugua and Ibrahim Omondi censured me for 'extreme statements' in my paper for discussion by the St Paul's staff but added, "Yet we cannot overlook the fact that some of the things he said needed to be mentioned." A former tutor was quoted as saying, "Anderson should have been allowed the freedom of discussing the paper he wrote in the confidence of a staff fellowship." The article connected the sermons in St Andrew's and the paper 'Christianity, The Church And Money' as the immediate causes of my deportation and concluded, "How can the church be the light of the world when cries of injustice are heard right from the pews?"

Bedan Mbugua eventually paid the price for such courageous editorial leadership. Not, I must make clear for publishing an article about my own case, but for authentic journalism in the Kenyan context of which the article about me was one example. 'Beyond' magazine was closed down and Bedan was imprisoned for a time. These were the birth pangs of the democracy movements of the late nineteen-eighties and nineties in Kenya. They bore fruit in time.

In the May edition of 'Beyond' the Secretary General of the P. C. E. A. the Reverend Plawson Kuria wrote a rejoinder to the article about my case. He likened me to Judas Iscariot and described the P. C. E. A. as "the most democratic church." He paid due deference to the President of Kenya and stated that anyone who tarnished the name of leadership in the church of Christ as well as leadership in the state would be deported. "The integrity of the church and of the state are not negotiable." What dangerous over-statement! Where is he now? More gifted men than he had been passed by for such a prestigious position in the P. C. E. A. But Kuria was generally held to be a stooge. I wonder who placed him in his exalted position?

Bishop Alexander Muge of the Anglican Church and Dr Timothy Njoya wrote articles of articulate bravery which were published in April and May. Muge's article "Let Us Be Bold" appeared alongside the one on my own case in the April edition. In May, Timothy published an article entitled "Surrendering Jesus To Pilate." I had been in good company, a point which letter writers noted. Muge, still a comparatively young man was later to lose his life after having been threatened by a member of the Kenyan Government. Timothy Njoya continued to speak Biblically about the great issues of human freedom. He was a spiritual progenitor of the democracy movement in Kenya. He survived and appeared on British television and was quoted in the British press.

Years later the journalist Mary Anne Fitzgerald wrote "In the row over the role of KANU (Kenya African National Union), Kenya's sole political party, the language of confrontation has turned parliamentarians into preachers and clergymen into politicians.......Shariff Nasser, an assistant minister (said)...."The voice of KANU should not be overshadowed by any institution in the country including parliament." Last month President Daniel arap Moi entered the fray when he accused a Kenyan church of circulating subversive pamphlets. Although the President did not identify his target by name, he was clearly referring to the Rev Dr Timothy Njoya, who in a sermon had urged Kenyans to challenge government leaders on decisions they did not agree with and charged that the wealth of the country was amassed in the hands of a few. The emergence of the church as critic comes at a time when both parliament and the national press are reluctant to challenge the administration. A government clampdown on opposition, that reached its height earlier in the year, has put more than 60 people in jail."

In its June issue, 'Beyond' informed its readers of the non-renewal of Albert Juffer's contract as a tutor at St Paul's College. The issue highlighted was 'African Theology' and the respective positions of my former adversary and myself were summarised. "He is known to have dismissed as rubbish the fact that the Bible is the ultimate authority on which theology should revolve.........Dr Anderson, on the other hand, advocated that the place to start in Christian theology is with Christ." Albert was quoted as having written, "The integration of traditional religion in theology deprives the cross of its salvific significance, and the cross of Christ is God's radical judgment over traditional religions, be they European, Asian or African." The 'Beyond' editors added comments about "the fall of moral and academic standards" at St Paul's. I understood at the time that the church leaders had favoured Albert Juffer's submission and I do not doubt that it helped in the maintenance of Christianity at St Paul's.

## Kenya In Later Years

The world knows that in the nineteen-nineties President Moi of Kenya has been forced by western funding agencies and governments to organise free elections. Dr Robert Ouko had been grievously murdered. Tribal warfare had broken out in many places. Ethnic cleansing had occurred without much opposition from the Government, Police or Armed Forces. How ironic it was that the Christian churches, those with whom I had been involved, whose leaders expelled me in 1986, rose up in argument against the President and took part in the various movements towards democracy in Kenya. The things I had said in my humble paper became commonplace. Some of the issues for which I had struggled were articulated in pulpits throughout the land.

To be sure, the various opposition parties could not agree on one leader to challenge President Moi and so he survived and was re-elected. Moi has been by no means the worst of African leaders though he with so many others seem to stay so long that like over-ripe fruit they become rotten before falling. The churches today are very outspoken about much. An Anglican student visited me in Edinburgh in 1993 and suggested kindly that I had been vindicated by history and events. I have never received an apology from the P. C. E. A. It was later reported that in that same year some $269,000,000 was found to be missing from the central Reserves of the Government of Kenya. Western governments have made it a condition of further support of the Kenyan economy that reforms are introduced to the political process and democratisation be re-introduced. Foremost in criticising the Government of Kenya in the mid-nineties were some of the people who were responsible for my rapid and forced exit.

A friend sent me a copy of the December 31st 1995 edition of "Finance" Magazine from Kenya. Such a magazine could never have been published ten years earlier. The cover page offered the title of the leading article "How KANU (Kenya African National Union - the Government Political Party of President Daniel T. arap Moi) will rig 1997 Elections." The first page carried an advertisement by Amnesty International detailing abuses by the Kenyan police against refugees. The 1993 'election' was derided for "widespread rigging." (p.10) The leading article included the following statements, "Millions of Kenyans, mainly from Opposition strongholds will be denied the opportunity of voting. Terror, violence, fear and voter intimidation will be intensified and escalated throughout Kenya." (p.12, 13) So much for Plawson Kuria!

It was because of the great freedoms that are in Jesus Christ that I felt able to speak. Each African was my brother or sister equal in God's sight. Why should I have patronised them with ineffectualities? I had not gone to Africa to colonise. I had gone as a member of Christ's universal church and as a member of the Kingdom of God. Whatever was argued about, discussed or disagreed about - whatever was done - was done in that context first and foremost. It is the politically conscious mentality that infects the freedoms of God's reign in human lives. And so many in the churches are these kind of animals. They hinder much before being exposed for their absurd hypocrisies, weakness, spiritual immaturity and cowardliness. But their conspiracies have their day – even if they have no eternity.

# 5 : It Is Your Cross

## Waiting Days

I began looking for a parish as soon as I arrived back in Scotland. I was contracted by the Church of Scotland to undertake speaking engagements in the two Presbyteries with which I had a missionary partnership arrangement. The purpose of these speaking engagements was to familiarise congregations with overseas work so that they would continue to support those who chose to work abroad. This duty took me to the Scottish Borders and to Morayshire, both idyllic places to visit in spring and summer months.

The system of free call for congregations was won at great cost in Scottish Christian history. I uphold its principle and support its practice. However, it places certain categories of ministers in difficulties. If you are not in a parish, it can be a problem to move into one. If you have been in a particular sphere of service other than a parish, it can take time to be accepted. If you have worked abroad and have no track record in parish ministry, you are at a further disadvantage. If you have academic qualifications, that creates suspicion. If you are single that handicaps you. If you are evangelically minded there are certain no-go areas. I did not have much going for me!

It matters not that you may have vision allied to commitment, a caring heart and God's blessing on your life - any amount of applications will be consigned to the round filing cabinet which sits on the floor. It is very hurtful to be rejected without as much as an interview. The church is often a difficult place for everyone because we are exposed spiritually to some extent or another. There is nowhere else to hide - nowhere to go.

The months of 1986 passed slowly and painfully for me. The interminable process of application, waiting for a reply, having a possible interview, preaching to a vacancy committee, and then hearing nothing for weeks (sometimes months) until you learn that someone has been called to that particular church wears on the soul like a punishment. But for the value of spiritual democracy and the right of people to choose their own minister, I would gladly have been appointed to a job by someone whose role it was to do just that.

Great of course is the joy that accompanies the call when it comes. It is a call of the people and has the significance and authority of such a call - something utterly precious in the Body of Christ in this world. Scotland retains this custom in its Presbyterianism even although some self-appointed power-brokers within the church would seek to change it or even abolish it. The principle is exemplary, but the practice is limited by the wisdom of the participants. Thereby hangs many a tale! And time dripped from the clock as I waited and waited and waited.

## Summer In Scotland

I was astonished at Scotland's beauty. One can miss the seasons and sunshine alone can become boring. It is the contrasts and the intensities, the scale and the richness of the contents which always impress me when I return to my native land. I continue to find nowhere on earth as beautiful as the west coast of Scotland from Helensburgh to Cape Wrath. It is an extravagant feast of landscape which cannot simply have been the result of impersonal, geological and atmospheric forces over long periods of time. It is the originality of the scheme, the sheer perfection of the asymmetrical, the encompassing of the human spirit in a natural home which ever delights my soul.

In mid-April, down-hearted at the silence which my applications had met, I walked a few miles from Dundonald to Drybridge and back. It was about 7 15 in the evening. I looked across the fir trees and saw my home village bathed in the evening sun, white and golden. I exulted and praised God for such a sign of peace and beauty, of providence and blessing. I came back home a happy person.

I might have been called to parishes sooner than I was. Interest was expressed on more than one occasion and I took matters no further. It is an instinctive response which one hopes is the result of divine guidance rather than of its antagonist. I was touched that the congregation in which I was brought up as a child, in which I had laboured as a Sunday School and Bible Class teacher and youth leader, in whose context my original call to the ministry had been confirmed, sought me as their minister. Yet I was absolutely sure that I should not go and I did not do so. I think I felt that my own person would come between the people and the preaching of the Gospel. I thought I would be compromised before I ever arrived. If and when disagreement arose, how would it be resolved? I would be a disappointment no matter what I did.

Furlough in Jedburgh Presbytery brought some relief. Borders history is worth much. Sir Walter Scott's home at Abbotsford is fascinating, with its collections of armour and artefacts such as Napoleon's coat-hooks, locks of Lord Nelson's and of Bonnie Prince Charlie's hair, the great Montrose's sword and much else.

Speaking was enjoyable and not taxing. A humorous commentary with picture 'slides' informed and entertained. I was able to preach on occasions and that was a source of personal blessing. I thought I might even be called to a parish in the Borders, but after due process, I was not required. That was a disappointment at the time. Morayshire has always impressed me as a warm and sunny place. My sojourn there allowed me to motor across to the west and gasp at the awesome beauty of Loch Maree. I visited sites of Highland Clearances. Pitiably few acres of grass - why such an inhuman struggle? It was not much that the landlords appropriated for their cruelties. I was appalled too as I read the lists of those who died in the First World War. There seemed to be no just proportion. Entire male populations of villages killed. Countless women left as widows. How many children grew up without their fathers? I was incensed at the brutal carnage of that war and even more so at the culture of exploitation of human beings by army generals. Even if Scots became soldiers out of misplaced loyalties and because of lack of other opportunities, they were considered as cannon fodder, expendable by the thousand. Now the culture of war has changed, at least for the time being, but great areas are barren and bereft of human community and that part of Scotland is but a wilderness, the last in Europe.

## The Pain Of Spirit

By July I still had received no call. I began to feel desolate. I have never had a relaxed temperament and so have always found delay hugely difficult to negotiate. Impatience has ever been a weakness. Perhaps it was necessary for me to slip slowly down from the plateau on which I had returned from Africa. It is easy to rationalise. I loathe theologies of compensation and these abound in church circles throughout the world. Kind people suggested that God was waiting to give me 'the right parish'. I however lacked faith at that moment that God had much to do with processes in the institutions of Christianity throughout the world. I did not spend my time idly and wrote a manuscript for a book on the subject of African Theology. Unsurprisingly, I was never able to find a publisher.

The problem for me was how to relate my spiritual history, my calling and those intimations of the divine which had come to me in my life to the Church in Scotland of which I was a Minister. I had to take my chances as every other applicant did. I knew few people and had no 'godfathers' to recommend me for appropriate charges. Reformed tradition is intellectual in emphasis and that is a great glory. However, I carried knowledge from beyond the confines of human intelligence. I accepted that these secret things were given to me and were not to be broadcast. However, I felt that I really should expect to be the instrument of an equivalent return on God's investment in me. It seemed logical and right that I should have a fruitful ministry.

I continued to pray much and although that was sometimes hard work in the circumstances, it invariably lifted me out of my discouragement into a more peaceful and patient disposition. Yet I did go down a long way. I began to question the value of nearly twenty years of Christian life and calling. I wondered if I would actually ever receive a call from a congregation. About the beginning of August, for no apparent reason, I came out of my valley of disappointment. I began to have a renewed confidence in the future and looked forward to exercising a ministry somewhere in my native land.

Five wonderful September days on the Isle of Arran lifted my spirits. To see the autumnal setting sun rip through Glen Rosa turning trees from green to gold and crimson, to gaze out from the summit of Goat Fell to east and west and north and south and become silent with admiration for the gift of natural architecture, to breathe the clean fresh air and sleep deeply of the night, makes you feel that you belong. Celtic Christianity has that genius of not divorcing the spiritual from the earthly. No-one could - who can enjoy such a paradise. Reformed thought also teaches that we may see the world with God's eyes. Evangelical Christianity speaks much of new birth and new creation. The redeeming perspective of faith in Christ transforms our view of the world. It is in relation to its Maker that the world is perfectly beautiful.

## The Call

I was offered a part-time temporary assistantship in Renfrew with the Reverend Peter Houston and gladly accepted. It was the humblest beginning imaginable and seemed in inverse proportion to my years to study and discipleship, my experience and calling. But I was most grateful. The connection was made by my former St Paul's College student Peter Cheboiywo who had come to Scotland to undertake his doctoral studies at Glasgow University. Regular involvement in Sunday worship would be advantageous. I turned down the possibility of a call from a rural south Scotland parish.

On Sunday 12th October I preached in the presence of two vacancy committees. I met with and spoke to the vacancy committee from Overtown because they had asked to meet me after the service. The other, from Aberdeenshire, returned home. On Tuesday 21st October, twenty years after my call to the ministry, Dr Kennedy telephoned on behalf of the vacancy committee to ask me to preach as sole nominee for Overtown Church. I accepted.

I was happy to do so. I felt that I was going to the right place. Overtown, overlooking the picturesque Clyde Valley in Lanarkshire was within the central belt and almost half-way between Glasgow and Edinburgh. It seemed unpretentious with a cross section of occupations and social roles. There were capable people in leadership positions and young people in and around the congregation. The manse was not unmanageable in size - an important factor for a single person. I was given a strong sense of God's guidance and providence when I drove up the hill and the sun shone on my future parish.

I preached as sole nominee for the charge of Overtown on November 16th 1986. One hundred and eighty-six people voted for me and five against. I was therefore called as minister. The date of my induction was set for 15th December. It delighted me that I would be in place for Christmas. The invitation to be sole nominee, the preaching as such and the induction took place in a way which related to the manner of the intimation of my call in late October 1966, my acceptance before God of that call and then beginning of due process in the Church of Scotland. There were three stages in 1966 and there were three stages in 1986. The timing was acute. It is important to recognise this because as we live our lives we often struggle and lose our way. We may become discouraged and lose faith in the longer term plan. In discerning actual events and their meaning the sequences which form the fabric of our journey through life may reflect a closer walk with God than we can see at the time. If we doubt God's love for us, God's presence in our lives and God's willingness to redeem us in both the small and great things of our living, we must record our gratitude for such exceptional evidence of Sovereignty when it is so obviously granted.

I began the worldly tasks associated with taking up my position. I needed to buy second-hand furniture and a second-hand car. I was given some gifts and scoured the classified advertisements for basic necessities. I bought furniture at an auction in the town of Hamilton. The minister is obliged to keep up a certain appearance. Filling a manse so that it resembled a home was not easy for me. My admiration of the motor car was humbled in purchasing a six year old Ford Cortina. It was an honest vehicle however and served me well.

I also talked to the head teacher of the primary school who told me that the children of Overtown had an isolated and introverted view of the world associated with the nature of the village. I was assured by another person that I would have minimal privacy and I gathered that there were turbulences within the relationships which constituted the congregation. I said to myself, "I am not going here to fight." I hoped that I would be able to survive. I enjoyed my last few days of 'freedom.'

## The Parish

I was duly inducted as Parish Minister of Overtown on the evening of 15th December 1986. It was a happy occasion. I was deeply moved when everyone began singing, "Praise waits for Thee in Zion, Lord." The great vows I took seemed to lie heavily on my shoulders. Close friends attended and after-the-event speeches were well received. I had the good fortune to have Peter Cheboiywo as a speaker. Polished and able, he made a great impression on all who attended. Much hilarity accompanied proceedings. I noted that the warmest room in the manse was the bathroom. I had considered using it to interview parishioners. "Have a seat..." I'd say, pointing to the W. C. as I sat cross-legged in the bath - a Mahatma Ghandi-like figure somewhat out of context in North Lanarkshire.

My first duties coincided with the Christmas celebrations in the community and these invariably involved the eating of steak pies and trifles. Many months later and weeks before the Christmas of 1987, I was walking down Overtown main street. In the distance I spied a redoubtable eighty-five year old woman member of the congregation coming towards me. "Ah jist pit ye doon fur braised steak," she exclaimed from what appeared to be a considerable distance. When we eventually reached each other, she repeated her unusual greeting and added to counter my confused expression, "Ye ken, at the Christmas dinner - Ah jist pit ye doon fur braised steak." "Ah don't want braised steak!" I rejoined, gaining in confidence. "Whit?" said she. "Oh well, wid ye like some chicken?" "Yes, that will do fine," said I. "Ay, I can get a special order fur ye." "Thanks very much," I offered, as we departed.

The village was wealthy in characters. Dull it was not! Intense it proved to be. The ladies vied with each other as ladies the world over do. "Ah fair cracked her enamel," I heard one sophisticate boasting as she lacerated the reputation of some unfortunate. "Ma ain craw is the whitest," explained a fine woman, sympathising with a mother's need to defend her children against all comers. Evocative nick-names proliferated. Tinny Glidden, Pianna Johnson, Squeak Johnson, Wizard Johnson, Links Tweedlie, Luggy Frew, Stookie Matha, Peel Wull (for he was a chemist) and Boosty McClew were real people. Every member of the primary school football team had a nickname. No-one was called by that name into which he had been baptised. The wonderful Jimmy McDowall greeted me extravagantly whenever I patronised the village sub-post office which he owned and ran with his wife. I used to return his healthy greetings as merrily and as loudly, thereby confusing those queuing up for their pensions, early in the morning. The sub-post office sold food and other household necessities. I noticed a 'fun set' for sale at £1 85p. It was a plastic set of glasses and false moustache. Week in week out, month in month out, I'd say, "I see no-one has bought the fun set, Jimmy." One year after I had first seen this item, I raised its unpopularity with Jimmy again. Exasperated, he turned to the shelf, took the fun set and threw it to me. I think I tried to use it as an illustration for a children's address. I saw my first 'pie buttie' in Jimmy's shop. This Scottish delicacy, the epitome of health food, was a roll with margarine, inside which was a hot Scotch mutton pie with the edges broken down so that the roll could be closed. School children preferred this treat at lunchtime to anything available in the school dining room.

The politics of the parish are as the politics of the world. Representatives of three traditional professions were there to be knocked down, the head school teacher, the minister and the doctor. Families would sometimes sign their relatives out of the local hospital out of distrust of medical staff. Occasionally, the general practitioner would not be allowed entry to the house of a patient through mistrust. The Minister was always on trial for his life, the jury permanently out, the verdict awaited by everyone.

I had watched Episcopal Bishop Richard Holloway's television lecture on the subject of AIDS. Troubled by the lack of Biblical, theological and ethical reference, I had written a letter to 'The Scotsman' newspaper. I also had a short article placed in 'The Glasgow Herald' and in January 1987 I took part in a television programme on the subject. Little did I know what this would cost me in later life.

The local councillor described my parish to me as an area of 'multiple deprivation'. Because it was officially a 'rural area' it did not receive grant-aid which urban situations merited. I was daunted by the difference between my hopes and the reality with which I was confronted. Visibility in the community was important. I actually enjoyed meeting people in their homes. I met spiritual heroes and heroines there, lacking fame and wealth, but not greatness of stature. The elderly seemed particularly admirable. They had struggled through life, raising families in straitened circumstances. They were wise and deep and had more Christian character than the well-dressed middle-agers who listened uncomfortably to my sermons week by week. I thought ruefully, "My problem is to avoid conflict and folly. It won't be easy."

I began to react spiritually, psychologically and emotionally to the area, its history, its presence, its people, its forms of religious understanding. Thus began a kind of invisible spiritual suffering associated with the burden of dealing with religious formality without equivalent content. Few ministers of sensitivity or perception will have escaped this process. Yet even fewer parishioners seem to recognise or understand it. Therefore a gulf of spiritual loneliness may accompany a ministry. This is accentuated in the case of the single person. It is multiplied by the factors of the place in which one lives and ministers.

One is transported and cast down. The rhythms of parish life are violent and unpredictable. Christmas Eve was magical. Listening to the large congregation gently singing "Still The Night" in the early minutes of Christmas Day was an unsurpassed delight. Spiritual rewards there are a-plenty in Christian ministry, but they do not come uninterrupted by the sin and tragedy, the messiness and sorrows of this earthly life. You can I suppose, insulate yourself. I felt that I had met many such insulated people in the ministry of churches. I was not likely to become such an automaton. Indeed, I would resist any pressure to be so moulded. Therefore my laughter would be real laughter and my tears would be real tears. Both I was given in abundance.

Fresh air has always been my favourite resort. I climbed Tinto hill in late January. I made my way slowly through the mists, seeing little behind or below. After an hour I reached what I thought might be the summit. I could not tell. It seemed a futile exercise. Then - the sun shone splendidly, an east wind blew and the fog scuttled away. A north, south, east and west panorama presented itself to me. I rejoiced in the sight of the rolling forbidding hills to the south east, the river winding its way west, and the fields and trees and sheep and sky and clouds and cold fresh air. I knelt down and prayed with thankfulness, for I thought that God had blessed my climb. When I started to come down again, the mists enveloped everything. Visibility was but a few yards. Inwardly I felt happy, warm and comforted. Aloneness, purity, peace, majesty, scenery, sunshine - these found meaning in fellowship with the Creator of all that is.

## Protestant And Catholic

North Lanarkshire maintained a hypocritical allegiance to sectarianism. There was a saying, "As lonely as a Protestant in Coatbridge." Many years later, while attending a football match between Hibernian and Rangers at Easter Road in Edinburgh, I heard a supporter of that club correct the match programme information concerning the referee's home town which was stated to be Aberdeen. "You come fae Larkhall, ya ————" the gentleman interlocuted knowledgeably.

While I was on furlough from my post in Kenya, I and a friend and his son aged eight had gone to Ibrox to see a Rangers versus Celtic Derby. We took our seats in the stand. A few minutes after the game had begun, an obese man came and sat in the seat immdiataely to my left. I could tell that he was a Rangers supporter because he had on blue shoes, supporters' blue socks, blue trousers, blue pullover, blue shirt, blue jacket, red, white and blue scarf and tammy. In each of the pockets of his jacket he had a half bottle of vodka. After the first fifteen minutes during which I and my friend and his son watched quietly, my blue-clad neighbour elbowed me in the stomach. "Your mother was a nun," he said confidently. Throughout the game he made occasional snide remarks to me from time to time. "You're no' wan o' us," he concluded as a consequence of my relative quietness and uncommitted clothing. His earlier suggestion had implied that not only was I not a Protestant, but that I was illegitimate and my mother had broken holy orders when I was conceived. I would have found this amusing except for the fact that as the game progressed, his consumption of vodka increased. At the end of the match, he threatened me with physical violence, staggered to the top of the steps of that part of the stand where we were sitting and waited for me to make my exit. I decided to stand beside a Police Inspector. I had visions of becoming involved in a brawl. The true blue was hopelessly drunk. I was not afraid of him. The Police, however, are not noted for their subtlety. Had there been a fracas, both of us would have been arrested. I did not want to spend the week-end in Govan jail and be bailed out on the Monday morning! The fan's objectionable behaviour continued until the Police Inspector forcibly removed him. I took to my heels and ran to Great Western Road where my friend and his son were waiting for me. I never attended another Old Firm match.

In reality there were many marriages between Protestants and Catholics in North Lanarkshire. At the family level there was much love and support, even if the public posturing continued. Within weeks of arriving I shared the marriage ceremony of the son of a member of the congregation to a Roman Catholic woman. The groom's father was a leader of the Orange Order. It was not easy for him. The marriage had to be in the bride's Chapel in Wishaw. There was an awkward silence after the vows were taken. Then the bride's mother rose from her seat, crossed the aisle and reached out to shake hands with the groom's father. He stood and returned the greeting. Everyone followed. Later I told him that he had behaved with great dignity, which was true.

In the second year of my ministry the Orange Lodge asked if they could come to worship in Overtown Church. Seeing the possibility of preaching the Gospel to partial outcasts, I agreed. In the event, there were no problems. They had their march. The tawdry cardboard crown and the Bible were brought to the front of the church. There was a large attendance. I compared marching to the last charge of the Polish Cavalry as a means of effective communication. But I also spoke about the love of Jesus for everyone one and all, not exempting any present. I know that that message touched a number of individuals. Respectable Church of Scotland leaders, desperate to appear reasonable in everything, tend not to extend God's love to the fringes of their own society while with indecent haste rushing to acknowledge societies at greater distance than their own.

I never found the Roman Catholic priests I met convincing. Lacking ease and spontaneity outwith their own circle, they seemed tired and nervous. I'm sure many would say the same about Protestant ministers. The spiritual burden which secularism places upon pastoral figures is difficult to quantify. But it is very real to those who live each day struggling against indifference, agnosticism and insincerity in congregation and community. The dynamics inherited by religious upbringing are not always healthy. Often Christians appear to be contradictions of the claims of their Faith. Beneath the enthusiasms of parochial Catholicism, I saw too often the psychological consequences of an unnatural grid in which many had been reared and in which they continued to try to find meaning.

Freedom seemed to be found in Protestantism. With it, a taking for granted of the spiritual roots of personal freedom which lie in the Reformation and beyond that in Christ Himself. Secularism is squandering the spiritual capital of the ages. Never have so many lost so much that was won by so few. Biblical authority has been diminished by science and higher criticism. Sure, the responsibilities of the past still live within the new generations, but in a less demanding way. Where faith is real, it is blessed. No-one needs to go to church. Many are the motives which bring people to public worship. At best there is a calling of the inner spirit and a response to that leading to communion with the Living Lord. In true encounter, neither Protestant nor Catholic labels matter. And so many now realise that this is so. If professional clergy could think so too, popular ecumenism would be institutionalised. The Church would indeed be one. The chaos of human imagination however will never let Christ's Body rest in peace. Nor should it. For there is life to be lived and work to be done. Creation itself testifies to difference and distinction. These define everything. We can worship in many ways the same God. Our hearts and our intentions are greater than the metaphysical constructs which pass for Christendom. Christ cannot be held within the confines of our own understanding.

## Anna Weir

People fall out with their congregations. There are many who are estranged from their spiritual home and family. It was a pastoral duty to visit all such and to invite them to return to the fold. So I met Anna and Jackie Weir. Anna later became seriously ill and I visited her in hospital. Her condition was eventually diagnosed as a form of motor neuron disease. But at the beginning of her illness we hoped and prayed that she would recover. In March of 1987, I held a healing service for Anna in hospital. Rivulets of sweat ran down my face although I was not warm. I felt the vibration and heat associated with laying-on-of hands. I felt a little 'out of this world' but there were no angels visiting us. The air was not charged with light or spiritual beauty although Anna herself brightened up towards the end of the service. Anna's husband Jackie feared that she was going to die. He said he'd heard of miracles but not in Overtown.

The days, weeks and months which followed found me carrying a great spiritual burden for Anna. I cried out to God for her life and recovery and fasted on occasions. I re-read Cameron Peddie's 'The Forgotten Talent' for inspiration. A few days after the initial service, I visited Anna in hospital and held her hand. She seemed bathed in golden spiritual light this time. I thought she was slipping slowly away but I could not accept that this should happen at that moment.

I telephoned George Fox, Scotland's most distinguished Minister of Christian Healing and asked him to pray for Anna. Later that day I learned that Anna had received blood (again) and was to be taken for an exploratory operation. At least she was surviving. After a few days Jackie told me that the doctors had found no malignancy and were interpreting her problems in terms of mental spasms. Anna herself was brighter. I told Jackie that I had asked George Fox to pray for Anna. By the end of May Anna was still recovering and was expected not only to survive but to return to a normal lifestyle. Inflammation of the muscles was diagnosed without further understanding being given to us. She returned home but later in the summer was taken into hospital in Glasgow. I saw her for the last time on Sunday August 2nd at about 5 00pm. She was so thin and weak and it was obvious that her time with us was drawing to a close. Yet as I looked at her, fifty-one years of age, lying in the peace of sleep, I said quietly and with conviction, "It is beautiful to die." I recalled this perception during Anna's funeral service. The doctors said that her clinical condition, once known had offered no hope. God did not heal her. Why? I agonised over my own failure to be an instrument of healing. I knew that Jesus could have and would have healed Anna. The Risen Jesus had not done so.

I don't like the theology of compensation, but the situation was not all negative. Anna might have died in February. She returned home with joy and optimism and it was there that she began to deteriorate. I learned that early in their marriage Anna's husband had decided that they should not have children although Anna's wish was to have brought up a family. She had been dominated by her older husband. Perhaps her illness was caused by years of inner silent suffering and frustration. Doctors accept that illness can be brought on by psycho-spiritual pressures, especially if present over a long period of time. Anna recovered in hospital and relapsed after returning home. I learned later that the situation on her return home was actually intolerable and contributed to her relapse, decline and death.

I bore no grudge against the Lord because Anna did not survive. I knew why she had been unable to continue in this life. Jackie himself did not live much longer and died suddenly of an asthmatic attack. He had agreed to sponsor the daughter of a former student of mine in Kenya through her schooling. To my astonishment, I learned that Jackie had left his entire estate in the form of a Trust, which I was to administer along with his lawyers, to help and educate children in Africa and elsewhere. Over the years that have followed The Weir Trust has helped many children and Jackie's thoughtfulness has been a great blessing.

Another young woman for whom I had prayed died of cancer after a brave struggle. She too recovered well and had a good spell before finally declining. She left two teen-age children. She gave me a clue to her suffering which was in relation to a poor and apparently unhappy marriage. Many people bear in their bodies the evidence of suffering which is emotional, mental and spiritual. Jesus understood the root causes of disease and healed with divine healing. Physical existence itself is imperfect and prone to imperfection. Disease is endemic in the human condition. But individual and personal suffering may also contribute to physical symptoms. If these are not recognised or admitted through genuine lack of understanding or to protect a social relationship, they can, in time, lead to a position from which it is difficult and sometimes impossible to recover.

There were occasional healings. I ministered to a little old lady who suffered from a painful leg which she associated with a disc problem in her back. She told me later that she felt she had been healed. Tracy, a bonny schoolgirl and a wonderful character was struck down in an accident. After weeks deep in a coma, she emerged at Christmas time, thus answering the prayers of many. When she appeared in church it was a joyful moment. Later I used to drive her to her horse-riding lessons. When I left Overtown, she was progressing slowly.

Just before Christmas 1988 and while I was within Shotts Prison on Chaplaincy duties, a senior officer asked me to pray for a little boy of two years - the son of a friend - who had lost one of his eyes due to cancer and was thought likely to lose his second eye. I remember crying to God that evening with tears for this poor little boy. His helplessness and vulnerability touched me as did the awefulness of his problem and the whole seeming injustice of innocent suffering. I asked the Lord Jesus that the little boy's good eye be saved and that the cancer be removed from his body. I also asked that this healing would be as a Christmas gift to me. On January 19th 1989 I asked the prison officer how the little boy was. He told me that he was responding to treatment, that his second eye was all right, that he was playing football in the ward of the hospital where he was being treated and that he was scheduled to go home in four weeks time. I quietly wept inner tears of joy and thanksgiving.

The churches offer kind pastoral euphemisms. Society is not geared to giving space for the radical healing option. We watch people die who need not do so. Jesus was not conventional, neither was he socialised. If you really wanted to be healed, He would heal you. But He knows the names of all who have died of silent cross-bearing love. I have the greatest admiration for those saints like George Fox who make the healing ministry their specialisation. It is a self-denying life which requires great discipline, endless patience and great faith. It is wonderful that now healing has become respectable and many congregations encourage healing services. John Calvin was wrong when he said that "the miracle has ceased." The recovery of this 'forgotten talent' is one of the best aspects of the church in the latter part of the twentieth century.

## Prison Chaplaincy

I had taken up a part-time position as a Chaplain at Her Majesty's Prison Shotts in 1987. I had not approached this task with enthusiasm and found my first visit utterly depressing. Prison is punishment enough. The atmosphere enervates. No matter how comfortable this new prison extension was, the impression created was that life as a prisoner is not pleasant. You are, for a time, sometimes for a long time, a non-person deprived of the basic rights of free choice, free association and free movement which everyone takes for granted until they are obliged to live without them. There is a kind of decay in the air - a sort of collective depression produced and execrated by men whose personalities are reduced and whose minds and spirits are enclosed just as their bodies are enclosed. There is a sense of explosive tension kept in check and of a culture of duplicity and deceitfulness in which men survive by their wits making the best of their enclosure and indulging in the ancient male archetypal practice of mental constructs, often relating little to reality, occasionally finding expression in rebellion. And in prisons there are market places, shop keepers, agents and suppliers creating their own alternative to the consumer society. You can get nearly anything you may want in a prison - but there is a price to pay.

One afternoon I interviewed six men. Each one was adamant that he had not committed the crime for which he had been imprisoned. Perhaps chaplains and mothers are the only people left to fool! Three of them did agree that they had been indulging in criminal activity but stated that they had been framed by police who, frustrated at not being able to catch them for crimes they felt certain had been committed, made sure that they did not remain free to continue their anti-social behaviour.

One of the men I listened to was twenty-two years of age. He told me that his father had spent his life in and out of jail and that his grandfather had also been imprisoned on several occasions. He was a third generation prisoner. I felt sorry for him. He seemed not to have known any other lifestyle than violence, infidelity, robbery and their attendant vices.

It occurred to me that the only way to make an impression on people brought up in such a culture was to set up Christian Schools in Scotland. I thought that such schools might offer a muscular Christianity and perhaps instil into young minds the possibility of another way of life than that into which they had been born. I did not regard this idealistically or paternalistically, but practically and caringly. I placed a motion before the General Assembly of the Church of Scotland in 1988 asking for a feasibility study into the formation of State Christian schools with the same status and privileges of Roman Catholic schools. The motion was overwhelmingly defeated. I also wrote an article on the subject in The Church of Scotland magazine, 'Life and Work' which was published in April 1989 and reported in national newspapers. I believe the Editor, Bob Kernohan, received some adverse comments from the Department of Education of the Church of Scotland for having published my article. It was 'against the party line.' I always thought that 'Life and Work' did not reflect the broad sweep of opinion in the Church, governed as it was by an overseeing committee and this reaction seemed to add weight to my suspicions. So much for freedom of speech! As the end of the millennium approaches, the idea of Christian schools in Scotland does not seem so outrageous. Holland has them as does England. Surely parents might have the choice between a Protestant secular school or a Protestant Christian school for their children. I was sure that if such Christian schools were operated within the state education system, they would be oversubscribed.

Although I accept that it is very difficult to have a motion of substance passed in the General Assembly without having gone through the committee structure of the Church, it seemed pathetic to me that those who had presided over the disappearance of Christianity from schools in Scotland should have taken such a negative attitude to what remains, in my view, an imaginative and altruistic vision of sharing the love of God with those whose family life and background precludes such a dimension. This was not utilitarianism, but rather a principle and a means of admitting God in Christ to the early lives of many who would otherwise learn of God at the occasional funeral, or indeed, at a service of worship in a prison. To be sure, I enjoyed baiting my Roman Catholic colleague in Shotts Prison about the large number of Roman Catholics who were prisoners. How, I asked, did this square with the thesis of the perfect church? I thought that strong evangelical Christianity would have an effect and though I did not expect every child taught in a Christian school to become a model Christian, I did think that at the very least they would know of the possibility of ceasing the cycle of crime and punishment into which they had been born and raised.

The Department of Education of the Church of Scotland was weighted heavily in favour of people whose profession was education. Education in Scotland has been a tool of vested political interests for most of the twentieth century. The agenda of the various teaching and academic unions was often the agenda of the Department and its conclusions were uncommonly like those of the various organs of the teaching establishment. Therefore a spiritual suggestion was interpreted politically and responded to as such. The teaching of Christ in state schools in Scotland has shrunk to peripheral status. The liberal agenda has failed but no vision of something better is tolerated. The blind lead the blind.

Some of the prisoners were larger than life characters. I remember conducting a discussion group one evening with about twelve prisoners. The subject was 'happiness.' (Such incongruity and naiveté!) I was interrupted in the midst of my explanation of The Beatitudes by one middle-aged, balding man with a deep voice who interjected, "Ah'll tell you what happiness is. Happiness is sitting on top of the Cuillins with £25,000 and a bottle of whisky." Another prisoner from Glasgow had his wife keep him supplied with life's little luxuries. She brought in what were ostensibly bottles of lemonade but in fact the lemonade was not laced, but positively embroidered with vodka. I sometimes took along people from the church and they brought cakes for tea. The prisoners responded well to these visits. The company of women was especially welcome as can be imagined. Normal life was available for a couple of hours. Those who visited the prison tended to gain much from doing so too.

It was with some fear that I paid my first visit to a man in solitary confinement. This was because such particular treatment often resulted from having committed an offence of a sexual nature, usually against a child. It was for their own protection that such men were kept alone, guarded twenty-four hours a day against the physical abuse that would be meted out to them by their fellow prisoners. There is a hierarchy of crime! Some are regarded as noble, others are not. Tabloid headlines influence us whether we know it or not. They create in our minds ideas of 'beasts' and 'monsters' - wild and uncontrollable men of violence and perversion. I found the opposite to be the case on my first such visit. The man was gentle and weak and thoughtful and concerned. What he had done was wrong, of course, and he was paying society's price. Dangerous to children are indeed the gentle ones with the quiet voices. Children cannot recognise the hidden agenda. But pathetic are these men who have given way to a peculiar instinct. The damage they have done is mostly irreparable. The sexual corruption of children must be about the most serious offence a human being can commit other than the taking of life. But on this first visit I found a human being not a monster and someone glad to be under protection, knowing all too well the consequences of any lapse in professional care. These did happen from time to time. One such prisoner was attacked while having a shower. All that was needed was a split second to kick his feet away causing him to fall, breaking his thigh bone on the edge of the shower base. Multiple fractures resulted and it was years before he could walk properly again.

Pastoral issues predominate and they vary in intensity. It is helpful to be able to liaise between prisoners and their families. Distance and time produce misunderstandings and suspicions and these grow their own imaginative offspring. Some prisoners become suicidal and it was not unusual to be involved in some serious prevention work along with others including outside medical staff. Desperation can set in and paranoia accompanies confinement. The rhythms are uneven and the highs and lows are many. Often it took me a day to recover my own equilibrium after just a few hours within the prison. On one occasion I journeyed to Edinburgh carrying a collection of £143 23p from the inmates to the family of a Roman Catholic man who had committed suicide. He had been imprisoned for life for murdering his own brother. Another brother of the same family was also serving a long sentence in another prison. I handed the gift over to the deceased man's sister and she told me that their father had been dead for many years and that her mother had died comparatively recently. She went on to tell me that her own son of thirteen years had been killed by a drunk driver. The woman behaved with impressive dignity in her trials and expressed gratitude for the kindnesses shown. I was deeply humbled by the catalogue of tragedy which had befallen this particular family.

In September 1988 tensions within the Prison rose sharply. Summer months confined and the influence of strong personalities engendered frustration which led to planning and action. I conducted Sunday Services. Usually there were about fifteen people attending. I brought my guitar and did what I could to make the service relevant. I always preached a strong message. One Sunday there were over forty men at church. I did not think that my preaching had been so wonderful the previous week as to increase the attendance three-fold. It was an uneasy experience. The following Tuesday, many prisoners rioted and caused extensive damage to cells and work areas. I learned that the original plan had been to take me hostage at the Sunday Service. So that accounted for the sudden large attendance. No-one explained why the original plan had not been followed through.

Being a prison chaplain changed my life. It opened my eyes to the enormous task that faces us if we are to redeem the world in Christ's name. It showed me how decent church folk are and how separated from this other world. I never despise those who live a quiet life. Our world needs the quiet of the land more and more. It is a great vocation to be a good and peaceful citizen. But the divide is enormous and those who are caught up in the culture of crime suffer much. I believe that divine power can change human lives from extreme bad to good. In prison, men think about God a lot. Their spiritual sensitivities are activated. Conversions take place. Some even remain Christian within themselves when they leave prison. Many unfortunately resort to their previous ways and values. Some prisoners regard chaplains as irrelevancies. We tried to offer a caring and a friendly face. Not associated with the prison management, chaplains can be helpful in many ways. I found that my representations on behalf of prisoners were taken seriously and I saw myself as a mouthpiece and advocate where possible. There were some successful outcomes to difficult problems. The issues were real and sometimes the pettiness of congregational life contrasted with the seriousness of the pastoral realities of prison life.

## Community

It is one of the greatest privileges that a Church of Scotland Minister is a Parish Minister and serves not only the congregation but the community as a whole. Although fewer and fewer people are attending churches, the spiritual needs of communities do not diminish. There remains a public attachment to Christianity and very many people still want to be a Christian when they die, even if they have not lived as such. What sense of community remains has Christian rites of passage at its centre. Offering divine and spiritual meaning and significance to human events is part of Christianity and always should be. Sometimes purely secular happenings require spiritual initiative and on the other hand perhaps nothing is necessarily completely outside the concern of a good Creator.

Mining villages have a tradition of Gala Days. I learned that the Overtown Gala had been discontinued many years before. I wondered if it could be revived. With the invaluable and indispensable help of Tom Sleith, owner of the local garage, and with the support of a small group of residents, we were able to plan to hold a Gala Day in Overtown on 28th May 1988. It was not easy holding the various 'political' strands together and there were some tensions on the way. The choosing of the Gala Queen raised perceived divisions in the community but this was happily resolved by the drawing of lots. The little girl who was chosen was excellent. People responded to the future event and floats were designed and produced on the day.

My especial department was in ensuring that the weather was good! I did not seek this meteorological role but I was clearly warned by various individuals in the weeks before the Gala Day that it had better be a sunny day! That - you see - would be a sign of God's blessing on everything. I was God's man. Therefore, if there was no sunny day, it meant God was not with me. My extravagant claims about God's love in Jesus Christ in weekly worship would be gainsaid. I did not conclude this - it was stated to me in terms that those belonging to a mining village in North Lanarkshire state their case. Bluntly. I certainly provoked me to serious prayer. Apart from my own position, the whole day would be spoilt if the weather was not good.

I rose early that Saturday morning. The air was still and breathless. The cloudless sky was blue. The sun shone everywhere. I exulted. The floats were beautiful and the Playgroup's Care Bears theme won everyone's admiration. A great deal of work had been put into making the spectacle worthwhile. When I saw the parade coming down the small hill from the school and through the heart of the village I was greatly touched. People lined the streets. The races and tug-o-war and five-a-side football provided  competition and entertainment. No-one plays friendly football! Children's races provided much laughter. It was all over by about 5 00pm. At 6 45pm a shower of rain arrived. The evening's dull weather exaggerated the beauty of the earlier day. My sense of God's providence was complete. I could remain as a credible witness to God in Overtown.

In September 1988, again with the help of a committed group, it was possible to present an exhibition called "The History Of The People." I asked everyone to look out old photographs and artefacts for inclusion. I hoped that the exhibition would offer a longer term perspective to God's providence in our lives. This was organised to coincide with Harvest Thanksgiving. We get all too caught up on our present problems and they seem overwhelming. Yet in retrospect, they are never as bad as they seem at the time and this is true historically as well as individually. The church itself provided the location for the exhibition and was open to the public throughout the week. Over one thousand people visited and everyone found it all fascinating. I did too. One hundred and fifty years of local history were on display with valuable symbols of farming and mining industries alongside fashions, home decorations and photographs which told their own wonderful stories. For me, it was the divine dimension that mattered as well as the human. Each life is a treasure, known to God. Fame and wealth do not of themselves bring such meaning to life. Richness of character and colourfulness of personality may be greater blessings and "The

History Of The People" certainly witnessed to that value judgement.

## Travail Of The Soul

I carried the inner burden of having been blessed by God in an especial way in my life. My personal spiritual history sometimes weighed heavily on me. I expected much of myself. I expected much of God. Every day and every incident had this hidden dimension. No-one knew. Assurance, confidence and articulation are not always forthcoming in Christian pulpits. They can be disconcerting to some. Neither was there any significant outpouring of the Spirit of Pentecost. I did not preach to a deeply prayerful people. The spiritual temper was not high. The Christianity was social rather than eschatological.

There were pockets of opposition to my ministry in Overtown. Not every member of the Kirk Session supported me. A difficult meeting in May 1987 caused me to consider my ministry. I even began to think of leaving. Elders sympathetic to me urged me to stay and said, "It is your cross." Every parish minister and priest of sensitivity knows what that means. You cannot transfer spiritual burdens. If you share them too often, your role is compromised. The unavoidable consequence of spiritual calling in a context in which you are inevitably separated from everyone else is a disproportionate weight upon the soul. I sometimes felt that I was slowly dying. Outwardly I maintained the expectations associated with my role. I enjoyed doing so and much was being accomplished. Perhaps it is the stress of being too many things to too many people that costs much. Perhaps it is because you are involved in so many joys and sorrows that you are constantly pulled one way or the other. Perhaps it is because your life is in some measure an outpouring of good will, spiritual energy and personal strength that you are yourself inwardly traumatised so often of the time. And there may be no respite. Every move is watched, every single thing you say is analysed. You can't have a day off but someone notices you have been missing. You have a public role and you are a target.

"We wrestle not against flesh and blood," said St Paul. That is still true but there is not a sufficient stewardship of spiritual resources, a great enough waiting upon and calling upon the power of the Holy Spirit by congregations in their entirety. Vicarious Christianity in which the minister is paid to be the Christian is ultimately blasphemous and a dereliction of proper calling. It is extremely difficult to effect a complete change of mentality and understanding in a parish. This may be done on occasions in special circumstances. Or it may happen over succeeding generations. In cities it is more possible where people may come and go. In a small community it is almost impossible. To want to change things is considered threatening. There are limits placed on God's intervention.

I have always retained an inner desire to live in peace. That has never materialised. Some would think the opposite of me. There is no peace, of course, in a world like this one. You pay a price for a special calling. You are marked out. Your paths are charted. They lead through difficult and sometimes dangerous areas. You are always exposed and always at risk. And you cannot make any claims for no-one will understand them. Your adversary incarnated in some local life, waits for you.  It is by the fruits of your life that you will be recognised, for good and ill. Yes - in eternity you may find peace and joy and friendship and recognition, but you will not find these on earth. Christianity is a future hope rather than a present reality. This fact is an offence to late twentieth century western society. True discipleship may even necessitate one thing or the other, the 'either-or' of Kierkegaard.

In August 1987 I visited Iona *incognito*. Seventy of us attended a nine o'clock evening service after which we traipsed around a quadrangle with candles. The spiritual significance of this escaped me and I concluded that performance and effect do not take place of personal relationship to Jesus Christ. Next day I saw one of the Community leaders sitting on the wall smoking a cigarette and that exemplified the lack of seriousness which I associate with the Iona Community. Elements of 'New Age' and feminism are influential in the nineties. Iona has fallen a long way from its original spiritual greatness and even many of George MacLeod's hopes have been blown away.

In October 1987 I arrived in mind at one single clear principle which I understood to be for me the purpose and goal of life, the highest meaning and status, the fulfilment and satisfaction of earthly human existence (the *summum bonum* of moral philosophers)... "to have one's prayers answered in personal relationship with God through Jesus Christ." Everything else seemed to me to be secondary. I have prayed a great deal in my life and for many things. The proportion of positive answers has in my view been small. Yet great industries turn over huge sums of money for a fraction in profits. So it must be with prayer. If at the end of the day there are spiritual profits from prayer and these can be seen and witnessed to, then that is a cause for rejoicing. I do not equate this with Calvinistic 'evidences.' Many decent souls have not seen their prayers answered in this life. Christianity is about eternal existence. How many look forward to some explanation and a time when answers will be available? But just the same, Christianity is about God's active love for us all and we need to see that manifested in our actual lives and not just cling to the Life of Jesus as our only indication of such a possibility.

Olympic athletes are few and their gifts and discipline bring them success. Great thinkers, writers, poets and musicians have often lived tortured lives, even if they have left the world the most exquisite forms of culture. Many inventors gained nothing from their ideas. Others reaped harvests. Missionaries blazed trails without seeing the future hope fulfilled. Jesus left this life alone and uncomforted. It is just the case that a price is paid for Christianity in the world. The higher the stakes, the greater the price. Those who are at ease in Zion have their reward. The Lord Himself was not an one.

I continued my personal struggle with God. There were moments of great joy amidst the routine and the inescapable sorrows of parish life. I did not feel complete in my life and probably would have admitted that I needed a wife. On Easter Sunday 1988 I awoke at 7 04am and took myself to the top of the hill overlooking the Clyde Valley, only a few hundred yards from the manse. I entered a field beneath which lay one of the mines of former years. The rising sun met me face to face. Mist followed the River Clyde through its valley home but evaporated just low enough to allow the dark trees to protrude on the east and to the south. The towns of Larkhall, Hamilton, Motherwell and Wishaw could be seen sleeping on the low hills in the distance. The blue-white sky encompassed us all.

I thought of how unhappy the women must have been who went to tend to Jesus' body. Their sorrow turned to great joy. I hoped that my sense of failure might yet turn to such joy. I felt that my ambition outstripped the gifts given to me. I felt sinful and ill at ease. I thought that I too often decided my own agenda and asked God to endorse it. I needed to abandon my striving and allow myself to be led by the Spirit. I felt touched that my early waking thoughts had been about The Lord's resurrection and my relationship to Him and service in His Kingdom. A busy day followed. A service at Shotts Prison was followed by worship at Overtown. Then a lovely drive to Dundonald and a birthday tea with my mother, sister Shona, her husband Ian and three children Kenneth, Ruth and Natalie. It was a special time and a great contrast to the loneliness of my own existence.

## The Weir Trust

It had been a shock to learn that Jackie Weir had left his estate for the purposes of educating children in developing countries. Not many people would think of such a possibility when making their wills. In death one has many sudden friends and relatives. Those who have not themselves lived and worked in places like Africa or India cannot know at first hand the value of such a bequest. Jackie Weir invested his estate in my judgement. There are many hard hearted people who look without compassion on the poverty of others. Television pictures of famine and of refugee camps do not move them. "It is their own fault," is an idea often repeated as a psychological means of deflection and of self-deception. Others wring their hands and do nothing. A very few take the issue of the poor to heart. Some spend their lives in the service of such. Some offer something from their income, month by month to alleviate individual suffering and promote personal development. The Weir Trust made it possible to contemplate significant help to individuals and to projects which might not succeed without the injection of financial donations which in themselves would be beyond the capacity of local groups to raise.

Over succeeding years, the Weir Trust invested many thousands of pounds in three particular areas. The first was in the payment of school fees for children who would otherwise be deprived of an education. The second was in funding an educational programme for orphaned children in Madras, India. This came about when I met an Indian clergyman called Jayasingh. He was very persistent and determined but I thought that he was a person of integrity who could be trusted. He was returning to India to set up what he called 'Life in Christ Ministries.' He needed substantial initial funding to do this. The goal of this Christian enterprise was to rescue young children without means of support, without family security and sometimes without normal functioning of a healthy physical body. 'Life in Christ Ministries' is a registered public religious trust in India under the jurisdiction of the church of which Jayasingh is a minister. Hundreds of children have since been offered a better life through this excellent Christ-like work.

It is clear from the New Testament that Jesus invited those who would follow Him to care for others, especially for those less fortunate and very especially for those who could not help themselves. Not every society has such a code of ethics. Not every religion has had such compassion at its centre. Even so, in the comfortable churches of the West the responsibility to help others is often ignored or diminished. Certain awkward texts are seldom used in preaching. For example:

**"Come you blessed of my Father inherit the Kingdom prepared for you from the foundation of the world. For I was hungry and you gave me food; I was thirsty and you gave me drink; I was a stranger and you took me in; I was naked and you clothed me; I was sick and you visited me; I was in prison and you came to me."**
**Then the righteous will answer him, saying "Lord, when did we see you hungry and feed you, or thirsty and give you drink? When did we see you a stranger and take you in, or naked and clothe you?**
**Or when did we see you sick, or in prison and come to you?"**
**And the King will answer and say to them, "Assuredly, I say to you, inasmuch as you did it to one of the least of these my brethren, you did it to me."** (Matthew 26: 34-40)

Many people are in a position to help others, to make a difference to their lives, to redeem them from poverty, futility and life long waste. No-one can earn a place in heaven. We are saved by Grace. But it must surely be the will of God for those who are comfortable and no longer in need themselves to organise their resources to help the least fortunate of the world.

For example, years later in January 1996 I was praying about how Weir Trust funds for 1996 might be allocated. I was given the clearest guidance in the form of an implanted idea that I should write to Bernard Muindi, Moderator of the Presbyterian Church of East Africa. I had not been in touch with the P.C.E.A. since my departure in 1986 but I remembered Bernard Muindi as being a totally different man from his predecessor John Gatu. I told Bernard about the Weir Trust and asked if he would be willing to recommend a suitable educational project or projects for funding. I also asked him whether or not there would be political objections to receiving funding from Scotland within or without the church.

Bernard wrote back positively expressing astonishment that my letter should arrive coincidentally with his beginning to organise a fund-raising day for a girls boarding school called Ngaita Girls Secondary School which was situated in a very rural area. The 'harambee' was being planned for July. He described the primitive state of school facilities such as unfinished classrooms and lack of sufficient dormitory accommodation and toilets.

Bernard wrote movingly of how he and his wife had been touched by the poverty of the people and had become involved in trying to help. The Weir Trust money, he said, would come like manna from heaven.

It was possible to send a substantial donation to Ngaita Girls Secondary School in time for presentation at the fund-raising event. In October, I received photographs of the school and of the fund-raising event. It was clear just how needy the school was. Girls had to wash their clothes in basins outside in a field. External walls of classrooms had been built but thereafter lay unfinished. The kitchen was a broken-down mud hut. There was no electricity in the dormitories which had no windows. There was no science block, very little educational equipment and no focal point for meetings other than under the African sky.

Thus the Weir Trust was able to offer significant help to a legitimate and deserving project which would benefit many young people in years to come. Jackie Weir's altruistic ordering of his financial affairs has brought delight to individuals and to communities. It is so difficult for rural people to raise the disproportionately large sums of money needed to make development possible. In supporting and adding to locally raised funds British pounds can accomplish much more in Africa than they can here. The gratitude is overwhelming.

## Interlude In France

I spent July 1988 in France. Through friends I had rented a bed-sit flat in Le Pradet on the south coast near Toulon. I knew no-one and was completely alone. I felt liberated. No burdens, no loneliness, no demons, no struggles, no doubts, no self-criticism, no cross - for a month! It took me fully two weeks to unwind and to de-stress and a further two weeks to recharge my personal batteries. The village was unspoilt and two bakeries contrasted with our supermarket provision at home. Nearby towns like Hyeres seemed beautifully clean in comparison with towns in North Lanarkshire. The bright sunshine contrasted with the reluctant grey-blue Scottish summer sky. The beach at L'Almanarre was perfect for swimming and sunbathing. Monaco is a ridiculous place, infested with false vanities of created pseudo-royalties as a means of tourist exploitation. Nice was wonderful.

I lived on a simple diet and eschewed the bread and potatoes, cakes and sweets which cluttered my system year in year out. Much exercise made me strong and fit again. I read. I rested. Anonymity healed. Some days were spent in prayer. The parish was killing me, I knew. I had lost my way. I had not maintained my relationship with God sufficiently. Whatever human imperfections were present in me seemed to be exaggerated in the exposed condition of parish ministry. I had not seen sufficient response to encourage me. The politics of congregational life bored me. I was unable to relate my own spiritual journey to those who listened to me week by week. Although there were great joys and great rewards in parish life, I was unsatisfied and unfulfilled. Yet I returned to Overtown with my spiritual and physical health and energy restored. I was buoyant and enthusiastic about the future. After a few days I was thinking, "I sleep behind the lines, in enemy territory."

## Power Struggle

I was preaching on Sunday August 14th 1988 and as I concluded my sermon I had the strongest feeling that I would, of necessity, leave Overtown Parish. I was saying things about hope, revival, renewal, calling and commitment, but inwardly I was sensing something else. Sometimes I wept of an evening, prostrate on the floor of my study. By mid-September blood-letting was occurring with one or two influential people rebelling against me. I did not return the hostilities and strangely enough did not feel threatened by them. There was plenty to do. European Economic Community supplies of butter and mince had to be distributed (with the help of John and Helen Jackson) from the church hall to needy citizenry with impartiality. Tom Russell's twenty-five years as organist was recognised - the more because he did not take a salary. Autumn brought to life all the organisations, including a Men's Club which with some excellent help had been resuscitated after many years extinct and a 'Monday At Eight' Bible Study meeting. Weddings and funerals and pastoral issues, administration and all the duties of ministry took up my time. But I felt that there was opposition and dissatisfaction with me and with my ministry from one or two people whose influence was greater than the Christian grace given to them.

In October the congregational fund-raising group sent a letter to me intimating their collective resignation. This was a serious issue. Sunday collections were not enough to meet all financial obligations. This group had been instrumental in topping up normal givings. Unfortunately, some seemed to think that this gave them a pre-eminence in the congregation. Their methods were not always wholly in line with the Church of Scotland's rules on congregational fund-raising. The timing of this protest was important. The Autumn Fayre was due in a month's time. This event raised a substantial amount of money without which the books would not balance at the end of the year. In effect, my ministry was being sabotaged by the withdrawal of fund-raising support by a few people, acting unilaterally. Money matters! I met my accusers and defended my principles and conduct. Some accepted my response, others did not. I was given the grace of calmness.

In the midst of these traumas, the October Holy Communion Service was especially blessed. I was almost bursting with joy in singing the hymns and the Eucharistic Presence of the Lord was so very real. A very high proportion of the congregation attended Holy Communion in 1988 (eighty-three per cent.) These were wonderful occasions on which to preach the unconditional love of God in Jesus Christ. I took my guitar and we sang 'Amazing Grace.' I felt that we should have Holy Communion every week and thought that if that were the case, I'd be a better man and a better minister.

The Autumn Fayre was organised and run by other members of the congregation some of whom had felt excluded from the group which had done so before. The money raised amounted to £2,400, some £700 more than in the previous year. I felt that my stand on principles had been vindicated and I felt that the group which had withdrawn their support had been taught a lesson and put in their place. I was very grateful to everyone who supported the event and its success proved that the congregation as a whole did not need to rely on and was larger than any small self-appointed group.

At that point in time, I was ruminating over an advertisement for the post of Chaplain To

The University Of Edinburgh. I had discounted it as a possibility at first sight believing that there was still work for me to do in Overtown. My longtime friends John and Ross advised me to apply. At the very last moment I did so. I was actually relaxed and laid back about the application. I considered it most unlikely that I would be given the job. However, I was concerned about the congregational events that had taken place. It occurred to me that if I stayed in Overtown, the same troublemakers might conceivably attempt another heist. There had been threats by the same people to take real or imagined grievances to the Presbytery and I knew that that would damage me considerably. I also had little confidence in the Presbytery of Hamilton to decide any case impartially and not on theological party grounds. I thought that if I stayed I'd need to stay for many years to establish the congregation and my own ministry. Finally, I foresaw the possibility of contrived and created complaints without actual substance but with dangerous intention being taken outside the congregation. It was for that reason that I opened up the possibility of leaving Overtown.

## Making Way

A wonderful day trip on December 8th kept my spirits up. I bought a huge loaf of bread to feed the ducks at Callander in the Trossachs, marvelling at the pecking order and the intense rivalries with cruelty which the ducks manifested. We humans are the same, I thought. In fact we are much worse. I walked along Loch Katrine. In mid-winter it seemed like a forgotten, newly-rediscovered magic kingdom. Surrounded by snow-covered bens, sheltered and quiet, the still water like glass and the white of your frozen breathe in the air before your face. Winter-grey trees stood out against the evergreens and distant waters lay still as if in hibernation. Scotland - how you minister to my soul!

The enemy within the congregation had been defeated. Much had been accomplished in the two years. Fifty people had joined the congregation in that time. Services were well attended. The new hall had been erected with Robin Russell's invaluable oversight. Chaplaincies to both primary and secondary schools and to Shotts Prison had broadened the work. Yet I had not ordained new elders and the congregation had a long way to go towards spiritual maturity. There was much to be done.

The pre-Christmas spell is as busy as the parish may ever be. Little time is left for introversion. At a meeting of the Kirk Session, one of my adversaries rose and said "I accuse you of being a dictator." No discussion followed and he was left feeling embarrassed. However, he represented the undercurrent that I had recognised for some months. I buried an elderly lady whose wealthy son said to me, "How much do I owe you for your services?" "Nothing," I replied, offended, "She was my parishioner." "I'll give a donation to the church then," he offered in return. Humble folks behave with greater dignity I thought as I returned home.

A laugh-a-minute session with the primary school children always brightened the week. I asked them what the name of Santa Claus's wife was and when they did not answer, I suggested that it was 'Aggie.' Then there was Henry Claus, Santa's brother, who looked after the reindeer and Santa and Mrs Claus had three children who were called the subordinate Clauses. But when I went home in the evenings, I was terribly lonely. I did not put up my Christmas cards that year and it was long after Christmas day before I opened such presents as I had received. I felt that the undercurrents were significant and they weighed heavily on my spirit. I began to contemplate failure as a parish minister. I thought that the real signs of the Kingdom being near were unrecognised and unappreciated. What could I do? I was approaching exhaustion. A two day stay at Dundonald helped.

I have never liked New Year. I remember 'first foots' coming to my parents' house when I was a child and the thrill of being allowed to stay up so late on that occasion. Christmas has always been truly beautiful for me. I am always touched by the fact of the Incarnation. Christmas Carols move me deeply and the relationship of their words to the music inspires me every year we sing them. New Year is nothing at all. It has no spiritual significance for me. I cannot take ideas of artificial new beginnings seriously. I feel no different on the first of January each new year. I loathe the contrived hype which appears on television and find neither meaning or comfort in the false greetings and celebrations.

I drew strength from prayer. I was conscious that I loved God and could say so to myself. I felt that I had flitted hither and thither, never staying long enough to achieve anything significant. Grace held me together as a personality, as a person and as a human being. At 'The Bells' of 1989 and quite alone, I raised a glass of apple juice and toasted "The Father, the Son and the Holy Spirit."

I thought that I would never be an influence in my Church. It seemed to me that the most valuable thing that I might offer would be to try to write a book of spiritual devotion and I longed for the opportunity and the peace, the place and the space to do just that. The cross of individuality is heavy. I wished to immerse myself in anonymity but I felt too that the uniqueness of my spiritual life and experience was in itself a gift and required to be set on a hill and not to be buried. This was a burden however and not a justification for egotism. I felt that I had to be myself and that in being myself I gave the best that I could. However, when I was hurt, it was deeply, and when I was rejected, it was a complete rejection. There was nowhere to hide. And I suffered too, from wondering about the conditions of the souls of those who did not understand.

I had friendships in Overtown and some have lasted ever since. Bill Moffat was my Session Clerk and a strong reliable and good man is he. I could go round for a coffee and a chat when I wanted to and I always found warmth and encouragement from him and Margo and their son Lee. Many a joke we shared too about the absurdities of life. The Browns, the Hornals, the Weirs and the Sinnetts offered generous hospitality and continuing friendship which touched me greatly and was more helpful than they might have ever realised. Isobel Girdwood is a woman of spiritual dignity. Matt Scott, our lively octogenarian challenged me to concentrate on what he was saying while he was saying it! It would be churlish in the extreme to suggest that Overtown was not also a marvellous place to be at times. The problem was myself and my intensities which found little relevance there. Had there not been a small minority against me, I would have persevered. I did not want to cause a split in the congregation. I think I saw trouble coming and was glad to realise that quite unexpectedly, I might be given the opportunity to leave.

I visited Edinburgh on November 21st 1988 and looked in on the University Chaplaincy Centre. I did not find the experience encouraging or uplifting. Ruminating on the issue the next day I thought that five years there would be frustrating given the rationalist secular ethos of the University. I received the information about the position of Chaplain two days later. I was sure that I did not have the remotest chance of getting the job but I also acknowledged that God could give me the job if God decided to. I completed the application forms with feelings of guilt about leaving Overtown and thoughts of future possibilities intermingled. To my great surprise on December 3rd I received my invitation to be interviewed on 5th January 1989. I prayed God's providence. I never prayed to become Chaplain of Edinburgh University, neither did I pray to remain in Overtown. December passed slowly with inner feelings of disloyalty conflicting with public ministry. I genuinely did not think I would be appointed and that brought peace to the ongoing stresses of the situation. I carried on as if I expected to remain for at least another few years. I remembered 'mean-spirited Edinburgh' from my days as an assistant minister. I thought of the stimulus and challenge of ministering in an academic environment. In deep mid-winter I was warmed by the amazing possibility that under God's providence I might be allowed to leave and take up a post which would use all of the gifts and skills that God had invested in me. I continued to work conscientiously and prayerfully.

I noted on 17th December that the riches and rewards of being a parish minister are unlike any other vocation but it was the desperate loneliness that made it so difficult to continue. I thought some of my parishioners recognised this in me. But as every minister knows, people see you and relate to you in your public and 'professional' mode and not to you as an individual person in your own right. People do not want to think or to know that you may have the same emotional framework as they have. You are not paid to share your private thoughts on life. You are expected to mediate a higher form of understanding based on the Christian Gospel and you must put yourself behind that at all times so that God and His Son and His Kingdom may be communicated and realised. The Roman Catholic Church has an entire system of support for its celibate priests. The Church of Scotland offers little for its unmarried clergy.

I drew a long breathe on the evening of the 21st of December 1988. Lockerbie was not far away and Overtown was not much off the pace of the flight path to America of many of the civil aircraft which overflew Scotland en route across the Atlantic. It could as easily have been our village which suffered.

Like many a minister at Christmastime, I was exhausted. Feelings of not giving of my best and not having done enough prevailed. I wanted peace, sleep, oblivion, anything. It was the spiritual warfare which drained me of my strength and buoyancy. I longed for solitude, time to write books, poetry - time to have thoughts. I was sure that life could be less stressful if one was not so much exposed. In trying to change the world, one is doomed to fail. To keep trying is to fulfil an impossible calling.

## Exit Stage Left

I was one of five candidates interviewed for the post of Chaplain to the University of Edinburgh. I knew two of the others. Nine people faced me across a large table in the Raeburn Room in Old College. I thoroughly enjoyed the occasion. Part of the reason was that it was nice to have someone to talk to! It is very flattering to be asked for your views on all sorts of important matters. I presented myself openly as an anti-establishment, non conformist minister without attachment to any theological school within the Church. Questions were asked about my ministry in Overtown and there was some amusement when I described my school chaplaincy course "How Christianity came to Overtown, beginning with Jesus and ending with me." - the course that is - ended with me! Professor Howie asked about performance indicators and misquoted me from a brief conversation over coffee before my interview. I corrected him and later, in introducing another question, he apologised for his mistake. I replied, "I thought you would apologise." I said to myself, "This man is a gentleman - eventually he will apologise." There was a farcical five minute video test. I made the best of it and said that distinction forms the basis of all life from geology, through plant forms, the animal kingdom, humanity and into the spiritual realms. I had asked my referees to say very clearly what kind of person I was and to advise the University people not to appoint me unless they really wanted my style of ministry. I duly departed, feeling much uplifted and walked all the way to Corstorphine, energised by the stimulating conversation I had just held with the nine people who interviewed me.

I returned home and went visiting in hospital of the afternoon. At 6 15pm the telephone rang and Professor John O'Neill offered me the position of Chaplain to the University of Edinburgh. I asked for a little time to think it over. I phoned my mother and the two friends who had encouraged me to apply. I also checked out my position with the Clerk of Hamilton Presbytery who was sympathetic and helpful. That encouraged me. I asked my Session Clerk, Bill Moffat to come round for a coffee. He later told me that he had a feeling that I was going to tell him I would be leaving. He was full of congratulations and happiness for me. That convinced me that I should go. I telephoned my acceptance the following morning at 9 30am and wrote my confirmation letter. I began to feel very happy.

It was coincidental that I had invited friends to come that evening to share my 'Silver Jubilee' as a parish minister - after all, I had been in Overtown for twenty-five months!! It was a happy evening at a certain level. However, when ministers gather there are often undercurrents of rivalry and jealousy even among friends. These were not absent.

The following days were filled with spiritual gratitude that my tears had been seen and my unspoken needs had been met. I had never asked of God to leave Overtown. I had not sought nor desired the Chaplaincy other than to apply to find Providence's direction. I felt it was a gift and a grace given to me. I was surprised and elated at God's knowledge of me and care for me. The Father of my soul answered my greater need.

Later in January I took a few days holiday in London, attending Question Time at Westminster on Thursday 12th January. The usual mixture of the puerile and the relevant was on display. People seemed to speak for effect and not with substance. Mrs Thatcher looked tired. Mr Kinnock was energetic but superficial. John Wykeham was answering questions on all sorts of things. What a silly process, I thought. Scots were disproportionately vocal. I was ever sure that this adversarial approach requires to be replaced by a conciliar form of discussion of such major issues of national concern. I went to see Derek Jacobi's Richard III and witnessed an astonishing performance which made the other actors look wooden. He played to and interacted with the audience at one point faking a Masonic signal. I also saw Stewart Parker's play 'Pentecost' set in Ireland in 1974. The message at the time seemed to be a typically artistically arrogant re-hash of Bonhoeffer's thought - that the Christ of the churches should be abolished and each one should discover the Christ within.

I have always liked wandering around the City of Westminster and on this occasion took a pleasure boat sight-seeing trip along the Thames. Anonymity is a great healer of the inner man. London is full of pseuds and poseurs, garish and cheap in quality if not in price. It is spiritually enervating for one used to breathing the cleaner air of Scotland. But as always when I visit, I understand again a little of this dis-united kingdom and the seemingly unavoidable problem of people divided by the differing accents of their own language.

I visited David Butler my former colleague in Kenya in Birmingham on the way back and enjoyed much hilarity with him and his family. I attended Evening Prayer at his son's Public School in Solihull. I mused that perhaps I was the only Oxford D. Phil to do so while wearing trainers. I returned to Overtown refreshed to continue parish duties.

On 31st January after morning service, an elder came to the vestry, shouted at me, threw his Communion cards down on the table, stomped out and slammed the door. Poor man! I felt sorry for him, knowing his personal background enough to forgive him. On February 14th, I noted that in 1988, 306 of the membership of 361 had taken Holy Communion and that of the £28,000 raised by the congregation, £21,000 was by direct giving. These were encouraging statistics reflecting the best of the life of the congregation as a whole.

Unknown to me a process was beginning in relation to the Chaplaincy at Edinburgh which caused me much anguish and had far reaching effects on my life at Edinburgh and thereafter. The University 'Student' newspaper telephoned to enquire about my views on AIDS. As early as January 19th the 'Student' newspaper had carried a front page article on this topic. It was tabloid gutter journalism! National newspapers followed the story up and this obliged me to write to my elders and inform them about my impending departure. I had been waiting to do so at the next scheduled meeting of the Kirk Session.

Nevertheless there was but a month and more before my departure. I felt that I had had a wonderful ministry in Overtown, knowing the heights and depths of my calling. I felt that the tendentious nature of the publicity being given to my appointment as Chaplain to the University of Edinburgh was unfair, ill reflecting my Christian life and commitment over the years. Some statements constituted both defamation of character and libel.

The last 'Monday At Eight' prayer meeting was especially blessed with Holy Communion and supper afterwards. I received a generous cheque and many lovely gifts from parishioners as I prepared to leave Overtown. Holy Week arrived and I felt the suffering of Christ and a new and deeper way. I thought that my ministry would be remembered. I had even pleased my enemies by leaving. I preached my last sermon on Resurrection Sunday, March 26th 1989.

The following day the 'Glasgow Herald' carried front page news about my article on 'Christian Schools' which appeared in the April edition of 'Life and Work.' 'The Scotsman' also carried a less prominent reference. I was glad to be known for something other than the issue tendentiously prosecuted by the 'Student' newspaper and bled dry by the Edinburgh 'Evening News.' I was surprised by the coincidence of these publicities.

I regretted leaving the picturesque view from the manse looking south west over the Clyde Valley. I had had many moments of spiritual peace in the privacy of that place and I knew I would miss the countryside and the fresh and bracing air. As I spent my last evening, I knew that it was right for me to go. I could never share the deeper spiritual things of my existence. Spiritual opposition exists everywhere. The Church of Scotland bases the conduct of its affairs on visible and rational phenomena. Fulfillment of the basic tasks of ministry does not guarantee anyone a sympathetic hearing on the issue of personal revelation. This is true of all Christian church institutions. Padre Pio was treated with suspicion by the Roman Catholic Church. You dare not make claims for yourself. Anyway, it is by the fruits of your life and ministry that you will be known, recognised and judged. You subsume your own identity to that of Jesus Christ. It does not matter that you may have a special calling, a living vision, a wonderful account to give of your Maker's active Grace in your life. You cannot earn a living for such. And if, in the unseen realm, your enemies though not knowing why still oppose you and the adversary is incarnated wherever you go, what else can you do but leave, not expecting peace nor remission, but a higher challenge and greater odds to overcome. But you must go.

Just before I left on the morning of Wednesday 29th March, the church treasurer Douglas McLellan arrived with papers for me to sign. I had always liked him and had got on well with him, sharing some daft humours from time to time. When seeking reimbursement of my travelling expenses, I once got down on my knees in his house and in mock supplication said "O great One - may I have my travelling expenses?" He had laughed uproariously. Now, as he shook me by the hand, firmly and warmly, some emotion was visible in his eyes. He gave me the ultimate accolade a minister could ever receive in North Lanarkshire, a testimony of respect and of acceptance at the end - "I wish you well, Sir, - you gave as good as you got."

# 6 : One Against A Thousand

## In The Eye Of The Storm

While still in Overtown I had learned about the campaign to prevent me taking up my appointment as Chaplain to the University of Edinburgh. As befits church history, the campaign began and was organised from within New College, the Faculty of Divinity, by ministers and trainee ministers of my own Church. These were people of liberal theological persuasion, some associated with the Iona Community, who objected to someone perceived to belong to the evangelical wing of the Church being appointed as Chaplain. What grotesque intolerance! The campaign, public in nature, reported by the Edinburgh 'Evening News' in particular, sought to mobilise liberal opinion in the University against me. Those who orchestrated the campaign had never met me and did not invite me to meet them and discuss perceived differences. Whereas one may doubt the future of a church whose trainee ministers act in such an unchristian manner, what can one say about divinity professors and lecturers who supported such a campaign against a fellow ordained minister of their own Church? Professor Duncan Forrester, Principal of New College at the time was prominent in the campaign. He had never met me and did not know me personally. On 25th February, I noted that I felt like a suffering servant, sensing the wounds of Christ on my spirit.

Some non-Christian academics supported the campaign and one telephoned me in Overtown on 10th March to tell me that he intended to have my appointment revoked because he did not want to return to the Stone Age in which, he said, I lived! John O'Neill later telephoned, ordering me to make no more public statements. These reactions of anger and panic dismayed me since they reflected ill on what I had assumed was a civilised and enlightened society. Interesting indeed it was to ask why such organised hatred had occurred. I took solace in a quotation from a prayer in Michel Quoist's 'Prayers of Life' in which the writer suggested that we who follow Christ should rejoice in opposition, petitions against us, pursuits and exclusions for the sake of Our Lord. But I was sustained by my personal spiritual history. I had not provoked any public issue at the time of my appointment. My adversaries and spiritual enemies (whom I myself did not know as persons) had done so. In acting unjustly, undemocratically and impersonally, they had strengthened my resolve to take up my position as Chaplain. In the Lenten days of March, I accepted the affair as a spiritual discipline to be repented of, fasted for, wept and prayed over. I felt alone in the world, amid the loveless Christianity of Scottish Presbyterianism. I considered the logic of Calvary and applied it to my own condition. I wondered what would happen to me in the cold and pretentious city of Edinburgh. My escape from North Lanarkshire was not to be into a haven of peace but a calling of a higher nature. On March 26th, Resurrection Day and my last Sunday in Overtown, I wrote, "Grace may go before me, Grace may guide me, Grace may gift me survival." Personal friends supported me. Professor Tom Torrance wrote a letter of encouragement to me. Since I regarded him as the greatest living Christian thinker in our country, this was most helpful. Letters of commendation arrived from different parts of Scotland. Devout members of churches prayed for me, including those in Holyrood Abbey Church, Edinburgh. I realised that if God gives you something, no-one on earth can take it away. But your enemies will make you suffer just the same.

## Arrival

I moved to Edinburgh on 31st March 1989. My appointment began on 1st April. My first working day would be Monday 3rd, my forty-second birthday. This was a pleasant coincidence. I attended worship in Greyfriars Church on Sunday April 2nd. It was as bad as I had expected. Pandering to agnostics and semi-believers, the sermon was short and of little substance. There was acceptance of doubt and no application to personal life. Self-congratulatory and self-indulgent indeed, it was unrelated to New Testament Christianity or to the deeper veins of Christian History, found in the better forms of Protestantism, Roman Catholicism and Orthodoxy. Edinburgh liberalism was as narcissistic as it had been in the mid-seventies, unchanging amidst unprecedented apostasy. I sat quietly. I had my thoughts. I kept them to myself.

I entered the University Chaplaincy as Chaplain with confidence on the 3rd of April. That day I was presented with a petition against my appointment which I did not look at but filed for possible future reference. It had failed to reach its target by a very long way. Nevertheless, the rudeness and unkindness of its import affected me, though disappointment was tinged with pity towards my adversaries and my aloneness was comforted by internal spiritual peace. My first week was as interesting as I had hoped it would be. The articulate student leader seemed relieved to meet me in person, perhaps realising that I was not the ayatollah figure that my enemies had suggested. A member of the University telephoned to say, "We have been needing someone of conviction in this University for some time." Colleagues rallied round and this was most encouraging. I was advised to keep quiet and not give the opposition the oxygen of publicity they sought. My article on 'Christian Schools' was featured in 'The Sunday Times' and quoted in the House of Commons. I began to respond most favourably to the stimulating environment of the University. I felt an affinity with the community.

There was no Chaplain's house as at the other ancient Scottish universities. Apparently there had been but it was now occupied by the University chauffeur. I had been offered a two-roomed flat somewhere and turned it down. I was then given temporary accommodation in Teviot Row for five months until a suitable flat in Buccleuch Place became available. In the early weeks of summer term I was making evening pastoral calls from the telephone booths outside the Royal Infirmary!

On the first Tuesday of the month I duly attended Edinburgh Presbytery and found it to be the most dismal experience. Someone was advocating the abandonment of some of the central doctrines of the Christian Creed in order to attract people to attend church! Ego trips, those who spoke in order to say something rather than because they had something to say, subtle theological political manoeuvring, obvious manipulations, false compliments and outright hypocrisy - the entire gamut of the faults of Presbyterianism were extant in this unvenerable gathering. However, in May I presented myself to the Presbytery for introduction. As I stood before the Moderator, a man of good humour, I felt blessed and anointed. He mentioned my embarking on a ministry 'to the educated masses' and rounded off with a reference to 'There is Hope,' punning the umbrella evangelical organisation of that name and title. I could only remain in Presbytery for an hour before the fibre of my being revolted against the contrived artificiality of the occasion. I believe in spiritual representative democracy. Edinburgh Presbytery did not seem to me to be a vehicle of such highly principled conduct.

## Without A Chapel

Edinburgh University has no Chapel. The University was originally a Christian foundation though not a Church foundation. Subscription to the Westminster Confession Of Faith was once essential for all professors but this custom later disappeared. There were many churches on the south side of Edinburgh in the early nineteenth century. When Old College was completed at that time, the University became a secularised institution. The Scottish Enlightenment was the adoptive parent of the modern Edinburgh University. Not having a chapel or worship at the heart of the University has meant that Edinburgh has evolved in a more secular way than the other ancient universities of Scotland. And although several church buildings have been gifted to the University, none has been retained as a place of worship.

After the Second World War a full-time Chaplain was appointed to care for men who had been in the armed forces between 1939 and 1945. What is now the Bedlam Theatre was apparently lively place in the nineteen-sixties, though doubts have always been expressed about the precise spiritual nature and Christian identity of Edinburgh University Chaplaincy.

In the seventies and eighties, chaplaincies in Scottish universities were the fiefdoms of the liberals in the churches. The Student Christian Movement (SCM) was ascendant and expected always to have its representatives in these positions. The SCM however became embroiled in secular politics following upheavals in European universities in the late sixties and seventies. Its spiritual strength waned as a consequence and it began to lose numbers and position. By the nineties, it was a shadow and a skeleton organisation. The Christian Union (CU), evangelical in character grew steadily throughout the seventies and eighties and became ascendant in the nineties.

In 1989 an evangelical was appointed to the Chaplaincy of a Scottish University, my own appointment to Edinburgh. This was greeted with anger and dismay by the liberals. Former SCM students were in positions of influence in churches and members of the liberal establishment of the Church of Scotland sympathised with their objections to my appointment. Liberals regarded university chaplaincies as their territory and preserve. Like the minority government whose tactics they excoriated, they sought to cling on to positions their numbers and opinions no longer justified. And they squealed with bitterness when they lost the most liberal, most secular of the university chaplaincies to an evangelical. No matter that an equivalent pattern of decline had been formed in the SCM and in the liberal run churches of this country, they refused to accept the logic of Christian history. Liberals have presided over three decades of decline in Britain's churches, always having the important jobs, always stacking the committees, always having their opinions read as those of the church as a whole, always being university chaplains. The form of protest against my own appointment was thoroughly unjust. People had failed to realise that times had changed. How reactionary and fearful and conservative are the 'lefties!' How superficial and immature is their radicalism! How hypocritical are their cries for justice! How intolerant is their demeanour!

## The AIDS Issue

I began to understand the dynamics of the previous six weeks. The student representative on my appointing committee, having agreed with all members of the appointing committee not to divulge the name of the new Chaplain until my appointment had been formally ratified by the Senate of the University, had broken that agreement. Someone had recalled my debate with Episcopal Bishop Richard Holloway in late 1986 and early 1987 on the subject of the moral and spiritual and theological and Biblical issues surrounding AIDS.

To me, Holloway's sociological description, accepting the phenomenon without further explanation seemed pastorally irresponsible and dangerous. It was for pastoral reasons that I myself became involved in the debate. I reasoned that there was a moral and spiritual solution to this problem which was available to everyone. I took the view that the problem was our problem and was a corporate infliction on our society and upon us as individuals. If God was to be brought into the equation, I argued that God could not be held to be morally and spiritually neutral. As to the origins of the disease, I understood it to be a manifestation of sexually transmitted disease, of a particularly virulent and fatal variety. As to the theological dimension, I never held that God designed the disease in response to human behaviour and targeted certain social groups, but rather that the disease was potentially present in the human condition and with certain types of behaviour became prevalent. I thought the connection between AIDS and particular practices indicated that the practices were intrinsically harmful and that the justification of these practices was morally and spiritually wrong. I knew that throughout human social history, homosexual practices and heterosexual abuses had often led to fatal consequences. The abuse of drugs of any kind has, likewise, always resulted in extreme damage to those unfortunate enough to be overtaken by the consumption of harmful chemical substances. It is the scientific categorisation, the world-wide scale of the problem in the late twentieth century and continuing media presentation which differentiate the AIDS problem.

Every theologian in every age has wrestled with the problem of evil and the prevalence of pain and suffering in the human condition. One question distils all the issues, "Why does God allow evil, suffering, pain and death to exist?" No one has ever produced a satisfactory answer to this question. God allows us the consequences of our actions. If and when we go against the highest and best advice mediated through revealed understanding, then we are exposed to the consequences of such conduct. God does not intervene normally to prevent the consequences of preferred human actions. God allows free-will at the expense of deterministic control. If free-will leads to self-destructive behaviour, God allows that process to follow to its logical conclusion. This is a self-conscious decision on God's part, a judgement as in a court of law with the evidence having been given on both sides. It is a discrimination between good and evil which God by God's own nature cannot but make.

In the New Testament, the Greek word for judgement means discernment and discrimination, clarification and distinction. This was what I understood I was trying to communicate in late 1986 and early 1987. It is however, very difficult to convey moral theology and spiritual doctrine, theological principles and Biblical exegesis in the public domain. I was one of the very few who tried to articulate this kind of thought at that time. The appropriate Church of Scotland people were silent and absconditi. The Roman Catholic Bishops in Scotland did not have the courage to enunciate their own highly principled teaching on the subject in question. Instead of being thankful for the positive introduction of divine revelation in human history by which we learn of the moral and spiritual nature of Our Maker, this crisis resulted in the justification of forms of living which resulted in death and the rejection of divine revelation as mediated in the Judaeo-Christian tradition. Christians were emotionally blackmailed into silence by the mental constructs of self-justification projected into theology. A society which calls good evil and calls evil good is surely heading for oblivion. My opinion and view was at least as equal as anyone else's and yet it was not tolerated. This negation of a better way can only lead to compounded misery and it continues to do so. How strange!

> **"However hard you listen,**
> **you will never understand.**
> **However hard you look,**
> **you will never perceive.**
> **This people's wits are dulled;**
> **they have stopped their ears**
> **and have shut their eyes,**
> **so that they may not see with their eyes,**
> **nor listen with their ears,**
> **nor understand with their wits,**
> **and then turn and be healed."**       *(Isaiah 6:8-10)*

There was someone else I had in mind when I took part in the public debate about AIDS. I had been a student of John McLeod Campbell and had completed my doctoral thesis on his life and thought. One of the ideas which Campbell had articulated in his book "The Nature Of The Atonement" was that the atonement was accomplished by Jesus Christ in part by his making a perfect confession of human sin to God (p.136.) I therefore intended to help people towards making such a confession of our sin in God's sight as a means and entry into the healing process

116

and eradication of the disease. My pastoral concern was that no-one should suffer and die in this way and I believed that an admission of the moral and spiritual dimension of the problem would be part of its solution.

Sociological descriptions seemed to me to be inherently dangerous because of their partial and limited perception of the problem. I regarded them as impotent to solve the basic problem of human self-destructive conduct. I genuinely believed that the disease could be eradicated through a moral and spiritual response. I still do. It has ever been a dangerous thing to think spiritually - and even more dangerous to do so in relation to churches which are led by politically minded and materially motivated people. It is possible for people to re-invent themselves. Part of such a process includes restating previously held opinions and views to fit changed climates of political correctness. I am not doing this here. There must be a video of a Scottish Television programme in which I participated at the time. It was recorded in St Andrew's and St George's Church, in George Street, Edinburgh. This can prove that I never meant to take a harsh and judgmental line from which I am now trying to disassociated myself. At the end of the programme a lawyer of some distinction was asked to sum up the various views which had been articulated. He attributed to me the severe 'Calvinistic' judgmental position on the topic in question. As I realised he had misunderstood me, I shook my head indicating dissent from his description. When the programme was broadcast, the camera had focused in on me as the lawyer's summary mentioned my name. I was therefore seen rejecting his interpretation of what I had said. As I left the building I felt troubled by such misrepresentation and thought that there was a gratuitous element to it.

A grievous distortion of my views and worse, a complete failure to learn, know and understand my motives for involving myself in the public debate in late 1986 and early 1987 was the basis of the campaign to prevent me taking up my appointment as Chaplain to Edinburgh University. I am a Minister of the Church of Scotland. I had been properly appointed. I accept the right of people to be unhappy about my appointment but I would have thought that the logic of Christianity would have meant that such unhappiness could be expressed after a tenure and not before it had even begun. In my Church I was entitled to a hearing before being condemned. It was against all of the spirit of the rules of the Church of Scotland to mount a public campaign against a solitary Ordained Christian Minister for views expressed years previously, taken out of context and distorted for theological party political reasons. At least I should have been given the opportunity to explain such views if I wished to do so. However, if these were a clear expression of conviction based on Christian theology, the Bible and the Church's teaching, which was the case, then no-one had any proper right to attempt to deny me my rightful appointment. It is intolerable that people sitting in New College who had never met someone should decide that that person is not a suitable person to be a University Chaplain. Erroneous allegations were made about my departure from Kenya to the effect that I could not reconcile my 'fundamentalism' with what was going on around me!! These allegations were not fostered by agnostics in Edinburgh University but by church people ignorant of the truth and of such poor character as to spread untruthfulness. Dangerous such can be - and wilfully determined to act unjustly. I was never invited to meet my detractors nor was there any attempt to organise a civilised debate on important matters. A cowardly unchristian campaign was as much as my enemies could manage. The members of the Committee which had appointed me and its Convener were put under some pressure. As a Minister of the Church of Scotland I am allowed freedom of opinion in matters not affecting the substance of the Christian Faith. Professor Duncan Forrester seemed to have forgotten that. Yet he is a Professor of Christian Ethics! Some balanced assessment of the legalities might have urged a different approach but the liberal church establishment of Edinburgh would not treat an outsider fairly. How blind are the Pharisees! Ah! Amateur politicians must have their fling. Tally Ho! A nice juicy evangelical is good sport. And there is always the pub for a drink after the blood is shed.

I was never a church party person. My life in adulthood has been an existential search for the reality of God. Church politics presented the battle as liberal versus evangelical. That was the historic issue at stake. The citadel of theological liberalism was to have an evangelical Chaplain. A crude attempt to prevent this happening took place. I stood my ground and won the day. My enemies bided their time.

For the record, it is instructive to note that in addition to unfair and out-of-context use of my thoughts, balancing and compassionate sentiments, though part of what I had said on the AIDS issue at the time of the public debate, were ignored. For example, I also said the following, "The caring role of Christian can never be denied. But Christianity must show a double loyalty, with Christian truth and with the suffering. Christians are part of the human condition of which AIDS is a symptom. They cannot ignore the disease or the dying. Neither must they forsake the theological implications of the disease in order to be acceptable to media presentations. God is not a terrorist but God is a strong parent. Judgmental truth is not helpful but liberating truth is!" ('The Scotsman', December 23rd 1986)......"The defeat of AIDS requires the expression of a collective will to return to a better way of life. Ours is a history of simplicity and it would be good if we could find our ethical roots again. We are meant to consider the effect of our conduct on all other people. Cancer treatment uses healthy cells to fight weak cells. It is Christianity that can defeat AIDS. Christianity also cares for those who are suffering and offers forgiveness and eternal life to those who can make a confession of wrong-doing. The individual must be treated with all compassion, but the disease must be eradicated by a return to Christian teaching." ('The Glasgow Herald', 21st January 1987)

All that I had been and done in my life was unknown to many and a distorted and grievously unfair picture of my person, my character, my Christianity and my vocation as a Minister had been created and publicised, obliging me to live with it for the rest of my life. There is an old saying, "If you want to kill a dog, tell everyone that it has rabies."

I claimed no special privilege, only the same right as any other Minister of my Church. My personal spiritual history gave me the strength to endure the isolation and loneliness that was necessarily a consequence of this time of trial. I did not have any martyr complex and had not provoked anyone purposely. I thought my cross was hard to bear and wondered if I would be able to survive long enough to succeed. It was hard to live with public distortion of my character. Whether or not and to what extent my enemies were opposing God in what they did, I must leave to God. I always had an inner understanding which made sense of what was happening externally. In God's treatment of me throughout my life, I had a reference point which could not be undermined or blown away. It was hard indeed to be caricatured as a rabid fundamentalist. Mine was a living relationship with a dynamic loving Maker and Redeemer in Christ. I never lived for the law but for the Spirit. It was a dynamic interaction between God and the human community that I sought in anything I had said. It was that that was never welcome in Edinburgh.

## The Adversary

Professor John O'Neill, the Convener of the Appointing Committee who was also Convener of the Chaplaincy Committee whose function it was to oversee the work of the Chaplaincy on behalf of the University administration played an equivocal role. He seemed to me to lack authority and confidence and he had no real appreciation of the kind of person I was, not recognising my own resilience, faith and experience.

I was prohibited from taking part in the public campaign. My hands were tied behind my back. I did not like that. He told me to agree with people in order to make myself acceptable and I found that extraordinary. On Thursday 2nd February he had told me that the Chaplaincy at Edinburgh University was moribund. My remit was to give it a higher profile. As soon as trouble arose and it arose very soon, he backtracked and behaved with the perfidy for which academics have been notorious throughout the centuries. A stronger and better man would have acted differently.

On Thursday April 13th I was summoned to the Convener's office in New College. In one hour he took his own frustrations out on me. I was told that I was on probation and surrounded by enmity. Very little would be required for me to have to tender my resignation. If the public case went any further I would have to go. The Convener suggested that I take counselling sessions with Professor Howie with whom I had had a brief mental spar during my interview. No reason was offered as to why the Convener thought this advisable or necessary. The implication seemed to be that there was something psychological or organically wrong with me. The Convener then suggested to me that I would commit suicide. I knew that I never would. I recalled the days of dark exploration of the spiritual world at Glasgow University when Max Magee had suggested the same thing. I deduced at that time that he was speaking falsely from a false spiritual perspective. I knew that the Convener was speaking from the same false spiritual perspective. His words revealed to me what was in his soul.

I had not been prepared for this kind of behaviour when I entered his office. The Convener was not gentle or pastoral but threatening and bullying. He then said that if they had known about my letter and article of 1987 they would never have appointed me. With that he angrily dismissed me. This was spiritual punishment and it struck deep into my innermost being. I returned to my flat devastated. The Convener had tried to manage the controversy as best he could but I thought that from now on I was totally on my own. I realised how flawed and dangerous for me were his perceptions and attitudes. It seemed that in his supposed defence of me, he was more interested in protecting his own reputation than anything else. This brutal treatment released the pent up emotions of the last two months. I wept bitterly and deeply. I do not think that I wept like a child but like a man, like a Biblical man before God, perhaps a little like Jeremiah.

I was unable to eat any food that evening and lay shivering for hours not from cold but from shock. I felt numb, and spiritually injured. At 2 00am I awoke from a troubled and fitful sleep with a dull headache and during the next hour vomited with such violence that I had never known. Three times I vomited in that terrible hour. (I could not remember when I had last been ill - throughout my life I had been blessed with robust good health.) At one point I wanted to die and be away from all the pain and hatred and injustice of the church. After 3 00am, I sat up and began to pray feebly in Jesus' Name. After some time, I drifted into a more comfortable sleep. In the morning when I awoke I felt a strange emptiness within me and I thought that I had lost my confidence and had become a shadow of myself.

It was a Friday. I decided to try to see George Fox, the Christian Healing Minister in Crossford, Lanarkshire. I was much relieved to find that he was available at 12 noon that day. As I unburdened myself a little to him I broke down again and wept bitterly again. I remember saying to him "They are very cruel people." George prayed over me and after one hour I began to feel better. I then decided to go home to Ayrshire. I nearly fell asleep at the wheel of my car on the twisty scenic route. My mother was wise enough to minister gently to me and in the evening I ate my first food for thirty hours. That same evening I returned to Edinburgh and decided to take up the offer of a week-end in Morayshire with a friend in the ministry, John Stuart and his wife Elma. Two days in the warm ambience of that lovely part of Scotland in the company of friends helped me greatly. I returned to Edinburgh in a calm frame of mind although I was not sure what was going to happen to me. I kept praying and trusting in God to see me through. I felt that my cross was far too heavy. As the weeks progressed the burden lessened.

Unspiritual minds will not easily comprehend the hidden dynamics of the spiritual opposition to my taking up my post as Chaplain of Edinburgh University. Easy it is to dismiss someone as inadequate. People thought Jesus a most inadequate Messiah. But as He Himself said, "They did not know what they were doing (to Him)." I thought that I understood the reason for the hostility to me and it lay in the hidden nature of my calling rather than in my visible status as a Minister of the Church of Scotland. I came to Edinburgh as a servant and I came in peace. I came not to wage war but to preach the Gospel and to care for anyone who may have required any help that I could give. That was how I had lived my life before and how I have continued to live since. However I did not share this understanding with anyone. Jesus did not reveal Himself in His resurrected state to those who had crucified Him. He did reveal Himself to His friends. In any case, one cannot make claims for oneself of a spiritual nature. By one's fruits one is known. The prophet Isaiah was himself banned from preaching in the Temple in Jerusalem. He wrote down what he was not allowed to say in public. What he wrote forms part of the Old Testament.

In keeping silent however, I was defenceless against the kind of abuse that I had been receiving. To have tried to explain the source of my confidence would have been futile. No-one would have believed. Personal revelation is lost in the telling. And no-one would have cared. Edinburgh is a particularly unsympathetic environment for any significant spiritual disclosure.

I joined Greyfriars Church, hoping to fulfil all righteousness. The Convener also belonged to this congregation. I sat patiently week in week out listening to extreme liberal preaching which undermined much of the teaching of the Bible. Everything that had happened to people like me on their journey through life was stripped away, minimised, relativised and ultimately negated. I attended Holyrood Abbey for the good of my soul. I always got something to think about from Jim Philip's sermons although I did not always agree with him. The praying fellowship of that congregation was a source of encouragement throughout my time in Edinburgh. I never became a formal part of the congregation but I was able to enter and leave freely. No questions were ever asked and no demands were made. The caricature of evangelicals is that they are somehow narrow and intolerant. It is totally untrue. Narrowness and intolerance there is in the church, but it is usually found elsewhere. One of the joys of working in Edinburgh University was the friendship and support of colleagues. And in my first weeks and months I received much of this and it made it all worth while.

By June it looked as if my enemies contortions had subsided. If they were not restored to their right minds, at least they seemed to be pacified for the time being. I began to expect to survive and planned the coming year's activities with much happiness. The summer months arrived with their especial blessings of warmth and light and picturesque sunsets.

## Awesome Assynt

In August I spent ten days alone in a caravan beside the beach at Clachtoll by Stoer near Lochinver in the far west highlands. 'Holidays' for me have often taken the form of spiritual retreats. Being relieved of the day to day responsibilities allows one to think and pray freely. I have always found it better to use holiday time like this rather than to indulge myself. The other great benefit is loads of fresh air. The combination is always stimulating and the effect of revitalising the mind, the soul and the body together was usually felt on returning to take up the tasks and opportunities of ministry with renewed hope and confidence and commitment.

The surrounding hills of Assynt threatened and protected like great policemen. Suilven rising unnaturally, without legitimacy or excuse and contradicting the treeless superficiality of the vegetation. The winds blow and there is no elemental peace. This is a place for cleansing. There are no distractions. The view from the summit of Quinag was breathtaking, the climb mildly hazardous without equipment or food and with trainers which quelched in the wet wet heather-peat soil. Against all common sense and written and unwritten rules I enjoyed the risk. Hill-climbing brings a sense of achievement, exhiliration at the top, physical fitness and much thankfulness for each safe return. I fell coming down but only skinned a wrist. As I looked back, the route seemed more severe than I had been thinking. In fact I was appalled at my wrecklessness.

Experienced climbers continually pay the ultimate price on Scottish hills and mountains. But the inner man is cleansed and 'office man' cast aside for a little while in the much more natural environment of that last wilderness of Europe which is Assynt. Wild blew the wind one night. The roof of the shower and toilet block on the caravan site was blown off. Take the elements lightly at your peril.

One of the most exquisite parts of the peninsula lies between Drumbeg and Nedd. There are turquoise inlet-lochs with white-hulled yachts at anchor. The burns cascade between the trees and clouds rush by to the east. Military exercises prevented a visit to Cape Wrath further north but I saw that north-west point from just above Durness. I shouted my prayers against the wind, defying its power to carry my seemingly lost words to heaven. On the same drive I visited Tongue and Lairg, disappointed by the blandness of central Sutherland in comparison with what I'd just seen. Climbing Suilven was unforgettable even though I did not reach the top. Stac Pollaidh to the south was my bearing, on my right going, on my left returning. This time I was even less well equipped. I had forgotten my watch. My eyes scanned the sky for the position of the sun between the grey clouds. Twelve wild deer started as I appeared from behind an overhanging rock. The mists rolled in from the east. Discretion took hold of me. I decided not to go all the way. Defeated, I set about the descent and the long walk to Lochinver. Wet it was. Rain it did. I could see little. Now I knew how people get lost. You can be walking in the wrong direction without knowing it. Miles and miles you are from your intended destination. Fatigue sets in. Cold cramps. The dampness seeps through to the marrow. No-one knows you are there. Don't fall and break an ankle. Take it gently. Take it slowly. Where am I going? An existential question! An hour later the mists briefly clear. There is glorious Stac Pollaidh further to the left than I expected. Correct your bearings. You expect to make it back. What a deep cleansing! The warm shower is bliss. And the sleep is endless.

## Fasting

It is only when you get away from all responsibilities that you can truly fast and pray. You review your life critically, more critically than you review the lives of others - but they do not know that. Like the prodigal, you slowly come to yourself and you decide to return to your Father. You pray for the Church and for your place in it. You ask to be of use. You surrender everything to the Living God in Jesus Christ. You find peace. You meditate on asceticism and love and on which path to follow.

> *asceticism is control : love you do not control*
> *asceticism is world-renouncing : love is world affirming*
> *asceticism is relationship renouncing : love is relationship affirming*
> *asceticism is discerning : love is blind*
> *asceticism is self-denial : love is self-surrender*
> *asceticism criticises : love forgives*
> *asceticism means poverty : love is family*

*asceticism implies abandonment : love requires inclusiveness*
*asceticism is a means to an end : love is the greater*

The appetites die and you retreat within yourself, becoming very still. Your movement becomes slow. The head is a little dizzy from time to time. You take the bandages off the wounds. Your Church has no place for you. You have been pushed around everywhere you have been. You offer up to God your tenure of the Chaplaincy at Edinburgh University, five years at most. You surrender it and wait to see if it is given back to you. It is. You ask the Lord to order your life anew. You ask the inner healing of your loneliness and spiritual grief. You learn how much of your mental energy is taken up by non-essential matters. You ask that the cup of failure may be taken from you. You mark the date and time, August 18th 1989, 8 00pm. Next morning you break your fast with thanksgiving and with happiness. And when you leave Assynt and come south again you come down from the mountains physical and spiritual and the air is warmer and the fields are greener and the trees are stronger and more luxuriant and life seems better and richer and more varied and interesting but you know that you have been to a true place within and without and you are much the better for your journey there.

## Ecumenical Strategy

My ecumenical strategy was to allow everyone to be and to do whatever was possible. I wished to have a broad coalition including the Orthodox and Roman Catholics on one hand and Northern Irish Presbyterians, Baptists and Independent Church people on the other. In the middle were the Church of Scotland, Methodists, Anglicans and Congregationalists. This meant that the middle caucus of traditionally liberal SCM types were obliged to broaden out to include others. New College student John MacNab was a good friend in early times. Andrew Steven's dry humour was much appreciated in later years. From the outset Andrew Hailey, Helen Beardsley, Stephen Hughes and other leaders of the Methodist students were great supporters of the Chaplaincy while the Christian Union was equivocal depending on the issue in hand. On being introduced to the Christian Union, the leader whose name was Colin Brough said, "We can support you as to your doctrine but not as to your person." Now there is a definition of European theological dualism! And of classical pharisaism! I could think of a few more 'isms' but these will suffice. This lack of recognition and of acceptance of those outside the peer group is as divisive within the churches as the pejorative extremes of the liberals. Later Christian Union leaders such as Nick Blair, Elspeth Paterson and Jürgen Tittmar showed broader judgement and better example.

Times had changed. The liberal route was no longer the only one on which young people entered the churches. Many students were travelling from outside Christianity into the churches via the evangelical route. The largest Christian student organisation was the Christian Union. I wished to recognise this social change and adapt the Chaplaincy to relate to and accommodate it. It was this strategy which allowed "The Case For Christianity" mission to take place in 1992.

The small liberal rump were however unable to live with this widening of the horizons of Edinburgh University Chaplaincy.

Inter-faith issues are always raised in the context of a university. Some people think that Christianity should no longer have a privileged status in British society. In the ancient Scottish universities there has always been an acknowledgement of Christianity. The universities have benefited greatly from this relationship over the centuries. Some would argue that if university chaplaincies are to exist then they should reflect the multi-cultural and inter-faith aspects of human society.

My strategy was to recognise non-Christian faiths and religious groups as distinct personalities in the spiritual family of humankind. Therefore they were always welcome to meet in the Chaplaincy and 'do their own thing.' I do not think that it is possible or wise to try to harmonise the premises of different religions and faiths. The most devout of each faith recognise one another. Those of genuine spiritual perception can see the best in each other's beliefs without agreeing with them. To pretend that these differences do not exist is dishonest and self-deceiving. Thus a truly Christian Scotland will be a better place for Jews and Muslims and Buddhists to live than a secular Scotland. Where there is no acceptance of the reality of God as in the former Soviet Union, all faiths and their adherents will suffer. Scotland is far from being a Christian country and is probably at this point in time in a retrogressive phase of Christian calling, understanding and commitment.

## The University Churches - Greyfriars and St Giles

How odd to have two University Churches which students did not attend! How Edinburgh! In Greyfriars no accommodation to the more modern forms of undergraduate Christian worship needs were made. The service was supposed to be 'high.' There was no talk for any children who may have been present. The organist was an Anglican. The worship was formal and impersonal. I found it 'low' in spiritual and intellectual content. There were occasional unintended hilarious moments. After one particularly solemn entry of the procession of choir and ministers and just as the Reverend David Beckett, Minister of Greyfriars turned towards the congregation, mouth open to speak, there was a loud crash. I looked to my right and saw that the leg of a pew had collapsed on one side. Mummy, daddy, little girl and granny slid down the acute angle and on to the floor. So much for pomposity! On another occasion, when we were preparing the Memorial Service for Professor James S. Stewart we were told that the Queen's Representative would attend (for Jamie had been one of Her Majesty's Chaplains.) The Minister of Greyfriars asked me "How does one address the Queen's Representative?" I responded, "One stands three feet away, bows to an angle of ninety degrees and says, "My Liege, I humbly welcome you to the Kirk of the Greyfriars." "Oh - I don't think we need to do all that." replied my questioner thoughtfully.

On June 30th, Pentecost Sunday 1990, the Celebration of the Coming of the Holy Spirit upon the early Christian community, I attended Greyfriars. The service was a mixture of unusual hymns, a weird anthem sung with a screech or two and the usual dose of flat-earth liberalism laced with provocative reductionism. We were informed that if the Virgin Mary were to be told today that she was to become pregnant it would not be by an angel because we do not think like that today - we'd say it was intuition. We were also told that the disciples did not suddenly develop a gift for foreign languages. It was the complacent superficial certainty of this type of individual pedantry which undermined the historic truth of revelation, the possibilities of creation and the very nature of Almighty God. I was troubled. If what I was listening to was true - I concluded - then I do not exist.

Once each year on a customarily cold February Sunday morning a few representatives of the University would share in a service of worship in St Giles High Kirk. On the first occasion in which I took part as Chaplain, the invited preacher was Derek Worlock, the Roman Catholic Archbishop of Liverpool. As he was saying 'Good-bye' to me, he put his hand on my shoulder and said prophetically and perspicaciously, "Don't let them browbeat you." From me he had known nothing of my appointment. It was not easy to follow his advice.

It was even harder to persuade students that it was of value to them or anyone else to attend a morning service in St Giles! Hundreds of students attended different churches in Edinburgh Sunday by Sunday. The spiritual instincts of eighteen to twenty-three year old under-graduates lie in worship patterns which reflect freedom and spontaneity. Beautiful though the sounds of the paid choir of St Giles may be, they did not encourage participation by others. Edinburgh people like listening to church choirs. It allows them to pretend that it is worship and saves them the price of a concert ticket. I had some personal respect for Gilleasbuig MacMillan although I could not agree with his urbane liberalisms. In this great place of Reform worship and protest, continual equations of Christianity and other faiths were now made. Homo Edinburgensis rules O.K. Evangelical experience and commitment were scorned. Spiritualised humanism was raised up, demeaning history, theology and tradition.

Iain Robb, the University officer responsible for public occasions liaised with me for University services. Thus he would telephone a week before the St Giles Service so that we could go along and see the church and plan the procession. It was a bit of a skive but also helpful because the interior layout of St Giles was being altered. A new organ was being installed. As we walked on one of our reconnoitres Iain told me that the new organ would be operational for the coming Sunday's University service. I replied that I thought the organ was not ready. Ian insisted that it was. I countered again by saying that although the new organ was being installed, as far as I knew it was unlikely to be ready for the coming Sunday. This argument went on until we arrived at St Giles. On entering the sanctuary we came across a number of cardboard boxes of various lengths. It transpired that these contained organ pipes. One of the largest was open and the sixteen foot pipe had been placed on top of the box. I went over to the pipe, cupped my hands, and opined into the pipe in a deep voice, "Iain, I have a feeling that the organ will not after all be quite ready for Sunday's University Service." "Take your point, Take your point," said Iain!

It disappointed me that so many students from England never sought to integrate themselves into Presbyterian forms of worship while they lived in Scotland. I had been a *de facto* Anglican while at Oxford. They however had a ghetto mentality and clung to their own traditions. The depth and sincerity and transcendence of Reform worship patterns would have done so much good to those who could have placed themselves under its discipline. Very few ever did.

## Return To Crowhurst

Thirteen years after my life-changing call at Crowhurst, I returned for one week's retreat and holiday. I simply rested, prayed and meditated. I found forgiveness, healing and inner peace at the evening Service there on Wednesday 21st March 1990, through no human intermediary. All the hurts and burdens of the last year which I had carried internally, in my soul, were taken from me. As I sat on the right side of the Chapel I saw a vision of a great Person whom at first I did not recognise. It was an august Presence. It made me gasp with astonishment, awe and fear. The Presence was wearing a white robe with a golden belt at chest height. Later in the evening I scoured the Book of Revelation for a clue. I read Chapter one verse thirteen, "...a gold belt round his chest." Had this been a vision of the Risen Christ? The vision had not been close to me and did not speak to me. Rather it was an entry into an eternal Presence to which my eyes had been briefly opened. I had not gone to Crowhurst to seek a revelation and I would not have put God to the test in that way.

God may choose to reveal Himself to whomsoever but it will not be to anyone trying to make it happen. But in being granted this vision I knew I had been forgiven and that I still belonged to and with My Lord. When I had left the Chapel at the end of the Service, I had raised my hands up and touched the low ceiling of the passageway from the Chapel to the main house in triumphant exhilaration, release and happiness. The lady behind said that she nearly tickled me but thought the better of it.

I fasted for a day and sat in the same place the next evening. My eyes were opened once again to this same Presence, this Person of the Risen Christ. Now I saw more clearly and more nearly. He was holding a lamb in His arms. The lamb raised its head and looked in my direction. The lamb was warm and alive and its eyes were beautiful, dark brown and full of spiritual light. The Person was stroking it tenderly. And now I understood what I was seeing. This was a vision of the Good Shepherd. It was a vision of peace and Grace and pastoral care and spiritual love.

I announced to Ralph Essex, one of the Ministers, "I am restored." As I reflected, I contrasted the provocative percentage of my own vocation with the substance of the vision. I was much affected and became softer in heart and mind as a result of the supernatural experience. It was a truly lovely way to learn a beautiful lesson.

I spent the remainder of the week sight-seeing, visiting Hastings, Eastbourne and Brighton and in reading and walking. I enjoyed a laugh with a Kensington-type woman called Brenda. I suggested that places like Crowhurst should be graded for amenities and service just like hotels. Instead of stars however, indication of excellence or the lack of it could be indicated by placing crosses after each name on a scale from five to one. I also suggested keeping a boat at Brighton for pleasure trips, holding one hundred yard zimmer races and angel car cramming as fund raising ideas.

Ray Jones the Warden told me that he had appreciated the wonderful quip of Lord George MacLeod, Founder of the latter-day Iona Community when he had attended the funeral of Harry Whitely, Minister of St Giles High Kirk in Edinburgh. Whitely had quarrelled with his predecessor Charles Warr. At one point in the funeral service a loud peal of thunder was heard. MacLeod was quickest to react. "I guess he's met Charlie Warr already," said the great man.

I returned to Edinburgh relaxed and happy and full of energy and optimism for the future. Above all, I was filled with gratitude to God for replacing my exhaustion and sorrow with joy and inspiration. It had been a long round trip to Sussex and back. I might not have gone. Seeking God is well worth the continual effort. The rewards of His Grace are extravagant.

## The Living Word

In late 1989 I had accepted an invitation to preach at the morning service in Barclay Church, Brunstfield in Edinburgh. F T Pilkington, the architect had been a man who understood the needs of preachers and listeners. The semi-circular design made it seem as if you could touch the congregation. Penicuik South Church on the south-west of Edinburgh, another of Pilkington's masterpieces, creates the same impression. The sermon I preached was entitled "The Value Of The Bible." One person described it as 'stirring stuff' and it seemed to have been well received. However a few days later, John O'Neill told me that he had received complaints about the sermon and he demanded to have a copy to read. He did not specify these 'complaints.' In discussion he criticised me for the sermon without making any substantial points. I asked that in future people might address issues to me directly.

The idea of Edinburgh University having an independent minded Chaplain might have been attractive as an idea. The reality was not as acceptable. But we had all been caught out by the public nature of the campaign against my appointment. I was obliged to try to survive. The Convener had his own position to defend. On Wednesday 20th December, he told me to suspend my critical faculty and lay aside my prophet's mantle for five years. In the midst of his harangue during an after lunch walk, while passing a tartan shop on the Royal Mile, my eyes caught an Anderson clan shield with our motto "STAND SURE". I pointed it out to him and roared with laughter

The Presbytery Of Edinburgh at that time was continuing to debate a proposition to have the Presbytery unilaterally reject certain doctrines in the Apostles' Creed - the very basis of Christianity. The Convener had spoken in favour of discussing the matter. In my Barclay sermon I expressed concern about the entire process. The Convener apparently had interpreted the sermon as a reflection on himself and had decided to discipline me. Six months later he apologised to me for the way he had treated me and conceded that I had been right and that he had been wrong. However, in 1990 a similar incident occurred with more serious consequences.

On 2nd December 1990 I preached a sermon called "Apocalyptic (Christianity Is being Squeezed)" at the morning service in Greyfriars Church. My address was a critique of the forms of liberalism I had countered since coming to Edinburgh some twenty months before. It was general and wide-ranging in character. I specifically did not reply to the theological liberalisms preached regularly there on such subjects as The Virgin Birth.

*"It is possible that we are at the beginning of the end of Christianity*
*as a coherent, visible, organised global spiritual force....Marxist-*
*Communism has lost its great historical battle with Jesus Christ.....*
*It would be wrong to suggest that our society is a tool of divine*
*purpose, a sanctified instrument of justice and truth. It is not."*

Towards the end of the sermon I turned to the impending war between Iraq and the forces of the United Nations.

*"There is no trust and there will be no trust. We must not put our*
*faith in material victory however, as others do....Christian nations*
*can still by their restraint and compassion prevent the fruitless futile*
*militarism of other nations from inflicting suicidal self-defeat.....*
*But neither side will have it."*

On Monday 3rd December, the Convener telephoned to say that the Minister of Greyfriars and a woman lecturer at New College, Dr Ruth Page had objected to the sermon and that the Minister of Greyfriars had said he did not think he could allow me to preach in his church again. Dr Page had verbally attacked me as she had left the service. A copy of the sermon was demanded. Surprised by this reaction, I asked a post-graduate student who had been present what he had thought of the sermon. His unflattering comment was "Low-key and forgettable." An elder of Greyfriars, Herbert Kerrigan Q.C. had offered a little more encouragement by saying on leaving the service, "You gave us a lot to think about."

I thought that my position as Chaplain would be compromised if I could not preach in the University Church. The Convener decided that a meeting would have to be called. It took place on Saturday 5th January 1991 from 12 noon to 2 00pm in the Chaplaincy Centre. I asked Herbert Kerrigan to attend to offset the expected persecution. I had also asked Dr Donald Meek who was a member of the Chaplaincy Committee to read the sermon to see if it was deserving of this kind of reaction. He had replied that in his opinion the sermon warranted no such reaction. He agreed to attend the meeting to speak on my behalf. The Convener duly set about punishing me for the sermon. The Q.C. gently suggested that I had had a right to say what I said. The academic said that he found no fault with the sermon. The Minister of Greyfriars, somewhat phased by the presence of two heavyweights, kept remarkably quiet. As the meeting wore on, the Convener used bully-boy tactics against me. "You can be dismissed," he said in a threatening manner. I replied, "Not for nothing I can't; there are employment laws in this country." However by the end of the meeting there was some improvement in the situation and although nothing specific was said, I took it that I would be allowed to return to Greyfriars Church and therefore that I could carry on as Chaplain. I did not know that the Convener in threatening me had overstepped his authority. As a University employee, I had rights not to be treated in such a manner.

The weeks of December 1990 and January 1991 saw a number of public statements by church leaders on the subject of the impending Gulf crisis. The liberals were very much against the war but they offered no solution to the problem posed by Saddam Hussein. Richard Holloway, the Episcopal Bishop, was quoted in 'The Scotsman' as saying that the war would not take place. The Minister of Greyfriars said so too in his sermon on January 6th 1991.

I had been concerned that I may have spoken presumptuously in my sermon on 2nd December. This would have constituted a serious spiritual sin. After the war had begun and had been quickly won by the United Nations forces, I felt relieved and vindicated. Had I been wrong, I would have offered an apology to the Convener and the Minister of Greyfriars. He, however, never apologised to me, nor did the Convener, nor the woman lecturer from New College. Holloway never wrote to 'The Scotsman' to say he had mislead people. I concluded that if liberals are wrong, it does not matter. If an evangelical is right, it may cost him his job!

In the Bible, the test of a genuine prophet is whether what he has said actually happens. Conversely, false prophets were those who said things were all right when they were not (Peace, peace, when there is no peace.) Did this mean that the December 2nd sermon was also right in its other aspects and topics? It may have been. But the Chaplain to the University of Edinburgh was not expected nor allowed to preach directly or truthfully in Greyfriars Church. The content of my sermon had not been a hunch or a lucky guess. I had risked my authority as a Minister of the Christian Gospel and my genuineness as a Servant of the living God in Christ. Something particular had occurred. In 1990, in distinction from the liberal and rationalist church culture of Edinburgh, a living Word had been uttered.

Here was demonstrated the relationship between God in and through Jesus Christ speaking by the Holy Spirit through a Minister of the Church. A historically verifiable prophecy had been given and later vindicated. Punishment and threat of dismissal had followed the living Word. No-one will be condemned for disliking the imperfections of another human being. Even Jesus said that sin against the Son of Man will be forgiven. But opposition to the Holy Spirit of Truth will not be so easily forgiven, said Jesus. When something is objectively true and called false, when something is objectively good and called bad, when something transcendent and divine is ignored, that constitutes an objective and eternal sin which cannot find resolution on earth. Why did this strange and disproportionate reaction occur? It was an example of the difference between the liberalism of Greyfriars and of New College and the evangelical Chaplain to the University. It was of the same genre as the opposition to my appointment in 1989.

I wondered if I could continue as Chaplain. The threat of dismissal in the presence of the Minister of Greyfriars had weakened my position, perhaps making it untenable. I thought that no matter what happened in the future I would always be wrong. I had been offered up as a sacrifice to Greyfriars. I began to suffer. I felt the onset of spiritual suffocation, crushing and inhibiting. The highest aspect of the real me - my relationship with God - could not be tolerated. This was and remains the somatopsychic-mental-spiritual basis of my personality, my individuality, my life and my call to the ministry in the Church of Jesus Christ. This was the best gift I could offer. It was unwelcome to the point of persecution.

The positive flow of energy and enthusiasm which had carried me through the latter half of 1989 and all of 1990 began to dissipate. I seriously considered resigning. If my living Christian ministry was not tolerable, then there seemed little point in remaining in my position. But I felt aggrieved. I had done nothing wrong. The opposite was the case. After some weeks I came to terms with the situation. In 1990 I had begun to raise funds for the refurbishment and modernisation of the Chaplaincy Centre. That goal was worth pursuing and seeing through. Also, I had initiated planning for a Chaplaincy sponsored University Mission to be held in November 1992. These projects were more important than my own personal fortunes, health or public acceptance. I decided to live 'underground' until these projects were completed and that for their sake I would try to keep an uneasy and unnatural 'peace.' It was self-denial but it was more than that. It was a compromise of the highest and best I could offer to Edinburgh University. Excellence was not expected or required of the Chaplaincy. Grey ineffectual mediocrity was its reputation. That was all that was wanted. I felt untrue to my calling. The Holy Spirit, the agent of truth and of revival was to be restricted. My Chaplaincy tenure became a kind of resistance movement. I had to survive to accomplish certain goals. Instead of continuing to be a free-flowing channel of stimulus, interest, challenge and renewal it became a percentage game with much inner unspoken anguish and pain. This was not caused by atheists and agnostics in Edinburgh University but by Christians and by fellow Ministers of the Church of Scotland, one a Professor of the New Testament, the self-same Convener.

In November 1991 I was due to present my annual report to the Chaplaincy Committee. The Convener insisted on vetting it beforehand. The report was upbeat and encouraging, listing a range of initiatives and evidences of growth and renewal. At the end of the report I included a paragraph entitled "Freedom Of Speech" in which I asked, "Is the Chaplain circumscribed by his role from preaching the Christian Gospel without fear or favour?" When the Convener, reading the report in my presence, came to this paragraph he leapt from his seat, picked up a pencil and scored through this paragraph. Angrily he said, "Take it out or I'll finish you." The date was the 25th October 1991. I still have the copy of the report with his pencil scores. I argued with him for some time and then decided to withdraw the paragraph. I said, "All right, but there will be a price to pay." Eight months after the January altercation, the two main projects of my Chaplaincy looked like being accomplished. I did not want to jeopardise them. I gave in. I despised myself. It was the spiritual cruelty which caused most pain. The blindness and injustice appalled me.

I had worked in Africa for nearly six years, educating ordinands for the ministry. I had always sought the best for each student, helping, encouraging and kindly challenging everyone to reach his or her fullest and best. I continued with this method in dealing with students at Edinburgh University who came to see me on a personal basis. Here was I, in my own country, a Minister of the Church of Scotland, in my capital city and in its great University being subjected to unreasonable conduct and harassment to the extent of bullying. For what? For saying something that was objectively true. The Convener had also asked me to submit my sermons to him in advance for clearance and censorship. I had refused to do so on the basis that I am a Christian Minister in a free society, working in a University which depends for its existence on the free exchange of ideas. I began to feel that I had lost all integrity. I followed One who had been outspoken and had paid the ultimate price. He had died younger than me. I felt the weight of my salary heavily upon my heart.

## Meeting The Pope

In the summer of 1990, I had visited Rome for the first time. I had been given an introduction to the Scots College by my colleague Rodger Clarke. Rome itself was breathtaking. To walk on the Palatine Hill, the Capitol and to go inside Coliseum, to visit Ostia Antica and Pompeii, to see the Pantheon, Augustus' Mausoleum, and Aurelius' Column were experiences which enthralled me. To actually visit the places where Roman history had occurred and where classical civilisation flourished was fascinating. As I looked around, I thought with admiration (and not with disgust as did the Emperor Julian) that Jesus had conquered all of this, one of the very greatest political, military, literary, organised empires the world has ever seen. "Thou hast conquered Galilean." The dimensions of St Peter's Basilica amazed me. I'd seen nothing like it. Christian 'culture' had surpassed the secular Roman. I thought that the Vatican Museum was one of the wonders of the world. Valueless! Priceless! And I met Pope John Paul II briefly on Wednesday 29th August. I had been given a privileged ticket for a general audience. I was phased by the mafia style bodyguards who surrounded him. But I shook the man's hand and told him I had come from Scotland and he grunted in acknowledgement, shaking his head upwards. He seemed strong with a peasant strength, remote and distant. His face was lit with prayer and celibacy of the years.

The Scots College was a safe place for me to stay in a corrupt city. I thoroughly enjoyed the after dinner chat of the ordinands and priests. This was so much missing in my own Church, I thought. Here I could talk theology without frightening people off. I tried out a few gentle provocations. John McIntyre and John Tormey were helpful and genial hosts. I joined a conducted tour of the vaults below St Peter's where Constantine's Basilica was. It had been built on the cemetary in which as legend has it St Peter's bones were found. I was not too impressed by the claims.

In the College Chapel I prayed with depth and agony and not without some consolation. I read Kenneth Leech's book 'Soul Friend' and found a list of reasons for unanswered prayer; refusal to forgive, anger and quarrelsome thoughts, refusal to be reconciled, distorted sexuality and lust, occult and magical rites, disobedience, refusal to confess one's sins in the community, greed and avarice. (p.168,9) Some of the conditions made sense of my own tears and disappointments.

Roman Catholic clergy may have had neither wives or families of their own, but to me, they were well cared for. I enjoyed their asset-stripping humour and self-mockery. I was surprised by the extent of their freedom of opinion and the frequency with which they exploited this gift. But I suspected that they were less open with their own congregations. Beneath the banter I also detected levels of 'angst' and psychosomatic symptoms of stress and interior torture. I was baffled by some of their theological myths and legends, accretions and false logic and their defences of all of these. The immaculate conception of Mary, her permanent virginity and her assumption, for example, seemed quite unnecessary to a bare Protestant like me. They told me St Peter had a daughter called Petronella and this was news indeed.

The extravagant ambitions of former Popes appalled me. And the 'authority' structure was one I could not accept. But - at a certain level, it all worked within its own logic. '121 George Street' seemed a small operation in the corner of Christ's church on earth in comparison. I loved 'The Tablet' with its clear and critical essays on topical issues. Protestants and Roman Catholics share The Apostles' Creed. Sad it is that what the human will has added should divide us still. I even got the sense sometimes that people felt that the Reformation had never actually taken place. But visiting Rome was a seminal experience, mind-boggling, stimulating and humbling. And in the catacombs I remembered those who had given everything for their Faith in Jesus Christ as martyrs, the seed of the church. I thought of the tawdry representations of Christianity which we clergy today offer our folk and the pale imitation of Christianity that they are content to receive.

Florence was beautiful and the Uffizi magnificent. The Duomo I thought was not so in spite of its dimensions. Naples was dreadful. And I thought it possible that anyone who saw it could most certainly die - of pollution. I loved the basking warmth of the sunshine everywhere everyday. I exulted in total anonymity. It was a truly great holiday and one of the highlights of my life.

## Skye

At the beginning of April 1991 I took myself to Geary on the Waternish peninsula in Skye for a week's holiday. It was still cold. I felt much pain in the inner man. I thought that I should be at the peak of my strength and here I was broken by conspiracy and weakened by the strictures placed upon me. Loneliness too still debilitated. I was drained by my experiences in Edinburgh, two years after I had become Chaplain to the University. I longed for the free expression of my calling. I felt stifled and crushed. The real me was bearing the burden. I did not want to become someone else - a cipher for others, a door-mat, a 'professional' clergyman who says the most apposite things and dodges the real issues. I expected to be able to grow and flourish in Edinburgh University's environment. It was a great shock to me to be kicked around as I had been. I contemplated failure.

On the Tuesday I walked eighteen miles along the road to Dunvegan and back. The weather was bright and sunny with two brief showers. Skye was a contrast to grey Edinburgh city streets. Wild and remote, unchanged for millenia, the lochs and fields and rivers seemed to echo my own sense of personal remoteness and disappointment and aloneness. So few shared the beauties of the place. Who knew they existed? Inverse proportion. I saw myself in the environment of still lingering winter.

On the morning of my forty-fourth birthday the weather was quite beautiful. I drove to Portree and bought myself a solitary celebration lunch of soup, haggis, tatties and neeps and plum duff. Afterwards I visited Glen Brittle and walked along the clear, clean deserted beach. The sun shone down. I sat on a milk crate washed up by the tide and sunbathed. In the evening I visited a mediaeval graveyard near Geary and the setting sun flooded the small sea loch and the way across to Lochmaddy where the big ferry was bound. It was what I had come to see. I was not disappointed.

I was suffering the inner tensions of the bullying of John O'Neill. Sensitised to spiritual life as I was, these unwanted abuses lacerated my consciousness. It was not that I exaggerated them. Rather, everything was exagerrated in pain and pleasure once you have seen life from God's point of view. Once you have been to the Heavenly City. Once the Lord Himself has opened your eyes to Him and to the true nature of the world. It was not paranoia nor schizophrenia. It was spiritual invasion. I felt that I was being beaten into submission. My confidence was going. I was shocked to discover my internal state. In the job you keep going, you present a persona, you struggle. You give much of yourself to others in ministry and friendship. You suffer unjustifiable abuse. You carry away in your soul the refuse of other people's lives. And in cold Skye at night in the darkness, the loneliness of it all enveloped me like a shroud. My birthday was such a day of self-understanding. I felt tired. The weight of the dry secularism of the University had exhausted me. I had expended huge quantities of emotional and spiritual stress over the last two years. Where the inspiration and energy to carry on was going to come from I did not know. I said to myself, if I am restored by Sunday, God is still with me.

For the remainder of the week I visited the usual tourist places, the Clan Donald Centre, the Glen Dale Folk Museum and the eastern Cuillins but I could not walk to Neist Point because of rain. There was peace in my heart. On the Saturday I visited Flora MacDonald's grave. Something of the special quality of the woman seemed still to hang in the air. According to Dr Johnson she was lady-like, feminine, attractive and with a quantity of highland grace such as has not been totally despoiled in some from these parts to this day. It was an awesome singular journey round the coast via Staffin to Portee. I thought I could live at peace on Skye forever. There were no great answers. Just an unremitting sense of need to learn faithfulness, obedience and devotion amid the temptations of this life.

The sermon in Portree Parish Church on the Sunday morning on the inevitability of death was archetypally west-highland. It was not inspiring. It was not entertaining. But it was theological *realpolitik*. You could understand why folks here had not been able to find much joy in their Faith. I was at the end of my holiday. It had been a great week of rest, reflection, recreation, introspection, life-repentance, peace and contentment. My body and my soul had benefited. I was in my right mind. But I knew this inner healing would be tested on the anvil of Edinburgh University. That night I prayed for the remainder of my time as Chaplain. I offered God what I thought was the waste of my life. My real life. No-one wanted to know. I could not tell them anyway. I felt crippled by consciousness of sin - of the man of sin - the sense of which was heightened by those intimations of God which had been given to me. Perhaps that was the only way I could be of use. Not I but Christ in me.

The breathtaking journey home confirmed my admiration for my Maker. Cuillins, Kyleakin, the Five Sisters of Kintail, Ben Nevis, Glencoe, the Trossachs, Stirling and the lower reaches of the Forth, Auld Reekie. What a fabulous country! How many Scots neither know or recognise the extraordinary beauties of their own country.

## General Assemblies

I was a Commissioner at the 1991 General Assembly of the Church of Scotland. It was easy for me to go into the Chaplaincy office and then go along to listen to the debates. I had always found the opening pageantry utterly unconvincing. The late mediaeval language of the Queen's address was so outmoded that it was risible. But I recognised the power of The Establishment. I saw how interwoven were social advancement and acceptance of class division, local and minor aggrandisement, aristocracy and monarchy. Monarchy still attracts and excites people. I have never known why. It may be a spiritual thing. It could be to do with ancient social perceptions so embedded in our racial memory that as creatures we naturally defer to our own leaders, however unworthy some of them may be. It may be the association of power - of being with people to whom others bow. I never would. On being presented to Prince Philip, Chancellor of Edinburgh University during one of his rare visits to the University, I asked him why he never attended any Graduations. He paused for a moment, looked at me in an arch kind of way and replied, "Because there are too many of them." Not a convincing excuse.

The set piece presentation of speeches at General Assemblies shows the best and worst of the Church of Scotland. The best lies in the extraordinary amount of work which is put into each Report of every Department every year. Scholarly and eclectic, these reports portray the Church's wish to understand the movements of contemporary society and to offer perspectives upon them. The worst is that they are sometimes presented by dull grey committee people, appointed for lack of charisma rather than for any other reason. The reports are usually fudges anyway. Inevitably, they tend to reflect the Kirk liberal establishment mentality. There are occasional exceptions. Poseurs seem to get up year in year out to present themselves to the Assembly. 'Rent-a-Speech' or 'Speech-U-Like' did brisk business. Bygone days were re-enacted by the ancients such as R Leonard Small. I saw the great Tom Torrance humiliated more than once. What an ungrateful climate is Presbyterianism!

On the Monday of the Assembly I climbed Ben More near Crianlarich. I was a diligent Commissioner. The weather was unkind - wind and rain and mist prevented me reaching the absolute summit. But I came close. I slipped and rolled and tumbled my way down. It took me two hours to find my car. I had not returned as I had ascended - a constant problem on the Scottish hills. I was exhausted. Soaked. I questioned God's personal Providence but arrogantly did not question my own foolhardiness.

The high points of General Assemblies for me have always been the evening legal cases. Here individuals or groups, perhaps a congregation, have the right to popular justice. To me this is the best reason for being a Presbyterian. However humble you are, you have a right to have your case judged by the entire Assembly of men and women there present. If your local church or area Presbytery has denied you, there is still recourse for you. In an age of increasing authoritarianism and manipulation, of disintegration of the political process and of 'management' ethics in churches, Scotland's Presbyterian tradition still offers a system of free representation which takes personal and local issues out of their context to be decided upon according to the evidence heard there and only then. Wonderful! Here the mandarins are often discomforted and their organisational prejudices highlighted. Here the subtlest movements of favour by a supposedly impartial Moderator are exposed and become manifestly counter-productive. Here - miraculously - evangelicals and liberals vote on issues presented and less according to party lines. Here the underdog has a chance. Here is a day in court - free of charge. Here is a shining light to the world still.

And so I saw a dear lady from the Island of Foula in the far far north petition the Assembly against a decision to remove the missionary-teacher who acted as a pastor to the people who lived in that remote place. She looked liked an islander. She sounded like an islander. The oily explanations of the '121' chap - a man called Russell - contrasted with her simple integrity. It seemed that much arrogance and lack of common sense had prevailed until now. The trouble is that so many of those who aspire to decision-making positions in the Church of Scotland seem to develop almost Jacobite megalomanias. They fail to observe the simple courtesies and they often fail to proceed correctly and constitutionally. This is so that they can get their way and push through what they consider to be in the best interests of the church as they see them. But the dear lady won her case. The Venerable General Assembly supported her petition to have the case looked at again. I pray that in the pressures of succeeding centuries, this light of popular justice will not be extinguished. If it is - it will not be by the people of the Church, but by those and their successors who baulk at running a church in such an outmoded way. But what really is at stake is power to decide.

The 1996 General Assembly has been asked to consider that Assemblies should no longer hear cases. Assembly Commissions (Committees) will be given the function instead. Thus smaller and smaller groups of people with their own agendas will decide cases. Experts may take the place of the broad *common sense* of the people of God. What yet distinguishes Presbyterianism from Roman Catholicism, Episcopalianism and Evangelical autocracy may be abandoned. Central committees will increase their stanglehold on the Church's mind. They will stack the Commissions with theological kindred spirits to get the results they want. Their own failings will be hidden. At the same time as there is a desire for criminal and civil sentencing policy to be in touch with popular opinion, the Church of Scotland is moving in the other direction, of narrowing the basis of justice in the Church. Scottish *common sense* may still have a place. Kirk people may with their collective mind disagree with those who manipulate the system time and time again. Good. Justice and fairness and transparency - these are among the most precious invisible commodities in the value system of the universe and the very life of Jesus Christ.

And the General Assembly can be ridiculous too. And hypocritical. And played like a puppet by the likes of Professor James Whyte of St Andrew's if it looks like the liberals may lose a vote on some theological principle. And even its procedures may be hijacked in the all important cause of defeating any uprising of evangelicals against no matter how suspect a suggestion, arrangement, idea or deliverance. There is a secret desire in some to have absolute control. They associate their views with those of God. They subvert due process to make sure the Church agrees with them. So what? The Church has always lived that way on earth. The end justifies the means, they say before meeting Jesus of Nazareth - a judicially murdered person - somewhere - someday.

If you want to see the most minscule cucumber sandwiches in the world - then go along wearing the finest corresponding to your gender to the Holyrood Palace Garden Party on the Saturday of the General Assembly. You will feel safe because Her Majesty's Company of Archers are there to protect you. They are elderly men in blue suits and hats with large feathers. They form a *cordon sanitaire* around any personage of special importance. The smelly commoners are not allowed inside. And there are three dozen strawberry tarts for four hundred folk. But the regulars know where they are and get there first every time. You can say that you have been. But don't let anyone ask you what you did there.

The General Assembly is not without humanity. Perhaps the wittiest remark I heard of was offered by a Moderator after a Commissioner had concluded his long speech with the remark, "Moderator, I had arranged for a seconder, but he has taken ill." "Is anyone else willing to take the risk?" quipped the man in the big chair. Perhaps when Scotland has its own Parliament, the General Assembly's role will change. It has been a parliament by default and this has encouraged the politically-minded of the Church to use it for political purposes. If, in returning to spiritual matters, the General Assembly finds again its proper role it may become again an inspiration to everyone and maintain for itself a blessed role for centuries to come. More likely it is that the General Asemblies of future years will be riven with theological strife as liberals use any means available to keep evangelicals at bay. Not a few consider that a second Disruption may happen. I think the liberals want to provoke it. And they will.

# 7 : The Case For Christianity

## Setting The Agenda

Universities are children of the Christian Church. The search for knowledge took place for centuries in the context of belief in and worship of God. Modern universities have become large secularised degree factories permeated by Thatcherite market philosophy. There has been a loss of internal cohesion, of the sense of community, of collegiate friendliness and of personal identity.

It was a privilege to try to invest such a place with spiritual and Christian perspectives, insights and creative projects, alongside the regularities of worship, of prayer and of pastoral care to everyone who sought the Chaplain's help. The helpfulness of colleagues contrasted with the 'aye resist improvements' mentality of church groups. Initiatives were welcome. Yet universities are very conservative institutions and real changes are tolerable only at a cosmetic level. The freedom to experiment was however a great luxury for a Christian Minister.

I intended that the Chaplaincy should set its own agenda and make its own unique contribution to the University on that basis. I took the challenge of excellence seriously and I had to sharpen up my own act. I found this stretching process exhilarating and stimulating. An important aspect of my psychological approach was my Scottishness. I value that metaphysical space that Scots have and recognise in some. We do not like to trespass on the souls of other people. Our silence is often respect. We may seem diffident and lacking in confidence, but we may have our reasons and sometimes they are to save the other person's dignity. We loathe the forwardness of some from other places (not too far away.) Today we suffer the imperial mentality and the colonisation of our spirits. By our very nature we cannot defend ourselves. To do so means to abolish that spiritual condition into which we were born and which we treasure. We do not want to become like the other person whose conduct embarrasses us.

I did not wish to attract a personal following. I preferred simply to offer my perspectives on any issues under discussion. If these be of God, then I was sure they would find hearts and minds in which to grow. I have always been troubled by the ignorance of those who speak on religious topics without any real authority other than their own opinions. And many within the churches do. I could not be an expert on a million subjects. You learn therefore to operate at different levels of understanding. Rarely does anyone ask you to go too deep. You protect your own soul too. In personal counselling much gentleness is required. You cannot live another's life for them. People seeking help have simply not found the way forward for themselves. You bide time with them. They find their way.

Pastoral care is the 'invisible' contribution of a Chaplain to a university. Some would argue that it is the only justification for having such an office in a modern university. Secular counselling is not adequate for all pastoral cases. The spiritual needs of students are recognised in this way and a statement is made that universities have not entirely closed their minds to the dimensions of the metaphysical, the spiritual, the divine. Therefore scarcely a day went past without some contribution being made to the well being of the academic community.

The Chaplain deals with numerous non-spiritual problems as well. One of the pleasing ways in which 'the system' can be made to work is when a student has academic difficulties. I found teachers receptive to advice from the Chaplain and in some cases, re-programming of a student's degree course was possible. It was most gratifying when an academic career was saved in this way, especially if the student had felt that there was no hope.

Tragedies do occur. Start of university is very stressful for some late teenagers. The deep mid-winter weeks are difficult for others, especially students of more mature years who can be very much on their own at such a time. You miss children and you miss the elderly. University is a rarefied atmosphere - a strong combination of the cleverest and of the youth of the land. It is a most privileged existence even although the stresses wrought by government policy have destroyed the ambiences built up over centuries.

The rescuing of an overseas student from 'The Unification Church' was a pastoral highlight. Weeks of delicate negotiations and a trip to Cambridge resulted in the student returning home to parents who sent a traditional gift to express their gratitude. It was a 'going the extra mile' pastoral role whose consequence far outweighed the time spent.

## Spiritual Bliss

There was a unique and blessed moment in each week of term throughout my tenure, immediately after the celebration of Holy Communion on Wednesdays at lunchtime. I introduced this service when I took up my appointment. Over the years the numbers averaged no more than nine or ten although different people came at different times and so the 'congregation' was much larger. The service seemed to be anointed. True to my tradition which does not administer the Sacrament without the preaching of the living Word, I gave a short address each week, sometimes on a topical subject, sometimes on a Biblical theme. Mental stimulus and sacramental communion were thus held together.

We always prayed for others, especially for all the students. I believe that the very small number of tragedies throughout my tenure was in some part a result of our constant prayers. We did not forget those who lived and worked in the University, interceding for staff of all grades and occupations including the Principal, Sir David Smith. Our worship seemed to be a Sacrament for the University just as the Body and Blood of Jesus was a Sacrament for us. It was a sacred moment, hidden away in the little chapel within the Chaplaincy Centre, ignored by so many staff and students and yet an occasion of the deepest blessing possible.

After the reception of the elements we would sit in silence for a moment or two. I could almost reach out and touch the Presence filling the place where we were. I would always offer a short concluding prayer the words of which I never prepared. These words seemed themselves to be a direct greeting to the Risen Lord of the Church and of the world. I could see a pathway to heaven and the removal of all spiritual and mental barriers to faith and belief in God. Sometimes I could have stayed there all afternoon.

## A Scottish University?

I had been dumbfounded upon taking up my appointment to find so many English people within Edinburgh University. I remembered one day in May 1989 when it was 3 30pm in the afternoon before I heard a Scots accent. It belonged to the maintenance engineer in the Faculty of Veterinary Medicine and Surgery. My Kingdom is not of this world but I did resent the fact that so many English people seemed not to realise that they were no longer living in England. I found their presumptions intolerable. The colonial attitude was alive and flourishing in my capital city. Assumptions of superiority peppered so many conversations. I did not think that I should apologise for being a Scot in my own country. Later I wore my 1990 Grand Slam commemorative sweater from time to time!

It was politically incorrect to be a Scot in Edinburgh University. In 1991 I planned to give a lecture called "Is Edinburgh a Scottish University?" If the Chaplain would not raise these issues, who would? I kicked against the attempted restrictions on freedom of speech which still remained as a threat against me. I never intended to be a pleasant fellow of no opinions drinking sherry (or whisky) in the Staff Club on Friday evenings! Neither was I going to be a cipher for anyone. I thought as I have always done, that I should offer my best thoughts. Integrity demanded intellectual honesty. I thought too that if the University was as civilised as it pretended to be, I would test its tolerances. If I could substantiate my argument then that would be a positive contribution to the life and future direction of the University. What idealism! What naiveté!

One week before I was due to deliver this lecture, I voluntarily submitted a copy to the Secretary to the University, the eponymous Dr Lowe. I considered my contribution to be a responsible one. I was not seeking media publicity and for pastoral and loyalty reasons I wished my employer to know what I intended. The lecture was referred to the Convener of the Chaplaincy Committee to read and his were the pencil marks of censorship which adulterated the copy when I saw it again. The Secretary to the University called me to a meeting and asked me to excise certain parts for delivery. These were some of the more personal observations and I agreed to consider doing so as long as the general thrust of the argument was not compromised.

There were clear embarrassments. I had calculated that in recent times out of the top sixteen academic and administrative posts in the University, only two had been held by Scots and two by half-Scots or Anglos. No-one could tell me how many of the academic staff at the University were English. As I went my rounds it seemed to me to be the large majority. Some indication was possible from published tables showing where members of staff obtained their first degrees. The figures were overwhelmingly English. I wondered what this was doing to Scotland over the generations. I was reminded of the impotence which had continually prevented any significant demonstration of political autonomy. The University of Edinburgh seemed to be a Trojan horse blackmailing Scots with its prestige. Boasting that it was Lothian's largest employer, the University never divulged the true nature of its relationship to the local community or to Scotland. This was cultural negative equity! The City of Edinburgh is so south orientated that Scotland could never become politically independent even if a majority of Scots wanted it so.

The most powerful things in life and in the universe are ideas. Here, in the capital University, so many ideas were offered without a Scottish perspective, an imperialism of the imagination - perhaps the most grievous form of colonialism. Economic reliance on huge numbers of English students suggested that there was no likely solution to the problem. The circle of dependence was complete. It was a rout. The University reminded me of Chogoria Hospital in Meru, Kenya. It was a superb district hospital staffed by white people and subsidised from overseas. The local infrastructure could not support it, did not own it and was intimidated by it.

The Secretary to the University sent one of his subordinates to audit the lecture. The Convener of the Chaplaincy Committee appeared and appeared agitated. He interrupted my welcome to ask everyone to say who they were and where they came from. We never did that. People are always free to attend open lectures anonymously. He was afraid that a member of the fourth estate might be present. The usual custom in universities is to listen to a lecture and then share in discussion afterwards. The Convener interrupted me repeatedly and I lost count of the times he did so. After the lecture, a student asked me who the 'wally' who kept interrupting was and the following week I received a letter from a member of the public expressing regret that my main opposition came from New College.

The substance of my talk was a practical application of George Davie's "The Democratic Intellect" to the current situation at Edinburgh University. I criticised the dependence on 'The Oxbridge factor.' I had a double right to do that! I also discussed the place of Christianity in the future of the University. I tried to point out what happens when a great academic institution leaves its spiritual roots and becomes something alien to the history of the culture in which it is set. I pointed out that the prevailing atheism and agnosticism of British universities may someday be as easily overthrown as was Marxist-communism in the Soviet Union. I concluded that increasing Anglicisation of Edinburgh University was so assumed that questioning Scottish voices seemed to sound discordant notes. I found this unacceptable. I recommended the adoption of a coherent philosophy and theology of corporate identity. I suggested that active recruitment of Scots students and academics should be undertaken to redresses the imbalances. I also suggested a new style of University management with democratic cells throughout the institution rather than centralised line management. I advocated freedom of speech for all University employees. I expressed the hope that the spiritual, ethical and metaphysical dimensions of the Scottish personality would count for something in the direction and ethos of the University. The Convener stayed behind to argue with me for about twenty minutes. There were no further repercussions. Sometime later a committee on 'Scottishness' was set up. I submitted my paper but I was not invited to share my views. In November 1995, figures published showed that Scottish students were increasingly being outnumbered at Edinburgh University. 6,156 out of a total of 14,653 came from Scotland. More than ever Edinburgh University is the first port of call for those who do not make it to Oxford or Cambridge. Colonisation of the Scottish spirit continues unabated.

The Chaplaincy team of Honorary Chaplains also reflected the disproportionate Anglicisation of the University. Honorary appointees reflecting respective denominations, these ministers and priests of local congregations supported the work of the Chaplaincy and mitigated the solitariness of the position by visiting each week for prayer and what is known as 'fellowship' in Christian circles. They also helped pastorally and provided links between the Chaplaincy and local congregations. The Orthodox Chaplain, John Moir was a spiritual example to us all and I found a measure of friendship with two of the Roman Catholics, Rodger Clarke and Tom Kearns. Some of the others were 'wannabes' who referred to themselves as 'University Chaplain' and some others numbered themselves among my detractors. During my tenure twelve Honorary Chaplains participated in the life of the Chaplaincy. Some arrived to replace others who were moving on to other positions elsewhere. Of these twelve, seven were English, one was Anglo-Scots, one was Anglo-Irish, one was Irish, one was Scottish-Hungarian and one was Scots. I found myself constantly rebutting the old chestnuts about Scottish Christianity and countering remarks such as "they have funny holidays up here, I've never been able to get used to them." I did not like being in such a minority in the capital city of my own country. I once asked a senior academic if he knew of any other capital city with such a preponderance of 'strangers'. He thought for a moment and then said in reply, "Puerto Rico."

The problem really is one of scale and the impact the quantitative factor continues to make on Scotland. Individually, English members of staff related to me as well or as badly as did Scots. Some were most helpful and co-operative just as some Scots were not. The real issues are the social, cultural, political and historical consequences of having such a huge Anglicised institution within Scotland. But if Scotland ever aspires to political autonomy, it will require to deal with the stranger within its gates. I would disperse parts of Edinburgh University to other universities in Scotand. Reduced in size, it might begin to serve Scotland with more effect, relevance, intellectual profit and perhaps even with some humility.

## More Lectures

I thoroughly enjoyed preparing and delivering talks and lectures. I received many invitations to do so. In the academic environment it was good to present as good a case as I could for what I believed. The Lesbian and Gay Society invited me to talk to them soon after my arrival. I prepared a detailed lecture entitled "Christianity, Celibacy And Sexuality." I took as my starting point the respective attitudes of the two thieves who were crucified with Jesus. One had berated Jesus for being impotent to help Himself and them. The other had made a moral distinction between them and Jesus and said, "This man has done nothing wrong." I argued that none of us should use Jesus to justify our own conduct. He must be held up as distinct from us or else He is not the Saviour and he cannot be Our Lord. I also traced the Christian Church's teaching on sexuality over the centuries. I suggested updating the commonly understood scale of wrong-doing based on the near two thousand years of tradition. I maintained that sexual abuse of children is the most heinous form of sexual wrongdoing. Consenting adult homosexual practice was placed a few steps down the list. I said that Christian moral teaching had to be taken as a whole. No one particular form of deviance could be isolated and picked upon. It is, however, only in acknowledging that Jesus is not made in our own image that we can find the true path for ourselves in this life. It was a civilised meeting with much discussion after the talk. We were obliged to break up the meeting when the Societies Centre closed for the night.

How extraordinary it was to me that in a University as prestigious as Edinburgh there were no formal lectures on the ethics of scientific research. Developments in reproductive biology are happening so quickly nowadays that a moral and legal framework for our decisions as to what is right and permissible can easily become outdated. Science as the unfettered pursuit of knowledge has been and will continue to be a dangerous enterprise. I shared in setting up a series of lectures called "Biology, Origins And Ethics" with two colleagues in the Faculty of Science, Dr Andy Vinten and Dr John Phillips (later Professor). Attendance of first year students was requested but there was no process to make attendance mandatory. Students with doubts, questions and consciences about our life and world did attend. My own lecture was called "The Ethical Basis Of Life" in which I traced the moral dimension of ancient societies which had influenced our own such as those of Judaism and of Greece. I explained how traditional religions in Africa and North America had ethical dimensions as have the religions of the east. Contrasting this with the history of scepticism in 19th and 20th century Europe and America, I tried to show that the 'end justifies the means' approach was itself a departure from the majority view. I mentioned David Hume and Neitzsche and returned to Christian teaching as the implicit or explicit moral basis of our own cultural inheritance. The do-it-yourself ethics of the eighties and nineties reflected a fragmented society in which scientific research could and in my opinion had in some cases lost connection with a broader moral framework and spiritual view of life.

I also developed a research interest in 'New Age' during my Chaplaincy and gave a number of lectures on the subject. 'New Age' is a supermarket religion including astrology, spiritualism, alternative medicine, therapies galore and even health food fanaticism. It has no consistent ethics and conduct is based on the theory of the comfort zone, that is, whatever you are happy with is right for you. 'New Age' is a representation of the gnosticism of the early Christian centuries and a rejection of the last two hundred years of scientific rationalism in the western and northern hemispheres. The churches have lost people of metaphysical inclination to this phenomenon. It has its own anti-Christian doctrine and is not neutral in its hypotheses and explanations of the world and its unseen dimension.

## The Hebrides

Towards the end of June 1991 I visited the Hebridean islands of Lewis and Harris for the first time. Stornoway was bigger and more beautiful than I had thought it would be and I was surprised by its tree-lined streets and by the presence of teen-agers in number. I called in to greet an old college pal called Roddy Morrison, Minister of one of the churches there. To my surprise he was wearing jeans! He had a lovely wife and two fine children.

Then I discovered the most wildly romantic place ever - the west coast of Harris. With spectacular beaches filled with golden-red sand, 'Caribbean' blue inlets and bays, the grey Atlantic in the distance, sunny blue skies above, the cry of gulls, and only a very few other human beings on the planet, this was a paradise I had not known existed. I exulted. The air was charged with excitement. Why? I could not tell. Some call it 'Hebridean magic.' All I knew was that being near Scarista evoked uncontrollable joy in being alive on earth. I visited the small cathedral-like church at Rodel as I rounded the south and met east Harris's moon-like terrain. Two planets in one. Such generosity. Here were houses built precariously on promontories. You could not take your eye off the road for a second or else you would be off the edge of the narrow, winding, up and down, round and back again single strip of tarmac that reminded you that you were on earth.

Thence by ferry to North Uist and to Benbecula where I was to stay with the Minister of my childhood, Rev. Colin McKenzie and his wife and family. He drove a Lada which he praised fully. I had a store of Lada jokes which I strung out over my stay of a few days much to the amusement of his wife and much less to his own. I climbed Ben Mhor on South Uist on the Sunday after Holy Communion. A huge golden eagle rose up only yards in front of me. Great wings beat slowly as this glorious bird took its departure with immense dignity like some monarch leaving a public gathering. And the view from the summit was glorious and I knelt and prayed. But on the way down the bog exhausted me as I waded ankle deep and waist high in rushes. Twenty seals and pups were basking near Eriskay on another glorious day. Crab and prawn fishers were hauling in great catches. I wondered how the ocean could sustain such hoovering. Surely greed will have its recompense. But - each generation takes its chance. A good salary is not spurned anywhere. The standard of living is good on these islands, as far as I could see and if there was remoteness, there seemed many compensations. What it is like in winter I do not know - nor winter after winter. And Barra was beautiful too. Every Hebridean island is different in character and in geography. Barra is soft and sunny and gentle. I walked all the way to Castlebay, basking in the high summer warmth. I loved the petrol-blue waters beyond the clean white sands.

## Fasting

I began 1992 with some days of fasting and prayer and thinking and reading. I retreated within myself. I did not like what I saw. It seemed as I reflected on my life that I had always been snookered wherever I went. People and events had conspired against me to limit my ministry to what was tolerable for them. Not for me. I bore within myself the contradictions and stresses of such enforced compromise. And my own sinful nature. I hoped for some moment in life when there would be a spiritual release for me and I would be able to live as myself and perhaps be of better service in so doing. I sought no position of power as such. I have never wanted to dominate others. Portions of my interior life seemed unredeemed. I was possessed of an overwhelming sense of not having fulfilled the truest possibilities of my calling.

I listed my blessings and there were more than I expected. Health, God's general providence over me, a reasonably well-ordered life, an excellent job, real prospects, a caring family, the special friendship of Jesus Christ, a place to stay, a motor car, a little money in my bank account, over sixty Christmas cards, helpful contributions to people in need in Kenya through the Weir Trust, some very good friends, brilliant colleagues, daily amusements and humours, the eternal hope of forgiveness and salvation in and through the life, death and resurrection of Jesus Christ. Not bad.

I found great comfort in reading Psalm thirty-seven. I began the year as I had wished on my knees in prayer, repentance, intercession and with hope. I put my life into God's hands. I felt powerless in myself to achieve what I wanted in the service of my Lord. I depended upon divine Grace and on the fulfillment of God's own promises to many throughout the ages. Rested, rejuvenated, forgiven, healed and blessed, I could not wait for the new term to begin.

## Conferences

Shortly after my arrival, Professor John Dale had given a talk entitled "Universities And Public Esteem" at King's Buildings in our Thursday Lunchtime Series. He had traced the decline of public respect for the university system of education. I thought that what he was saying was important and deserved a wider audience. We formed a steering group and planned a Conference for November 1989. I worked very hard to ensure that it was a success. Although ninety-five people attended, I thought that the University community could have been more responsive. Chaplaincy things were not taken too seriously. Academics are a snobbish lot. They support their own. The generalist approach of the non-specialist was looked down on. Even the University Information Office was less than helpful. I decided not to have long formal speeches but to have short to-the-point summaries of the main issues followed by equal amounts of plenary discussion. The formula worked.

The following year another Conference entitled "Scottish Universities In The 1990's" was held supported by sponsorship from 'The Scotsman' newspaper in the form of articles publicising the event as I had requested. One hundred and twenty-two people attended. A by-product of the organisation was an enjoyable business lunch in the Staff Club with the Editor of 'The Scotsman' Magnus Linklater, the Principal of the University Sir David Smith, James Seaton, the redoubtable Owen Dudley Edwards, Dr Ian Campbell (later Professor) and others. The point was made that the segments of Edinburgh society did not seem to talk to each other or co-operate as well as they might. I recalled that Edinburgh's city leaders had attempted to copy Glasgow's great success with its 'Glasgow's Miles Better' slogan by marketing its own uninspiring and quickly forgettable 'Include Me In' equivalent. The experiment had failed miserably.

In 1991 we organised a Conference called "Managing Change In Higher Education." Michael Forsyth, later Secretary of State for Scotland agreed to speak and this added considerably to the attraction. One hundred and eighty-five people attended, representing schools, colleges and universities from all over the country. This was a gratifying response. It was also noted that the Conference had been held at a time when Edinburgh University was suffering an onslaught of bad publicity due to financial mismanagement. It must have seemed like bravura indeed. Dr Ronald Crawford of the Committee of Scottish Higher Education Principals said later that the conferences of 1989, 1990 and 1991 "had been important for Scottish education and had put Edinburgh University Chaplaincy on the map."

The work of the Chaplaincy was burgeoning and I saw no prospects of organising another Conference in 1992 unless I was given extra secretarial staff. My excellent secretary Christine worked well beyond the conditions of her contract to help make the conferences successful. It was not possible even to ask for another member of staff in a climate of cut backs and I recognised that. I handed over organisation of future conferences to the Centre For Continuing Education which had been involved in the conferences so far. The 1992 Conference attracted less than half of the number who attended in 1991 and in 1993 a half-day Conference attracted fewer still. Instead of moving outwards, the conferences had become more specialised, a fact which Dr Ronald Crawford regretted.

In February 1993 with the help of another steering group, I organised a Conference entitled "The Ethics Of Genetic Engineering" which was a pleasing success and received extensive reporting in the 'Times Higher Education Supplement.' I thoroughly enjoyed being part of these conferences. Even the Information Office had begun to take them seriously. They were not intended to be 'money-making' ventures but a service to the academic community. Fees were low and generous hospitality was offered, but there was no financial loss to the University.

## Czechoslovakia And East Germany

In June 1992 I flew to Holland and met up with my former colleague in Kenya, Albert Juffer. He and I, his son Anne-wym and his friend then departed on a camping trip to Czechoslovakia and East Germany. It was a step back in time. Empty roads and huge factories with no-one present, dull and dirty buildings with unpainted windows, criminal pollutions of the air - these were my first impressions. Abrogation of personal property responsibilities contrasted unfavourably with Holland's manicured and weedless gardens, brightly painted houses and well tended infrastructure. Did anyone really think that undiluted communism was good for the human spirit? Prague's jazz players and trinket sellers on the King Charles Bridge welcomed visitors but after Rome, Prague's churches were modest. Government buildings were unspectacular. The chiming clock with its skeleton sculptures signifying vanity attracted many.

Heading north we visited Terezin Concentration Camp. It was small in comparison with other more infamous places but it had been no less lethal in its institutionalised barbarity. In their extremities, the inmates had defied fate by scrawling humorous cartoons where they could. The overall impression was sobering and sickening. European civilisation was ever but a veneer. Underneath was macrocosmic bestiality. And fifty years afterwards in the former Yugoslavia identical traits were again hung out for all to see.

East Germany seemed poor. Roads were bad. People drove Skodas and Trabants. Berlin retained an aura of greatness. The Lutheran city centre Evangelical Church was still bullet-marked from the Second World War. The wasteland near Hitler's bunker seemed strangely pointless - a contradiction to the organised evil that had once been disseminated from that locus.

The Brandenburg Gate was magnificent as were the museums and opera houses and public buildings in that part of the city. I bought my piece of the 'Berlin Wall' to bring back as a souvenir.

## Humours

Scarcely a day went past in my time as Chaplain without some laugh. The stresses and pressures of modern higher education weigh heavily. My attempts to lighten loads were not always pastorally conventional. On one occasion, I telephoned a colleague, imitating the voice of a police constable and informing him that he was to be prosecuted for driving a Fiat Uno. This, I said, was anti-social behaviour and carried a large fine. There was a deadly silence. Eventually I broke it with a peal of laughter. "Thank goodness it's you," he said, "I was speeding on my way to work this morning and I thought for a minute that they had caught up with me." The coincidence made the joke more valuable than I had intended. Sometime later I devised what looked like a parking ticket and placed it in a cellophane wrapper on the windscreen of the same colleague's car. He had just been given a chair in his subject at another university. The ticket read "Fixed Penalty £150" and when he opened it up it continued "Incommensurate with new academic status."

Dr Ian Campbell was a fund of hilarious stories and Owen Dudley Edwards could always be relied upon for a witty and sardonic slant on everything. Dr Hugh Montgomery's sense of humour brightened every Thursday Lunchtime Talk at King's Buildings. Typical of his humour was the story of an unpopular colleague who had retired but kept coming back to his former Department. Scrawled on the door of the office he used one day were the words "Forgotten but not gone."

I thoroughly enjoyed the company of the servitors. Poorly paid in my view, they nevertheless counted among their numbers men of skill and success in previous occupations. One chap called Hughie suffered from a breathing condition. Sometimes he looked quite ill. He could not give up smoking. I had not seen him for some weeks when I literally bumped into him on a corner in one of the passages in Old College. "Are you still alive?" I asked. "Indubitably," he invariably replied. It was his favourite word. "Amazing!" was my wondering response. This became a long-running joke with him suggesting that I could not wait to bury him. But I was genuinely surprised and delighted when I was able to say "Hughie - imagine you seeing 1994."

I remember driving my car out of Old College just after five o' clock one evening. I waited a long time behind the car in front which was being driven by another servitor whom I knew. I blasted on my horn in mock anger. In response he shot out into the flow of traffic narrowly missing a bus. Next day everyone enjoyed the joke except me. I learned to my chagrin that the poor man suffered from a heart condition. Providentially the Chaplaincy servitor was called Robert C. Anderson. I used to call him 'Rab C Anderson' after the television character. He confessed to me that the 'C' actually stood for 'Catholic' although he had been lapsed a long long time. Isa, our cleaning lady was a woman well past retiral age, of strong views and opinions and equally strong language. One morning in my office she was offering her customary diatribe when her throat became parched. I glanced at the bottle of sacramental wine on the bookshelf which was kept for communion services and offered her a plastic cupful. This allowed her to continue with her indignations. It was all right. I had bought the wine at the Catholic bookshop on The Mound. It was approved by the Scottish Hierarchy.

The Chaplaincy team shared the occasional humour. We used to meet for weekly prayers. Early one Friday as I awaited the brethren, I was amusing myself by playing the jazz theme "Lullaby of Birdland" on the Chapel piano. A more spiritual person would have been meditating or playing a hymn! Then I heard a noise and turned round and spied the two Honorary Roman Catholic Chaplains, Rodger Clarke and Gilbert Markus coming through the auditorium door. I said to myself, "Crivvens, there's the Dominicans - I'd better play something religious." I could only think of "Ave Maria" and began playing. Whereupon the two fathers began to dance a Viennese waltz together round the auditorium.

During the 1993 Edinburgh Festival Fringe there was an exhibition of paintings and photographs in one of the rooms in the Chaplaincy Centre. Unlike everything else in the venue, it had not received a review. I wrote a spoof review under the name of the 'Stornoway Gazette' and posted it with the other genuine notices. It contained sentences like "The exhibition is well planned leading the viewer automatically to the cash till." Fascinating it was to see the *cognoscenti* stop and read it, murmuring their approval. I also sent a spoof letter to an exhibitor asking if it would be possible for H.R.H. Prince Charles to view his exhibition during his forthcoming visit to Edinburgh. The letter-headed notepaper was too convincing. I had a hurt ego to attend to.

These anecdotes are simply examples of the fun that I shared with others throughout my tenure as Chaplain. Chaplaincy may have its crosses but one has more than a measure of personal freedom and the space to live a more natural existence than in the parish. In spite of the spiritual suffering - I thoroughly enjoyed the whole time.

## Refurbishing The Chaplaincy Centre

Prince Charles would have abhorred the Chaplaincy Centre. It was another of those soulless hangar-like concrete boxes reflecting seventies architecture. The main auditorium had never functioned as its name suggested it might. Experts had suggested that its acoustics were among the worst of any modern building in Edinburgh. An office file going back many years showed my predecessors' repeated ideas and schemes to try to do something about it. Nothing had even got off the ground. I initiated an appeal to raise funds to install a lowered false ceiling constructed of acoustic tiles which would be complemented by a new lighting system. Other facilities in the Centre also required standard upgrading. It was not easy to raise the required money. Historical barriers had to be overcome. The Chaplaincy had no reputation such that would attract funds quickly. The University Development Office's Director, Dr Diana Henderson was very positive and most helpful. Without the dogged persistence of Bryan McClure and a £5,000 donation from the University Development Trust, the project would have failed. £18,000 was raised in total and this was enough to complete the project. Colleagues from the Works Department of the University were also most helpful. Bob Prentice designed the new ceiling which was intended to absorb the sound vibrations which had inhibited communication. John Calder's lighting system brought a warm and welcoming ambience to the place for the first time in its existence. The project was more successful than we had hoped. It was a great occasion when at the beginning of the October term in 1991 students were welcomed into the newly refurbished auditorium. Classical musicians playing in the auditorium during the 1993 Edinburgh Festival Fringe especially commended its value.

## Tiree

In August of 1992 I gave myself a little respite from preparing for "The Case For Christianity" by driving to Inverness and then across to Gairloch. It was always difficult to find a single bed and breakfast facility in Scotland. But in the evening the setting crimson of the sun in the far far west gave way to a huge silver lunar orb above highlighting the grey black hills and mountains. And the passive sea loch stretched content around the little highland village. I slept like a top. Next day I found that Torridon's midges were so appalling that I continued south. I reached Oban. I noticed a sailing schedule for Coll and Tiree and realised that I had time for a brief visit to these islands for the first time. I had also managed to book accommodation on Tiree. MacBrayne's 'Lord of the Isles' took us passengers through the Sound of Mull to the nearer Atlantic. This was a magical enough journey in itself with castles on Mull and remote villages on Ardnamurchan on either side. The 6 00am sail meant that the sun began to rise while were were but half way on our voyage. There was no wind and so it was like passing through a fairy-tale. In mid-winter gales, I dreaded to think how it must be for the real people who lived there. In the passing Coll looked to be a bare place but over Tiree peace and warmth and sunshine reigned. And in the afternoon I began the walk to the south-west of the island, to the Civil Aviation Authority radar station, passing interesting houses with thick walls and roofs which did not overlap but instead stopped on the inside. And each generation had built a newer addition to the old so that three or four generations were represented in the architecture of the original black house, added to and upgraded twice and three times. And now European Economic Community money brought new roofs and stone cladding and electrical rewiring and everyone was pleased.

I climbed through the purple heather and half-way up the small hill and stopped in utter peace and blissfullness. There was not another soul in sight. From the little valley-niche, no other building could be seen. I knelt down and prayed. I discarded the detritus of my life and unburdened my soul with tears. I then turned over and lay in the heather on my back, facing out towards the Atlantic. I drifted into a kind of spiritual dream. The warm sun beat on my body and the warm Presence of the Holy Spirit hugged and cuddled my being. I felt invaded by an overflowing power of cleanliness, forgiveness and divine love. It was one of the most remarkable and lovely experiences in my entire life - so strong was it - so needed - so unexpected. I cannot forget it. Friday 14th August, 3 00pm!

I enquired about Professor Donald Meek's home and was told where it was. And when I reached the mainland again, I took the long route home via Lochgilphead, Inveraray, Crianlarich and Stirling before returning to Edinburgh after my fabulous short break from responsibilities and tasks yet to be accomplished. And I felt like a trapped animal after the call of the spiritual wild.

## The Case For Christianity

It had been many years since Edinburgh University Chaplaincy Centre had organised a university mission. The liberal tenants of the seventies and eighties were not interested. I felt that something had to happen during my tenure. I had in mind not a 'Billy Graham' type of mission but one which would challenge the establishment and orthodox agnosticisms of university life. The objective was to present "The Case For Christianity" on a level playing field, meeting and debating non-Christian interpretations of life. A sound steering committee of staff and students prepared the groundwork. I had to lead from the front. Had the enterprise got bogged down with ecumenical and theological politics or church party divisions, it would never have taken place. Opposition to 'mission' is more likely to come from liberal church insiders rather than from those outwith the churches. I thought that it was essential to raise the entire funding required from outside the University. The institution was suffering severe financial restraints at that time. It would have been hard to justify doing otherwise. There was no money anyway! I also thought that those opposed to Christianity whether from the agnostic point of view or from another faith perspective might consider University financial sponsorship of a mission as undesirable. In the sense that the University Chaplaincy was organising the mission, it was a University event.

"The Case For Christianity" was presented to the University in November 1992. The broad coalition of ecclesiastical and theological opinion which I had fostered held together. There were some anxious moments when it looked set to splinter. Rory MacMillan, a law student was helpful at a crucial moment. Andrew Wilson was also supportive. There was sufficient trust in my intentions for the mission to succeed. We were united by the vision of reaching out to the non-Christian University community. Each of us had to put certain aspects of our own understanding and preferences aside temporarily and concentrate on the main issue in hand. A measure of self-denial was exercised by everyone involved and without that "The Case For Christianity" would never have been made.

Two years of delicate planning succeeded. The budget of £9,000 was raised from outwith the University. My idea of using a leaping salmon as a logo suggested vitality, extraordinary achievement and a realisation that Christianity is not only struggling against the tide in today's society but requires supernatural inspiration to survive. We used the University's corporate colours for our publicity. A newspaper with biopics and articles, Alex Noel Watson's cartoons and a hilarious send-up of academia by Bill Shackleton was distributed to as many places as possible. The Principal agreed to offer a word of commendation as did the Rector Donny Munro.

More than three thousand five hundred people attended the lunchtime and evening meetings during the eleven day outreach. The highlights for me were the public debates in the McEwan Hall on "The Case Against God" and "The Case Against Jesus Christ," and the science and religion presentations. In addition, 'New Age', sexuality, literature, church leadership, ecology, politics, music, psychology, other religions, feminism, Biblical authority and the truths of the Christian faith were discussed. Distinguished guests such as James MacMillan, Lord Ronald King, Lord Kemp Davidson, Bishop Mario Conti, Episcopal Bishop Holloway, Brian Souter, Daphne Hampson, Donald Macleod and more than forty others took part. Charlotte Baptist Chapel sponsored a Romanian evangelist called Doru Popa to bring a refreshing perspective to the mission. He came to us as a suffering servant and his testimony of persecution under communism and of recent liberty was so authentic that those who heard him were humbled.

I had hoped that the lectures, debates and discussions would act as feeders to the closing rally. This did not happen in the way I had envisaged. People came to the parts of the outreach in which they had an interest. One student summed up the response of many, "I know what a mission is; I don't want to be converted just now; I do want to learn what the issues are." Someone else said, "I wish there had been something like this when I was at university." It is a false perception that Christians compartmentalise their minds. We were able to demonstrate that Christians in the nineteen-nineties have the highest intellect and expertise in many fields of human interest. Christianity as a living force has much to say to the concerns of today's world.

One of the loveliest aspects of "The Case For Christianity" was the contribution of Christian students. In their white with red and blue 'Leaping Salmon' T-shirts they were helpful ambassadors for Christ. They conducted themselves with dignity and thoughtfulness, with commitment and maturity, with enthusiasm and with grace and many people commented on their presence throughout the mission.

There were real disappointments. 'The Scotsman' newspaper and the 'Evening News' ignored this unique event, as did B.B.C Television and Scottish Television. B.B.C. Radio Scotland did publicise "The Case For Christianity" on more than one occasion. Students often get a bad press. Minorities of politically motivated people manage to grab headlines from time to time. Here was an opportunity to redress the balance. The percentage of students attending individual events during "The Case For Christianity" meetings varied between ninety and fifty per cent. Unsurprisingly, the church leaders Question Time attracted the lowest percentage of student attendance. The mission had been designed for the entire University community. There was a significant student response. A new dialogical style of Christian communication was attempted. Here was no 'talk-down' evangelism, no 'take it or leave it' attitude. Christianity at the end of the second millennium was meeting its adversaries on their own territory, giving them the opportunity to make their points and offering a constructive and credible account of its reasons for holding to Faith in Jesus Christ. "The Case For Christianity" made its mark beyond the University of Edinburgh and similar outreaches were held elsewhere.

I thought that it was something of a miracle that "The Case For Christianity" mission had actually happened. Throughout the planning and organisation there had been no real traumas or worries. Nothing else that I ever planned had caused such little stress. I felt borne on wings as if the mission was the work of another Person. I believe that it was. After the mission was over I felt myself carried on a tide of spiritual warmth and happiness. It is an immeasureable joy to be within God's will even if one has to return to lesser things thereafter.

## Christmas Carol Service

The Edinburgh University Annual Carol Service was held in Greyfriars Church in early December each year. Members of the University read lessons and everyone sang carols. The Chaplain opened the service with a welcome and closed it with the Benediction. In 1989 it was a pleasant if somewhat uninspiring experience. Six hundred and twenty people attended. Students later suggested to me that I should give an affirming address and I agreed to do that next year. In 1990 I introduced the Salvation Army City Corps Band because the Greyfriars organ was out of service while being replaced. I was also making a social statement in doing this. The Salvation Army is associated with the best of Christmas in the public mind and with concern for the poor and the outcastes of our society. Therefore I wished to remind our elite community of the outside world.

I asked leaders of Christian student societies to read lessons rather than faculty representatives who may or may not have had any Christian commitment. These three changes transformed the Carol Service. In 1990 and 1991 numbers increased and Greyfriars became uncomfortably full with people sitting on steps and on the floor unsighted and not really part of a worshipping congregation. The University had instituted an administrative scheme to make ten per cent savings across the board. When announcing that coffee and mincemeat pies were available after the Service, I added concerning the latter, "However, they are ten per cent smaller than last year." The Principal Sir David Smith, a man whose great tolerance I must have tested said to me afterwards "At least you can laugh at it, Robert."

I decided that it was time to return the Carol Service to the McEwan Hall, the University's main auditorium, used mainly for graduations. I did not intend that the Carol Service should be anything other than a Service of Worship. I did not want it to become again an example of Edinburgh's own demythologising syncretism - a Carol Party - that is Christmas without God. It took one year to persuade the Chaplaincy Committee to allow me to do this. The Convener was doubtful and did not want to offend Greyfriars. Another New College Professor, Gibson by name, expressed doubts as to whether the change would be justified. However in 1992 the Carol Service returned to the McEwan Hall. It was good to have the University organist, Dr John Kitchen because of the range of his musical empathies and his excellence. One thousand five hundred people attended. So many more students came because they identified themselves with a University occasion.

My address began with the statement "The results of a recent survey on the subject of Christmas were published in 'The Scotsman.' Young people between the ages of 13 and 20 stated by a large majority that it was the spiritual and moral meanings of Christmas that are really important." There was a place for humour and I included a local application of the well-known parody of the disciples of Jesus. I read a 'letter' as follows...." From Magi Management Consultants PLC (for the University was in the hands of management consultants at the time) to Jesus of Nazareth:

Dear Jesus,

Our representatives called just after your birth. Over the years
we have kept a discreet interest in your progress and we are
now renewing our professional relationship. It is our opinion
that the twelve men that you have picked to manage your new
organisation lack the background, education and vocational
aptitude for the type of enterprise you are undertaking.
According to their star charts they do not exercise team spirit,
being totally incompatible with one another. Simon Peter shows
emotional instability and is given to fits of temper. His brother,
Andrew, reflects no qualities of leadership. The other brothers,
James and John, place personal interest above company loyalty.
Thomas demonstrates a questioning attitude that would tend to
undermine morale. We also feel it our duty to inform you that
Matthew has been blacklisted by the Greater Roman Association
for Banking and Income Tax (GRABIT) for exceeding his monthly
quotas. James, the son of Alpheus, and Thaddeus have radical
leanings, and both registered high on the manic depressive scale.
One of the twelve, however, shows great potential. He is a man
of ability and resourcefulness, and has a keen business mind. He is
highly motivated and ambitious with contacts in high places. For these
reasons, we would suggest that you make Judas Iscariot your chief
adviser and right hand man. Wishing you every success in your new
adventure, Yours etc...."

I preached the redeeming Christian Gospel before concluding with the words " The Christmas Story of the Birth of the Saviour Jesus, who was born, who lived, who died and rose again from the dead and is present here with us this evening in and through the Holy Spirit, is the only thing of unsullied romance and true goodness that this world has ever known. I say to you then 'If you want to be the right person, at the right time and in the right place, then confess yourself a Christian this Christmastime and throughout your life.' Amen."

The satirical letter was not lost on colleagues. In view of the internal politics which afflicted me following the University Mission and throughout 1993, the parody was an exercise in dramatic prophecy. But there was an indescribable joy in asserting the truth of the Christmas Story at University Annual Christmas Carol Services and for the remainder of my life I will remember the ecstasy evoked in my heart by the sixty voice University Choir, the full sound of the McEwan Hall organ, the Salvation Army brass band and one thousand five hundred voices raising up together the loveliest of Christian hymns and praising the Living God in the Incarnation of Jesus Christ.

## Leaping Salmon Theatre

For many years the Chaplaincy Centre had been a venue for the Edinburgh Festival Fringe. By the early nineties the Fringe had grown and changed. It had become more commercially competitive and the quality of events and performances had become more variable. The University Conference Office let the Centre directly to theatrical groups. The Chaplain had no responsibility for the choice and suitability of groups or performances. The result of this management style was that increasingly undesirable theatrical companies were allowed to hire the Chaplaincy Centre for the three weeks of the Festival Fringe. It was hard to function as a Chaplain when the Centre became a mini-theatre. During the summer there was always a continuation of pastoral work. People came in for counselling, advice, the arrangement of marriages and other pastoral requirements. Post-graduate students dropped in for a little encouragement from time to time. I had noted in early annual reports that the situation during the Festival Fringe was not tolerable but I had received no backing and nothing had been done.

In 1992 things came to a head. Once again, the Chaplaincy Centre had been let to a theatrical company without any consultation with me. Under pressure to make a commercial success, the London-based company decided to use every available space within the Centre. They decided to use the Baird Library as a coffee bar. I was not amused. I thought that this was a desecration. I refused to allow them to do so. I informed the University Estates Office and I was asked to reconsider my opposition to the let. I declined to do so. They investigated the matter and then told me that the theatrical company had threatened legal action if they were not allowed to use the Centre as they wished. It transpired that the contract was so badly worded that the University could not have defended such legal action. I was therefore asked to allow the let to continue on the understanding that in future letting policy in relation to the Chaplaincy would be reviewed.

The Fringe began. The entire Centre was taken over. Productions included a woman giving astrology sessions and female strip-tease late at night. The Chaplaincy servitor thought that the latter show was worth seeing. However, I did not take his advice. I do not like the reactionary 'shock-horror,' knee-jerk attititudes sometimes associated with Christian Churches. I do not regard myself as a prude. But I did not think that these types of performances were appropriate for the Chaplaincy Centre of Edinburgh University. During the summer of 1992 I was in the latter stages of organisation for "The Case For Christianity." I was raising money throughout Scotland to cover the costs. All Fringe events receive publicity in the national press for the three weeks of the Festival. I received enquiries as to what was going on in the Chaplaincy Centre. It was hard to persuade people that I had absolutely no control over how the Centre was used during the Festival Fringe.

It was the treatment of legitimate users of the Chaplaincy Centre which offended me more than the poor quality of the productions. This theatrical group expected everyone entering the Centre to purchase a ticket for a show. Otherwise they prohibited entry! Members of a wedding rehearsal party who had an appointment with me were turned away one Friday evening. I found the poor folks wandering along the street. A post-graduate student whose thesis I was supervising was asked for money when he came in to keep an appointment. A middle-aged woman who was talking to me about her violent husband was also asked to buy a ticket for a show. The Greyfriars Church Officer was accosted with the words, "Where the hell do you think you are going?" I did not escape. I myself was asked to pay to enter my place of work!

I thought that the best way for future years was that I should run the Centre as a Festival Fringe venue myself. Neil Oliver, the Director of Estates agreed to allow me to do so in 1993. I knew nothing about the theatre. I decided to use a secularised version of the mission logo and so "Leaping Salmon Theatre" was born. This touched people's imagination. I decided that "Leaping Salmon Theatre" should have two points of identity, Christianity and Scottishness. I wished also to avoid heavy theatre props and "canned" music and to offer light, bright settings and acoustic music where possible. I had some contacts with people in the Christian arts scene. Ian Fraser of the School of Scottish Studies put me in touch with James McDonald Reid. This was a stroke of genius. Jamie had many contacts in the theatrical world and together we produced a programme of productions which suited our vision and purpose.

The 1993 Fringe Festival was great fun. For the first time I had control of the venue. The reviews of our productions were favourable. Some were received with enthusiasm. Budding playwrights were given the opportunity to present their work. We operated on a profit-sharing basis which meant that artistes did not have to fork out large sums of money in advance. I owed it to the University not to make a financial loss. In the end, there was a modest profit. James McMillan and Sir Peter Maxwell Davies came along to hear the superb young Moriarty Saxophone Quartet. James McDonald Reid's "Sgeul" - a combination of Gaelic story-telling, traditional and contemporary music and contemporary dance was very well received.

A touching play on the "AIDS" theme was presented. A local Christian band called "Rock The Boat" featuring the songs of two University colleagues, Alan Murray and Tony Bramley (Applemint Music!) held two concerts and Alan presented his one man show on the theme of the Life of Christ. There were other events and an exhibiton of art and photographs which alone attracted well over a thousand visitors. It was a happy time and I realised why the Edinburgh Festival Fringe is such a stimulating event for all who participate. I found satisfaction in having the Centre properly used. Positive publicity resulted for the Chaplaincy Centre and for the University and the reputation of both were enhanced by "Leaping Salmon Theatre." I knew however that this experiment required years to be established if Christianity and Scottishness were to be identified in the public mind.

## Looking To The Future

In 1992 I had begun to think about my future. It seemed to me that Edinburgh University's Chaplaincy Centre required me to have a longer spell of tenancy than my five year contract allowed. I therefore contemplated seeking renewal or extension of contract. I thought that recent successes would count for something. I hoped that my theological enemies would perhaps have recognised significant achievements. I wondered if I might even receive an apology for the events of 1989. But the internal political struggle resulting in my departure from Edinburgh University was to prove as distasteful and in some respects even more so than that which had accompanied my arrival.

# 8 : Natural Injustice

## End Game

Jesus of Nazareth is known more for the last week of his life than for anything else. His failure made cosmic headlines which have never stopped. The man lost everything, status, family, friends, hopes, reputation, dignity and finally His life. We have the comfort of knowing that that was not the end. He rose from the dead. He was who he claimed to be. He is alive for evermore. But - He had to die an ignominious and painful death first. He suffered religious vengeance, social annihilation and judicial murder. He took upon Himself dimensions of spiritual hatred unknown to us. He stood in the tradition of the persecuted prophets of Judaism. His exposure of spiritual truth brought out the worst in His contemporaries. Their religious hypocrisy became transparent. It was in Jerusalem that the prophets were murdered as in any city where supposed sophisticates live, where the good schools are to be found, where the social networks include or exclude at will, where people dabble in new ideas but don't take much seriously and where the authentic critic is rejected and discarded and finally ostracised. Nothing changes. Edinburgh is as any city ever was. It has its religious establishment. Its members are at ease in Zion. They are most comfortable with their own thoughts. They enjoy their own opinions. Ministers are paid to tell the people what they want to hear. Congregations are dying for the want of truth. No-one cares.

It was hard for me to be an evangelical preacher without a pulpit. Liberal churches did not invite me to preach because I might challenge their complacency. Evangelical churches did not invite me to preach because I did not toe the party line on everything. I had looked forward to preaching in Edinburgh and I was disappointed but unsurprised.

## Familiar Pattern

Wherever my vocation had taken me I had found myself struggling against odds greater than my singleness. I sometimes felt that I had little right still to be alive and marvelled at God's providence over me. I had gone to Edinburgh in 1989 aware of what I was taking on and unphased by anything that I had found there. Confirmed as I was in my scepticism about Edinburgh's Christianity I had allowed myself to consider the possibility of remaining as Chaplain to Edinburgh University beyond my five-year contract. By the end of 1992 much had been achieved. I was still basking in the afterglow of the Mission and the Carol Service. 1993 brought only a process of discouragement, frustration and opposition, designed to prevent me from continuing in my position. If someone is by nature an enthusiast, it is doubly cruel to kick the enthusiasm which drives that person out of his system. I had to be stopped. It had been decided. No reasons given. Everything that happened remains to me a contradiction of what a university should stand for. The issues are important and it is for that reason that they must be explored.

I believe that if any of my predecessors had shown as imaginative an approach to the

Chaplaincy as had been in evidence between 1989 and 1993 they would have been well regarded. I, however, was an evangelical. I had bearded the liberal lion in his own den. What would I do next? I might grow in strength and influence and students might enter the church through the Chaplaincy. Some might confess vocations to the ministry. What the liberals took for granted as their right was to be denied to me. Neither was I to be allowed to live down the controversy which surrounded my appointment. And there would be no apologies from New College for 1989.

## The Contract Business

On Friday 11th December 1992 at 2 30pm in the Lee Room of Old College, I attended a finance planning meeting, chaired by Deputy Secretary Melvyn Cornish. I had resisted the recommendation of the management consultants to the university that the Chaplaincy should become an aspect of student services. To me its contribution was unique, incorporating University worship, education, pastoral care of all grades of staff, students, post-graduates, graduates and the families of all of these. In order to retain its spiritual distinctiveness, the Chaplaincy had to retain its individual departmental identity. Otherwise, the role of the Chaplain would be diminished. This was beyond being simply a personal matter. Edinburgh University needed a strong Chaplaincy.

At this meeting we discussed the following year's projected expenditure for our respective departments. I said, "My own contract expires at the end of March 1994 and I have an open mind on the subject of whether I should stay or go. By the nature of my vocation I require a year to find another job." In the evening, I recorded in my diary, "For the first time also, I raised the issue of my own future and whether or not I should or would leave in March 1994. I am glad to be able to talk to someone about it."

There never was any discussion. The routine spring term Chaplaincy Committee meeting took place on Wednesday February 3rd at 2 15pm in the Chaplaincy Centre. The Convener had been in my office on January 26th and he came to my office again before the meeting on the 3rd February. At neither of these meetings was the issue of my contract mentioned. I had begun to prepare a paper on "The Development Of The Chaplaincy" which I expected to use as part of discussions about my own future relationship to the Chaplaincy.

On Thursday 4th February, while I was working on this paper in my office, I received the following letter:

Dear Robert,

As you know your period of appointment as Chaplain to the university comes to an end on 31st March 1994. It is not intended that we should depart from the normal practice which is not to renew the appointment.

I have discussed the position with Professor John O'Neill and with Melvyn Cornish and I thought you should know that, subject to the outcome of the forthcoming budgetary round this Spring, we will be taking steps in the Summer to initiate the appointment of your successor.

May I thank you for your energetic efforts on behalf of the University and wish you well both for your final year with us and for the next stage in your life.


Yours sincerely,


Martin


Secretary to the University


My immediate reaction was one of great anger. I was appalled by the trivial and immature tone of the letter. It was the fact that this decision had been made without any discussion with me having taken place. This was probably illegal in terms of employment law - but I did not know that at the time. In 1995 Glasgow University was found guilty of illegally terminating the employment of short-term contract staff on the very grounds of lack of proper consultation. In terms of the civilities and courtesies which universities attempt to portray, this procedure fell far short of what was proper. As to the Convener's role - I cannot say in print what I felt. John O'Neill had known that this decision had been made. He was party to it. He had not prepared me for it. If he had considered the possibility that I might seek a second term, then this was his incompetent and cynical strategy to make sure that it did not happen. What hypocrites academics are. They demand that you be polite and not to upset people with your preaching and yet they are blind to their own more grievous handling of relationships. I was incensed that I had received this letter on the day after the Chaplaincy Committee's meeting, thereby circumventing the possibility of my raising the matter for discussion at that meeting. That this was not deliberate I will never believe. It has all the hallmarks of the lowest tactics of academia. A great wrath rose up in me as I looked at my paper on "The Development of The Chaplaincy" on my desk and held the crass and puerile letter in my hand.

I understood the import of this letter for me. It made me a non-person. Opportunities for a suitable post in university or church were proscribed. My liberal predecessor had found a post at Glasgow University. I was an evangelical, single, academically qualified and forty-six years old. I knew it would be hard for me to find a good job. I thought that the treatment I was receiving was unjust. The University of Edinburgh was under no obligation to negotiate an extension of contract with me. But I had made a significant contribution to the Chaplaincy and to the University and by its own standards I would have been as entitled to consideration for extension of contract as any employee who had made an equivalent difference in his or her department. I never expected fairness from people in the Church of Scotland who taught at New College. I did however think that a University which claimed to take the personal and professional development of its staff seriously would at least discuss the possibility of a further term or extension.

I did have a longer term plan for the Chaplaincy. I had expended much time and energy but I wanted to try to grow into and with the position. This would take a longer time. The basis of my plan was to be the writing of a book which would, I hoped, open up new understandings of the possibilities for relationship with God in our time. This would certainly be against the trends of liberalism in western society for the last two hundred years and would contradict the sceptical tradition in theology, philosophy and in the social and human sciences as to the spiritual nature of human life and relationship with our Maker. I hoped that the book would be come an important contribution to human knowledge. It seemed appropriate that I should write the book as Chaplain to Edinburgh University. It was precisely because I would in writing and publishing have become stronger and more influential that I was not to be allowed to remain in Edinburgh University. As an evangelical, I would continue to challenge the status quo. I would always be an outsider. But the combination of evangelical faith with some scholarship would have been unwelcome in that position. Unwelcome to people in New College. Unwelcome to Episcopalians. Unwelcome to liberal Edinburgh Christianity. Professor Duncan Forrester specifically said at a meeting of the Chaplaincy Committee that he did not wish the Chaplain to become an academic. He himself had travelled such a path. It is all right for a liberal to gravitate from Chaplaincy to academia but not for an evangelical. I was astonished at such blindness and prejudice and such determined intention to fulfil personal and private agendas. I had come to Edinburgh in 1989 in defiance of the bigots. They were very sure that they would not let me overstay the non-welcome I received.

When the anger had subsided I found that I bore no hatred nor malice of spirit against anyone though I questioned the conduct of the Convener of the Chaplaincy Committee. I continued to produce my statement about the development of the Chaplaincy. The Secretary to the University agreed to receive the paper and look at it with the Convener and Deputy-Secretary Cornish. I said that that would do no good since they were the three who had already made the decision about my future.

## Internal Politics

Somewhere in the University in 1992 it was decided that there should be a centralised system for allocating University space for teaching. Without any discussion with me, the auditorium and two rooms in the Chaplaincy Centre were included in this system. Policy was made bye-law without reference to those whom the policy affected. I regarded this as management of the poorest quality. This style of rule had reduced morale among staff of all grades to pitiable levels. The Chaplaincy had recently been refurbished with much the greater share of the money having been raised outside the University on the understanding that the use of the Chaplaincy would not be changed. To allocate teaching to the Chaplaincy would destroy its value as a spiritual, human and social resource with its own individual and beneficial contribution to the well-being of the University community as a whole. Whereas the Centre always had been used for academic seminars from time to time each week of term, there was a difference between such allocation in consultation with the Chaplain and the direct allocation of regular teaching schedules to the Centre.

The Chaplaincy Committee met to discuss this crisis on September 8th 1992. The meeting was chaired by Professor John Southam in the absence of the Convener who was on holiday. A very strong resolution was passed deploring the scheme to include the Chaplaincy in the centralised system for teaching allocation and for putting unfair pressure on the Chaplain. It was stated that if teaching was to be scheduled in the Centre, its past and continuing purpose and use would have to be abandoned. The Secretary to the University agreed verbally on 11th September that the Chaplaincy's use should continue as normal. However, the real issue was about power. Who controls the University? Is the Chaplaincy to be allowed to deviate from the grey impress of an impersonal management? When people who run universities are frustrated in a matter they find out when the uncomfortable colleague is due to leave. They can be patient. They will have their day.

The University of Edinburgh has an obligation to utilise its buildings as economically and as profitably as it can. The Pierce Commission had said as much. I knew however, that the University administrators could choose to abstract the Chaplaincy Centre from the overall picture in order to let it continue to function as a Chaplaincy Centre. This was justifiable because the Chaplaincy Centre was cost-effective on the service side for the large numbers of students who used its facilities. In a University without a chapel, I hoped that someone with even a modicum of spiritual perception would place a strategic value on preserving the Centre for Chaplaincy purposes. The University Sports Centre functioned only as a Sports Centre. Its function and identity were the same. I thought that the Chaplaincy Centre should be treated in the same way. I knew that other departments cast envious eyes on the Centre's refurbished facilities but that was no good reason, in my view, to unilaterally negate its historic role. The argument was won at that point in time. Martinets do not like to be opposed.

Universities have changed from being simply communities of intellectually seeking people. Now those who control the money supply control everything and everybody. The academic process is subject to accountancy and academics themselves to failed academics who have gravitated to positions of disproportionate and unmerited power. A harmless chaplain is tolerable. Someone who will do his master's bidding. A liberal apparatchik, a known face, an unspectacular grey person who will not shine any light on the machiavellian harassments meted out to decent hard-working staff by people whose competence is in inverse proportion to their salaries. I did not belong. I was not one of them.

No sooner was the issue of allocation for teaching purposes overcome than another similar problem arose. Universities are now under political pressure to function as businesses. They have residential accommodation and meeting rooms and can therefore enter the lucrative conference market. This is good sense. In holiday times there is no reason why university premises should not be let as often as possible for as much money as is possible albeit with respect to those who work there and remaining mindful of the reputation and image of academic institutions.

A "one door" entry policy for conference lettings was introduced. This was another form of centralised control. Edicts arrived determining that control of the Chaplaincy Centre would pass to the Conference Office. As I studied these documents I realised that if I accepted these edicts, which, of course, had not been discussed with me, I would have had to apply for the use of the Chaplaincy Centre's facilities for my own work of ministry within the University. Neither would I any longer have discretion to offer the Chaplaincy Centre for spiritual, educational, humanitarian, social and recreational purposes as I saw fit. No-one seemed to know what went on in the Centre, how often it was used, by whom and at what times. Yet, in my Annual report of 1992, I had included an Appendix giving detailed information of such extensive use. No-one had read it. No-one had come to ask me how the Centre functioned, what it did, who used it, when and how.

There ensued a lengthy correspondence with Deputy Secretary Cornish. He sent three and four page letters on the simplest of administrative practicalities. Was this how he justified his existence? I became exasperated as 1992 moved into 1993 and I found myself wasting precious time replying to what were supposed to be management negotiations. It appeared to me that he did not grasp the central issues. The Chaplaincy Centre deserved to be recognised for its distinctive contribution to University life. Its premises were properly utilised on behalf of the University. The same argument that was used in the struggle to avoid allocation for teaching was employed again, namely, that the Chaplaincy Centre was by definition a Chaplaincy Centre as the Sports Centre was by definition a Sports Centre. A colleague suggested that they were just trying to grind me down. I'm not sure that that was as deliberate as my colleague thought. What was going on was empire building by employees responsible for accommodation and conference facilities. But the effect was the same. Time and energy were diverted away from spiritual and pastoral tasks to combat this ill-thought out scheme to take over control of the Chaplaincy Centre. It set me against the management of the University again. I foresaw that if and when I left, the opportunity would be given to transfer control out of the Centre before my successor took up position as Chaplain. In this way the role and status of the Chaplaincy would be diminished. I am prepared to say that it might have been by default that this would have happened rather than by deliberate intention, but the result would have been the same. At the very least a combination of dreadful management and opportunism would have reduced the autonomy of the Centre, rendering it much weaker in identity and practical availability for the purposes of Chaplaincy. This actually happened after I left the University. In the summer of 1995, the senior officer in overall charge of accommodation and conference letting was dismissed by the University on grounds of impropriety.

I recognised that the moral basis on which the University had accepted donations to build the Chaplaincy Centre in the seventies and to refurbish it in the nineties would be undermined by administrative unilateralism. That was nothing new. The same University managers had sought to sell part of the Torrie Collection of paintings without informing two of the hereditary trustees. It seemed to me that the colonial mentality adheres within Edinburgh University. Colonialists rarely have a feeling for the culture they colonise. It is expendable. It might be tolerated and patronised. There is no "inside" commitment. In consequence, off-hand decisions are made, harmful in the extreme, lacking in understanding and empathy and reducing this great academic institution to internal decay. Edinburgh University's teachers and researchers carry it through time after time. In my view the management is by no means equal to the academic reputation.

## Duplicity Rules Not O K

The paper that I submitted on 31st March 1993 was entitled "The Development of the Chaplaincy." It was ten pages in length. It suggested that the University (ie., the University management) should take a longer term view of the Chaplaincy's development. This might include the provision of a University Chapel. A plea for intellectual autonomy within the pastoral role was made. Control of the Centre should remain with the Chaplain as a responsible officer of the University. "The Case For Christianity" had shown the validity of the Reformed theological tradition with its strong emphasis on explaining things in a credible way. Development such as had been seen since 1989 should continue. The Chaplaincy should remain as an independent department within the University's administrative structure.

On April 21st a meeting took place to discuss the paper. The Chaplaincy Convener was asked why there had been a decision to limit the Chaplain's contract to five years. He replied by saying that Chaplains run out of steam. I countered that response. Two senior professors, McCormick and Miller recommended an extension to my contract. The paper was referred to the Chaplaincy Committee for discussion. Specifically, Martin Lowe the Secretary asked for three items to be addressed, the lack of a University Chapel, renewal of contract for the Chaplain and the role of the Chaplain in relation to the spiritual and welfare needs of students and in Christian outreach. He said to the Chaplaincy Committee Convener at the end of the meeting, "There is funding to continue the post at the present salary."

The Chaplaincy Committee met on 26th May at 4 15pm. The Convener was agitated. His chairing of the Committee throughout my tenure had been less than acceptable. I sat on a number of University committees. On no other committee, did the chair decide the outcome before the meeting took place, talk over every item of business thus inhibiting free discussion, introduce annual reports on behalf of those presenting them and then decide which parts of annual reports should be discussed. The Convener did all of these things.

I had requested that this meeting to discuss my paper should not be chaired by the Convener but by an independent chairperson. I myself stood down as minute-taker. But the Secretary to the University replied to my request saying "I would not presume to advise such a senior and experienced colleague as to his duty in this respect." The Convener had the option to stand down as chair and prosecute his case against me. He did not do so. He prosecuted his case against me from the chair. At the meeting he attempted to have the matters raised in my paper discussed in abstract as if they had nothing to do with me whatsoever. He informed the Committee at the outset of the meeting that the Secretary to the University had already instituted procedures for the appointment of my successor. This contradicted the last words of the Secretary at the meeting of 21st April. One member of the Committee asked to discuss my particular case. The Convener said that that was a new item of business. He decided that I had to leave the meeting. "You have one minute to state your case," he said. I was appalled. I simply asked that any decision should be based on my performance as Chaplain over the past four years.

I was a long time sitting in my office. The longer the meeting went on, the worse it was for me, I knew. At 6 45pm the Convener and Dr Hugh Montgomery came to my office. I was told that the meeting had been adjourned until the 2nd of June, that the Committee was not resolved and that an independent assessor might be asked to look at my own position. The Convener left. I asked "What happened Hugh?" Dr Montgomery told me that they were sworn to secrecy. However, he said that he was so upset that he felt he should tell me what had happened. In my absence John O'Neill, the Convener had raised "charges" against me. These had not been intimated to me at any time and I had been given no right of reply. They had not been substantiated. They were not doctrinal or moral  or anything of that kind. They referred to the controversy at the time of my appointment. I said to Hugh, "So, he can get away with it?" "Yes," he replied, "I'm afraid so." I did not sleep much that evening. I thought that the Convener had been true to his word. He had finished me. I was not surprised at all.

I loathed the childish conspiratorial handling of the Committee and was appalled at the weakness of decent people who sat quietly watching this abuse of position. Why cannot academics ever grow up? What spoilt, petty minded, unjust and dishonest people some of them are.  It was the New College members of the Committee who had done the damage. The Convener was the Professor of New Testament and a fellow Minister of the Church of Scotland. The chairing of this meeting of 26th May did not conform to natural justice. At no time had I ever expected that it would?

Dr Hugh Montgomery resigned from the Chaplaincy Committee on the grounds that he had broken the vow of secrecy. He did this as a matter of personal honour. He wrote a letter of resignation explaining his decision and sent me a copy. I sent a copy of his letter to the Secretary to the University. Dr Montgomery stated in his letter that he felt that I had had a right to know what had been said about me in my absence, that John O'Neill had attempted to sway the Committee against me and that the "charges" could be interpreted in various ways. This was evidence that my request to have the Committee chaired by an independent person had been justified.

I thought that Dr Montgomery's letter would have shown the Secretary that I had not been treated fairly. I actually thought that the Convener would have to resign. He did not do so. He was intent on ensuring that I did not have my contract extended or renewed. How he did this seemed not to matter as long as it happened.

The Chaplaincy Committee met again on 2nd June. The Convener (perhaps under advice) handled this meeting more fairly. I was allowed to be present. There was a civilised discussion on relevant issues and my own position. I was allowed to remain while a vote was taken on my own future. The result was as follows:

| | |
|---|---|
| No extension or renewal | 0 |
| 3 year extension | 1 |
| 3 year + 2 year extension | 10 |
| Tenure | 1 |
| Abstention | 1 |

I felt happy at this decision. Had the Chaplaincy Committee not supported me I would have accepted their verdict. Some of the Committee had known Edinburgh University's Chaplaincy for many years, long before I had arrived. Some had been personally involved in recent projects. The Committee was always broad-minded and representative of the University as a whole. These people were in a position to give good informed advice to the Secretary to the University. External assessment was unnecessary. But it was another line of attack for the Convener.

## External Assessment

The Secretary to the University did not accept the advice of the Chaplaincy Committee concerning renewal of contract for myself. Instead an external assessment, mooted at the first meeting of the Chaplaincy Committee on May 26th and not discussed at the second meeting on 2nd June was contrived as a means to an end. Colleagues warned me about this procedure which no academic liked. I prepared a three-year plan for the Chaplaincy outlining ideas to be implemented should I remain in post. On 15th July I attended a meeting at which I was to be told who the external assessor was to be. "It will be one of the Secretary's cronies, I said to myself." It was - none other than his former colleague at St Andrew's University, Professor D.W.D Shaw. I accepted this against my better internal judgement. I hoped that if he was a just man, there would be a favourable outcome. I also consciously decided that if a liberal were to recommend that I continue, then that would be a helpful factor in bridging the divide between liberals and evangelicals in the Church of Scotland. This was a high risk strategy. But I genuinely wanted peace. If fair-minded liberalism and open-minded evangelicalism could meet and find some common outlook, then I thought that the future of the Church would be healthier. Manipulations by the liberals at successive General Assemblies grieved me. Rumours of an eventual second Disruption pervaded the courts of the Church. There was nothing contrived about my decision. I never saw myself as a liberal or as a conservative evangelical. I did see myself as an evangelical. In matters of doctrine I was with them. In having a calling to confess the uniqueness of Jesus Christ and His Lordship over all, I was with them. In embracing the humanity of Jesus and in advocating non-violence, I was with the liberals. In taking a broad 'catholic' view of creation rather than a dualistic one, I was with pre-Reformation Celtic Christianity. Two things gave me hope and optimism. The Chaplaincy Committee had roundly supported my request to remain as Chaplain and I had just been given a most positive University staff appraisal which also recommended renewal or extension of contract. Dr Lowe had earlier acknowledged that I felt that I would not be given a fair hearing. What dimension of cynicism does this represent?

On Wednesday 29th September I spent two-and-a-half-hours with Professor D.W.D.Shaw. I had originally been given one hour by the Secretary's secretary, an Episcopalian, and I had objected. I was concerned too, that I was only allowed to make my submission in the middle of representations and not at the end, thus being unable to answer points raised against my continuing in post. Neither did I know who else was being invited to testify for or against me. This troubled me more than anything. I would gladly have had an open approach in which I could have replied to criticisms of my performance as Chaplain. I thought that in the interests of natural justice I should have known the case against my continuing, I should have had leave to reply, and then a decision could be made. That did not happen. I still do not know what was said against me during this external assessment. I was particularly concerned that the old chestnuts of 1989 would be dragged up by my unimaginative but determined foes. Here however was the age old game of secrecy, preferences, the abuse of power and the manipulation of people. Academic communities are unreal. They are not subject to sufficient public accountability to order their affairs properly. The external assessment did not conform to natural justice. Why should I have ever expected that it might have done?

Another month went past. It was now October. On 11th December 1992, I had stated clearly that I needed one year to find another job. My contract ended in March 1994. I still did not know where my future lay. The Secretary wrote to say that Professor Shaw had not come to any conclusions but had suggested various options with possible consequences. He never thought to discuss these with me. I was tired of being treated like a second year high school pupil. Why can they not treat you like a man? Correction - like a mature human being! Can you not have a responsible and serious dialogue about important issues with anyone in this life? On Monday October 25th, the Secretary to the University accompanied by Vice-Principal Miller came to my office at 4 15pm. I told the Chaplaincy Secretary in advance what the outcome would be. She did not believe me. Martin Lowe told me that he and the Principal had decided not to extend or renew my contract. He commended me for my work as Chaplain and offered to give an excellent reference for future employment. I asked on what basis this decision had been made. He replied, "I'm not going into that; legally we are all right." He left. Professor Miller remained to chat. I was grateful for his consideration but he had nothing helpful to say. I said, "It is the wrong decision." I was not thinking only about myself but about a University that acts in such a way, about a Divinity College whose teachers suffer so profoundly from spiritual blight, about Edinburgh churches and their miserable tolerance levels of anything that might remotely be representative of living Christianity and about the Church of Scotland, that one of its Ministers should be treated so shabbily.

No-one can do any job without someone somewhere making observations or complaints. The question is whether these are true and whether they justify not extending a contract of employment. Professor Miller suggested that it had to do with New College. I was advised that I could be told who Professor Shaw had interviewed. The Secretary gave me these names in a letter on 2nd November. They were :

> Professor John Richardson
> Professor Duncan Forrester
> Melvyn Cornish
> Professor John O'Neill
> Rev David Beckett
> Quentin Somerville
> Vice-Principal Andrew Miller
> Professor John Southam

What a transparent stitch-up! John Richardson had signed the petition against my appointment in 1989. He was an ex-colleague of Martin Lowe's at St Andrew's. An Episcopalian non-stipendiary priest, he was involved in the Anglican Chaplaincy's unsuccessful contortions to survive as a functioning entity in the University. His local congregation was part of the clique of liberal city centre churches to which few students ever went to worship. Professor Duncan Forrester was the only member of the Chaplaincy Committee not to vote positively for me to remain. He had abstained. Melvyn Cornish was the Deputy-Secretary whose incompetence was partly to blame for the fact that no proper discussion had taken place with me about my future before Martin Lowe had sent the letter I received on February 4th. He was also the officer with whom I had struggled to retain control of the Chaplaincy Centre. Professor John O'Neill was the Convener of the Chaplaincy Committee. Rev David Beckett was Minister of Greyfriars Church. Quentin Somerville was President of Edinburgh University Students Association. I doubt if he took any soundings among the significant Christian student body before making his own views known to Professor Shaw. Vice-Principal Andrew Miller would have advocated an extension of contract for me as would have Professor Southam who had conducted my staff appraisal. Out of eight, five were against me, the student President might have been swayed against me, and only two were for me. How to stack a committee in one easy lesson. You pick the people who will give you the outcome that you want. These people were not representative of the wide-ranging nature of my tenure of the Chaplaincy nor of the University staff with whom I had accomplished a number of important tasks.

## The Sacrifice

I had not been surprised at the decision not to extend or renew my contract. I never thought that it would happen. One of the reasons I wanted to remain had to do with the treatment I had received from the Convener over the previous four years. Had I been given a three year extension, for example, I would perhaps have been able to do my job without interference and bullying. I might even have been able to preach with more freedom though that was unlikely. I would then have left in peace. I wanted that for Edinburgh University, for the liberal congregations associated with it and for Edinburgh's churches more generally. I had hoped that justice would prevail. It did not. Professor Shaw had asked me what would happen if after another three years, I still wanted to remain as Chaplain. I replied that the Chaplaincy Committee would know whether that was appropriate at that time. He did not like that answer. I recalled Father Antony Ross's long tenure of the Roman Catholic Chaplaincy and made the point that credibility takes time just as university departments take time to become established. He really did not like that answer. I asked why it could be such a problem if I wanted to write a book and have a wider ministry. He squirmed. No answer to an open question. How incredible it is that the University of Edinburgh could not allow its Chaplain to foster his own academic development. Had I been going to write about unilateral disarmament or socialist politics, I'm sure that would have been acceptable. But - I was an evangelical. I might write a book about God. That would be terribly upsetting to people in New College, in which the same Professor Shaw had once taught. You see - when people have all the power and all the influence, they are insensitive to real justice. They assume that what they want is right. Spoilt brats they are and slimy as eels. Poor of character and shallow of understanding, they fear anyone of commitment who cannot be bought. And they cannot give equal space. One does not seek favours - only a level playing field. Not given! No doubt the sherry tasted particularly good that evening.

I cannot ever minimise the spiritual burden that was placed upon me by the decision not to extend or renew my contract. I took some punishment in order to take up my post in 1989. I had been bullied and threatened with dismissal for no good reason. I had worked hard and well. I had brought no scandal to the University and had done it much good. All the pain and wounding of the last four and a half years returned and fell on my back. I went through a series of spiritual sobbings and private heartbroken griefs. Where was my God? I was defeated. I had been outmanoeuvred. I had offered up my life and ministry to my enemies and they had not perceived what I had done. I felt used and degraded. I was amazed at the persistence of the adversary. Some of the spiritual wounds of 1991 re-opened. I thought that if I bore on my physical body the wounds that were in my soul, it would be a bloody sight. I recalled famous words:

> **"..we despised him, we held him of no account,**
> **an object from which people turn away their eyes.**
> **Yet it was our afflictions he was bearing,**
> **our pain he endured,**
> **while we thought of him as smitten by God**
> **struck down by disease and misery. "**
>
> (Isaiah 53:3b-4)

I had wanted to remain in university life. Perhaps I might have found a teaching post in time. I knew all was lost. Seeing the names of those who had been interviewed filled me with anger. Once again Episcopalians had had a disproportionately bad effect in my life in the church.

They whom I had tolerated and who shared the Centre, had undermined my opportunity to have a second term. I thought of Glencoe and the Campbells. I was sure that what they had done had weakened the Chaplaincy. New College's influence, disproportionate to their numbers in the University had counted like the tail wagging the dog. All the work I had done throughout the University was countermanded by the in-house theological parochialism of New College. Edinburgh University is large. Over six thousand students belong to the Faculty of Science at King's Buildings alone. The arts and social sciences faculties teach thousands of students. The Chaplain to the University must not simply be the creature of New College. Small and physically remote, its particular occupation gives it an unfair interest. Justice would have allowed me to remain, at least for some time. For all their language of political justice, those who work in New College do not, in my view, represent personal justice.

Relations with Greyfriars might have been a concern. But expediency rather than principle is hardly the basis for the long-term presentation of Christianity to the University. Again, blighted theological liberalism had intervened to my detriment. There was no point in writing a paper on the Virgin Birth and sending it to the Principal! I had tried to emancipate the Chaplaincy from its restricting relationship with Greyfriars and to a certain extent had proved the point that Christianity can flourish if and when it is freed from such enervating theology and worship patterns.

I thought that if the University would have its own chapel on the south side near the halls of residence, and if the worship was suitable for eighteen to twenty-three year old students, it would be a viable aspect of University life. But the University of Edinburgh would not want to turn two hundred years of semi-secularism on its head. Not for me anyway. I appreciate quality in music as much as anyone. But liveliness and informality are essential for relevant worship for young people.

The spiritual good of many students was sacrificed on the altar of Greyfriars Church. This monument to the National Covenant signed in their blood by men who sought spiritual liberty had by the nineteen-nineties become a contradiction of everything that such men had struggled for. Selling plastic souvenirs of Greyfrairs Bobby was very 'low' church to me. Not a few Americans thought that the Church was built in honour of the little dog. By 1993 it may as well have been.

As for the Convener - I cannot imagine what picture he painted in order to get the result he had planned for. All I can say is that someday he will have to answer to God for his treatment of me throughout my term as Chaplain. I do not believe that the decision not to extend or renew my contract was made on a fair assessment of my performance as Chaplain.

The issues were about the University of Edinburgh in the nineteen-nineties, it's image and corporate identity. To some, my appointment had been a mistake. The Principal had allowed me to have a go. I had done my best. There was no obligation to extend my contract. What would it say about the high temple of liberalism if an evangelical was allowed to remain Chaplain for a few more years? It did not matter that the publicity surrounding my appointment had been defamatory and unfair. It did not matter that by the University's own standards of achievement,

I deserved to continue in post. Edinburgh's Chaplain was not to jar with the liberal fundamentalisms of the place. A less distinctive approach would be required in future. Stepping back in time to the seventies and eighties was what was acceptable. Whether this was planned as a way of eventually closing the Chaplaincy remains to be seen. A night watchman might do. I had to be removed.

## Justice Not Seen To Be Done

I was due to present my Annual Report to the Chaplaincy Committee on November 3rd 1993. The Convener had decided not to chair the meeting because he feared being asked about the resignation of Dr Montgomery and had asked Vice-Principal Miller to take over for the meeting. I had been very busy preparing for two University Services which were to be held on 6th and 7th November. The first of these was a Memorial Service for Father Antony Ross and the second was the Centenary Service for the Faculty of Science & Engineering. It was an infelicitous coincidence for me that before any question of an external assessment of my work as Chaplain had arisen I had recommended Professor D.W.D.Shaw as preacher for the latter service! It was an awkward lunch.

On Friday 28th October I spent part of the morning at King's Buildings. On returning to my office I learned that the Convener had attempted to obtain a hand-written copy (which in fact did not exist) of my Annual Report from the Chaplaincy Secretary without my knowledge or consent. This was wholly unethical. I protested to him by telephone. I then wrote to him expressing my views on his conduct and sent copies to Vice-Principal Miller and the Secretary to the University. On Monday 1st November the Convener handed in a written apology to the Chaplaincy Secretary.

I produced my Annual Report and sent it to members of the Committee ahead of the meeting scheduled for 3rd November. I included a 'Personal Statement' at the end of the Report which dealt with 'Freedom of Speech' and referred to the events of 1991. I recorded *inter alia* that I had not been allowed what is generally known as academic freedom or freedom of speech. I stated that after a service in December 1990 I had been told that I could be dismissed and that a similar threat had been made when I had wanted to include a paragraph on 'Freedom of Speech' in my Annual report of 1991. I did not go into details. Then I learned on the morning of Wednesday 3rd November that John O'Neill had resigned as Convener of the Chaplaincy Committee.

The Chaplaincy Committee duly met on 3rd November. The Committee minuted its unhappiness that their deliberations and advice on the length of contract for the Chaplain had been ignored by the Secretary to the University, that no mention of their views had been made and that no reason had been given for the decision which had been taken with respect to my own position. The Committee also minuted that they had not known the remit given to Professor Shaw and they questioned the extent to which he had sounded out the position in the broad University.

The Committee concluded:

"..in relation to the present Chaplain
justice has not been seen to be done."

I felt angry with myself for having let all of this happen to me. I protested in writing to the Secretary to the University that I had not been treated justly. I felt utterly degraded by the whole affair and felt a deep longing to get away from Edinburgh University. I began to look at advertisements for vacant parishes.

I was offered a four month extension to my contract to allow the University more time to appoint my successor. This would also give me more time to find a position but it was still three months short of the year one might take to move into parish ministry in Scotland under the Presbyterian system. I wrote to the Secretary to the University on 16th November sending him a copy of the Chaplaincy Committee minutes and adding, "I am taking further advice about the management of my request for an extension of contract and about the treatment I have received from Professor O'Neill throughout my time as Chaplain."

I had briefly toyed with the idea of making a legal challenge, possibly through the industrial relations court. In writing thus, I did not say, "I am taking legal advice" nor did I mean to imply that in the sense of external legal proceedings. I received an oral communication the next day (November 17th) telling me in disguised and evasive language typical of universities that the offer of an extension of contract would be withdrawn if I did not accept the finality and irrevocability of my position.

It was possible that a legal challenge could have been made on the basis of lack of consultation with me when the original decision to adhere to my contract had been made. I am sure that I have a substantive case against Professor O'Neill for his intimidation and bullying behaviour which resulted in much stress, psychological suffering and psychological damage. Several things prevented me from taking this course of action. Firstly, I am a Christian who tries, however failingly to follow Jesus Christ. His teaching does not encourage legal suit. (Matthew 5:25) Secondly, I did not think that those who had been in charge of my case would tell the truth in any court case. Thirdly, I had no confidence in the legal establishment of Edinburgh to judge my case fairly or objectively. Fourthly, I simply did not have the financial resources to conduct such a law suit. I asked Professor Neil McCormick for his opinion on the matter. Over the telephone he said that his view was that the treatment at the time of my appointment had been unfair and the external assessment had been unsatisfactory but not unfair. I thought these were strong conclusions from a lawyer. I later found out that Professor McCormick expressed himself differently when he was sitting as part of the Central Management Group of the University.

I wrote to the Rector of the University, Donny Munro on 8th December appealing to him against the decision of the Secretary not to extend or renew my contract. I had no real hope of a reversal of the decision. I thought however that it would be interesting to see if the ancient Office of Rector had any residual influence or power. I had supported retention of the Office of Rector when it had recently come under threat. Some held that it was anachronistic to have someone outwith universities elected to chair University Courts. Modern management theory would hardly recommend the continuation of the ancient Scottish practice of protecting the rights of students and staff in this way. I would not wish this example of egalitarianism to be swept away by people who want to be as little accountable as is possible for them to be.

I had by now lost any wish or desire to remain as Chaplain. I thought that it was important not to submit psychologically to the treatment I had received. The issues were serious. They required investigation as much for the University's sake as for my own. A University which treats employees as I had been treated is a great contradiction. As Chaplain, I felt I could make that point although I knew that it would be sacrificial for me to do so. I thought I would give my opponents no rest until 31st March 1994, when my contract (without the four month extension) was due to end. I asked Vice-Principal Andrew Miller "Is the Secretary to the University the servant or the master of the academic community?" He met this question with silence.

John O'Neill sent me notice of a vacancy in the Scots Church, Sydney, New South Wales, in the Presbyterian Church of Australia. I returned it to him forthwith. It is a measure of how completely he had failed to understand me that he should have imagined that I would ever go and live in Australia. Apart from having my aged mother in Scotland, anyone who knows me is aware that in Christ I have an existential relationship with and commitment to Scotland. Whatever is left of me to give, I wish to live out my life here. It is not a rewarding country. The spiritual temperature is cold. The Church of Scotland is riven between liberal and evangelical. There is no peace. O'Neill recognised that as far as advancement in the Church was concerned, I was finished. There would be no academic post and there would be no prestigious charge. How easily is commitment mistaken for ambition One is pigeon-holed and stereo-typed for convenience. I regarded it as a profound and grievous insult that John O'Neill should wish me to leave for Australia while he, an Australian remained in Scotland. His wife, also from Australia and a convert to Roman Catholicism had wanted me to go to America, she had said, some time previously. The pair of them seemed very keen to get rid of me.

The Annual Christmas Carol Service in the McEwan Hall uplifted my spirits greatly. I knew it would be my last. My address was called "O Little Town Of Scotland."

"There is a fine line between true and false religion..
The simplest way of discerning whether a religious
group is good or bad, indeed a congregation or
and individual or even a University more concerned
about its corporate image than the apprehension
of truth, is whether each of these practices freedom
of speech and freedom of association."

I added a funny little monologue based on the lugubrious Scottish television character, the Reverend I. M. Jolly.

> "Hullo, Season's Greetings to you all. I hope you
> are as full of festive joy and exhilaration as I am.
> Ephesia and I had retired the other night. (My
> parishioners wish I would retire for ever) I was
> actually hoping for a little conjugal bliss, but
> Ephesia was reading her horoscope - in the Church
> Times. "Your partner is in need of some emotional
> support just now," she read, and added somewhat
> unkindly, "Yes - and for the last forty years." I got my
> own back. Sitting there in bed, we pulled a Christmas
> cracker. I got both favours. There was one of those
> pithy sayings, 'A bird in the hand spoils the broth'
> and a small plastic hippopotamus. "It looks just like you,
> Ephesia," I ventured. She replied by hitting me on the
> nose with the Church Times. "No conjugal bliss tonight,"
> I concluded, and fell sadly asleep.

That and other humours over I ended the address with the ringing tones of Christianity, savouring the moment of addressing such a large congregation with so many young people present and wondering whether I would ever do so again.

> "There are many people outside and inside the church
> and in theological colleges who will tell you that they
> do not agree for one minute that the Christmas story is
> actually true. Pleasant it may be, beautiful indeed, but
> no more than a folk-tale or a fairy story... I want to
> suggest to you that if you study the kind of people that
> were involved in the nativity of Jesus, that there is a clue
> to the truth of the whole thing. These people were open
> in spirit to the possibility of God intervening in their lives;
> they were not deists, agnostics, or atheists, not into
> nature religion, astrology or the occult. They did not get
> drunk every Friday night. They had no social prominence
> or power. They were not wealthy. It was possible for a
> mighty spiritual work to be done in them because there were
> no psychological barriers to prohibit their response to the

divine calling..It is possible for some people to apprehend the truth of God today. Jesus Christ as God incarnate was born as you and I were born, lived as you and I live, and died because the human community in which he lived could not assimilate him...The gift of faith raises us up above every thing we say and do for a living, for recreation, in personal creativity, in family life. It is the extra dimension, the Grace that is freely given to us to enjoy our lives, to live properly and well, to find our destiny and to live for ever. This utterly unique and precious gift is given to you this evening, in the Risen Jesus Christ. Take it thankfully and hold it in your heart for evermore."

## Procedural Issues

Donny Munro was highly respected and had shown intelligence and strength of character as Rector. He grasped the central procedural issues clearly. He wrote to Martin Lowe on 28th January 1994 and while making some comments and observations, asked the following questions:

"1. At the point where the decision was made not to extend the Chaplain's contract, why was he not called upon to give formal notice of his intention or not, to stand down in the terms of his contract. Also, given that such a key figure within the University was to leave, having instigated many changes with his department/Centre, why was he not called in for discussion as to the success or otherwise of his period in office?

2. Why were the views/recommendations of the Chaplaincy Committee not acted upon with regard to the most suitable period of contract, ie., 5 years, plus 3, plus 2 years, as voted for by the large majority?

3. Given that the Chaplaincy Committee felt that, as they were not the appointing Body, and recommended that the University appoint an External assessor to look into, and make appraisal of the work of the current Chaplain and further that this should be with the intention of reporting back to an Appointment Committee, rather than to Line Management, why was this recommendation not followed?"

Universities are expressions of the human spirit. Academics have a peculiar mind-set. They deal in multiple theories of everything. They find it difficult to make concise decisions. They also wish to survive in the longer term. That requires not sticking one's neck out for anything or anyone. The social dimension of university life necessitates forms of external politeness which involve each person saying what it is thought the other person wants to hear. Thus in one hour you may meet six people and hear in reply to an observation, say, about the weather, "Yes, it is cold," "Yes, it is warm," "Yes, it is very wet," "Yes, it is not raining very much," "Yes, it is windy," "Yes, at least it is not windy today." Even allowing for the proclivities of Scottish weather, and besides, this is just an example, such polite insincerity is bound to lead to chaos when permeating conversations of greater import. Imagine such serpentine conversations being carried out on a wide range of issues in a large academic institution with around two thousand academic and administrative staff! Try to administer such a place. Central management is actually impossible and any attempt to make rail roads for people's thoughts is bound to destroy the essentially free nature of intellectual enquiry and the administration of those institutions which specialise therein. Truly, the right hand doth not know what the left is doing. Conspiracies may or may not be present. It would be hard to grasp an object which is always changing like a chameleon or slithering like a snake. And though it is impolite to suggest so, original sin has not passed by those who work in academia. There is evident a deliberate and calculated insincerity bordering on deviousness with untruthfulness when it may seem expedient to some to be so minded. Further there is social and career murder. It is an invisible crime and its stench is everywhere.

Ideas, opinions, research, findings, and conclusions are the currency of universities. Minds are sensitised. The imposition of any management system will restrict the interactive processes and superimpose a collective weight upon the spirits of all who work in universities. In the age of political correctness, conformity to the flavour of the month will be expected. A single corporate image for a place like Edinburgh University is a blasphemy. Yet - there were attempts to create this and impose it where it was not wanted. What is happening in universities is reminiscent of the killing of the human spirit under communism. The poison asphyxiates; the mental stresses are intolerable. The role of a Chaplain in such circumstances is most definitely, in my view, to speak out and to buck the trend and under no circumstances whatsoever to be part of such a system. Liberal ministers of my Church however time-serve the system without conscience.

Universities are also both stages and battlegrounds for personal careers and ambitions. In this they are no different from any other human organisations including churches. It is not easy to maintain a collegiate atmosphere in a modern university, especially if it is a large and multi-sited university like Edinburgh. One of the great joys of working in a university should be the quality of the democratic participation of its employees at all levels. Management strategy should always be to facilitate the academic process. All support services should have the same aim in view. If management becomes an end in itself to the extent that it cannot admit errors of judgement, actual mistakes in procedure or even partiality in favour of or against particular members of the community, then it becomes a quasi-demonic force which in time must lead to the destruction of the collegiate character associated for centuries with universities. Of course - there has been much skullduggery throughout academic history and much justified with appeals to the Name of Jesus Christ. In the post-Christian era, there is no common appeal to prayer or divine forgiveness or the sacraments. You have gray stale secularism 'personified' in robot like beings with uni-speak and printed edict.

Huge quantities of energy are required to hold on to a semblance of humanity in modern universities. If those in management positions have no spiritual resources other than their own personalities then only abstract and impersonal and anonymous defensiveness prevails. This is countered by personality cults and sycophantic accession to whoever is in vogue for a moment or to whoever has the power to hire and fire, promote and demote, release funds or starve people of resources to do their work properly. Management of universities is probably among the worst of any major employer in the country.

What can a humble and marginalised Chaplain do in such circumstances? Praying for everyone is not enough. Modern universities need a lot of good Christianity. They need a lot of the Living God, of the risen Jesus Christ and of the Holy Spirit. They need a lot of the best type of Christians. A depth of understanding of human nature, a vision of a higher purpose, a broader individual selflessness mark the very best of such people out. Others suffer by comparison. The powerful and influential twentieth century atheistic and agnostic consensus fostered and promoted by British universities may be running out of steam. It may be self-destructing. If Marxist-communism can be defeated without warfare then the atheistic-agnostic consensus of British universities can too. This is no rallying call for what is caricatured as 'fundamentalism.' It is rather a request to invite the cleansing, regenerating presence of the Risen Son of God in all His liberating joy into the lives of academic communities once again and to include the dimensions of existence which His life represents in all explanations of the universe, this world, human nature and behaviour, the arts and theology.

Christianity throughout its life on earth has been fraught with division and schism and disagreement. But Our Maker will not go away. If we could learn to deal democratically with God in our midst we could have the best of all possible worlds. When we leave the Living God out, that does not work. If we usurp God's place, we institute a tyranny.

It is hard indeed to be just to those with whom we disagree. Life in the churches is conspicuous for its lack of personal justice and this leads to abuse in positions of power. One need not sign or repeat any creed to work in a university. Sadly, however, one concludes that for all the rhetoric of corporate idealism, justice is as much lacking in universities as it is in the churches or anywhere on earth.

# 9 : The Establishment And The Kingdom

## Without Honour

Vice-Principal Andrew Miller, who was sympathetic to me said one day, "The Establishment has ways of dealing with people like you." How often is it said, "You can never beat The Establishment." It is possible. It depends how you understand and how you value your life, what is important to you and to what extent you have been true to yourself. Christians have a greater loyalty than that of social acceptance or peer recognition. This requires being faithful to whatever vision of spiritual truth one has been given. Perhaps this is not fully possible in paid employment. Perhaps it is not possible in the church. It may require the abandonment of dependence upon the attitudes of others to be true to Jesus Christ. I would have thought that Edinburgh University might have been able to cope with a spiritual challenge. It is a big place. Unfortunately it has some small minds and great egos, complicated in some cases with religious falseness. When I applied for the position of Chaplain in 1988, I noted that the information sent out described the University as "Essentially a secular foundation." There were many Christians working in the University. Most kept very quiet about their faith. The University has a public Christian face on occasions though this may appear to some to be no more than a representative connection with the past. The Chaplain who would normally suit this situation would for the most part be someone of adaptable and liberal views. Assumptions always seem to move towards more and more liberalism and not towards proofs of the claims of Christianity.

In answering certain questions regarding my own application for the post in 1988, I stated *inter alia* "I have viewed Edinburgh with interest and suspicion over the years...I have been suspicious of Edinburgh's ambivalence during the Reformation in Scotland, and its disproportionate influence during the political Union of 1707..I am not convinced that the city reflects the spiritual identity of Scotland well...It has disappointed me that there is no tradition of Sunday worship within the University."

It had been a great surprise to me that I was appointed as Chaplain. Once there I never had any great problem with the broad University community. I was always willing to listen and to talk to anyone. The academic community tolerated my views even if they did not always agree with them. I did suffer some ill-treatment and abuse from occasional agnostics and atheists. But those who caused me most unhappiness called themselves Christians, professional ministers or priests or academics, and others were less than able members of the central administration of the University.

I had been forbidden from indulging my hobby of amateur journalism by John O'Neill. As he put it in May 1989, "We are not interested in you." I found that a strange doctrine. Here was a University Chaplain with a mind that was not supposed to think, with a voice that was not to be heard and with a pen that could not write. The reason for this was that my thoughts and words and writings were perceived to be "anti-Establishment." They are.

Lord George MacLeod, founder of the latter-day Iona Community belonged to The Establishment. He preached in private schools to the children of the wealthy. He lunched at Edinburgh's exclusive New Club. He had rejected the militarism of his youth, but he remained a Lord in lifestyle and values as well as being a famous Christian leader. He had an upper class privileged education. He retained money and property. He was always acceptable because he belonged to the circles where power and influence reside in Edinburgh, in Scotland. The churches in Scotland are as snobbish as any in other places. Whether Presbyterian, Roman or Episcopal, an English education, money and a title carry great weight.

Edinburgh University is a brilliant society, the most brilliant in Scotland. It would take long to list the ongoing achievements of those who live and work in Scotland's flagship University. Throughout my time there, the Principal Sir David Smith made a number of public statements criticising the attitude of successive Conservative governments to universities. I agreed with much of what he said. But the University itself is no model of organisational rectitude. Management falls short of the standards set by the academics. It probably should be a matter of public concern. If a simple matter like a chaplain's contract can be handled so unworthily, what is being done with larger scale issues, humanly speaking, of greater strategic and economic importance?

In my view a chaplain should not uncritically validate any enterprise. Scottish preachers throughout history were reknowned for their cutting edge. Now grey and stale conformity is traded for a living. Improvements could be made to university culture. Secretive means of decision-taking should be abandoned. Access to personal files may come in this country. We no doubt require a freedom of information act. This would reduce the arbitrariness of selection and dismissal but it would also reduce the power of the few who select and dismiss on personal whim. Universities should lead in social change but they are desperately conservative and fearful of anything which would reduce the power and increase the accountability of a few. I wonder if clever children who succeed early in life ever mature as human beings? Intellectual maturity does not breed personal or spiritual maturity. Arguably it retards both of these. Certainly if you want to meet some of the most petty-minded and spoilt of the human race, you go to a university. The Chinese used to send professors to work on farms for six months each year. What a good idea!

Not many are distinguished for straightforwardness. For circumlocutions, evasiveness and outright untruth you need go no further than a university. This culture affects students. They learn the tricks of the trade early. They breathe in the stultifying atmosphere for three or four years or more. They are intimidated. They take their revenge later in life. Some enter politics and starve the system of financial oxygen. Most leave without any sense of attachment or regard for the institution which has educated them.

I strove constantly throughout my term as Chaplain to be as much of myself as I could be while retaining my position. But Christian immediacy is hard to deal with wherever it is expressed. One may write a thesis about the Old or New Testament prophets and preachers but one is not expected to prophesy or preach oneself. Week in week out the Bible is read in churches. It is acceptable to read the words of the prophets and preachers as long as they are referred to ancient history. Any suggestion of something akin happening today brings misunderstanding, panic, persecution, rejection and ostracism. Like those who crucified Jesus, some persuade themselves that they are doing the right thing. I wonder if they sleep well of the night.

The prophet Isaiah wrote:

**"They are a race of rebels, disloyal children**
**..They say to the seers, "Do not see" and to**
**the prophets, "Do not prophesy the truth to us."**
**Tell us smooth things. Tell us falsehoods. Turn**
**aside. Leave the straight path. Take the Holy**
**One out of our sight."** (Isaiah 30:9-11)

What a timeless description of congregations!

The prophet Jeremiah fared worse. Single and alone, he was physically abused for telling the politically unacceptable truth.

**"Be on your guard each against his friend; put**
**no trust even in a brother...friend slanders friend**
**..They deceive their friends and never speak the**
**truth. One person talks amicably to another; while**
**inwardly planning a trap.."**(Jeremiah 9:4ff)

What a timeless description of institutions!.

Honesty, bearing no false witness, straightforward dealing with one another, keeping one's word are marks of a civilised society to me. They are more important than Mozart's symphonies or the Brandenburg Concertos. They are in less and less evident as social coarseness and crude ambition take over in an age without the sense of any final responsibility to God for life and conduct.

## Vichy Edinburgh

In Scottish church history there has for many centuries been a place for those called to preach and teach what we may call 'the objective Word of God' that is, the understanding already recorded in Scripture of what Christianity truly is. It may be uncomfortable on occasions to listen to applied Biblical theology. But it is also painful to take part in a rigorous training session for a sport. A good preacher will challenge listeners to deepen and to expand their understanding of their faith. In Edinburgh, preaching is more concerned with social acceptability than with transcendent authority. You cannot survive on the cocktail circuit if you are critical of the custom itself. You cannot get money out of people in business if you are critical of their tastes and preferences. Christianity is desperately weak. It can be forgiven that. It is also presumptuous. That is its dangerous and abiding problem. In Edinburgh it is considered most acceptable to have intellectual questions about the truths of Christianity. To voice these is much encouraged. Yet the Living God has spoken to you in your life and you know in your own experience of mind that the claims of Christianity are true not only for you but for many others throughout many generations and ages and you are privileged to conclude that the claims of Christianity are eternally and objectively true. The postured spiritual ignorance of the comfortably-off embarrasses you much. You squirm in their presence. They think you gauche. A dirty washing of little faith and understanding is blowing in the wind. A prejudicial intent not to seek the truth and discover it has taken the place of openness of mind and spirit. But doubts are most welcome - the stuff of ministerial careers, of dinner parties, of theological discourse and of cremation services.

There is a fear of evangelicals in the liberal churches of Edinburgh. You can smell it! One female member of the Presbytery of Edinburgh, some kind of semi-professional radio journalist perhaps, stated quite deliberately to me, "Of course, we are fighting a rearguard action against evangelicals." There is a kind of theological ethnic cleansing in the church which acts prejudicially against evangelicals at all levels of church life. In General Assemblies procedures and protocols are stood on their head to ensure that the liberal agenda remains in place.

The following farce occurred in the Presbytery of Edinburgh in 1990 in my presence. Statistics showed that the Presbytery of Edinburgh was losing members at a faster rate than other presbyteries. The answer of a 'New Age' person seemed to be that we should all become Unitarians. An evangelical and academic historian called David Wright suggested during the debate that in previous centuries, when the church was faced with adversity, people held days of prayer together in order to rediscover their sense of calling and purpose. A prominent evangelical Minister called Peter Neilson pointed out that Pentecost Sunday was not far away. He proposed that this day be designated as a day of prayer for the falling membership of the Presbytery. A liberal minister, Jack Kellett by name, rose to counter this suggestion because he said, "It is not procedurally correct." Richard Baxter - a member of Edinburgh's liberal gerontocracy seconded the counter motion. A vote was taken. The motion was defeated. What future is there for such a body, such a mentality, such a decision, such people?

There is a fear of fundamentalism too and for some there is no difference between evangelicalism and fundamentalism. Many evangelicals are well educated and intelligent people who can make a credible and reasonable case for what they believe to be true. Deliberate and strategic opposition to someone simply because he is an evangelical must be contrary to all the rules and practice of charity and of Christ's church throughout the ages. Yet that is what I encountered from church people throughout my five years as Chaplain to the University in

Scotland's capital city, Edinburgh.

A Christianity which places human beings first and God second as in liberalism is antipathetic to a Christianity which places God first and human beings second as in evangelicalism. How extraordinary that churches can be divided by as much as the difference between the first and second commandments to love God and one's neighbour in that order. (Luke 10:27) The correct attitude to any spiritual claim at any time in history should be that of Gamaliel who advised the Jewish authorities who had ordered the apostles not to preach in the Name of Jesus Christ. He said, "If what they have planned and done is of human origin, it will disappear, but if it comes from God, you cannot possibly defeat them. You could find yourselves fighting against God." (Acts 5:38-39)

Had the attitude of Gamaliel been adopted in response to my sermon of December 2nd 1990 in Greyfriars Church the remainder of my time in Edinburgh would have been very different. I was denied the opportunity to give full expression to the gifts of ministry entrusted to me. This was never a University of Edinburgh problem. It was a New College and a Greyfriars Church problem. In Edinburgh, the Gamaliel principle is applied to liberal expression which includes or presumes agnosticism about much that is contained in Christian tradition. It is not applied to committed Christians if they happen to be evangelicals. There is an air of irreconcilability about it all. My own case is a warning example. Liberals may flout the law of the Church in relation to freedom of opinion. Past Moderators of the General Assembly who had been given office to chair discussion without bias may join a public protest against an individual whom they have not known and to whom they have given no opportunity of defence. An individual Minister of the Church of Scotland may be both libelled and slandered and his fitness for the office of University Chaplain be denied publicly without reason or evidence. He may be stigmatised and typecast so that people are prejudiced against him throughout his life. He may be denied proper inclusion in the courts of his Church and such reasonable access to continuing service as his gifts and talents and education and calling may merit.

If evangelicals had ganged up against a single liberal minister in the way that liberals ganged up against me in 1989 I have little doubt that they would be derided in Church circles and in the national press. There would have been motions of protest to the General Assembly. Levers would have been pulled to provide an academic post. There might even have been calls for compensation. In Edinburgh in the 1990's liberals behave unjustly and get away with it. Baiting evangelicals is good liberal sport in the absence of deer hunting opportunities in central Edinburgh. Liberals occupy the best seats and the influential positions. They can do any amount of manipulating and justify their conduct to themselves and to one another. In mistaking a man of God for a self-induced image bearing no relationship to reality, liberals have exposed themselves for what they are. People without much depth of faith or understanding who are subject to panic and the repression of their own inadequacy. From there they objectify on to the other - the outsider - their own lack of reconciliation with the Living God and their fear of their own destiny. Like the Pharisees who encountered Jesus, they find themselves uncomfortably exposed. Instead of admitting their spiritual immaturities, weaknesses and outright sinfulness, they justify themselves by attacking the person who bears actual reconciliation in his own person. If these are the methods they must use to counter a freely appointed ministry, then the Church which they presume to govern must surely die.

## Theological Politics

It is terribly dangerous to bring the tactics of politics into the Church of Jesus Christ. Putting human society before the possibility of God is catastrophic. This is precisely what those who crucified Jesus of Nazareth did. They thought they were doing well. The Church is a spiritual organism in which God must always be free to act. It is a seriously dangerous thing for any one person or group to deliberately seek to inhibit or restrict or cripple or finish the ministry of a called servant of Jesus Christ. That is what happened to me before, during and at the end of my ministry in Edinburgh. It was a form of spiritual warfare. Long-term interests were at stake. Transcendent issues were involved. Had I been allowed to remain as Chaplain to Edinburgh University I would have sought to write and publish and so increase in usefulness. It would have remained a contradiction for Edinburgh to have an evangelical Chaplain. Public perceptions were determined by the campaign against my appointment. Continuing success would represent a further rebuke to Edinburgh's nominalism. The University itself might have had to respond to evidence of truth and verification. Its enlightenment adolescence would have been challenged. It would have been obliged, perhaps, to make a spiritual decision. If liberals pursued me there might be controversy. Edinburgh University does not like religious controversy. It was expedient that one person should be sacrificed. Justice did not matter. Spiritual recompense was not even considered. There was no courage to grasp that creative disagreement might be in the interests of everyone. Lively religion will ever be controversial. The influence of Christianity is declining. How extraordinary that someone with a contribution to make, spiritually and intellectually should be expelled from a situation of such transparent need.

Leaving an academic community can very painful, especially if you had hoped that perhaps therein you might have been granted enough space to survive and contribute. English 'New Agers' teach in New College. They deride Scottish Christian tradition. A Scot who can make some sense of the historic forms of Christianity in his native land cannot find any such position. But was John Wesley not also barred from preaching in Oxford for many years? Did not John Henry Newman reject the superficiality of 19th century Oxford Anglicanism? Was C.S. Lewis not tolerated only as long as he did not confess a personal Christianity?

Historic Calvinism includes transcendent seriousness. Roman Catholicism and the Orthodox Churches differently distinguish God and humans. Scottish Episcopalianism lacks this *gravitas*. Historic Calvinism witnesses to the transcendent Living God in Jesus Christ. Roman Catholicism witnesses to the Incarnation of God in Jesus Christ continuing in the Church. Orthodoxy rejoices in Christ's resurrection. Scottish Episcopalianism seems to witness to itself and to use the ecumenical movement as a main chance to obtain disproportionate influence and power. It reflects human society rather than transcendent mystery. Scottish Episcopalians present themselves in ways which more devout and serious believers do not. There is a combination of apparent over-confidence and insensitivity to Scottish history and theology. There is no basis of authority, neither Biblical or traditional. The human mind suffices. Doctrinal and ethical relativism rule.

Edinburgh is an Episcopal-friendly city. A leading Church of Scotland Minister once opined that Presbyterianism does not work in cities. There is an old adage that Presbyterianism is no religion for a gentleman. Edinburgh is English. It is not a Scottish city. So many English come to Edinburgh to be educated, to find employment and settle there. Many Scottish school-leavers do not apply to go to Edinburgh's universities for that reason. The University of Edinburgh is the most significant influence for Englishness in Scotland at the present time. The south-looking Edinburgh establishment prefers bishops to presbyteries. Scottish Episcopalian bishops court the media, buying time and air space at the cost of Christian depth and theological rigour. When 'The Scotsman' aggravated a public discussion in late 1993 and early 1994 on the subject of the Virgin Birth of Jesus, this was done in a way that was likely to provoke division in the Church of Scotland. My letter questioning the motives of 'The Scotsman' was not published. But the liberal Episcopalian bishops were not asked for their views. Neither were Roman Catholics asked to justify their Mariologies.

Preaching is now disrespected as a means of communicating Christianity. This is surely because those who denigrate preaching have themselves nothing much to say. Liturgical aesthetics have taken the place of declaration of the Living Word. What pittance of residual city religion remains as a hotch-potch of liberal theology, lack of confidence in the New Testament, feigned neighbourliness by means of dilettante political opinion and a relativistic code of ethics. Scotland's strong indigenous moderatism finds fellow feeling with Episcopalianism in today's 'New Age.'

## The Breaking of a Covenant

It was some three hundred and fifty eight years ago on the 28th of February 1638 that the document prepared primarily by Alexander Henderson and Archibald Johnston and known as The National Covenant was signed in Greyfriars Kirk. The context was the attempted imposition of Anglican liturgy in Scotland by Charles I. The first part of the National Covenant stated doctrinal differences with the pre-Reformation Roman Catholic Church. The second part detailed over sixty Acts of Parliament which had established the Reformed faith and Church Government in Scotland. The third part bound the signatories to maintain the freedom of the Church from civil control, to defend the true Reformed religion and to decline the impostion of Laud's Liturgy until the General Assembly had ruled on these matters.

Monarchical episcopacy was rejected. For those who signed in their own blood, the National Covenant was an assertion by the Kirk of freedom from royal or state control, a personal oath of allegiance to Jesus Christ, the only Head of the Church, the King of Kings, and a dedication of life to Him. This was not a political rebellion against the King as Head of State but these people could not have known where their principles would lead them or whether their actions might even someday cost them their lives. The following day the National Covenant was signed by many others and thence it was taken throughout the land for support. Charles I called the contents of the National Covenant "those impertinent and damnable demands." (Dictionary of Scottish Church History & Theology) The National Covenant served its purpose.

Times have changed! You cannot imagine the Edinburgh Establishment of today signing much in their own blood, certainly not for much Christian. The congregation of Greyfriars Kirk which trades the tourist track using in part an appeal to the heroic example of those men of 1638 at the same time contradicts in spirit what they stood for. As one student from overseas said to me at the end of a University Beginning of Session Service there, "Could you please tell me where I can find a Presbyterian Church?" Today, Scotland is unable to attain spiritual selfhood. Why? Because the connection between the Living God and Scottish history has been broken. Many historical reasons may be cited. One contemporary reason is the new form of episcopacy which rules the Edinburgh Establishment. Is not the unofficial bishop of so many Edinburgh minds none other than the former Anglican Bishop of Durham David Jenkins? He it is who replaces history with his own ideas and cuts the tie between the God of historical possibility and relationship and people who might believe.

In 1712 Patronage was reintroduced to the National Church in Scotland. Patronage was the role of landowners in the appointment of parish minsiters. After the Reformation patronage had been condemned in favour of call by the people of each congregation. After a long struggle it had eventually been abolished in 1649. This abolition was reinforced by the Act of Settlement in 1690 though there remained scope for conflict at parish level. The Patronage Act was restored by the English dominated Westminster Parliament in 1712. This was a flagrant violation of the Treaty of Union of 1707 and was enacted to advance the return of Episcopalianism in Scotland, thereafter to facilitate a Stewart return to the throne. Every General Assembly until 1784 called for its repeal, describing it as "grievous and prejudicial to this Church." It caused various secessions and led to the Ten Years' Conflict which culminated in the breaking of the back of the National Church during The Disruption of 1843 when over four hundred ministers and their congregations left the National Church on point of principle and formed the Free Church of Scotland. Patronage was abolished in 1874. Lasting damage was done to Christianity in Scotland. It has never recovered.

It is the imperial mentality, the monarchical impress, the crass historic insensitivity, the mental cruelty, the law-breaking, the lack of respect for Scottishness, the political bullying, the spiritual jealousy of something God-given - it is all of these and more. Arbitrary and secretive processes, manipulations of individuals, lack of justice and fair-play, of truthfulness and openness - these too often reflect the activities of Establishment groups with their own self-interested agendas. There is a patronising assumption that others know best. Subtle is the realm of ideas though it affects conduct and history. Patronage resides in the idea that the Establishment knows best. They will place their own candidate in a particular job. There are no regards for integrity, endeavour, imagination and visible success. Patronage exists today - it is alive and well in Edinburgh. It permeates the Church of Scotland. There is an intensity of wrong in the way things are conducted and how secret counsels are formed and in the abuse of positions of power. The liberal establishment gathers together to get its own way irrespective of truth, honour or decency. In the abuse of management positions, elective dictatorship, arbitrary and personalised decision-making and in the manipulation and distortion of facts and history and truth, lie the faults of an introverted society unrefreshed by the scale of justice represented in the Judaeo-Christian tradition. And workers are demoralised because they are not consulted before decisions affecting them are made. And there is an arrogant refusal to justify decisions once they have been made. So the life of the soul of a person is stolen, if not completely, at least in part, leaving a kind of living death. It is a spiritual crime to steal something good from another person, that is out of that person's own inner being. Those at the top feed off the life forces of those below. They suck the energy out of many by debilitating management improvisations. Bloated in their personas for a time, like sharks, gouging out the souls of those whom they dismay with incompetence, pretence and deliberate injustice. They sow the seeds of some future revolution with their arrogant complacency and utter incapacity to act with grace, humility and justice.

There were also the days described in Ian Henderson's book, 'Power Without Glory' which unmasked the unconsitutional attempt to foist episcopacy on the Church of Scotland in the second half of this century. Now the ecumenical movement is threadbare. Anglicans jilted Methodists at the altar. Roman Catholics and Anglicans have only held hands and not kissed. In Scotland there is much need for honesty. Great differences exist between the churches. These may represent strengths not weaknesses. Ecumenism is too often about false and polite insincerity. Who wants to be patronised? Or deceive? Or be deceived? The Kingdom of God is beyond the confines of ecclesiastical disagreements. The ultimate issue is Truth and our approximation to that Truth which is in Jesus Christ.

## Knowing God

God can be discovered although hidden from the naked eye. Spiritual truth is not linear, social or historical. Theory about the orbit of the earth or the composition of its crust may be ascertained by human intellectual development. The spiritual and the intellectual search are not the same. Some scientists may hold that physics resolves into theology but theology will never resolve into physics. Spiritual truth does not evolve. It is given in moments of personal revelation. The language of the evolution of spiritual truth belongs to ancient gnosticism, to its modern counterpart 'New Age' and to the multiplicity of spiritualistic sects, groups and cults which abound throughout the world. It has an academic alter ego in the kind of religious philosophy which David Jenkins and others offer instead of an acute and certain understanding of and dependence upon revelation in the Judaeo-Christian tradition.

It is to those who individually seek the very Person of God in Jesus Christ that the Subject of their search is revealed. If people only want the intellectually reasonable in any age, then that is all they will find. They have their reward. Late twentieth century Europe is much too narrow and much too culturally specific an environment for anyone to be making large and lasting counter claims about the origins of Christianity and the Person of Jesus Christ. The poor little village of Edinburgh with its emaciated spiritual orphans and its ricket-legged spiritual dwarfs should not be so presumptuous as to consider that it knows very much about the Invisible Church, or the Kingdom of God, or the Eternal Word that is in Jesus Christ. Ah - but a university degree and a comfortable living standard seem to allow much freedom to decide the cosmic destiny of everything and of everyone.

The basic constituent of knowing God is the personal relationship in which we embark on a lifelong journey of exploration. Many have followed this imperative throughout the last two thousand years. The most successful have been the most mistrusted, misinterpreted, persecuted and marginalised. One of the signs of a true and transcendent calling is to have a discomforting relationship with human society and culture. Jesus Himself is the perfect example of this, suffering as He did the ultimate penalty inflicted by His peers. Christianity which is most acceptable is probably so compromised that it is powerless both on earth and in the hereafter. There was a time in Scotland when people welcomed information on transcendent spiritual matters. Edinburgh has always kept such ministry at arm's length while tolerating and encouraging civil and social religion.

Will precedes intellect according to great Christian thinkers like Augustine, Luther, Calvin, Barth and others. The status of the intellectual exercise in relation to science is different from the status of the spiritual exercise in relation to God. In forming judgements, theories and opinions about the physical world we reflect on what is already there. The world precedes our 'discoveries.' We do not create 'out of nothing' no matter how sophisticated our inventions may be. In relation to God, we never obtain complete understanding, control, predictability or mastery. The mind does not reflect on what is given. It is part of a personal relationship of invisible quality and transcendent verification. This can be seen in historical retrospect in the lives of Christian mystics and saints and also in those committed to social care, missionary enterprise and prophetic ministry. God is known personally or not at all. God is not transferable from one person's understanding to another. Each must relate personally and not vicariously.

The life of Jesus, His Ministry, Death and Resurrection are complete acts in themselves. They are not theories about the cosmos. Relationships were made. Ideas were communicated, received and retained. Blood was shed. A tomb was empty. Jesus was seen again. The Church was born and still continues in existence. All we can do is relate to this Person and try with our minds and other faculties to understand what has happened and why and how it matters for today and tomorrow. Intellectual voluntarism will always be with us. Innovations have always occurred. There has never been and there never will be anything like the Death and Resurrection of Jesus.

Mental accession alone is not the way to find or to know God. Presenting Christianity as a rationally comfortable system at one point in human social evolution will in itself fail to advance personal knowledge of God. The creative distinction between human beings and God must be maintained. To state this today does not conform to the criteria of political correctness. The scientifically influenced community of the late twentieth century cannot ever be thought to be any final form of intellectual completeness such that can qualify or dismiss the actuality, meaning and continuing purpose of the Death and Resurrection of Jesus Christ. Who knows what spiritual and mental sensitivities may yet be employed in the human condition throughout the next one thousand years and more. There is as much likelihood of the Person of Jesus being more truly understood in future times as not. It is only bigotry which will not admit this possibility and not make it one of the polarities which assesses current theological liberalism and reductionism. This does not imply spiritual evolutionism. It means that someone in the far future may be given access to a deeper personal relationship with God in Christ than we have today. This must be held to be practically and theologically possible. Throughout Judaism and Christian history individuals have been granted some specialised knowledge of God. They have not found that this knowledge was directly communicable at the time when they lived and received it. Prophets and mystics and contemplatives therefore wrote down their visions for future generations so that they may reflect on prior experience.

## The Scottish Dimension

In Scottish Reformed Christianity God has been held to be known in Christ by intellectual recourse to the Bible corroborated by the teaching function of the Holy Spirit in the life of each individual seeker. English Christianity retained an equal place for human reason as a ground of authority alongside the Bible and episcopacy. It is the latter form which is now prevailing in Edinburgh. To make of one's own opinions an authority equal to the Bible is what episcopal bishops do. So do some who presume to teach in university faculties of divinity. Nineteenth and twentieth century scientific discovery and theory have affected both epistemological traditions. People think, by and large, that the English form is more suited to contemporary life. Evangelicals place their seeking of God above and ahead of enquiries about what is given in creation and about descriptions of human society and personality. Some like Tom Torrance then interpret what is seen and discoverable in the light of the knowledge of God given to them. In dealing with God there must always be a gap in our knowledge. To fill that gap with mere individual and personal opinion as is so frequently done in our society is an act of spiritual rebellion, a continuing type of 'The Fall.' It is doubly regressive to rubbish those who make the effort to seek and know God on God's own given terms. The spiritually lazy and uncommitted do ill to mock and abuse those who make a conscious effort to know God. There is a conclusive difference between those who acknowledge the 'repenting' tradition within Christianity, either as Protestant evangelicals or as devout Roman Catholics or as pious Orthodox and those who peddle political justification of human conduct as an expression of liberalism in the churches. These are irreconcilable. One is right and consequently, one is wrong. There is in the heart of every meeting with God that dimension of forgiveness which must be recognised. It is all too clear from the Bible and from Christian history that it is unwise to second guess God.

It has ever been a hazardous occupation to share personal revelation. Spiritual jealousy abounds. The sharp edge of challenge and of criticism which typifies a message with a transcendent component within the human community is really not welcome. The cry of repentance is no longer heard. It is not wanted in spite of the decay of social and national life. Polite and superficial reflection is all that one hears today in most Scottish pulpits.

Human self-expression is not equivalent to transcendent truth about God. The dispersal of Christianity into the secular society will benefit no-one if the recognisable source and river and pool of Christian truth and experience disappears at the same time. Different religious forms take the places of those abandoned and rejected. Other christs appear. Many become their own christs and christas. No-one wants to be wrong. No-one wants to be mistaken. Less do people want to be exposed - even to themselves.

We have inherited generations of compromised Christianity. People are patronised and lulled to sleep in pews. It is a dangerous business to invite such folks to discover how far they are from God in Christ, especially if they have been working their passage in the churches for years. The logic with which Jesus addressed his contemporaries was that if they really knew and obeyed The Law and if they loved God, they would at least have been able to tolerate Him and at best recognise Him and believe in Him. They did not and they could not.

It is by the common sense standards of just personal dealings, admission of lack of knowledge of God and openness to anything that might conceivably be of God that each of us betrays or displays our spiritual state and our relationship to God. None of us can hide. People have their opinions. Words reveal the soul. It is possible to know God in Christ and to articulate a personal faith.

Edinburgh society is the closed society. A well-known television pundit once described Edinburgh as "A tight arsed town with an ugly soul." Generous. On Christmas Sunday 1992 I went to Dunblane Cathedral to worship. I found myself sitting beside an elderly woman. Her face was bright and her eyes shone. Her black coat belonged to a different era. Before I got up to leave she asked me where I came from. I gave my standard reply to that question, "I come from Ayrshire but I work in Edinburgh." "Ah," she said, "My son works there now. He used to be a nice person."

I have never been allowed to be at ease in Zion. Neither have I found a place to lay my head for long. Nor peace on earth. I do not think I lacked the breadth of mind and spirit to be able to handle living in Edinburgh and in its University community. It may be said of me that I did not quite make it. Unfair. To be sure an easier personality and a less brittle disposition on occasion might have helped. But - there remains something within me which is of God - and it has been repressed, crushed, wounded and stultified, persecuted and ostracised. Perhaps it is this which is not welcome. To conclude so would make sense of the events of my adult life and public ministry.

## University

On 11th February 1994, Martin Lowe replied to the Rector's letter of 28th January. He stated that my appointment had been for five years and that the University was under no obligation to renew it. He said he understood that in 1992/3 I had asked to have my 'contractual position' confirmed. This was wholly untrue. In relation to the External Assessor, the Secretary wrote, "The Chaplaincy Committee's views were not acted upon because of the reaction of the Principal and myself to the contents of his report." I have never been told what these contents were. Neither was the Chaplaincy Committee. When the external assessment took place, two cardinal features of natural justice were missing. I did not know who my accusers were. Neither did I know what they were saying against my continuing as Chaplain.

The Secretary continued, "The process involving an external review of the Chaplaincy and report to the Principal and me was discussed and fully agreed by the Chaplain himself, in the presence of Professors McCormick and Miller, together with Melvyn." This was wholly untrue. There was no discussion whatsoever about the process at the meeting on July 15th 1993. All that was communicated during the meeting was that Professor D.W.D.Shaw had been asked to be the external assessor. I had agreed to his being so. I did not know that the process was to be in secret. I would never have agreed to such unjust procedure. I would have withdrawn from the external assessment on grounds of unfairness. Martin Lowe's letter of 29th October 1993 to members of the Chaplaincy Committee stated, "When it was agreed with Professor Shaw at the outset that his report would remain confidential.." There was no agreement with anyone else as to confidentiality. No-one else knew about it.

Martin Lowe accepted that (in early 1993) there had been a lack of communication but apportioned no responsibility for it. Finally, he wrote " It would be very unusual in the University to set up an Appointing Committee to review a post on a fixed term (of which the University has many) and there was no reason to suppose at the time that this might prove controversial given the Chaplain's willing acceptance of what I proposed. Moreover, it was necessary to respect the conditions under which Professor Shaw had agreed to act." I had known nothing of this agreed confidentiality. I did not know who would be chosen to state their opinion on my future. I was never told what was said about me or why the decision went against me. I would much rather have taken my chances with an open and above board process monitored  by the Chaplaincy Committee of the University. But, of course, that might have brought a different result. Neither did I campaign or organise support for myself. Dr Lowe himself even commented that I had conducted myself with dignity over the months of inquest and indecision.

The Secretary's letter of 11th February is evidence of much. The art of management, I am told, is to get your own way. This I suggest, is the management of Annas and Caiaphas, of Herod and of Pilate. How interesting it is that throughout the struggle I was always at a disadvantage. I was always wrong-footed. There was no voluntary or organisational openness, truth, justice or honesty. The goalposts were moved many times. In my view the end was morally worthless. How sad that a great institution like Edinburgh University, rooted in the majesty of Christianity should wish itself managed in this way.

I was not alone. The University made many decisions in this way and larger issues, humanly speaking were as badly handled. Due processes were often subverted. Corners were cut. People were ignored. It was just a matter of who had power and if some did not have it constitutionally, they assumed it. Insufficient scrutiny and accountability prevented exposure. Each person protected the other. After all, they decided each other's salaries and benefits. And they continue for long and many years. Proof of this is found in the published salaries of Principals of Scottish Universities. They themselves may not be overpaid according to the standards of the time but within universities senior officers have proportionately high salaries. I question the processes by which these salaries are negotiated and determined.

Dr Malcolm Macleod, he who as President of the Edinburgh University Students Association, had told me told me upon my arrival that "an atheist could do your job" published a letter in 'The Scotsman' on February 2nd 1996 in which he defended the historic office and role of the Rector in Scottish universities. He also listed some reforms which he as Rector had been instrumental in introducing to Edinburgh University, such as an increase in the proportion of women in the decision-making process, planning for a register of interests of members of the University Court and publication of Court minutes within the University. He must be a thorn in the side of the administration! But his views lend weight to my own observations and criticisms about the sterile introversion of university politics and the less than open styles of administration which allow abuse of position and victimisation and partiality in relation to some employees.

## Society

Edinburgh University's corporate image sets store by Edinburgh society. Its relationship with Scotland is more problematical. A Chaplain's value would be seen in the part he or she played in helping the University to relate to the community. It would be assumed that the liberalism of society would be reflected in the University's public persona. My own tenure of the Chaplaincy contradicted that assumption. Whether a positive and significant contribution had been made mattered not. Theoretical sympathy with obtuse lifestyles was what was wanted. A general practitioner is not incapable of helping patients with whose lifestyle he or she disagrees. Members of Parliament help everyone is their constituencies, irrespective of how they may have voted in elections. Lawyers defend people they know are guilty. Ministers baptise, marry and bury all sorts of people of varying percentages of Christian faith and understanding and of none. There would have been a continuing creative opportunity in having someone of commitment and theological definition as Chaplain. Edinburgh wanted to move into the broader realms of post-Christian existence. The University Chaplain could not be seen to be striving against this particular tide. Tolerance in Edinburgh is only one way - it does not extend to those who may bear something of the truth of Christianity in their own lives.

In relation to God, the social life may matter little. In Christian vocation, it may be a disguise for what is true and what is true may be beautiful. Life in churches may also be a disguise for what is truly ugly. And wicked. The greatest of those who have found some realisation of God in their lives have lived hidden lives. They have had to. It is a dangerous world. There has been and there continues to be much spiritual thuggery, brutality and murder on the streets of Christendom.

And the wider conspiracy ensures that a person with something to say will be marginalised and silenced. Perhaps when that person is old and harmless, it may be safe to acknowledge his existence. Then is the time for honorary degrees and the freedom of cities. There are apologies and hand-wringing. But no-one needs to take the original message seriously. The person is applauded. God is ever kept at distance.

## Church

We live in interesting times. Not times of expansion but times of contraction. Not times of faith and confidence but times of doubt and questioning, of wandering and of apostasy. James Weatherhead, Moderator of the General Assembly of the Church of Scotland in 1993-4 fostered a controversy about the truth or otherwise of the 'Virgin Birth' (ie., Conception) of Jesus. It is always most acceptable for a liberal thinker to question aspects of Christian Faith. It is never acceptable for someone to provoke discussion in the other direction, in ways which might encourage people to discover the truth of Christianity, truths that exist permanently, Jesus Christ, invisible, but knoweable and reachable, not by human effort or understanding but in response to calling and divine intimation.

Thus if the same Moderator is not allowed to preach in a certain west highland pulpit those who prevent him doing so are held to be bigots. If he is banned from visiting a harbour, those responsible are held to be narrow-minded. A liberal can make an evangelical unwelcome and that is acceptable. A liberal may prevent an evangelical continuing in employment and that is deemed appropriate. There are double standards in the Church of Scotland. It is arrant hypocrisy to make theological liberals into martyrs for their doubts and lack of knowledge of God in Jesus Christ. They occupy the social and academic establishment (the best seats in the synagogues.) How many evangelicals teach in Scotland's divinity faculties? What price do they pay for survival? When will the Church of Scotland's committees fairly represent the growing strength of evangelicals? When will the General Assembly actually allow free and fair voting on important issues?

Extreme liberals and very conservative evangelicals do not reflect the mainstream of church life. Arguments become polarised. Ancient enmities are fought out time and time again. Actual spiritual war continues. Centre liberals support extreme liberals when necessary. Evangelicals are dismayed by outright manipulation of people and procedures and truth. Surely the church of the future will depend on the committed remnant of today? Such people should not be marginalised and abused as they have been and continue to be. Justice demands that liberals while retaining the right to their own thoughts and beliefs and opinions should acknowledge and include evangelicals whose faith is crucial to the survival of Christianity in Scotland. Liberals are allowed to use pejorative language but evangelicals cannot use definite concepts without being charged with lack of intellectual breadth. What would they have made of Luther? Or Calvin?

190

# Kingdom Of God

Today's liberal dominated church is concerned with politics. The Church of Scotland's Church And Nation Committee has for some time not addressed Christianity in its transcendent spiritual power to the nation, but has sought to offer applied ethical remonstration to the political process. What a misunderstanding of its role! In New College divinity as a particular entity is compromised by involvements with sociologies and other human accoutrements. Theological and ethical relativism abound in theory and in practice. Making Christian teaching relevant by dilution is advocated. Friendship with the world is most necessary for ministerial advancement. The Establishment reflects the decay of British nationhood and the abandonment of public and private Christianity. Establishment values, conduct and politics are not tied to political conservatism. Socialist and communist countries have had ghastly Establishments of their own. Indeed, who knows what horrors may yet be visited upon Scotland if forms of retrogressive atheistic political left-wing militancy and minority campaigning groups achieve actual power and decision-making bases in a devolved parliament?

The Kingdom of God is different from all of this. The Kingdom of God exists in dimensional parallel to all life that is visible and understandable. The radical teaching of Jesus is as true today as it was when Jesus Himself explained its essence to His disciples. It is by way of negation, self-denial, self-renunciation, suffering and even death that one may find it. New College with its luxury cars and private number plates, its multi-thousand salaried sirens and its comfortable sometime alcohol-laced living represents the opposite of the Kingdom of God. No wonder the church is dying. Voluntary surrender to the higher will of God is the beginning. Being under direct and sovereign personal authority is a living experience. The psychological direction is not linear or social or visible but transcendent, divine and invisible. Mere human intellect is contradicted. Voluntarism is not required. Life abandonment is.

When Jesus of Nazareth was given the opportunity to defend Himself in face of execution, He is recorded as having said these words, "My Kingdom is not of this world." (John 18:36) The true church is to be found in approximation to and in relationship with this invisible Kingdom. It is not to be found in identification with human political society. It is not to be equated with the sum of human learning. "The best," says Mallory, "is the enemy of the good." True spiritual calling sits uneasily with the social church. There is an intrinsic incompatibility between liberal political Christianity and the spiritual distinctiveness of the Kingdom of God. The dynamic of God's intimation has always contradicted established ecclesiastical order. Bearers of immediacy have always suffered.

# Indirect Communication

You can't operate at an eschatological level and live a normal life. Jesus could not do so. How can you remain in your own Church and follow your vocation in its ministry? Firstly you can try to make a positive difference wherever you  may be. However the way forward is often by correct and critical analysis, criticism and diagnosis. Even if you limit this to the levels of tolerance of those with whom you are in contact, in the spoilt and comfortable institutionalised churches, you have problems already. If you open out at any time, then the whirlwind returns to crush you. You don't tell the whole story. You don't reveal the truest picture. You give people a chance to respond from where they are. So often they cannot respond even to that simple invitation. Jesus said, "We played wedding music for you, but you would not dance, we sang funeral songs, but you would not mourn." (Luke 7:32) He also said that people would remember playing in the streets with Him when it was too late to do them any good. It is not possible to communicate the Kingdom of God directly. In not defending yourself with all powers at your disposal, you sacrifice yourself so that others may have time to consider their souls. They do not do so however. In disarming yourself - they take advantage and cut your down. But there is a Christ-like basis to your conduct. Perhaps that is why though you are far from perfect the Living God will vindicate you. God knows what you are doing, even if no-one else does. And some may complain that you did not tell them. But Jesus did not explain much to those who asked questions out of spiritual enmity. "What right have you to do these things? Who gave you this right?......"Neither will I tell you, then, by what right I do these things." (Matthew 21: 23-27)

You are high and dry. There is no scale of context to make communication bearable. You are like a monarch without an aristocracy. When preaching you spend your life as it were driving in third gear. Occasionally you may get into fourth. You never use fifth! You could - but chaos and division would result. Yet - at that cutting edge of Christian communication revival and renewal might be stimulated. Those who could be expected to provide the context for such a spiritual challenge to the country and people with whom you live are themselves uncomfortable with you. Indeed they are against you. Jesus said that the Holy Spirit (the real Holy Spirit) would prove to the people of the world how wrong it is about sin and about what is right and about God's judgement. (John 16: 8) And so much misunderstanding occurs. And you bear most of the pain yourself. And you become virtually unemployable. And you are advised to seek psychiatric care or psychological counselling. Because for all the Christianity of their language people have little spiritual discernment of what motivates and guides you. But within your soul lives the New Heaven and the New Earth. The inner core alongside the outer shell. Incarnational. The church sees only the outer shell. There are occasions when you decide to speak from a deeper level of your spiritual consciousness - and there are rare occasions when you may be called to speak the Living Word of God. And just when people were beginning to be at ease with you and thinking you might at last have been tamed - that you could conceivably be normal, or at least approaching it from a distance, another just cause prevents your absolute silence and turmoil ensues once again. This point of crisis, of trouble, of controversy is exactly where God meets people. This is where the churches could be renewed. How can they be renewed if they continue with their dying process? Yet they will not tolerate the controversy which will save them. Jesus lived a public life not noted for peace and tranquillity. His ministry was prophetically disruptive to the religious institutions of Israel. They could not tolerate Him. They murdered Him. Likewise His prophetic forebears. The churches, given the choice of life or death, invariably choose death. And they are dying. And so is western Christendom. And the society in which it sleeps.

Churches with hierarchies maintain social positions from which people may speak from behind protected barriers. But why are their words so insipid and apologetic? Why do they conform to the world so easily? Because to get into these positions you need to have left your idealism a long time ago somewhere in a comfortable mansion. And you have learned not to upset the media by saying anything extreme or even provocative. You say "Peace, Peace" when manifestly, there is no peace. You appease the depths of people's spiritual rebellion because you cannot face the mess that results if you for once acknowledge that you discern what is wrong. And you are most reasonable in everything, and acceptable to Royalty and the Establishment of the land. But your church is dying beneath your feet.

To live as a real human being in the real world carrying the precious knowledge of the Living God within you is a dangerous and exciting life. If you have a sense of humour that alone can create havoc. The devil hates wholesome joy and laughter. And people who take themselves very seriously while working their way to heaven don't like to be laughed at. Yet you may have as part of your ministry to ask Christianity to depart from its false pathologies rooted in the historic past and the unreconciled present within each person. The world can be a dismal place. There is much suffering. The spiritual person who has no sense of humour is not fully human nor fully divine. He or she may be much too inclined to interpret self-will as God's will. Imposing the burden of unjustified seriousness on others is inadvisable. Liberals like to laugh at others. But - if you laugh at them - from a position of spiritual strength - they don't like that at all. Clever people without Christianity like to laugh too, unkindly, but they do not like to be laughed at, even if this is but to stimulate them to real discussion and thought and repentance. The Gospel according to Saint Matthew, chapter twenty-three is full of irony, satire and outright derision. Secular authors and poets and writers and musicians don't like to be laughed at. They don't expect meek Christians to do that at all. They are the only ones who can mock others. In their plays. In their books. On television. In films. You must not expose the shallowness of the artistic enterprise. You must not take away the justification of the human spirit. Don't dare. (Not as a feeble Christian anyway.)

So there are mild and bespectacled clerical figures with reports and books and papers. Goldfish. So many are sincere and doing respectable work. You cannot mock or despise those who give of their very best according to their vision. You have no quarrel with them. You recognise them. You commend them, encourage them. It is with those who seek to lead in wrong ways that you have a quarrel and a disputation on earth. And they come from the left and from the right. Merciless. Mistaken. Incapable of repentance. Consumed with an enormous jealousy that God might choose a poor man of humble origin to shake them up. And discomfort them. In their pride and arrogance and manipulation of the system and in their pursuit of wealth and respectability and comfort. And in their false teaching which has mislead generations. And in their crushing of the Holy Spirit in the Church time and time again. But you have no quarrel with those who follow Jesus Christ with great devotion. You dare not. You answer to Him.

And so you write. And what will become of you if you publish thereafter, God only knows. You ask an opportunity to preach and teach and discuss and talk and minister and serve. But - you are on the outside - unwanted. And your writing may be your nemesis or your opportunity. But - can you live up to your calling? Will not everyone be utterly disappointed in you - in your poor humanity - and physical form - and Scottishness - and Reformed, Presbyterian Protestantism - though you cling to no tradition as of final value in itself. And your ordinariness. Neither can you answer every question that is asked. You can only say "It is all true - this Christianity - it is all true." That is what you need to say. For you are called to witness to Jesus Christ and not to yourself and you will find salvation in remaining true to that vocation. And that yoke is easy and that burden is light and you will find rest for your soul. In fidelity. Humility before God. Seeking nothing for yourself that belongs to God. Making no claims but for God's providence in your life. Therein is joy and survival and the key to life and ministry in your Church and in your country.

In sharing your vision God may affirm or deny you. God is God. God can confirm what you have said. But already your personal history has determined much though you could have half your time yet to live. You offer yourself up again as a sacrifice. You lose your life to gain it on earth temporarily, then in heaven. And for how long - here - you do not know - months, years, decades? But God never left a generation without a voice or Himself without a witness. You are not alone. Many great Christian men and women share your Faith. On their knees in private places. Unknown but to God. Together you may accomplish much, who knows?

Dimensions of evil lie awaiting your next move. Ready they are with quotes and texts. Ready too are your detractors. Many. For if you are critical of them, expect no mercy in return. Within the churches lie your greatest enemies. No paranoia. Just realism. Discernment. The Son of Man had nowhere to lay His head.

## Turning The World Upside Down

Christianity is a revolutionary force. It signifies a reversal of the orders so visible in the world in politics, business and society. Jesus rejected the arrogances of authority. "It shall not be so with you.." said He. (Matthew 20:26) Unfortunately in the history of institutionalised Christianity it has been so with many. And those who have the most prominent positions are often themselves the antithesis of their Master in attitude. Christianity is very tolerable provided it is espoused by tame clerics. Lap dogs. Yes men. Yes women. Conformists. Looking after number one. It is thought foolish to actually try to be altruistic in the churches. And to actually go out on a limb for GOD - well that is only for those suspected of lunacy. As Chaplain to Edinburgh University I took part in a discussion with members of the student services group on the extent to which condoms should be made freely available in every area of Pollock Halls of Residence. One academic said "It is a radical step to do this." I replied, "That isn't radical. It would be radical *not* to have any condoms at all in halls of residence." It is not radical to legitimise and sanctify obtuse expressions of sexuality. It is radical *not* to do so. It is not radical to pretend to be armchair socialists while earning annual salaries of fifty thousand pounds and sending your children to fee-paying schools. Vicarious Christianity is most welcome among polite circles.

What Christianity offers is a complete eschatological redress of what happens to so many decent people in the world. It is a matter for rejoicing that this is so, that there is a God who will act finally in such a corrective manner. The example of Jesus of Nazareth is frighteningly accurate in its portrayal of the consequences of offering humankind a preview of the criteria of the last assize. What a fair-minded Creator to let us know in advance. But how many seek to manipulate and reinterpret and finally to negate that clear example. How many actually use the values of the world to oppose Christian truth when it is in turn presented with at least a measure of determination to be faithful to its original vision and reality.

The world is full of myths. But Christianity is not a myth. Some miserable theologians have said that it is. Christianity is an active and threatening power. The leaders of the Jews were mightily uncomfortable about Jesus of Nazareth, so much so that they contravened their own Law to have Him put down. Does anyone seriously think that He would survive today's Christendom of the world? Is it not a replica of the corrupt institutions of the Judaism of His time? These ludicrous figures in layers of robes and hose and mitres! Ha! The languid convictionless left of the churches! The repressed and hypocritical right! The posturing of the rich and influential. Bowing to Royalty indeed! What nonsense. "It shall not be so with you" was a command. It was not an option. It is the basis of the eschatological assize. The foundation of the Kingdom of God on earth. And many have taken its meaning seriously and have lived its import. Many still do so today throughout the world. Unheard of. Unfamous. No recognition. No reward. Known to God - supremely. Of such is populated the dimension of heaven.

## Farewell

In March 1994 I applied for the post of Lecturer in Theology and Development in the Department of Christian Ethics at New College, University of Edinburgh. My qualifications and experience in Kenya should have made me a strong candidate for the post. As Chaplain I had been pastorally involved with overseas students on the Theology and Development course, and a pastoral capability was asked for in the advertisement. I had also tutored one student through his Masters dissertation and had successfully defended his work against Professor Forrester at the External Examiner's meeting. The University claimed to operate a policy of job preferment for its own employees. I did not even get an interview for the post.

In April 1994, John O'Neill published an article in the Bulletin (The University of Edinburgh News) in which he offered advice to colleagues on how to handle committees. "Committees are not able to run anything. The affairs of the university...have to be managed by individuals who lead teams. Committees are to see that the show is well run, to approve any major change of policy and to feed in new ideas...The university works on trust. If we don't trust those who are taking the responsibility we should not resort to trench warfare but go for help."

Practical suggestions included the following gem. "Convener (of Committee) has thought ahead about sensible outcomes but makes it clear that the decision lies with the meeting.." As an exercise of transparent hypocrisy this defied belief. That it was acceptable in the University Bulletin is clear evidence of the culture of practising dishonesty which pervades Edinburgh University. But many years before John O'Neill had been one of George MacLeod's converts to partial Christianity. He had belonged to and had remained part of the political church.

Vice-Principal Andrew Miller took it upon himself to organise a farewell party for me. Reluctantly, the Office of the Secretary to the University (aka my old friend Iain Robb) became involved. A generous financial gift collected from colleagues was presented to me. It was later used towards the purchase of a multi-media personal computer. My farewell speech lasted fifteen minutes. I said my thanks to those who had been of best help to me. I used irony and sarcasm against those who had opposed, harried and hindered me. I called the University Administration 'Dad's Management' in comparison with the famous television series 'Dad's Army'. I concluded with verses from Robert Burns' poem "A Man's A Man For A' That" and from the Book of Revelation chapter 21 verses 1 to 4. I kept my powder dry.

Between January and March 1994 I had written an account of what had happened to me at Edinburgh University. Chapters six, seven, eight and nine of this book represent the core of that book which I called 'Without Honour.' I did this to stay alive. In January 1994 I felt utterly diminished to the point of non-existence. I felt that I had been judicially murdered but - I was still alive on earth. My career prospects were nil. I had no home of my own. Little money. Few friends. Being involved in great issues does not commend one to vacancy committees. My applications were sometimes ignored, sometimes discounted, sometimes rejected. Occasionally there was a bite but it never became a catch. My friend from Kenya days, Alan Ross and his wife Kaye helped me to produce "Without Honour" in a home printed and bound form. From April to July I had these copies under wraps. Advice given was not to distribute them while still an employee of the University. I desperately wanted to do so. I presented only a few copies to personal friends. "Without Honour" concluded with the words "I hope still to articulate what has been given to me to see and know and understand. This might in time become a joy and a blessing for many." (p. 92) Only in the broader context of my personal history did the issues of the Edinburgh University period make sense. Only in this way could a lament become an hymn of praise. And that is what I did. "*Intimations Of Love Divine.*" And you are reading it!

In July 1994, Rev Iain Whyte was appointed Chaplain to the University. He had been Chaplain at St Andrew's University. He was known to Dr Martin Lowe, Professor John Richardson and Professor D.W.D. Shaw. He was also a friend and acolyte of Professor Duncan Forrester. Iain Whyte had long connections with the Iona Community and was recognised as an unspectacular liberal party apparatchik. He would do his masters' bidding. There had been younger more gifted applicants for the position. Such transparent favouritism only confirms the validity of the observations made in this book. It is indefensible behaviour from people who claim to be Christians. Where is personal justice now? But - no further evangelical experimentation would be tolerated. Edinburgh's Chaplaincy returned to its liberal keepers. They on the political left talk much about social justice but perhaps in God's sight they are devoid of integrity. In August 1996 I met a former academic colleague by chance on the street in the Newington area of Edinburgh. He told me that Christianity had by and large been diminished at the Chaplaincy Centre since my departure.

St Augustine distinguished the Earthly and the Heavenly City of God. Amid complete social chaos on earth no-one could deprive the Christian of membership of the latter City, he said. John Calvin made a critical distinction between the Visible and Invisible Church. The former, he thought, contained a large measure of hypocrites. I myself wish to distinguish the Church Political and the Church Spiritual. In Scotland a struggle is taking place. I have been caught up in this struggle and have been a victim of its ferocity. Over the years, Edinburgh University's Chaplaincy had been the preserve of the Church Political, to which it has returned. The tiny Student Christian Movement has its own Chaplain once more, paid for by public funds. Some of Duncan Forrester's students are taken on trips. Introverted liberal chaplaincy rules again. The methods used to oppose my calling as Chaplain in 1989 and in 1993 belong to the Church Political. But for a little while - a Prague spring? - Edinburgh's Chaplaincy was part of the Church Spiritual.

My last graduation Benediction read as below. It received gracious comment. However an Episcopalian member of staff asked me where I had got it from. I replied that I had written the Benediction myself. "Oh", said he, "I thought it belonged to someone more famous than you."

> *"And the warm breezes of summer caress your face,*
> *the lightness of the evenings uplift your spirit*
> *may true love await you,*
> *a Faith to live by, an eternity to expect*
> *and the blessings of Heaven and of earth*
> *be upon you and those who are dear to you*
> *now and always. Amen."*

# 10 : It's Christianity - but not as we know it

### Drifting

The early weeks of 1994 found me in a calm state of mind. I suppose a condemned man feels the same. The struggle is over. The judgement has been given. You await events. A certain bemusement inoculates the inner being from the abuses which every false conversation brings to your sensibilities. There is something more honest about those people who acknowledge that something has happened in comparison with those who pretend that what they have done has never happened. I said to Tom Kearns "Perhaps it's better to lose,Tom." I knew that he, as a follower of Jesus, understood what I was saying. In spiritual terms nothing can be truly accomplished without the process of self-emptying.

If you are desperate for pitiless discouragement, try applying again for a Church of Scotland charge. Your application may or may not be acknowledged. Months (not weeks) will pass before you learn that you were never even on a short leet but that your application was excluded at the first consideration. Some idealists wait for 'the right charge.' I applied for a number. I was most desirous of being called to a rural charge and in fact came close during the spring months of 1994. Generally however, those who spoke to me wondered why on earth I wanted to go to their particular rural location, given my background, education and experience. I was unable to persuade anyone that I had always harboured a genuine interest in rural ministry in Scotland.

### Fasting

When times are difficult and things are not going well for you, you can give up. You can seek help. You can talk to people. You can organise yourself. You can campaign. I was never able to do any of these things. I usually took the opposite path. I went into personal spiritual retreat with prayer and fasting. It was a kind of aversion therapy. It was like jumping into freezing water just to offset the feeling of cold outside. When you came back out - it no longer felt cold but warm in comparison with the freezing water. And when you fast, you do not eat and your body does not receive fuel and it does not create energy and you do grow cold. You 'die.' And, miraculously - you come back to life. The dying is difficult. The waiting is long. The coming back to life is splendid. And you learn there what you had forgotten or what you did not know. And a mirror lays bare your innermost being and it is not very pleasant. And you realise how much of daily life is taken up by vainglories, irrelevancies and stupidities. How ungodly you are as a minister, as a Christian, as a man. All on earth seems trivial and of little account. Eternity opens up before you as the only reality.

So it was that on Friday 25th March 1994 that I began an eight-day fast through Holy Week which I hoped would be a blessing to me. I drank water but took absolutely no food whatsoever throughout the fast. The purposes of the fast were to return to the Father of my soul through Jesus Christ, to find forgiveness, blessing, refreshment, cleansing and renewal in body, mind and spirit, to seek help, guidance and direction for my life in the immediate and long-term future, to pray for another job on leaving Edinburgh University, to find out God's will in everything and to pray for such people and their circumstances as it seemed right to do. At the outset I said to myself that if God participates in my fast, then it will be blessed and graced. If not - it will be torturous and invalid.

My basic feelings in prayer before God have often been those of inner spiritual pain and suffering. This is hidden from view. People outside do not recognise its existence. Some are accessories to the fact. I have seldom been free to rejoice in the inner person before the Lord my God. I have never spoken in tongues. I have always identified primarily with the sufferings of Jesus Christ and the joys and ecstasies have been gracious if intermittent respite from the general tenor of my adult life. That is why humour has always mattered to me. I have suffered from lack of proper use and usefulness and proactive abuse in the church. I kept living for the day when this unused dimension of vocation would be released into a positive creative force for good. But the deeper realms of God's Kingdom conflict with Christian stereotypes and on the occasions when I tried to come out of my shell, I found myself attacked on all sides and driven back into silence and spiritual idleness. It was never safe to speak from the depths of my soul in a world such as this.

And so at the beginning of this fast, I reminded God that I had not seen the travail of my soul and I was not satisfied with my lot. The promises of the Gospel had not been fulfilled in my life to date. Good reasons for this, I was sure, existed, but that did not help me to persevere. So few of my prayers had ever been answered that I was discouraged beyond speaking. My efforts seemed to be for nothing. Whatever sacrifices I had made, counted less, it seemed than the judicious milking of the system so typical of many of my professional colleagues in the ministry. I had been crushed at every turn, or 'snookered,' or outmanoeuvred, and certainly defeated in social and public terms.

Yet I was thankful to be in good physical health. I have always marvelled at the robust resilience of my body, considering the huge quantities of stress which it has been asked to bear. I sometimes wonder if I will drop dead of a heart attack. At any time. Any day. I take not a breath for granted. I felt that I was not without a measure of respect from some who knew me. I was not entirely destitute though hopes of a job were not great. Life was not without love or beauty.

I genuinely sought God's will for my life. I felt like the Prodigal Son. I *always* feel like the Prodigal Son in the closer presence of Almighty God. I actually had five prospects of work. I was on the short leet for two parishes and was in the running for two others. I also was hoping at that moment to be interviewed for a job as a lecturer in Theology and Development in New College. It was difficult to bring God directly into these prospects. Never is self-deception so easy as when applying for posts and positions. Never does the providence of God seem so anarchic, capricious, unfathomable, confusing, dismaying, disappointing.

I thought about those who had treated me unjustly at Edinburgh University. Was I expected to forgive them? Could I? Lack of silence, peaceableness, discretion - these berated my conscience. Christian truth, truth, truth about God - these were what others interpreted negatively as unruliness and lack of trustworthiness and loyalty. Nothing had changed over the decades of my call. There was no space to be myself. I could not prophesy. I could not share the heights of vision given to me. No-one wanted to know. And no-one ever asked the right questions of me. No-one ever perceived what was really going on. That was forgivable. But what was less so was the arrogance of those who presumed their own rightness in place of mine. Because that was all it was. Just a battle for supremacy, one over another. A power game. And what if in me there was something more of God than people seemed to be able to understand?

Once you stop eating, you slow down. Your system actually 'rests.' It is a wonderful feeling. So is having an empty stomach. It is bliss. We spend so much of our time stuffed with more food than is necessary. A holiday from ingestion, digestion and expulsion is wonderful. It is like a trip into an exotic land with all the delights of sight and mind to transform the grey impress of daily existence.

I was tired of the struggle of my life. Life as a student, in Africa, in the parish and at Edinburgh University had never been easy. I wanted to live in peace. Where could I live at peace with integrity? I hoped a rural parish would minimise the opportunities for conflict and make me less of a target than I had hitherto been in my public ministry. In the fast I was beginning to 'bottom out.' Dying to self is not easy. You have to let go. The stimuli of society depart. You have become attached to them - the daily newspaper - the 'buzz' of city and University life - faces - the roles you play - people's expectations of you - television news - personal dreams - and they all recede into non-existence.

It seemed that to become a monk and spend my time in prayer and contemplation and in writing would be a good thing. Yet I could not subscribe to Roman Catholicism and what I had seen of monastic life seemed far from ideal or even healthy to me. The discipline of the best practice of monastic calling might be good for me but I loved the earth and its beauty and personal freedom and anonymity far too much to be able to live in a community regulated by arbitrary guidelines.

How much of my rebelliousness was of God and how much was simply my own sinful self-expression? It was hard to accept what God seemed to ask of me. Rewards and encouragements from God seemed to be in inverse proportion to my lot in life. I longed for God to answer my prayers before I had asked them. I longed not to have to struggle with God so much. I was exhausted by the effort of being a Christian. And of failure. Here was I with real prospects of unemployment and homelessness looming. I wondered if my years of Chaplaincy had been years of personal indulgence. I had had a prestigious position, gifted colleagues and for the last two years a comfortable salary for the first time in my life. Why should I expect that to continue? Many of those who served Jesus Christ in this world were worse off.

To him who is given much, much is required, I thought. And I have not returned sufficient for God's huge spiritual investment in me. And that was the heart of the problem. I did not consider myself a good Minister. The Chaplaincy had given me space to live in relative peace. Christians had pursued me, harried me and disposed of me. Yet over me there had ever been a kindly Providence, more beautiful, eternal and real than all human emotions, joys and sorrows. While fasting I lost a stone in weight and that did me some good. The living truths of Scripture were more accessible and understandable and instantaneous. Prayer was relationship and not estrangement.

I realised too that on Easter Sunday coming I would be forty-seven years of age having been born in 1947. A hope was raised within me for a watershed in my life on earth and in my relationship with God. I prayed that I may be enabled to live better from now on - there was a wish to do so - and a prayer also for gifts of sight and understanding of what the relationship between God and spiritual vocation may be. There was prayer and hope for practical guidance in practical matters, to know God's will and to make the right decisions. I saw the need to seek God's will rather than my own. My spiritual history seemed chaotic and full of trauma and defeat, saved only by such intimations of God's Love as had been given to me.

While fasting, the idols of the society in which we live loomed larger and uglier, especially wealth and its luxurious concomitants. Simplicity was beautiful by comparison. Eternal reality missed by so many contrasted with the falseness of human pursuit. So much theological teaching in our universities was wrong and harmful and evil. So much was merely an expression of unredeemed human will and spiritual ignorance. The churches were most profoundly corrupt. So many false prophets spoke in the name of Christianity and of God. The faithfulness on earth of Jesus was made more of a divine miracle given the nature of the world. The remaining and absolute mystery of God mitigated by the generous provision in Jesus Christ for our friendship with God and for eternal salvation. The miracle of divine calling to live for and witness for God in Scotland for the rest of my life. Heightened intercession for others. A blessed Maundy Thursday Holy Communion Service in Holyrood Abbey Church. The expectation of a joyful return to eating. Substantial inward rest and peace, sanctification of the soul, cleansing of the mind and heart and voice and temperament.

All these were riches which few in this earthly life may find. I felt utterly blessed. I could not deny that God must love me, that God must have some time for me and that there must be a place for me on earth as well as one in heaven. This feeling was worth everything I had ever known, experienced or possessed. I could freely worship in my soul. Above all, I thought that a change had occurred. My life up to that point seemed full of striving and self-will, personal choice, decision and resolution. It seemed that from now on I would be less in charge of my own destiny than I had tried to be. I would live more by faith than I had hitherto. There was a deepening and a surrendering in the inner man.

I suffered no pain or distress throughout the fast and felt upheld by God from beginning to completion. I did not sleep as much and the morning wakings were filled with peace and blessing. I found that I could not climb the ninety-two steps to my flat in the last days of the fast as quickly as normal. Holy Week 1994 was a watershed for me. It was a state of blessedness. I sought to be a better servant of Jesus Christ than I had been. Sunday 3rd April was Resurrection Day, the Lord's Day and my birthday. Was there a happier man than me on earth? I did not think so.

## Carberry

Although I was on the short leet for several pastoral charges, by May of 1994 it looked as if none of them would call me as their minister. I was due to leave my position in July but I had asked if I could stay on temporarily in the University flat if I had nowhere else to go to. The new Convener of the Chaplaincy Committee, Mr Roy Pinkerton made it clear that I should not be around by the start of term.

By July, I was no longer expecting to have a job to go to and my concern was simply to find a place to stay. I wrote to the Reverend Jock Stein, Warden of the Church of Scotland's Conference Centre at Carberry Tower situated not very far away in East Lothian to ask if he knew of any accommodation which I could rent. To my great surprise he telephoned to say that he could probably help with accommodation and that Carberry was looking for a Development Officer and was I interested? I was.

I had visited Carberry only once or twice in the past. I had never found it prepossessing although the memory of the cross in the garden outside the Chapel always remained. Jock Stein had actually invited me to speak at Carberry during my tenure of the Chaplaincy, once at a Carberry Festival and once at a Christmas House-Party. He had given me the title "Dear God, why is it not working?" for one of these presentations and I had gone into great detail about this - a little to his discomfiture. His wife Margaret is also a Church of Scotland Minister. I had invited her to preach at the Bi-Centenary Service for the School of Agriculture in 1992. She had preached very well indeed and had impressed everyone, including sceptical academics who were present with her grasp of the occasion and the suitability of the message she delivered.

I did not know Jock Stein well. He was by reputation an evangelical. I was invited to attend a week-end brainstorming session on 'The New Carberry.' It transpired that the Church of Scotland Department of Parish Education which owned the title to Carberry wanted to dispose of the property and use the funds to develop St Colm's College. Carberry is a Scottish castle dating from 1480 which was gifted to the Church of Scotland in 1961 for a nominal fee by the Elphinstone family for use as a centre for young people. Carberry has twenty thousand guests each year, including local and day visitors. It is one of those places where God meets people in their times of personal crisis. It is a place of healing where many have found Christian Faith and spiritual renewal. But it is also a place where broken people have come to be made whole again. And the healthy have discovered something while at Carberry in themselves or about God which they had not previously known. It seemed a suitable place for me to be at this point in my life. I would never have chosen to be at Carberry. I had nowhere else to go. The image of Carberry held by many within the Church of Scotland including myself was of an old-fashioned and out-of-date place with a kind of claustrophobic and suffocating piety which put people on the defensive.

And so I was asked to join the effort already in progress to save Carberry from closure and sale and preserve its spiritual and humanitarian work for the future. It seemed a noble enough cause. I enjoyed some early humour with the unfairly named Albert Bogle. For some reason, my first impression of what was going on at Carberry was not entirely favourable. Often in my life, I counter such impressions with humour since to confront them would make life impossible. But I did say to Albert when thinking about the future, "We could have photographs of Jock and Margaret Stein in our lounges and in public places." And I did say to Margaret Stein that we who would be part of the new venture could be called "The Steinies" (after the Moonies). She grimaced! First impressions are sometimes worth remembering. They may not be substantive nor have evidence to justify them. These may come in time.

I was interviewed for the position of Development Officer by six people over lunch. I had agreed to come initially for a trial period as a volunteer, beginning on 1st September 1994, receiving board and lodging and a monthly allowance. I was very glad simply to have somewhere to go to - somewhere to lay my head. I realised that much harm had been done to me and that it may be a long time if ever, before I would be rehabilitated in my Church. O'Neill had got his wish. I was finished.

I registered as an unemployed person at the beginning of August 1994. I did not enjoy attending the Employment Office in Lauriston. But my future was uncertain and I wanted to have my National Insurance record protected. It was desperately painful to stand in that queue to 'sign on.' I wondered if any other Chaplains to the University of Edinburgh had been left in such poor circumstances. I doubted it. Yet they balanced the ignominious nature of my beginning. The Lord gave, and the Lord took away. Blessed be the name of the Lord!

At the beginning of September I began living and working in Carberry. I was given a two roomed flat with a bathroom but without a kitchen at the back of the main building directly above the house kitchens where all deliveries were made and where rubbish was uplifted in large green wheely-bins. There was much internal pain - an agony of bitterness in fact - and I realised that I had been in no fit spiritual state to embark on a pastoral ministry of reconciliation. Not that that was why no-one had wanted me. Single, in my mid-forties, without a lot of parish experience and academically inclined - I was no-one's ideal ministerial profile. I had inoculated myself against rejection - but - it always hurt just the same. I had so much to give - to share - to preach - to teach. It mattered not. Deep within, however, I thought I recognised a wiser guidance. I could not go on expending my life so sacrificially for so little return. In trying to fulfil my vocation as truly and as honestly as I could, I simply set in motion reactions and counter-reactions which destroyed me. This could not go on. I needed a time of internal healing, a time for reflection, a time to find a better way forward for myself, or at least, a time to recharge my batteries for another struggle. I had never been a community person. Not by choice but of necessity was I here. But I accepted this as humbly as I could - as a learning process - as a spiritual discipline if that was what it was to be. God's will.

The silence of the nights embalmed me. No more noisy city police, ambulance and fire brigade sirens throughout the night. At Carberry the gentle toll of the clock and the communications of the owls lifted me a little from my light sleep - only to emphasise how still and peaceful this new place was for me. There were early indications of laughter. During a Painting and Prayer Retreat, attended mainly by elderly ladies, a young male streaker (a practical joker from a nearby village) had disturbed such an one. The matter was raised at the Staff Meeting. Someone said that this had been a foolish and dangerous thing to do. "One of the ladies might have had a heart attack." I thought to myself irreverently, "Perhaps the event made her week for her." Elderly women are extremely redoubtable and tough. I doubted whether any such person would at all be phased by such an occurrence. The overladen concern amused me. It transpired too that a police dog, called in to chase some young vandals from the grounds, had inadvertently frightened yet another of these Painting and Prayer ladies. It was obviously full of hazards - to be on a retreat at Carberry! And a hapless gentleman guest who, having forgotten his keys and being locked out, had been trying desperately to attract the attention of someone by throwing stones at a window when a zealous watchman had set the dogs upon him. And there was a wonderful story about a young apprentice groundsman who spied a cat belonging to the Steins mewing pitifully outside their door in the rain. The Steins' letter-box is large. The young man took pity upon the cat. He squashed it through the letter-box. And then he found that the door was not locked after all.

I was introduced to Pencaitland Parish Church by Donny McAlpine, Carberry's Senior Groundsman and an elder in that congregation. I began worshipping in Pencaitland Parish Church. I think it was the drive through the countryside that made me want to worship there. At the end of the Service, with the sun streaming through the south windows and much peace in my heart, I knew I was in the right place.

And sometimes I wept briefly. So much had gone wrong. I had been against great odds throughout my life. Jesus had borne many sorrows. I myself knew that He had not easily or cheaply redeemed the world. I have sometimes said to Jesus in prayer that it was easier for Him than for me. He had not had the weight of consciousness of sin that I had borne throughout my life. And - for Jesus - it was bad - it was intense - it was terrible - but it had not lasted long on earth. For such blasphemies, I always asked forgiveness.

And I found myself not striving nor driving nor competing nor struggling. I was not the main man here at Carberry. I had an advisory role. It was a relief for a time and I welcomed it. But - I knew I was not expressing the full range of my gifts and calling. And, of course, I wondered if I ever would again. I began not to associate my life any longer with any purpose of God. I was in bereavement. When university term began in October - my adrenaline flowed - and there was nothing - but a numbness and a disbelief. On October 16th, Professor Tom Torrance visited Carberry. He introduced me to his friends saying, "The best University Chaplain Edinburgh had - and Duncan Forrester and others blocked his second term." I was surprised by the first part of his sentence which was a kindly exaggeration. And the second part made me realise that there is a perception and you don't need to strive to make people understand. His words were much more helpful than perhaps he could have known or intended.

## The 'New' Carberry

I was concerned by a number of indicators which I perceived in my earliest days at Carberry. While Jock Stein and I shared an evangelical doctrinal stand-point, there was a deeper dividing of the ways. I felt a collision 'in the air' one moment one day and I inwardly felt that I was being assessed along psychological lines. I did not like that. Invariably such assessments are wrong in my case. I do not deny that a psychologist may find me a treasure of contradictions and analysable characteristics. Psycho-history is an interesting exercise of the human imagination. But it is quite wrong to put the rigid template of a narrow theory of human personality over a complex life and try to define it in such terms. I kept quiet about my relationship with God far too much and too often for my own good. The consequent space was left to be colonised by any theory which was handy to those who wished to obtain control over me. Jock and Margaret Stein had been encouraging certain 'New Age' types of personality testing courses at Carberry and it was strongly put to me to attend at least one of these. I never did so. I do not decry these absolutely. My free choice is to live my life in relation to God primarily and to see where that takes me and how I may respond to whatever happens. I accept that psychologically recognisable characteristics may follow for those interested in that level of explanation but that does not bind me to accept such a level of interpretation, especially if I think that it will simply negate the very relationship which is the meaning and mainspring of my life. This personal strategy is taken by some to be pride and arrogance, oddness, extreme individuality or perhaps even a manifestation of primary delusion.

A second indicator of difficulty was given when, after Jock Stein had read a copy of my account of my time as Chaplain to Edinburgh University which I had presented to him, he dismissed its import by comparing me with one of his house-keepers who he had been unable to eject from Carberry upon retiral. He took John O'Neill's side against me and I realised that Jock Stein was part of the same Establishment against which I had struggled for the previous five years. It was a particularly frightening and sobering insight into Jock Stein's mind. From that moment I knew that I was not safe with Jock Stein. Spiritually safe. We inhabited different places. As a useful functionary at Carberry, I may survive. If I dared to share the realities of God given to me, I would not. And if I struggled for righteousness, I was as likely to suffer at Carberry as I had done anywhere else in my life.

'The New Carberry' seemed to be modelled on an English public school (and to such an one Jock Stein had been sent from Scotland as a child). Those Friends of Carberry who were closely involved with the rescue bid were politically Conservative. Some were wealthy and some were outright Thatcherites. I protested immediately upon arrival against the decision, already made, to dismiss the entire part-time domestic staff of Carberry, hard-working, poorly-paid local women as they were, when 'The New Carberry' was to come into existence. This infamous strategy was concocted ostensibly with the dual purpose of saving money and bringing in more amenable personalities who would work for board and allowances out of their own mixture of personal agenda and searching. I compared this strategy to the Highland Clearances. I thought of

Carberry's own history as a 'big hoose' built and maintained by the exploitation of low paid workers over the centuries. I could see no blessing of God upon such a venture being ordered in such a way. I did not agree that the domestic women would keep the spiritual development of the new community back and I did not think it wise for Carberry to disassociate itself from the local community and labour force. Over the first months of my time at Carberry I pursued the issue of how much money would actually be saved by replacing the local part-time domestic staff with twice the number of volunteer staff who would require board and lodging, allowances and pastoral oversight. My own calculations contradicted the stated claims that I had been given. When I questioned why there was such a discrepancy, it was suggested to me that I leave Carberry.

I was concerned from the outset that the main strategy for 'The New Carberry' depended on receiving large sums of money from wealthy people, wealthy trusts and businesses. I thought Carberry should earn its keep more honestly. It had not been able to do so but I thought that under better management there must be the possibility that it might. I was troubled that there was no clear spiritual rationale to justify Carberry's future existence or to attract people to Carberry in sufficient numbers to justify its future existence. It was not Iona.

On the other hand I knew only too well how hard it is to do anything spiritually significant in Scotland. Jock Stein was part of the evangelical caucus which was badly treated by the liberal establishment of the Church of Scotland. He was trying to move beyond a particularly restricting type of Presbyterianism as represented by certain committees in 121 George Street, the Church of Scotland's administrative headquarters. I sympathised with these things. I may have known something of the mind of God but I had to test prayerful perception and Biblical teaching against what I was seeing and hearing. Jesus had tough things to say to some. Though I suspected that there were serious if not fatal flaws in the plans already prepared, I knew that God might tolerate what was wrong for a greater good. As far as humans are concerned, God only ever plays a percentage game. We are imperfect. He cannot go against His own nature.

And there was a greater good. Carberry was a place where young people came and found freedom of Christian expression which made sense of local parish life in a way that otherwise might not happen for them. Older people came in life crises, broken and bruised (and some battered) and found at Carberry a healing experience, a reforming of personality, a renewing of the inner person and an encouragement to move on to better things. Carberry was worth saving. Carberry was worth the effort. Carberry deserved my commitment.

And so I continued in my work as Development Officer, with a modest salary from 1st November. I thought that God's will would become apparent through Providence. My instincts might prove justified. I would work hard and diligently for the cause. I would offer the best advice I could even if it was not always welcomed. I would learn God's ways again. If I was significantly wrong at the end of the day, I would be willing to say so. Thus I lived with my conscience. I had nowhere else to go. I thought occasionally that maybe God had wanted me at Carberry for those higher things and less for the unspectacular graft connected with fund-raising, marketing and pastoral duty around the House. God may have done so but no-one else did.

And from the start I took my coffee and tea breaks with the staff and not with the Wardens. This was as natural for me as it had been to work on building sites as a student. I loved their company and I grew to love the Carberry staff. And I began to see in them much that others seemed not to see. And I tried to give them dignity as they gave me the healing of their humour and the example of their endeavour.

I recalled that years before while a Minister in Overtown I had written a note in my diary on Thursday 18th February 1988 which was to become more understandable in the months that lay ahead. "I met Jock Stein who was speaking at our Woman's Group last night; distant, humourless man but able and committed." Less flattering and more accurate was a further note on Friday February 3rd 1989. Some weeks before I had sent an extract of a book I had written on African Theology in the hope that it might be published by Jock Stein's Handsel Press. "I phoned J Stein about my book and got the coldest possible reception. Oh how I wish sometimes I could treat people with such cruelty. How can you be a Christian and be so hurtful?" This lack of humanity, of real empathy with the human condition was apparent in the way Carberry had been run. A privileged upbringing, a public school education and wealth unusual for a minister had created a 'little rich kid' personality, used to getting its own way, recognising no alternative and undermining and rejecting anyone whose understanding of Christianity might conceivably be deeper.

No-one would deny that Jock and Margaret Stein had been dedicated Wardens of Carberry over the years. Jock shared the view that the liberal Church of Scotland was in terminal decline. Carberry could be exempted from the consequences of such decline if it could be allied to the growing evangelical wing of Scottish church life, both within and beyond the Church of Scotland. This was a sound policy as far as it went but it also made ecclesiastical and theological enemies for Carberry. These were found not so much among ordinary church-goers but in the centralised committees where decisions were made. A curious range of experimentation in pseudo-psychological 'New Age' self-discovery courses and mild charismatic revivalism had come to dwell together at Carberry. This was paradoxical even to some who were of good will towards Carberry. But it appeared that whatever Jock thought was all right was all right. Carberry had become a personal fiefdom, run autocratically, not without occasional humanity or personal generosity and certainly not without hard work - but - problematically semi-independent from the democratic principles and checks and balances of the Presbyterian system of accountability.

Wealth does make people arrogant. And God is just and does not give the proud all of his own wisdom. Jock Stein seemed to be a very poor judge of human character. Indeed this represented a fatal flaw in a community setting in which people would always be the key to whatever success might be achieved. Jock Stein was off-hand with people and off-hand with his decisions. Had he given up his personal wealth and become a worker like the others at Carberry, dependent on a job and on other people, he would, I think, have treated us with greater care and made his decisions more thoughtfully. He had not. Yet the Bible as far as I can understand it advocates God's justice and compassion for those without power, influence or wealth in this world. Had nine years of this style of management done Carberry any favours? The throughput of staff had been extraordinarily high. You always got the feeling that it was all like the little boy who would not play football unless he wins. Should he not be winning, the game has to end there and then. It is *his* ball!

But it was not. Carberry belonged not to Jock Stein but to the Church of Scotland. The staff were employees of the Church of Scotland as Mr and Mrs Stein were. I thought that the issue was not ownership at all. It was stewardship. Yet Jock Stein's treatment of staff in the mid-nineties was reminiscent of that endured by working people in and through and after the industrial revolution. There was an instrumental view of labour. Personal distancing laced with paternalism. Examples of genuine concern and kindness and gross favouritism. You cannot make people feel dependent and expect to get the best from them. Often after I had left Jock Stein's company I felt diminished. Sometimes while talking with him and afterwards I felt myself under extreme spiritual distress which I tried to disguise. I noted this regular occurrence and considered reasons why it should be happening. I encouraged myself with a word spoken to myself more often than it should have been in what was supposed to be a Christian place. "I work for Jesus Christ not for Jock Stein." It would not have been tolerable otherwise. But 'The New Carberry' was an attempt to gain ownership and control over Carberry. And the way this was planned left me with many misgivings. I hung in there out of a sense of broader vocation and hopefully higher and longer term divine purpose.

There was much enjoyment from time to time. I shared in an "Encouraging Men" week-end conference. Marion Dodd, a former opera singer and now a parish minister came to teach a bunch of men to sing. One joke followed another. When we were introducing ourselves, I said: "I get out of here in 1996. I've tried to escape several times. The alsatians got me. So did the perimeter fence." And I Christened the place "Carberry Maximum Security Retreat Centre." At one point the following minor conversation took place:

> Marion - You can serenade your wife
> Robert  - That will be hard for me
> Marion - Why, where is she?
> Robert - I haven't got one
> Willie - You can serenade mine

At breakfast, Jock gave me a most generous introduction and asked me to say Grace. I stood up and said:

> "For orange juice, cornflakes and buttered toast
> Praise Father, Son and Holy Ghost."

And then there was a hilarious moment which I will always remember.

Jock - This book "The Singer" is a metaphor for the uniqueness of Christ.

Robert - I know another book with a similar theme

Jock - What is it called?

Robert - Wan singer, wan song

Jock - I've heard of it - who wrote it?

This type of week-end conference also justified Carberry's existence. Some of the men had been told at school to "Shut up" because the teacher (female) said they sounded awful. They had always wanted to sing and to sing in church, but they felt inhibited. In fact, two were good singers and one in particular had a lovely tenor voice. Marion Dodd's tuition took us back to our primary school days. "Sit up straight!" But - in being together we found a release from our inhibitions and we sung heartily and well as a result.

## Strategy And Politics

The basic issues involving Carberry remain complex. As a gift, the Church had to find a use for Carberry unlike another Church of Scotland Conference Centre called St Ninian's, Crieff, funded by the Department of National Mission which grew out of the ministry of the legendary D.P. Thomson. Carberry's annual subsidy by the mid-nineties was about £80,000. The fifteenth century castle was expensive to run. Twenty-four hour fire protection duty is required. By this time the Church of Scotland was having to prioritise its work. There was not enough funding for all its obligations. With the Department of Education's St Colm's College expanding its teaching role, Carberry was the worst off of the Church's three Conference Centres. St Ninian's has a ministry and evangelism training function within the Church of Scotland. St Colm's has found a market niche in complementary areas of parish education. Carberry was associated with liturgical renewal and experimentation, some revivalism and some forms of personal education. Carberry was not known for one distinctive thing. Carberry did some things moderately well. It was the place itself, the character of the house, the lovely grounds and perhaps a 'swinging' dimension as might befit a fine house of one-time aristocracy which attracted those who came and who returned. Jock Stein fitted the bill. He was, in effect, the laird.

There were theological politics. St Ninian's is perceived to be evangelical. St Colm's is liberal. Carberry under the Steins is perceived to have become evangelical although some of its 'New Age' type of courses raise evangelical eyebrows. In a system which only a Church could devise, the Carberry property title was owned by the theologically liberal Department of Education and the work funded by the evangelically minded Department of National Mission. Carberry was no-one's only child. Looking to the future, the gnomes of '121' decided that it would be impossible to justify spending any large sum of money on repairs to and upgrading of Carberry. Their studies had shown that significant work would have to be undertaken to the roof in particular.

Thus a plan was formulated to present the case for closure and sale of Carberry to the May

1994 General Assembly. A Friend and supporter of Carberry by an amazing Providence had found himself serving on the relevant central committee at 121 George St. When it looked certain that the General Assembly would be asked to sell Carberry, he withdrew from the committee, informed the Wardens, Jock and Margaret Stein, and with others began the rescue bid. The initial task was to present a counter deliverance to the 1994 General Assembly asking for time to prepare a business plan to take over Carberry as a self-governing trust. This was done. There was much sympathy and good will for Carberry at the General Assembly and Carberry, supported in debate by key people such as John Bell and Will Storrar won the day. My own involvement began in September 1994.

In February 1995, The Friends Of Carberry were offered the possibility of a most generous lease by the Education Department of the Church of Scotland. A twenty-five year lease with an eight year rent free period was suggested. It was turned down. My advice was to accept it but this was ignored. I thought that the Elphinstones had given Carberry to the Church of Scotland and that it should remain closely linked to the Church of Scotland. If people at 121 George Street did not have the inclination or expertise to run it properly, then indeed a group such as Friends had every right to try to make it work. But - I thought Carberry could be made to work for the Church of Scotland and not against it.

However, Jock Stein was by temperament an Episcopalian and made no secret of his admiration for the Episcopal system. That 'will to power' dimension of the human spirit is common in Episcopalianism. I saw the issue of service to be more important. Stewardship, not ownership; people, not money; service, not will to power. But - I had come in when the basic strategy had already been laid. And I had nothing in this life, no money, no property, little influence and few friends. All I had was an understanding of how I had seen God work throughout my own life. This was not my show.

Friends of Carberry thought that they might acquire Carberry for nothing because they were willing to carry on Carberry's valuable work. There was merit in this hope. Carberry had not cost the Church of Scotland much in 1961. The Church did not want to carry the work on. Therefore, the property could be transferred to a sister charity for little. Some of the Friends even thought that the Church of Scotland's Department of Education was being difficult, obstructive and mean-spirited. Some talked about leaving the Church of Scotland if it transpired that there was no way for them to acquire Carberry. I suspected that the Scottish Episcopal Church would be the beneficiary.

It seemed that so much of the planning was about money and not about people. The staff were almost totally ignored in the planning process and I myself had more substantive input than those who had worked at Carberry for years. I understood that Jock Stein did not want to lose momentum in a death of a thousand fears and objections to his plans from members of staff . But - I also thought that had he been alongside his staff there would have been no cause for such fear and paranoia. In fact - members of staff had many helpful and constructive ideas - but these were not considered. It looked more and more as though Jock Stein wanted only his ideas and plans to be put into practice. I thought that in not taking the staff with him, in not even trying to do so, in deliberately and strategically excluding them, he had stolen something precious from them as human beings, as Christians, as workers and as living members of a Carberry Community which already existed.

Extraordinarily we held meetings about property development without having the highly intelligent Factor present. I requested that Mr Lunn be invited to serve on the Steering Committee. This was done and Mr Lunn's sagacious and invaluable advice was thereafter utilised. Indeed when I strongly supported David Lunn in his contention that we were wrong in accepting only the seller's valuation of Carberry as Jock Stein had wished to do and I myself presssed for our own valuation to be undertaken, George Burnet followed through and this process saved the Friends £100,000 on the purchase price. Neither David Lunn nor myself received any acknowledgement or thanks for our significant help. It was not acknowledged either that my own representations necessitated having to oppose Jock Stein in committee. The wisdom and humanity and common-sense of others were ignored. How paradoxical to present the formation of a Christian community by denying the existence of Christian people already in community! It was put to me quietly from time to time by people outwith Carberry that Jock Stein did not consider the staff of Carberry to be 'Christian' enough to take the place forward. He seemed to pick out the local part-time domestic staff for particular attention in this respect. He longed for a dedicated evangelically minded staff and chaffed at what he thought were negative, argumentative and unspiritual aspects of people who worked at Carberry. Perhaps Jock Stein had never got along side his staff sufficiently, had never understood them well enough and had never got close enough to them to realise that he had been given treasures which he had not been given the grace to recognise. Thus Jock Stein may ever have strained at gnats and swallowed camels. Was this a contributory factor in Carberry's apparent decline?

Jock Stein had told me that we would have £500,000-£600,000 gathered by the time of the 1995 General Assembly in May. I asked where this money was going to come from. He replied, "Don't worry, it will come." So assured was he of his own rightness and of God's will. He told me that he had personal contacts who would raise the money required. He had asked God for and prayed for this money as an earnest and proof of God's approval of his plans. By March there was nothing. I saw him decrease in stature before my eyes. I knew he was suffering and I was tempted to take advantage of the situation. Instead, I did the opposite. I tried to help by suggesting alternative sources of funding so that his prayers would be answered. I hoped that God would make His will known and I wanted to leave space for that to happen. I had strong reservations about what was being done. Especially, I continued to find the decision to dismiss the local domestic staff to be morally without foundation, historically problematic and in practical terms, absurd. The 'money before people' strategy was to me a denial of what I understood to be God's will as seen throughout the Bible. And the demoralised staff and their humiliations and tears made me deeply angry that anyone should get away with such inhumanity.

There was a climate of fear. People did not speak out. They were afraid of the Warden's retributions. I experienced these. Especially after meetings in which I had taken a different view of things from Mr Stein! I waited the following day for the outburst or the derogatory remark, the cold shoulder or the ritual humiliation. It never failed. And as I got to know the staff better, we shared our common suffering. If something had not gone well - we used to line up to see who was to take the punishment. At least Jock Stein was fair. We took it each in turns. At Carberry there was no organised staff representation. Here was a throwback to the eighteenth and nineteenth centuries, to a mill or a colliery or, indeed a brick work! One person with absolute control and with an attitude to working people quite without acceptability except perhaps in post-Thatcherite sweat-shop Britain.

At the end of March we received word that two trustees of the N.E.P. (New Era Philanthropy) Trust would visit Carberry with a view to donating funds. This was not a 'New Age' organisation but a Christian one inasmuch as any large financial concern originating in America can be Christian. Jock Stein was late for the meeting. Before the meeting I discussed with our lawyer Richard Filleul the hugely optimistic request of Jock Stein for £750,000 from this Trust. We both agreed this was unrealistic. I suggested we ask for £100,000 each year for three years. He agreed. Jock Stein came to the meeting so late that I had already negotiated this sum and they had agreed to let us know soon whether it could be given. And we went to the Chapel and prayed for Carberry. Such piety! Two days later Jock Stein received a letter confirming the gift. He was ecstatic. His prayers had been answered. God had recognised his plans. 'The New Carberry' was to be.

But one week before the General Assembly of 1995, the 'Guardian' newspaper carried an article informing everyone that the N.E.P. Trust had filed for bankruptcy protection with huge debts. At the same time, Jock Stein received a telephone call from one of the men who had visited Carberry in March during which he was told to expect the worst. It was also alleged that the American Director of the N.E.P. Trust who had also visited Carberry in March, had been operating a pyramid type scam. Thus in my view, Jock Stein's proof of God's approval of his plans was set at nought. I did not think that God might not have a plan for Carberry, but I equally did not believe that Jock Stein's plans were acceptable in their present form. At best, I thought that this was a dramatic warning of the future bankruptcy of the proposed Carberry Trust. I thought that that could be a warning so that such a bankruptcy could be avoided rather than be an inevitable consequence of continuing to try to save Carberry. But to me it was a definitive moment.

I thought that my advice to accept the lease agreement seemed to have been vindicated and I still advocated a reconsideration of that route. That did not happen. A day before the General Assembly was due to debate the Carberry issue, Jock Stein told me that they were going to agree to the Department of Education's insistence upon a commercial purchase of the property and offer a deposit of £250,000 with a loan agreement for the balance of payment. I suggested an acceptance of the earlier lease offer but if that was not possible I said that I thought that if we got five years without any capital or interest repayments we would have a fighting chance to see if the rescue plan could work.

At lunchtime on Thursday 24th May 1995, three hours before the Carberry debate actually took place at the General Assembly, a deal was agreed by negotiators for the Friends of Carberry and the Department of Education of the Church of Scotland for the transfer of the property at a mutually agreed price on the basis of full commercial value with a deposit and a loan, the conditions of which were to be worked out. If no agreement could be reached, a Commission of Assembly was to decide the conditions of sale. This astonished me. I felt that a huge risk was being taken without sufficient thought, consultation or authority from the Friends of Carberry. We were being committed to a purchase and to an upgrading and development plan, the combined costs of which were likely to be upwards of two million pounds. It seemed to me to be a double or quits strategy - an outright gamble. So great was the desire to have the title to the property, and thus control of the work and of the people who made the place function, that this was what happened. And the day after the decision of the General Assembly to accept the resolution agreed by both parties, when I went to Jock Stein's office, I thought we might have had a time of prayer together for the future. Instead, I was given a brutal question. "What are your priorities for fund-raising?"

## Religious Introversion

The church is the church is the church. Whatever you make of it, it is identifiable. Its processes may be arcane and open to abuse. Where there are hierarchies, there are secrecies. Everywhere there are power struggles. Sects form frequently in all ages and cultures. Sects may hold to some or all of the doctrinal principles of the churches while specialising in closer forms of authority and in adding peculiarities of practice. There may be good sects. Is the Society of Friends a sect? Surely there have been and there are also bad sects. A cult forms when restrictions on freedom of movement, freedom of association and freedom of speech are demanded as conditions of membership. Control of the thinking process may follow. This prevents the critical exercise of the mind on what is being experienced. Spontaneous reaction, often seen in a sense of humour, for example, may be discouraged, quenched or forbidden. There will be a dominant figure with acolytes. There will be secrecies. There may be obvious distinctions of wealth and loss of financial independence for some. Dissension will be punished and if continued will lead to expulsion or to such psychological coercion that forces conformity.

Early in my time at Carberry I put some first impressions of what I understood was happening at Carberry down on paper and shared them with Jock Stein. I recalled Martin Luther's doctrine of the dignity of human labour and gently made other suggestions. This was a civilised meeting but I don't think there was any significant change which resulted from it. And on 6th January 1995 I wrote some comments and shared them with Guy Douglas who chaired the Friends' Steering Committee. I warned about Jock Stein's tendencies towards the Carberry staff. "Discipline without charisma equals cult." I suggested that 'The New Carberry' should be a community of Grace. I compared Jock Stein to the sole proprietor of a small business or to a bossy English public school teacher. I raised concerns that volunteer staff were to be obliged to take part in 'personality testing.' Although I did not have strong views on the wisdom of this obligation, I was very concerned that applicants were not to be told of this obligation before coming to Carberry to work as volunteers, or short-term staff as they were to be known. Jock Stein's answer to this expressed doubt had been extraordinary. He actually said to me "If we tell them, they won't come." I could not believe that I was hearing this from a Minister of the Church of Scotland. Why was personality testing thought to be necessary? To mould people into a team? To breed conformity? To eliminate criticism? To form a docile work-force? Just for an experiment? How different this would be from having to endure what Jock Stein referred to as that 'power base,' the local part-time domestic women with their humours and positively healthy attitude to life!

I raised other matters at that time too. I thought that Carberry should not become a personal fiefdom. Better if it remained under the wing of the Church of Scotland. I could not understand why Jock Stein's plans were subject to no serious review, analysis or criticism. The members of the Steering Committee were passive receivers of information. They trusted Jock Stein. They received no other view-point until I arrived on the scene. Then they found the receiving of another viewpoint uncomfortable. I questioned whether it was right to base the entire strategy on receiving money from rich people, rich trusts and businesses. I thought that this 'top down' strategy was flawed. I suggested that Carberry would find greater blessing and a more generous Providence in being the result and consequence of genuine ongoing interest from ordinary people. This 'bottom-up' strategy would simply have accepted a lease agreement, built the new Retreat Centre with money available, cut costs by good management by which means it would be possible to find out in the years ahead if there was a market for Carberry's spiritual and humanitarian work. If Carberry could do this much, there would then be a case for raising large sums of money to purchase the property and continue development. This seemed sensible. It was still a possibility - offered at that time by the Department of Education of Church of Scotland. It was rejected by the Friends of Carberry negotiating team.

Jock Stein also had a soft heart for those struck by misfortune in life. Jock and Margaret Stein have helped many people and have been personally generous to a number of them. Perhaps however they had attracted some of such people to themselves in supporting them. These may not have been sufficiently set free. There has always been a problem with this kind of religious leadership. Dependence. Carberry may have become a place of personal consolation, turning in on itself, making acceptance by the Steins the sole criterion for engagement with the Carberry Community. This, rather than becoming a dynamic outgoing witness to the better things of Christianity. It is possible too that the Steins wanted to be surrounded only by acolytes who would be respectfully appreciative and obedient in everything. This too subjective way of living and working inevitably would breed trouble. Any over-emphasis on individual human personality determining the nature of a Christian community is damaging to everyone concerned.

This was the Church of Scotland's property and money. Ordinary people gave collections, Sunday by Sunday to support the Church's work. There never seems to have been sufficient scrutiny of Jock Stein's management of Carberry. In 1992, Eric Lougheed, a man of integrity who was performing the duties of an honorary auditor, found himself having to inform the Church of Scotland about what he thought were problems with the keeping of the Carberry accounts. This was probably what Jock himself unapologetically called 'creative accounting.' Jock Stein went to Eric Lougheed's home at 11 00pm one evening and tried to dissuade him from this course of action. But he resisted much pressure that was wrought upon him. Auditors were appointed. They decided not to take retrospective action but to monitor everything from that point in time. Eric Lougheed's view was that in order to run a large ship aground you only need to alter course one or two degrees. And he felt that Carberry was being fractionally diverted from a straight and true Christian path. Jock Stein could sit all night in his study and work out papers with ideas, schemes, strategies, projected sums of money and likely outcomes. The trouble was that so often these did not seem to correspond to reality.

Jock could often make members of the Carberry staff feel stupid, even if they were both sensitive and intelligent. I had come from working for five years with some of the most intellectually brilliant people in the country. People with good ideas were often sidelined and isolated by Jock Stein. He could not properly delegate and everything had to revolve around his executive-playing function. It was a one-man-band although silent in the wings, there were deeper souls with greater gifts of 'musicianship' ordered silent by the conductor. As early as the 6th of January 1995 I had asked, "If the strategy to raise funds from large trusts fails before the 1995 Assembly, can we ask ourselves if there are spiritual reasons for this connected with the problems in the present vision for 'The New Carberry?"

Jock Stein could loose his temper with members of the staff. He was often not at all pastoral or even civil in normal daily routine. I was shocked to receive memos in my tray without my name on them. I asked him to please put my Christian name on memos. Why did I do this? The impression in a spiritual context was one of negation. It was not oversensitivity. It was negation, diminution of me as a Christian person. It made me less than a number, not a person, not one redeemed by Jesus Christ with a Christian name, known and loved by a loving God. It took one month for Jock Stein to do this, reluctantly, seeing no need himself for such pedantry. Whenever he left a memo without my Christian name on it, I returned it unanswered. He started and then stopped, testing me to see if I still had the resolve to continue the fight. I had.

And he treated everyone in this pugilistic way, seeing how far he could ride rough-shod over them, diminishing them, making up, offering warmth and coldness in equal quantities, reducing some of the weaker ones to emotional chaos. And he gathered up our energy unto himself and lived off our spirits and out of our souls. He the great worker of the world, tireless in his service of Carberry - so it appeared to those outside who did not know or would not know the whole truth.

In February 1995 I wrote in my diary that I was demoralised by Jock Stein's tyranny. I had struggled to bring some humanity to the regime which was being planned for 'The New Carberry.' Morning chapel was to be obligatory for everyone. Nothing wrong with that. However, if someone had been working until late evening, say 10 00pm and the following day was such a person's day off, he or she was to be expected to come to chapel just the same. I found this inhuman and said so. Jock Stein relented on this issue. I felt deeply uneasy that I had to intercede in such a way. I pointed out at that time that people in 'The New Carberry' were to be expected to live together, work together, study together, eat daily together, worship together, relax and recreate together in a place without any immediate diversion such as a city outside the main door and with little public transport. I said that no monastery had ever instituted such a regime. Monks and nuns have always had much space to be as individuals and their being together has always been a complement to their personal life before God, the exercise of their skills, interaction with others and frequent releases from the tensions of community living.

It was the harsh disciplinary nature of this proposed regime which made me uneasy. Christianity, I surmised, could not truly be fostered in this way. Examples of Grace were more likely to encourage faith in young people. I feared for the weak who might find their way to Carberry. A community did exist at Carberry throughout my time there. It was a kind of underground community which existed in spite of Jock and Margaret Stein. It was the community of workers. But it was this community which was to be destroyed so that 'The New Carberry' could be formed. This community was made up of real people. Coming from local villages, they refreshed Carberry by their daily presence, bringing common sense, humanity and humour in abundance. They were a window for Carberry and I looked into the future to see the window closing on the outside world. Jock Stein's brother-in law had long warned that left to his own devices, Jock Stein would turn Carberry into a monastery. No. Not a real monastery where everyone shared the same economic standard and where leaders were elected and where they led by transparent examples of piety, humilty and service. This was more a private religious grouping without such personal openness and with a Board of Management whose members, drawn from outside, would decide the fate of participants in the community while not sharing in the life of the community themselves. The spiritual dynamics of 'The New Carberry' were to be conditioned by this strategy. Can the Holy Spirit freely move in and through such constraints? Is this truly a work of the Spirit or is it too much the will and mind of human beings? Is it too much about money and too little about people? Is God invoked but not really made the Centre of everything? I did my best to be a mitigating pastoral figure in the circumstances. I carried a few wounds myself.

The first draft of Jock Stein's Business Plan concerned me. There were no people there. No staff seemed to exist. It was Jock Stein's one man show. I raised this problem at a Steering Committee. I said that people must come first and I was ignored. But later Professor Ewan Brown, a city financier and Christian made the same point and he was listened to. The Business Plan had to be rewritten. Significantly for me, I was not given my full title in the Business Plan. My spiritual persona was negated, my calling excised, my history and ministry diminished. Supposing that this was not done deliberately - what does it say even thus? I was a functionary, an office boy and I thought that I could have been of so much value to Carberry as myself, a called Minister of Jesus Christ. My protest was partially and reluctantly acknowledged. The

Business Plan mentioned me in the same sentence as a mature American female temporary volunteer. I asked Jock Stein in a very civilised manner that I be given a paragraph of description to myself in the Business Plan. I did not do this through spiritual pride. It was simply a correct and fair way to treat me. It was denied - combatively - in the way a boxer puts a man down on the canvas. No-one should rise to be truly themselves - if - they were of a spiritual order, perhaps closer to God than lived Jock Stein. And here was the crux of the problem. Jock Stein diminished and actually did persecute those of spiritual depth and maturity who came to Carberry. He did this to me. And it was for this reason above all, that I doubted the integrity of his plans for 'The New Carberry.' But another one degree off the proper course may lead to spiritual shipwreck in time. I stayed on board in the hope that perhaps I might be able yet to pull the ship back to the direction in which we should have been heading. Vainglory! On February 24th 1995, I noted in my diary, "I shudder to think what the place will be like as an independent trust run by Jock Stein."

I did not want to fight continually with Jock Stein. When I saw him 'down' I prayed much for him. I began to realise what abused women and men in marriage must feel like. I thought too of children abused by cruel parents. The abuse multiplied the wish for acceptance thus keeping the relationship going. I saw people at Carberry like that. I kept my deepest inner counsel. How little Christianity was here at Carberry after all. Was this why in spite of appearances to the contrary, Carberry had not kept pace with the other Church of Scotland conference centres? And on March 10th I noted, "I'd never trust in rich people to save Carberry. I'd trust in the Lord Himself to see us through."

## Carberry Characters

Carberry has always been blessed with some great human characters among its workforce. While I myself lived there coffee times often erupted in hilarious laughter. In particular the extraordinarily funny Liz McKellar kept everyone's spirits up with her outrageous humour, sometimes a bit over the top, but wonderful for staff morale and a happy complement to religiosity. Space does not permit justice to be done to everyone but a few quotes give a sense of the buoyancy of Carberry's community of workers. Liz: "Pick yer windae, yer leavin!" Rena: "Cough, cough, cough, cough, cough," Nettie: "Whit's wrang wi' you?" Rena: "Ma knees are sair." David: "Sex is good for God." George: "Ah'm havin' an awfy job convincin' Donny that this is Friday." May: "We've spoilt the Moderator's heid." Robert: "Ach, he's got a face like a torn pocket anyway." Donny: "David's drying the Chapel with a hairdryer." Margaret H: "Robert, you're like a packet of refreshers in that waistcoat." Margaret D: "Rob (the cook), you're goin tae get a mousse in the face." Viv: (about the Warden's hospitality) "Is this the night the crawlers go for their dinner?"

Most of this humour passed Jock Stein by. Indeed, it seemed as if he was embarrassed by the sound of the raucous laughter which often cascaded from the staff room. One by one the great characters were driven out. Jock Stein thought us impious and was embarrassed before his evangelical friends. I can't help thinking that Jesus of Nazareth might have found our company tolerable. I always thought that a community which was only the fruit of Jock Stein's pathology could not be a happy place.

## Hard Work

I found it hard to work well at Carberry. I seemed to make more mistakes than I normally would in a job of work. An early problem brought much hilarity. I had been producing various types of promotion literature. A company in Manchester was contracted to print thousands of colour leaflets describing Carberry and its setting and giving details of prices for accommodation. For a laugh, and it was very necessary to try to have a laugh in Carberry, I made a spoof copy with a few altered sentences. One paragraph waxed eloquent about the amenities of Edinburgh and East Lothian. For fun I added the following sentence describing a council-house village near Carberry. "Wallyford, with its own tourist gems, high culture and shopping facilities is within easy reach. Local sage David Lunn is a fountain of wisdom about the social customs of the local population." After advising prospective customers about our night watchman, I added for mischief that he might be accompanied by a friend and a friendly dog with good habits. I showed this spoof to some of the staff who found it very amusing. This nonsense backfired on me however. The company producing the promotional literature faxed me the proof copy of the leaflet before running off the thousands of copies. I was glad that they had done so. Inadvertently, I still do not know how, I had sent them the spoof copy rather than the genuine one. I was deeply embarrassed by my folly and incompetence.

I struggled to concentrate and often had to keep a perpetual discipline of prayer throughout the day to make sure that I was mentally alert. I did not think that this was so much a problem within me. Rather it was a battle with the ethos of Carberry, especially in comparison with the stimulating environment of my last employment. It was also a struggle against negative spiritual equity and at least one large person was the locus of this gravity pull. Throughout my two years at Carberry, I made many mistakes in the daily routine. I found it frustrating. I thought that there was possibly something which positively hindered mental sharpness in the place. That might be typical of a place of spiritual retreat but I thought it was something not necessarily of the Kingdom of God at all. Had this also kept Carberry back over the years? My being gasped to get away at week-ends. The duties of the development officer were to participate in the planning process for 'The New Carberry,' to prepare for a fund-raising campaign, to seek out and find new 'business' for Carberry, to share in some of the planning of conferences and courses and to share in the life of Carberry as helpfully as possible.

I had to be self-starting and self-motivated. Jock Stein left me to get on with the job and I appreciated that flexibility and freedom. I was charged with building up from scratch a database of trusts which would be asked for money. I was given a target of eight hundred but I reached thirteen hundred before stopping. I added to that a database of eight hundred Scottish companies. Everything went well until I began to put alternative suggestions for the future at planning meetings. Then I realised I was there as a means to someone else's grand design and not as an partner with considerable experience and education and with a grip on reality. Building up a database of charitable trusts was not my idea of a good day, but it had to be done. Starting to make contacts which might help at a later day constituted an important part of the job. I had learned about this from Bryan McClure at Edinburgh University. Dogged persistence and stamina were the keys to success. You might work many months without a breakthrough and then everything might be made suddenly worthwhile.

There was an air of unreality about these planning dreams and I feared for the future. But my own duties were sufficient to occupy the days, researching present use of Carberry, designing new promotion literature, finding new avenues for marketing, seeking advertising outlets and opportunities to make people aware of Carberry's qualities and amenities, raising funds for preparatory projects, inviting business and professional people to Carberry to see the facilities, helping to increase the numbers of Friends of Carberry, thinking about and recommending people for particular jobs, duties and functions, physical planning, administration and undertaking unofficial deputy-warden duties where required.

I was a minister and I never ceased to be one. I enjoyed welcoming guests and looking after them, seeing that everything was running smoothly for everyone who visited Carberry. It was often interesting and rewarding at a personal level. I found the lack of personal freedom irksome and felt that I gave more of myself to the community than was appreciated while trying to maintain a deeper spiritual privacy. I felt that I was able to offer a moderating pastoral influence. However I usually got into some kind of trouble for trying to temper the furious nature and the sometimes errant direction of the drive towards 'The New Carberry.'

I did not think that a happy spiritual community could be created by force. I thought money was being wasted on expensive consultants. The internal management was far from good enough to ensure the eventual success of the project. So many small steps could be taken to improve Carberry but these all seemed to founder. There was resistance in Jock Stein against new ideas which he himself had not thought of. He seemed to take constructive criticism personally as a slight on himself whereas anyone coming into Carberry needed to have new ideas to help the place survive and prosper. He did not like me asking why Carberry's interior corridor decor had to resemble that of an early nineteenth century asylum! But others had worked at Carberry for years and had had plenty of ideas which had been discarded. It was never a team effort and there was its greatest fault. Personnel management was as bad as it could be. The internal structure and practice did not, in my view, sufficiently reflect the Kingdom of God.

## Inner Consolation

I was not personally unhappy. Often I felt blessed. I liked living at Carberry. Outsiders did not recognise the problems which existed within. Spring reluctantly began to appear. In March 1995 Anglican Archbishops arrived for a week of meetings. I took Holy Communion with them each morning. On the Tuesday, as I sat in Chapel, I was aware of heaven being opened up and the Lord Jesus and all His saints and the populace of heaven being there - the Communion of

Saints - actual - 'visible.' I felt part of them and that I belonged. Our Holy Communion was like children playing at tea parties with plastic cups and saucers compared with what was to follow in heaven as the real thing. And I thought that whatever I may have or wherever I may be - if I have God's blessing, that is more important than all other factors and issues.

And on the last day of March Ben Lawyers was covered with the whitest snow. The day was glorious with bright sunshine, clear blue skies and air that was fresh and clean. And you could hear yourself breathe - so peaceful was it up there in this late still winter wilderness. It was a purifying contrast to our life of grime and business.

I fasted during Holy Week 1995. The reasons for this fast were to thank God for His faithfulness over the previous Christian Year, to seek guidance and blessing for the future, to pray for Carberry, to pray for others, to consider the life and last days of Jesus and to maintain my relationship with God.

I knew moments of the most profound peace and stillness that week, even though I continued to work as normal and no-one knew what I was up to. The house was quiet too, thankfully. On Maunday Thursday morning Jock Stein picked a fight with me. I was in the fourth day of my fast. He was tense and was holding back his anger. I calmed him with innocence (real and not contrived.) Paranoid as he sometimes was, he had taken umbrage because I had wished to share some suggestions for the future of the Carberry School of Faith and Life with those members of the committee planning the School who had not been present at its most recent meeting. I noted that he had treated me unjustly and without reason and with anger on Maunday Thursday while I was on inner retreat. That same evening I attended Holy Communion at the Baptist Church in Dalkeith. As the elements were uncovered I was possessed of a heightened sense of the beauty of their presence.

And nothing could detract from my inner peace that week. I praised the Living God in prayer. And for the last hours of my fast I was touched and caressed by the Holy Spirit - intensely - as I had been that summer's day on the island of Tiree, as I lay on the western slope, looking out to the sea, praying to God. It was a privilege to know such joy on earth. The contrast with my daily struggles and the squalor of human relationships was marked. I also felt my sinfulness very deeply. And rather than this occasional interlude, I hoped that someday I may live as if I was *always* on retreat.

# 11 : The Christian Right

## Curiouser And Curiouser

I continued to work hard, fulfilling the terms of my contract as best I could. Only if I did so could I expect to be taken seriously if and when I suggested modifications and changes in strategy and policy. It was the Christian right ideology behind 'The New Carberry' that continued to bother me. It represented what I call power evangelicalism (I am not talking here about power evangelism.) Power evangelicalism looks at the churches dying of liberalism and points out that where strong doctrine is preached and personal response and commitment are invited there is a bucking of the dying church trend. This is true and there are many examples of strong congregations within and outside the established churches of this country which testify to life, growth and faith. Accompanying some of this renewal and revival there is an attitude to the world which does not fully reflect that taught in the New Testament. Power evangelicalism takes money, business ethics and market forces seriously. And so it can without conscience put human beings including Christian human beings after power, money and success in status and priority, treating people for whom Christ died as means to ends.

Now it was quite obvious to everyone that Carberry had been trading without viability for years. That was the Church of Scotland's policy. Carberry was not allowed to charge commercial rates and was subsidised to provide a particular resource and ministry. That was good and right. It was also good and right for the Friends of Carberry to try to continue Carberry's work as a self-governing trust. This meant that significant savings would have to be made. Item one on any business savings agenda is wage cost. It has always disappointed me that business strategy far too often has no problem with excessive capital expenditure but always has problems with the salaries and wages of workers. A policy of people first might in fact be more productive in the longer term. And you might have thought that a Christian business would be the very one to try to make such an ideal work in practice. And you might have thought from the Carberry Business Plan that it was going to be such an experiment because it talked about being a sign of integrity for a broken world.

Of necessity 'The New Carberry' would have to earn its living in a competitive environment. But the rhetoric of evangelicalism invoked God as the great Provider. Pray hard enough and the money will pour in. This was good faith up to a point. What bothered me was that the God of the Old and New Testaments is a God of personal justice. I thought therefore that God may not provide oodles of money if the strategy and policy did not offer sufficient respect, dignity and practical love to those who already formed the community of workers at Carberry. I thought that it would be a Christian thing if in 'The New Carberry' the staff were raised up in dignity and recognition, even if there was not in the initial years or so, any money to increase their salaries. I thought that such a policy would indeed be a sign of integrity for a broken world. I was not speaking from a political consciousness or commitment. I was not part of any Christian socialist movement. This was the Gospel as I understood it from Scripture. I still could not see the justification for discarding hard-working part-time women, making them redundant and replacing them all with short term volunteer staff.

## Carberry And Iona?

In June 1995 I gave a paper on the subject "Carberry And Iona - Correcting The Balance?" to the Scottish Evangelical Theological Society. The paper sought to discuss the nature of the influence of the Iona Community in relation to the Church of Scotland and to suggest ways in which Carberry may in the future attempt to offset the Iona Community's narrow theological agenda. Jock Stein was present. I indicated that George MacLeod's establishment based radicalism was no different from the academic radicalism which he had despised. Carberry might be able to counter the defeatism and theological reductionism which had brought the Church of Scotland to its present impasse. Carberry had nothing of the history, pedigree, presence or romantic atmosphere of Iona. Yet its reputation had been of a place where Christ interfaced with His people at the personal level. Iona had been for centuries "The Glory of the West." Carberry had been the home of wealthy and privileged families who had belonged to the Scottish aristocracy. This body, I noted, had not covered itself in glory over the centuries of Scottish history. Numerous betrayals, including that of William Wallace, the material interests of the Reformation Lords, the disgraceful sell-out in 1707, and the cause of The Disruption - these had done us no favours. More recently, the Episcopalian Alec Douglas-Hume had spoken out against Scottish devolution before the 1979 referendum. How could Carberry overcome its history? It had in part been redeemed by its being presented by the Elphinstones in 1961 to the Church of Scotland. Yet under decades of Church of Scotland management, it had remained a 'back door - front door, upstairs - downstairs' place. For years domestic and trades people had to defer to those who worked in the offices in the 'front' of the house. There had been social improvements under the Steins but the 'us' and 'them' mentality still infected the place when I arrived in 1994. I thought that Carberry could be redeemed by becoming a serving community in which those who worked there could be treated as equal members. I saw no need for secrecy. Why could the finances not be discussed openly? People are not stupid. They have a vested interest in the survival and success of Carberry. For some - it is a matter of livelihood. Workers understood how badly the place was managed and could have made many suggestions for improvement. They represented a threat to total control.

George MacLeod was a lord all his days. But - he did have an understanding of working people. The rebuilding of Iona Abbey was a symbol of employment in the depressed thirties. It was only a symbol - but it was an important one. 'The New Carberry' was going to begin its life by putting people out of work. I said that I suspected that this would haunt it for years to come. MacLeod may have been a bully, a man possessed of outrageous contradictions, a showman and more besides, but he did have a sense of humour and he could and did laugh at himself. Jock Stein often complained about my making humours which involved him and in one pitiable moment he even outlawed jokes for 'The New Carberry.'

The early Iona Community saw itself as witnessing not just to Christianity but to political involvement. MacLeod stood against fascism and communism. The dominant ideology of the nineteen nineties is 'the market.' The Business Plan of 'The New Carberry' reflects Christianity and 'the market.' It shares market ideology and does not stand in distinction from it as the early Iona Community had stood in distinction from fascism and communism. I pointed out that throughout Christian history, experiments in community life had only ever been partially successful. Community in itself is a false absolute, I said, as Martin Luther had discovered.

I reiterated that the message of the Church of Scotland establishment in the mid-nineties is "We don't like or want evangelical Christianity." Carberry had been a victim of institutional blood-letting just as George MacLeod had felt that he had been in the year 1949 when he was forbidden to hold the office of parish minister of Govan for the second time while remaining Leader of the Iona Community. The Iona Community had been a conduit for people into the Church for many years. Carberry offered private individuals an opportunity for discovery and renewal of a living faith in Jesus Christ. Pacificism represented a commitment but also an intermediate theological principle which identified the Iona Community for decades. Carberry was not identified by such an established principle. Ideas like 'service' or 'renewal' or even 'revival' might become in time equivalent identifying principles. Words like 'spiritual,' 'retreat' and 'Christian' would be important too. Carberry's profile was not high. Its multi-faceted ministry could not easily be marketed or communicated to an unknowing audience. Spiritual reputation is won slowly and at cost.

I suggested that George MacLeod had been publicly associated with political socialism, whereas the Friends of Carberry, inasmuch as they had any collective identity, were politically conservative. MacLeod had maintained a moral ideological consonance with many people throughout the nineteen thirties, forties, fifties and sixties. It was possible, I reminded those present, that within a short space of time there might be a Labour government again. Market ideology alone may seem quite out of touch with people's general sympathies. Thus it would be difficult to present Carberry as an ideal of Christianity - a sign of integrity to a broken world.

I questioned the fact that Carberry was to be run by a Company with a Board of Directors. This was necessary in order to properly reclaim V.A.T. on development expenditure. But what would it do for the spiritual dynamics of the community? Can the Holy Spirit work in this way? It was to be top-down, elitist management by people who did not live within and share in the life of Carberry. It was bound to crush the spirits of workers, making them fearful and insecure. How could the Holy Spirit invest such a community with freedom and infectious spontaneity? Would there not be a sense of exploitation of cheap labour and the resentments which might result? The declared strategy was, in Jock Stein's words "to work people hard and let them go," to put people through personality testing schemes to induce conformity, and to have one of Jock Stein's personal friends Archie Mills, lecture them vicariously on community and on conflict resolution. The overall purpose of Jock Stein was to have complete control of everything that moved in

Carberry and to manipulate people with 'spiritual' which in Jock Stein's case meant psychological warfare tactics. Jock Stein probably never saw any of this as bad.

George MacLeod was interested in 'New Age' ideas. He was an anti-Calvinist and the Iona Community has done its best to destroy Scotland's Calvinist inheritance. Jock Stein seemed to me to represent a kind of this-worldly evangelicalism which allowed him to remain wealthy, allowed him to seek and exercise power over people, allowed him to experiment with psychological theories both for himself and others and contain Christian revelation within the limits of his own understanding. When he took daily prayers we braced ourselves for a too directly applied lecture on our own conduct. We were seldom raised up out of ourselves into that free and 'objective' worship of God that is the hallmark of true Christianity. If Jock Stein had lost an argument the day or week before, he would have something to add to the same argument when he took prayers. This was particularly vexing because it destroyed that sense of personal freedom in prayer and worship which is essential. In a community where the same people are always worshipping together, it may be even more problematical.

My paper suggested that Christianity in Scotland required a more defined theology than that purveyed by the Iona Community over the last thirty years. At Carberry, as a place of personal events, individual spiritual discovery, as a place of character, of characters and of humour, there was the possibility of continuing a living Christian ministry which might avoid the pigeon-holing labels of all detractors with Scottish Christian circles. George MacLeod had disagreed with Tom Allan on the Christian's right to make political comment. Tom Allan, a prominent Scottish evangelical preacher in the nineteen fifties and sixties had held that a person needed to become a Christian first before embarking on political campaigning. The Iona Community did not accept this condition. And so the Iona Community came to represent what I have called The Political Church in which people mistake political commitment and viewpoint for Christianity and seek to conduct the affairs of the Church as secular politicians conduct the affairs of political parties. This, in my view, has been disastrous. Carberry could perhaps in time balance this error in Scottish Christianity.

MacLeod loved the Church of Scotland. He was a thoroughly realistic participant in ecumenical dialogue and argued vociferously at the perceived sacramental injustices perpetrated by Roman Catholicism and the traditional perfidy of Anglicans. But some of the Friends of Carberry had decided to leave the Church of Scotland if they were prevented from assuming control of Carberry as a self-governing trust. And in meetings the people at 121 George Street and St Colm's College were often demonised.

My paper concluded with a warning about the 'James Jones' syndrome. The danger in a place associated with personal healing is that certain types of people are attracted to life there. Thus it is possible for one person to dominate the others in a way that becomes less and less desirable. Workers from local communities would always offset tendencies to absolute control. They would come in and go out - seeing and hearing - refreshed by the outside world - they would bring views to bear which would keep the community in touch. In an independent trust, too much power may be in the hands of one person. Unless such a person would prove to be an example of sainthood, renunciation, charismatic love and transparent honesty - something would be being born which might breed a bitter harvest in future years. Keeping the balance between freedom and discipline was, in my view essential for 'The New Carberry.' There was an opportunity to balance the less desirable aspects of the Iona Community in Scotland. And there was also the possibility of perpetrating the same mistakes and carrying with these, some even less desirable characteristics which in time would do Christianity in Scotland no little mischief and damage.

## Glorious Summer In Scotland

I made my annual pilgrimage to the West Highlands in June 1995 just as the most wonderful summer weather for a long long time appeared. I had never seen Torridon so clear with all the grey black peaks defining the blueness of the eternal sky. And I saw my first pine marten - so well dressed in brown fur and cream collar, visiting for a little while of the still warm evening. And a deer bounded gracefully across the road in front of the car and leapt majestically into the high brush. Herons stood guard on the islets near Plockton and seals basked by the dozen. And I looked out to Skye, shimmering, misty in the distance from two thousand feet and more on The Pass of the Cattle. Gairloch, Aultbea, Dundonnell, they and theirs, An Teallach, Gruinard Bay, it goes on and on. Such a wealth of natural beauty - peaty streams which make you drunk just listening to their excited greetings. Golden white sands - untrodden - it seemed - quiet and alone as you see the enormous crimson setting sun go home. You are in your element, your natural environment, the world your Maker made for you to be at home in and to enjoy and look after. And you find rest for your soul. And you are glad.

The sun did not rush away from Scotland as usual, busy with other things to do. Our star had time for us this year and waited weeks and months, giving generously of a blissful radiance and a midnight fire. And the islands in the firths and lochs were painted on to our corner of God's cosmic canvas without symmetry so as to be perfect indeed as no human could make them perfect. And you had thawed out of winter's cold by July. You basked in August's light. And even September's ambers glowed each day insuring you against an early coldness and the unwelcome return of winter.

## Fancy Footwork

In July 1995 during one of the Carberry Festivals, Jock Stein called a meeting for guests interested in finding out what Carberry's position was at that time. He did not invite staff but three of us attended. A concerned supporter of Carberry asked how the staff were coping with the uncertainties. Jock Stein replied that in business the practice was to withold information on redundancies until the last minute. He said that on balance the Carberry staff knew too much. I found this language unacceptable. Carberry was claiming to be a Christian place. The staff were *bona fide* employees of the Church of Scotland. They had a right to know about and to share in decision-making. Jock Stein treated the Church of Scotland's property and its staff as if they were his own. I determined not to let him away with this and at two subsequent Friday staff meetings asked him to explain his remarks. Jock Stein hated being challenged on anything.

The Annual General Meeting of the Friends of Carberry was due to take place on September 8th 1995. I was expected to produce an annual report of my work for that occasion. I did so, giving an account of my own stewardship, stating what had been accomplished and offering some personal views on the state of play. I prepared the report and placed two copies on Jock Stein's desk. Five days later I sent out copies to members of the Steering Committee which was due to meet immediately before the Annual General Meeting. When George Burnet, Chairman of Carberry Limited, received his copy of my report he asked me to come and see him. He was not apoplectic but he was getting there. It was Section Nine on "Policy And Principle" which was causing him a problem. Here I had stated that "I believe that as a Christian Minister called by Jesus Christ I have a responsibility to express my own view point on important issues."

I then expressed my regret at the enforced redundancy of the part-time domestic staff, at the exclusion of the Carberry staff from much of the planning of 'The New Carberry,' and the rejection of the Church of Scotland's Education Department's offer to the Friends of Carberry of a twenty-five year lease of Carberry with an eight year rent free period. I also expressed reservations about the narrowness of future plans, about possible treatment of short-term staff and about management strategy. I stated that I thought that Carberry would struggle to raise the large amounts of money envisaged because Scotland is a small country, Friends of Carberry did not know many wealthy or influential people, Carberry's public profile was not high enough and spiritual excellence and reputation are not easily won.

I defended my inclusion of these points on grounds of proper information disclosure to people who were giving sums of money to support Carberry's venture. I thought they should have the opportunity to ask questions. I thought real issues should be debated. The commitment to purchase had not been made with the agreement of the Friends of Carberry. Now they were to be asked to rubber-stamp the actions of the negotiating committee at the time of the General Assembly.

George Burnet forcibly rejected my defence and specifically denied to me that it was my calling as a Minister which had motivated me. I did not like that. He was wrong. Perhaps he thought I was trying to stage some sort of coup against Jock Stein. That - I was most certainly not doing. He said that I lacked judgement. He also stated that if Section Nine of the report was seen by people in 121 George Street the entire rescue attempt would be sabotaged. I thought that this suggested that there was truth in what I was saying in my report. But it was not my intention to wreck the saving of Carberry, if indeed that was what we were doing. I disagreed that he was right. Truth never did hurt a genuine work of God. He asked me to politely to withdraw Section Nine. I said that I would consider doing so.

Members of the Steering Committee were already in possession of my Annual Report. I decided therefore to produce copies with Section Nine re-written, omitting the offending sentences.

I intended to table both copies of my Annual Report to the Steering Committee and ask them to decide which copy they wished to go forward to the Friends' Annual General Meeting. The responsibility for full disclosure of facts and prospects was thereby placed in their hands. I agreed to abide by their decision. I felt relieved and spiritually happy that I chosen this path. I had no wish to jeopardise the rescue attempt of Carberry. I had shared my own best advice with those responsible. It was their decision not to share these matters with the Friends at their Annual General Meeting.

And so Friends were told by Guy Douglas, Chairman of the Steering Committee that the contribution of the N.E.P Trust had been God's sign to them to gain ownership of Carberry. Such a statement defied all spiritual and moral logic that I had ever encountered. Friends supported what had been done. I kept quiet, bemused, and watched. Does God give a sign of bankruptcy as an encouragement to purchase a building and its grounds at the commercial rate without having received agreement to do so? Is this the God of Abraham, Isaac and Jacob? Of Isaiah and Jeremiah? Of Jesus? Of Paul? I could not see it. In the Christian Right, the will of human beings takes over. It is then justified by taking God's name in vain. Power and money predominate. Ownership not stewardship, power not service, money not justice towards members of staff, economy of the truth rather than the transparency required of a Christian organisation rule the mentality of those involved. Secular business ideas more than the Kingdom of God are part of the mixture of motives. And these are justified because the overall intention is stated to be to save Carberry for God's own work. The necessity in business to present a positive front overcame the humbler option of confessing to reality. Strategic withholding of full information was favoured over an egalitarian sharing of truth and responsibility for the future. I did not think that this was God's will at all. Yet - no matter the sinfulness of us humans and the follies of our pride and self-will - I believed that God might indeed wish still to save Carberry in His own way for His own purposes. There are some doubtful moments in the Old Testament and though I can find no duplicity in Jesus Christ, Christianity has lived in a world of compromise and the choice of relative goods. In any case, I wished to allow the project to have its fullest possible opportunity to succeed or fail. I had sought such liberty for myself in times past and had been denied. I was not going to deny it to others even if my best judgement spoke against the means chosen. It was for those reasons that I decided not to tender my resignation. I wanted to see what would happen and still had much to learn through suffering - but I did not know that on September 8th.

## One Flew Over The Cuckoo's Nest

On Tuesday 21st November 1995 the Chairman of the Steering Committee Guy Douglas telephoned and summoned me unceremoniously to a meeting to be held on Thursday 23rd at 1 00pm. "We'll sort this out once and for all," said he. I asked what the meeting was to be about. He would not tell me. "Have I to get the sack?" I asked. Pause. "No." "Oh well, that's not so bad but I need to know what the meeting is to be about in order to prepare for it." " A paper will be read to you at the meeting." "I will not see it in advance?" "No." "Sigh - OK." And so I sat in

Room 25 awaiting my fate. Why are people so superficially pleasant when they are putting the knife in? They get their jollies while you are down. Job's comforters! It's the goody-goody hypocrisy that gets me more than anything. Guy Douglas, John Mitchell Q.C, Secretary of the Friends of Carberry and George Burnet entered and sat down. Guy Douglas then produced an impersonal document and read it to me much as if it had been a charge sheet in a police station being read to a man arrested for some crime.

My adversary stated that I had "built up a history at Carberry of confrontation with those in a position (sic) of authority...This culminated in a draft report to the Friends AGM..which would have created the impression.....that the project as a whole was seriously flawed.....The lack of co-operation (sic) between Robert and Jock Stein became apparent to Ian Mulholland, our fund-raising consultant, at their first meeting. Others...have reported that they do not trust his discretion....A report reached a member of the Steering Committee that at a meeting in Edinburgh, Jock spoke followed by Robert who contradicted much of what Jock had already said. The source of the report said, "Carberry is needing to get its act together"....Recognising that Robert has built up a track record in previous posts of the kind of confrontational behaviour we are experiencing, The Committee of Friends of Carberry is anxious to help him deal with this problem and break out of this pattern. To this end the Committee wishes Robert to go to a skilled counsellor for assessment. The Committee offers two alternatives...and expects a decision as to which one within three days. After this the Committee will arrange for assessment with the chosen counsellor. The Committee wishes a report from the counsellor by mid-December. Robert should be prepared to undertake further counselling, if advised, with a view to helping him change his behaviour. The Committee of Friends of Carberry has therefore resolved that representatives should meet with Robert to give him a final warning in the form of this feedback. Conditional on Robert accepting the offer of counselling, a further review will be held on or around the 19th of January 1996." Then there was a statement saying that if reports of confrontational behaviour were received in the intervening period, "the Committee will consider terminating his contract. If, however, Robert has been able to modify his behaviour during the intervening period then an outcome of the January review could be that he continues in post. The findings of the counsellor's report may be taken into account as part of the review in January. The committee also reserves the right to act upon the report at an earlier date." No signature. No salutation. No personal ending. No names. No God. No Jesus Christ. No Holy Spirit. No Church. No Ordained Minister.

I was invited to respond but I said that I would not do anything to incriminate myself. I also recognised the spiritual realities behind the facades. I looked John Mitchell in the face and saw only a self-conscious unease. I thought I detected in George Burnet's eyes just the faintest hints of compassion and embarrassment. I walked out. I was angry and tempted to slam the door shut. I closed it quietly and gently. If the intention was to get through to my anger it certainly worked. I despised this cowardly conduct. There was no space for me to answer these allegations. I was assumed to be guilty and in need of counselling. I thought that this was against natural justice. I doubted if it was legal. It numbed my soul and made me feel very cold inside. This was their way of dealing with me. The power game. Cloaked in righteousness and self-justification. George Orwell rides again. Were we in the Kremlin? I had not thought so.

A general staff meeting had been called for November 24th. We expected that formal announcements of staff redundancies would be made. I had written a four page letter to George Burnet on 14th November pleading in a last ditch attempt for reconsideration of the redundancies to be served on the domestic staff. In this letter I made the point that throughout the year none of us had ever heard the names of these women mentioned at any meeting. I therefore 'introduced' Vivian, Rose, Agnes, Rena, Nettie and Sadie, describing briefly their skills and value. (Earlier in the year, Helen, Mary and Isobel had found other jobs for themselves.) I asked the basic question, "Does Carberry really intend to make such poorly-paid, hard-working women compulsorily redundant?" (If this was to happen, I could not live with it. I was sure that I would have to leave.) Then I made as good a case for retaining 'the girls' as I could and concluded with these words. "I am asking you as a Christian gentleman to consider if there is any way to retain our part-time domestic staff. I believe this is a Christian thing to do and that blessing will result. I cannot square the thought of these good people being cleared from Carberry as a starting point for a Christian enterprise." I made other representations behind the scenes and at least one other person was also advocating the retention of the domestics to one of Jock Stein's allies.

Jock Stein had arranged to meet Vivian, Rose, Agnes, Rena, Nettie and Sadie prior to the general meeting of staff. I was still numb from my experience the previous day. I had not slept. A friend had invited me for lunch to ease my own personal pain. I decided that I should be with 'the girls' when they were given their formal notice. But as we walked towards the room for the general meeting, I heard laughter - that lovely sound in a place like Carberry - the laughter of working people - the girls' laughter. Why? I whispered to Rose, "What happened at your meeting?" "We've to be kept on," she said. And I could not believe it. I sat silent throughout the general staff meeting as Jock Stein informed us that a way had been found to retain the domestic staff. The announcement was made without emotion, certainly without contrition and with that false paternalism with which wealthy people so often betray themselves. And for me yesterday's numbness was visited by more numbness, though of a differing quality.

And when the meeting was over, I went to my room and wept. I do not know why I did this. I had agonised for a year, prayed constantly and struggled for these women and other members of staff to be treated properly. I think it was the nature of the last minute reprieve. And the way it was communicated. And the high spirits of 'the girls' at that moment. There was something more. I thought that the righteous anger of Jesus Christ upon us all had been averted. I thought that perhaps I could now live with 'The New Carberry' project. I thought something of Carberry's history had been redeemed in this new decision. And I was grateful that hard work and faithfulness was to be properly recognised and that after a depressing year for them, 'the girls' were accorded the dignity which was appropriate and deserved.

On Friday evening Jock Stein knocked at my door and sheepishly said that he knew about a document and if I wanted to talk about it to come and see him. I did not do so that evening, or the next day or the next, but I did go to see him on Monday 27th at about 9 30am. It was a strange meeting. Jock Stein's spiritual shallowness and lack of human understanding was apparent from the beginning. When I said that the decision to retain the domestic staff had changed everything for me, he asked, "What difference does that make?" It is hard to deal with such cold inhumanity. There are no reference points to get hold of - no bridges in sight. I said that between Thursday and Friday I had been emotionally wrung dry. Jock Stein did not want to talk about any major issues. He said that I like him tended to avoid confrontation if at all possible. When it happened neither of us handled it well. On several occasions throughout the year Jock Stein had commented on how alike he thought he and I were. I had not been flattered by the comparison and was relieved that Margaret Stein had taken this burden from me by expressing the opposite point of view. Jock Stein said that he knew I had had my troubles with liberals at the University but there were no such theological disagreements at Carberry. He gratuitously suggested that I had had confrontational problems in four of five different working situations and then in a moment of negative perspicacity which may ring through the Christian centuries to come he added, "If you were an alcoholic, we would want to help you." Jock Stein ended the meeting abruptly and coldly. We had a meaningless prayer. I did not think that I had been in a Christian meeting. I remembered that God does not reveal Himself to the proud and wealthy and arrogant but to the humble of heart and spirit. The Christian Right may have its commitments but does it truly reflect the will of God? I doubted it.

On Monday 27th November I took my written reply to Guy Douglas's home. I stated at the outset that I recognised a genuinely held concern that the Carberry project could not succeed if it was beset by internal conflict. I also said that the decision to retain the domestic staff had changed everything for me, enabling me to respond very positively to this new situation. I said that to force me to take counselling assessment at such short notice and under threat of dismissal from my job would be counter-productive in my case. I suggested that no professional counsellor would be happy with this enforcement. I therefore asked for the review document to be suspended to allow me time to think things through. I said that I had asked Jock Stein for the opportunity to talk through the issues affecting Carberry but he had refused and I asked whether he, Guy Douglas would be willing to do this. I concluded with a statement of contrition for my own imperfections, failings and sinfulness.

On Tuesday 28th November I was told to expect a telephone call from Guy Douglas at 5 30pm. At 5 45pm he telephoned to tell me that he and his wife were going out that evening and would I ring the following evening at about the same time? I thought to myself, "What kind of people are they to treat me in such an pitiless and careless manner?" Is this Christianity that so diminishes a person? But I duly telephoned as requested and Guy Douglas spent some time explaining some of the reasoning behind the action that the Committee of Friends had felt it necessary to take. This was actually helpful and Guy Douglas's manner towards me was not unkind. He expressed the concern that internal conflict would spill out into the public arena. He suggested that it already had to some extent. I disagreed. It was again about money, you see. The Appeal was to be launched in the spring. They wanted to know from a counsellor whether I was the type of person they should have to take part in such an Appeal. Ominously for a Christian Minister - worse for a man like me - Guy Douglas said "We want corporate loyalty." Was Christianity founded in this way? I'm sure the Pharisees and Saducees wanted 'corporate loyalty' from Jesus of Nazareth. They got the rough edge of his tongue on occasions. The Sanhedrin wanted 'corporate loyalty' from Peter and he famously replied "Is it right in the eyes of God for us to obey you rather than him?" (Acts 4:19) Throughout Christian history 'corporate loyalty' has been the excuse for numerous persecutions. And the Christian Right with its eyes on money and success could not recognise an honest spiritual struggle taking place in a man of conscience. Rather - he was someone to be controlled, emasculated, neutered.

I would have been so easy to deal with if I thought that 'The New Carberry' was being well-planned and properly ordered. If there were substantive issues in the way affairs had been conducted which a reasonable person would find problematic - then I did not need counselling. I had said to Jock Stein, "One Flew Over The Cuckoo's Nest, Jock - it is a serious thing to make a healthy man sick - if it ain't broke don't fix it." But if you are not sick, then in order to remain at Carberry you must become sick. And that is a classic sign of bad and false religion and of a 'cult' mentality which if left unchecked must inevitably lead to grief for others in the future. And it is for this reason that I write as I do. I have no other justification. But that I can do so is, I hope, evidence of my inner sanity and the Grace of Christian salvation present within. Because collective pressure can be strong and you can be tempted to give in. And if you have no home and wish to earn a living in this world then you are able to be blackmailed. The law does not help you. You have very few rights as an employee of just over a year's duration. And you cannot begin to talk to people about such preposterous problems. Who would believe you?

My strategy was to try to cool things down and to buy myself time. And, although this may seem pious, I had within me some pastoral concern for people so blind to the real dimension of God's Kingdom and the necessary struggles which it involves within the human community on earth. Yes - of course I had had struggles and confrontations throughout my life. But - were there not good reasons for them? Had they not been important issues? Had God not been with me in my sufferings? Had some of it all not been precisely for the Lord Jesus and the honour of His Name and Kingdom? How could these members of the Christian Right not recognise the Christian dimension of my struggles? They had not.

The best news now was that they would not insist on me taking immediate counselling assessment as a condition of continuing in my employment. This was most welcome. I was asked however to consider the invitation to go to counselling and respond. On 30th November I replied expressing gratitude for the fact that the demand to accept counselling assessment upon pain of dismissal had been removed. I said that I recognised the need for public discretion and suggested that I had done my best to ensure that 'The New Carberry' began in the best way. I could now simply work away in the background and share in the work of the Appeal as required.

In other words, I offered to cease the struggle. And that was what it was all about. Jock Stein could not stand having an alternative viewpoint expressed. His view of a community was a place where everyone did what he wanted. In which he was allowed to rule without contest. In which, as always, the little rich kid got his way. The Friends of Carberry were really the Friends of Jock Stein. The Committee which had decided to put such stricture upon me had not included George Burnet although he had complied with its decisions. I had asked that since the decision day for Carberry's future was coming near, because I had a lot of work to do and as Christmas was approaching, I would prefer to return to discussions about my position and future in January.

But on the 22nd of December - so close to the happy time of Christmas I received another document which expressed the strong recommendation that I seek counselling. The main issue here expressed (for the first time - I was always learning) was that the result of my behaviour in time of conflict is destructive rather than constructive. The final paragraph was conciliatory and even caring. Was it necessary to send this letter in order that it arrive two days before Christmas? It was demoralising, although I did my best to recover my spiritual equilibrium. This to me was oppression. It was a clear attempt to control me, to control my mind, my thoughts, my words, my opinions, my views, my suggestions, my criticisms, my alternatives. Let there be no mistake - this was the late twentieth century equivalent of mediaeval torture and burning at the stake. I could stay in my job as long as I became a cipher, an office boy, an obedient drone. Myself - I was not wanted - my ministry - was not wanted - my spiritual calling - was not wanted. And it was that which would have been the best that I could have offered Carberry. It was however a clever and ruthless way of dealing with me. In binding me spiritually, mentally, vocally, descriptively, certain management decisions were able to enacted without protest and counter-advocacy from me. I found myself on no policy-making committee other than in connection with fund-raising. In my mind, however there was an inextricable link between overall policy and fund-raising. I did not think you could act unjustly and expect the heavens to shower you with cash.

I was to be silenced so that certain things could be done. That was the reason for my being put to counselling. Not that I needed it at all, but that to make its possibility a continuing factor would make it impossible for me to advocate alternative ideas, plans and strategies. Is this honourable? Is this Christianity? In the confines of a community is this healthy, desirable or good? In God's sight is it just and fair? What do these tactics say about 'The New Carberry?' If Carberry has been run this way for so long - is this part of the reason why it has been brought to its knees? The mixture of the Christian Right, outright self-will, personal favouritism, the seeking of absolute control over property and people and the diminution, exclusion and persecution of mature-minded Christian people seemed to me to be dangerous for any supposed new venture. Yet it was there. It was happening.

Jock Stein and I had attended an Evangelical Alliance presentation by Sir Fred Catherwood in Edinburgh on the subject of social involvement. For more than a decade leading evangelicals in England had been trying to encourage evangelicals to show greater awareness of and interest in Britain's social problems. This was a genuine attempt to balance the doctrinal only identity of evangelicalism and to build bridges with others in the main churches. I had listened to David Anderson, the Director of Evangelical Alliance Scotland read part of Psalm Forty-one as he introduced the guest speaker.

> **"Happy are those who are concerned for the poor**
> **the Lord will help them when they are in trouble.**
> **The Lord will protect them and preserve their lives;**
> **he will make them happy in the land;**
> **he will not abandon them to the power of their enemies.**
> **The Lord will help them when they are sick**
> **and will restore them to health."**

I was uplifted by this living Word which spoke to my condition. Whether Jock Stein understood its relevance I never knew. And when, a few days later, I was worshipping in Dundonald Parish Church on Sunday 3rd December 1995, one of the readings for Advent was from Isaiah Chapter eleven.

> **"He will not judge by appearance or hearsay**
> **he will judge the poor fairly**
> **and defend the rights of the helpless."**

As these words were spoken, the sun began to shine through the windows in the gallery where I was seated. And I was bathed in welcome winter light. And a great peace entered my soul. And a sense of the fulfilment of that calling of many years ago was given to me and I was blessed and comforted.

## Decision Day

Friends of Carberry met on Saturday December 16th 1995 to vote on the terms and conditions offered by the Commission of Assembly. The purchase price was to be £747,000. The deposit was to be £250,000. One per cent interest was to be paid on the balance from year one to year five. Then bank base rate interest was to be applied for years six to ten. Thereafter bank base rate plus two per cent was to be charged. A schedule of repairs costing about £250,000 to the roof was to be completed within the initial five year period. These terms were presented in the most favourable light possible. No mention was made of the February offer of a twenty-five year lease with eight years free of rent which in the light of the mounting costs seemed to me in retrospect to have been most generous. I was obliged to keep silent on pain of immediate dismissal. Ruthless is the Christian Right in getting its own way. But there is a God and a Lord to reckon with someday. Neither was there any alternative. By this time it was purchase or close.

There were seventy-two people present. We all voted to accept the terms. And there was a blessing, it seemed at that moment. There was a warming of the spirit. Jock Stein looked elated - but not in an unacceptable way. I myself was lifted by the occasion and felt blessed also. In spite of all the problems and the serious errors of judgement and the less than admirable treatment of staff, the Christian Right had got its way. Control of Carberry was theirs and with it came control of anyone who lived and worked there. And so Jock Stein assumed the mantle of managing director and produced an elaborate one hundred word letter-head with his friends' names on it telling the world that he had become what he had always wanted to be - a wee managing director. I begged him to withdraw this nonsense else he expose himself to ridicule but he would not do so. And I looked for charity and trust and Christianity and looked hard. The women domestic staff were offered less wages and more work and some accepted and some declined. Those who left did so because they were uncomfortable with the plans for forced religious observance and because they lacked confidence in themselves to participate in the Carberry School of Life and Faith. A little genuine pastoral insight would have quietened these doubts. Carberry needed them and when they left the place was the less for their going. The pressure for internal conformity increased. And you felt that you were frightened to think, let alone speak. Attempting to force me to counselling took away any compunction I may have had about remaining. There was more to see. This form of Christian Right behaviour concerned me. I suspect it will provide its own questionable harvest in time. What its contribution to Scottish Christianity may be over the decades ahead I do not know. Surely it will be as harmful as the worst excesses of the Iona Community have been harmful. Only from the differing perspective.

## The Unconverted Unconscious

Spiritual jealousy has always existed in Christendom. The liberals are blind to be sure and they mug you almost to extinction and leave you by the side of the road. But when you are down there more premeditated aggravated blows rain upon you from the Christian Right. And you lie there bleeding. In your heart and soul and mind and spirit. As Jesus did - long before Calvary. For they are assured that they are Christians doing the Lord's will. They cannot distinguish spiritual enmity from spiritual advocacy. Nor consider that God may be with someone who calls those who call others to repentance to themselves repent. Thus the unconverted unconscious rules the hearts and minds of human beings in the churches throughout the world. Eternal life is not so easily won after all and the dying churches testify to shallow understanding and self-interested posturing and the use and abuse of the Name of Jesus Christ for human ambition. God is not mocked. We have our reward.

But nothing and no-one is beyond God's Grace in Jesus Christ. Even these words are meant to save and not condemn. Pain indeed they will cause but that may be the only way to true redemption. It has been the only way that I myself have known. I do not force it upon others. They must find their own way in Christ. But you cannot negate a man of God with impunity. The lesser trouble is to be found here on earth, the greater not to know what you have done and to journey in ignorance towards an uncertain eternity. The Christian Right is judged by its own words and actions - not by me. What is within the deepest soul will surely reach the visible surface. Our words and actions bespeak what lies beneath, within. The process of redemption is through consciousness of sin. Repentance. Forgiveness. Grace. It is only by the way of negation that these are found. Whoever gains his or her life will lose it and whoever loses her or his life for the sake of Jesus Christ, will gain it. Christianity is true. Always was. Always will be. Let no late twentieth century pedant or martinet try to avoid its consequences or lead others to do so.

And I saw my first white Christmas - though it was fiendishly cold. In Dunblane Cathedral on Christmas Eve I rejoiced in all that Christmas is. The message was humanistic but its poor content was dwarfed by the eternal beauty of the carols and the perpetual gift of personal prayer and the love of God in Jesus Christ made known, transparent, sacrificial, victorious, ever ever present.

## I Have Fought With Wild Beasts At Ephesus

My review took place towards the end of January. It was as positive as the previous one had been negative. I was actually commended. How strange! A further review would take place in three months time. I was told that it had been decided not to offer me a job on the expiry of my contract in late summer 1996. I asked why this decision had been made without any consultation with myself. However badly it had been handled, I was told, the position was the same. And any introduction of alternative policy would be deemed sufficient cause for discipline and possible dismissal.

The Carberry Trust took possession of Carberry on Thursday, 1st February. The 'sasine' ceremony (the cutting of a turf and the placing of a stone symbolising transfer of house and grounds) was carried out by George Burnet and the Very Reverend W. Roy Sanderson, a former Moderator of the General Assembly of the Church of Scotland, representing the Church. Ian McCarter who had chaired the Commission which set the terms of purchase began the proceedings by saying that he thought that we, gathered together as we were on the grass, looked as if we were attending a funeral. It was cold and grey and dull. No sun shone through the cloud - not a single ray. Jock Stein was ecstatic.

Thereafter a 'sweat-shop' atmosphere was created and there seemed much dullness in the daily worship. Young George McIntyre summed up something we were all feeling, "At coffee-time, you can hear the clock ticking." David Lunn said brusquely, "This place is like a morgue."

If you act unjustly, can you then ask God for millions of pounds to fulfil your private dreams? Even if these be cloaked in Christian language? What if, when the real decisions are being made that Christianity is set aside and only desire and expediency inform? For all the language of commitment and dependence, the strategy is pure humanism dressed up in pious language. Money is a messy business and the trust and corporate donation business reflects that. One year previously I had urged a 'bottom up' approach to the future. Hope had been placed in rich people. They had not so far produced the goods required. Anyone could see that Carberry would struggle to succeed under the present arrangements. Saddled with a debt of £500,000, with statutory roof repairs of £250,000 and a development plan requiring more than £1,000,000 The Friends of Jock Stein had bitten off a great deal. By April it was clear that although money would be raised, it would not happen in the large proportions expected or wanted. I was impressed by the sharpness and realism of people like Ewan Brown, Sandy Struthers and Sir Charles Fraser. I admire the quickness and the politeness of those who make their ruthless way in the world of money. Why do these types of people always settle for such second and third hand Christianity? Edinburgh is full of them. The suburbs of our cities are also full of them. When they take part in church courts, their acumen departs them. I had begged for such people to be at the centre of Carberry's survival planning. But - they were too powerful to let Jock Stein get his way all the time and so he kept them at a distance.

Carberry has not yet answered any of the big questions. According to the strategy in place a quantum leap is required, in funding, in business or in Christian provision. But does a Christian enterprise proceed in such a way? Can a Christian enterprise not begin by trying to earn an honest living? Humbly? Treating employees with justice? Being transparent in financial accounting? Risking everything as a genuine charity? So what was it to be? Business? Christianity? Power evangelicalism? Was Carberry to change irrevocably from what it had been over the previous thirty-five years? Could it survive?

Privatised religion has its problems. A situation where a very few people control everything from the spiritual orthodoxy to hourly wage rates is not, in my view healthy. There is far too much pressure to conform to a single person's personal agenda. It is too easy to 'play god.' To actually want to exercise control in such a way over people is to me evidence not of Christian commitment but of its opposite. It is ever a bad thing to get all your own way in a religious setting.

I had always favoured the lease agreement and the retention of a strong relationship between Carberry and the Church of Scotland. To work away and raise what funds could be raised and make Carberry viable, if indeed it can be made viable as part of the Church seemed to me to be the continuation of the Elphinstone bequest in spirit and in fact. For a very small group of people including Jock Stein to wrest title and control to themselves seems to me not to conform to the better history of Christianity. The Christian Right thinks itself more committed than the vacant liberalism of the established Church. But - the Christian Right does not truly fulfil the will of God in Jesus Christ in its harshness towards fellow human beings, in its desire for control and in its pursuit of money. Right doctrine and commitment are much to be admired. But it is a great error to think yourself correct in God's sight in everything. The will to dominance is not the Christ-like way.

And it matters how things are begun. It has ever been thus. The Reformation in Scotland was different in character and content from its English counterpart. Christianity's beginning was manifestly different from that of Islam. The taking over of Carberry was, in my view, not transparently honest enough, not motivated by the highest reasons, not accompanied by the best practice for it to succeed. It was achieved at the cost of the humiliation and negation of Christian staff and of my own suffering in silence. Yet Carberry could be baled out by some wealthy patron of the Christian right. But what fruit in times to come would be harvested? Carberry itself is worth the saving - but not in my view as a fortress for the Christian Right. If these words serve to shed light on hidden abuses and thus to oblige those concerned to bring back Carberry to a proper course then they will have fulfilled their purpose. The example of the Algrade Trust in Humbie nearby has served as a warning as to what can happen when unchecked religious zeal is mixed with human will to power and the love of money.

Carberry might survive if the intention is service and not power, stewardship and not ownership, people and not money. Where the public rhetoric is an expression of actual conditions and not a created myth. Where people want to come because something is happening that draws them. Maybe if Carberry's own secular history was redeemed and corrected, and if the justice of the Bible was enacted and the faith of the New Testament lived more openly, Carberry could survive. Serving the Church and the churches. Belonging. Accountable. But Carberry is a rich man's house and it does require investment. It may be that for all the good that happens at Carberry, it's day is over. A quantum factor is required either in major philanthropic funding, in a multiplication of those desiring to stay at Carberry for spiritual purposes or in significant access to the corporate business and entertainment market. Only the second of these alternatives will preserve and build upon what Carberry was given to the Church of Scotland for and what it has meant to so many.

The world is littered with the ruins of Christian places no longer needed or in use. Nothing has the right to survive. Reform Christianity holds Jesus Christ to no place or location on earth. He did not live in a rich man's house. Only in becoming a just and open place will Carberry live. It was intended to be so. Assuaging the guilt and conscience of centuries. Christ-like. The Cross At Carberry is known world-wide. Therein may lie the key. In full surrender to Jesus Christ, in dependence, in going forward in faith, and learning what that Cross really means.

## "Collogue"

"May one be permitted," said the usually mildly spoken Richard Filleul, Carberry's lawyer, "to say that one thinks the name is dreadful." Jock Stein had planned to have a 'School of Life and Faith' for short-term volunteer staff working at Carberry. He had originally envisaged about twenty people taking part but by January 1996 there were hardly any short-term volunteer staff at Carberry. Undaunted, Jock Stein had decided to have a 'dummy run' dragooning the core staff to attend. The name 'Collogue' was Jock Stein's idea. It had to be. He received many better suggestions for a name but, of course, he could only choose his own idea. The word, he had told us, in the Scots tongue, meant a 'meeting perhaps with subversive undertones.' A member of staff passed me a photocopy of the Oxford Dictionary's entry on the word in question. It was much less ambiguous! The actual connotations were of duplicity. I shared this at one of the planning meetings and suggested the name be changed. Jock Stein would not have it. The quisling committee members who had agreed that the name should be changed succumbed to Jock Stein's stubbornness. So 'Collogue' it was. He actually wanted to call those who attended 'Colloguers.' This far no one would go.

I had hoped that the Carberry School of Life and Faith would be innovative in learning strategy and techniques. In particular, I hoped that it would offer something different from the often dry formalisms of university theological education. Could it, for example, begin where people were rather than confront them with pre-packaged second and third hand 'knowledge'? To my great disappointment Jock Stein rejected my views on this and invited Iain Provan, a lecturer in Old Testament from New College to formulate the syllabus. Jock Stein's close friend, Archie Mills suggested topics on the theory of community! The syllabus was presented to one meeting as a final draft. I had supposed that the meeting in question was to share the groundwork ideas for the syllabus. I said that what we had was just a replica of a second year Bible college course. Jock Stein later told me that that was good enough for him. I asked for a different style and an argument ensued in which I was in my customary minority of one. I did submit some thoughts to Iain Provan and a few were incorporated. The tone and style was set however. There was nothing original or new in the approach at all that I could see. The 1997 syllabus is designed to begin further back in the educational process though its content raises questions.

I suggested from the outset that the Carberry School of Faith and Life should be a revenue earning service to the public. Jock Stein refused that advice. One year later, with plenty of space in Carberry's booking diary for 1997, he took this advice. Jock Stein did not acknowledge my foresight although Archie Mills did. I had taught in Africa for nearly six years. The existential life questioning approach was something I had practised since being a student. I was well qualified and had experience in academic administration. Jock Stein had to be in charge of everything. Even if there was someone better qualified than him available, he would do it himself. Carberry was not the Lord's work really. For the Lord chooses many people and gives them real responsibility.

I was asked merely to formulate a concise series of catch-phrases to describe 'Collogue,' as for example in a leaflet flier. I did so immediately after the meeting in question. The phrases were: Divine Initiative, Jesus As God Incarnate, Faith Seeking Understanding, Learning In Dialogue, Living In Community, Addressing The World, Serving Everyone. These were received and buried. They never appeared in any future literature about the Carberry School of Faith and Life.

In January and February of 1996 I was given three seminars to conduct. Members of the Carberry staff attended, including domestic staff and ground staff. My first seminar was entitled 'The Importance of the Christian Mind.' At least I would try out my own method of 'bottom up' communication. It was 'bottom up' too. Literally. I began my first presentation with an overhead projector drawing of two identical human bottoms. Above one I had written 'Christian Bottom' and above the other 'Ordinary Bottom.' I asked "What is the difference between these two bottoms?" "No difference," came the reply from Nettie Young. I then proceeded with the discussion on what differences exist between Christianity and ordinary views of life. Does your Christianity make you see the world in a different way? Does it change your values? Does it affect your family and personal relationships. In what ways? There were, I recall some twenty-four people there. It was a lively time and I cut the scheduled three hours with one break to two and a half hours with two breaks. I made the point later that no university asks students to sit for three hours on one topic. But Jock Stein wanted to ensure that the staff who were paid hourly until five o' clock remained there until five o' clock.

For my second seminar I took those who came to visit Jewel and Esk Valley College to see the educational choices and facilities that were on offer. I wanted to do this to put Carberry's 'School' in perspective and to get out of the suffocating atmosphere of living, working and learning in one small place with such a narrow personalised agenda. From there we toured the desolate Craigmillar housing estate, contrasting the privilege of education with its inhibiting and restricting environment. Lastly that morning we visited Newbattle Abbey College, famous in Scotland for being the nurturing home of many late developers and a place where indeed latent talents were encouraged and fostered and guided to fruition and maturity.

Jock Stein decided to attend my third seminar. I had asked him not to attend my first and fortunately he had withdrawn from the second when he realised we were going out of Carberry. I had attended some of the other presentations of the first 'dummy run' of the Carberry School of Faith and Life. Jock Stein had fallen asleep at those which I attended, much to the amused embarrassment of the Carberry staff. Margaret Stein, sitting alongside her husband had also fallen asleep on one occasion. Very encouraging for the presenter - to have Jock and Margaret Stein fast asleep as you seek to take the content of the syllabus seriously! In my third seminar entitled 'Developing The Christian Mind' I began by outlining the main points of world religions. I put the Ten Commandments into humorous common social usage. "I am Numero Uno, No home-boiled gods, No effing or blinding, b'ing or C'ing, Rest one day a week, Look after your mum and dad, No killing, No shagging someone else's man or woman, No thieving, No blackening of names, No wantin' what does not belong to you." I summarised the Sermon on the Mount as follows: "You are the goodness of humanity, Don't get angry with anyone, Don't lust after someone else's partner, Just say 'Yes' and 'No', Don't take revenge, Love people who don't like you, Love God in private, Don't depend on money or possessions, Don't worry about the future, Don't criticise for nothing, Search continually for God, Discern true and false religion, Follow Jesus, Do what He says." This may seem trite and obvious but I found it stimulating to 'sloganise' the profound teaching of the Bible in order to interest people who might not think theoretically about Christianity or know what the Bible says. Above all - I wanted the Bible's teaching to be a 'living' and not a dead thing, immediate and not abstract, applicable and not just reflective.

By now Jock Stein was fast asleep. I was delighted, I spoke in a hushed tone to make sure he stayed that way. "Sleep, sweetly sleep," I crooned quietly between sentences. I was about to introduce some hilarity into the proceedings and I was keen that Jock Stein should not wake up until this happy interlude was over. I put up an acetate sheet on which were transcribed 'The Ten

Principles of Lunn.' These reflected my summation of the personal life philosophy of David Lunn, the Carberry Factor, a man of individual character, abstracted from his conversations at coffee times. Just then Jock Stein awoke. Horror! Should I skip 'The Ten Principles of Lunn', I thought. Too late! The acetate was already visible. People were reading it. Laughing. I proceeded to enunciate David's collected wisdom. "Never trust naebody, Ae cover yer back, Nae disrespect when putting the boot in, Always be qualified for the job you are in, Never lift onything heavy, Reminisce frequently, Eat a balanced diet, Gamble and pray, Drive an automatic car, Have a happy childhood." I also picked out texts from the Bible which corresponded in some fashion to Lunn's principles. Halfway through this erudite exposition, I noticed two short-term volunteer staff who had come from eastern European countries scribbling down everything I was saying. "You're not taking this down," said I in consternation, "This is just a bit of fun." And I had a vision of these young people returning to their native countries and sharing their newly acquired learning with their compatriots, saying, "Scottish philosopher Lunn says......" I did not dare to look at Jock Stein in the middle of this happy chaos. Later I was told that he had laughed much himself and seemed to enjoy the fun. In all my presentations, most of the time was taken up by serious consideration of issues. The humours were ice-breakers and interludes, even if some were possessed of their own momentum for longer than I had expected.

'Collogue' tutors were asked to submit reports. Jock Stein summoned me to a meeting with Archie Mills and Margaret Stein and himself. Before the meeting I received a document which purported to be a synopsis of evaluation forms completed by those who had attended 'Collogue.' One sentence appalled me. "There was only a small sample of eight returns to assess: of the tutors, Iain Provan, Archie Mills, Margaret Stein got the consistently highest ratings, but no one was consistently low." I was deeply wounded by this sentence. I felt negated. Buried. Dead. I went to my office, locked the door and knelt down on my knees in pain and asked Jesus to help me bear this spiritual assassination, this living death. Lest anyone should see me through the curtainless windows, I did not remain in prayer long. At the meeting, I stated that twenty-four people had attended my first seminar. "Where have all the other responses gone?" I asked. It was quite possible that in fact there had been only eight returned questionnaires. Most of the Carberry staff had not returned forms for fear of victimisation. Iain Provan's heavy monologues on Neitszche had not been appreciated. He had offered undiluted stuff from New College to working people. They had found his lectures stultifying. I had warned Jock Stein of this possibility some months before but he had dismissed my counsel. As for Margaret Stein, she had offered those who attended her seminar some 'New Age' type personal assessment techniques, 'positive stroking' as, I believe it to be called. Rena, one of the most humorous of the Carberry staff informed us at coffee time the next day that she had been classed as gladioli, an elephant and an owl! What this had done for her relationship with Jesus Christ no-one could tell. Some had found Archie Mills interesting but David Lunn's perceptive question about the narcissism of the entire presentation had been greeted with a stirring of the pot gesture by Archie Mills. In other words, no-one was to ask too clever a question or expose the questionable nature of 'theories' of community. Jock Stein agreed to alter the sentence which had bothered me. I think Archie Mills realised what had been done but he did not have the integrity to deal with it openly. He did however acknowledge there and then that I had advocated organising 'Collogue' as a revenue earning service to the public one year previously, which step was now to be implemented. It takes Jock Stein years to see what others grasp quickly. This must surely be another reason for Carberry's predicament.

## Personality Testing

Personality testing in a religious environment carries significant dangers. In the context of the Christian Right it may be even more sinister. If an employer insists on personality testing as a condition of employment in a religious environment, issues of personal freedom are raised. Jock Stein said that he 'expected' all Carberry employees and volunteers to take part in a Myers-Briggs personality testing week-end soon after the transfer of Carberry to the new independent Trust. When I asked him why there needed to be such haste with this, he pointed out that this personality testing week-end had been planned many months before and it was only because negotiations for the transfer of Carberry had taken so long that the week-end followed so closely on the actual property transfer. I accepted this answer. I did not, however, agree to take part in the Myers-Briggs week-end. At a general staff meeting, I said quite clearly that I wished to be regarded as a Christian human personality not to be categorised in one form or another. I was aware that some of the staff were unsure whether they were obliged to take part and my lead made it clear that if I was not forced to take part, each person was free to decide to participate or not to. The word 'expected' carried its own pressure. Some members of staff took part, others did not. One was concerned that personality testing evaluations would be entered in employee records. I was concerned about Jock's Stein's motives.

You could argue that there is nothing sinister about Myers-Briggs. Many people have participated in such testing without much or any visible harm being done to them. Carberry was not the only 'Christian' organisation which used Myers-Briggs. Indeed, the Carberry week-end was to be led by an Episcopalian priest who had written a book called 'Knowing me, Knowing You.' I must admit I guffawed when I was told the title of the book, remembering a popular song of the same title by the 1970's band 'Abba.' The members of the Carberry staff who took part came to no grief.

However my concerns were not alleviated. What troubled me was that Jock Stein, limited in understanding of and in empathy with human beings had turned to these personality testing categories in an attempt to gain some understanding of people. Lacking perception and discernment - spiritually blind to a pitiable degree, he had begun to take these shallow personality-testing representations seriously and to base his judgements of people on them. This frightened me. He applied non-Christian or a-Christian categories to Christian people. The consequence was that whereas he began with little understanding of people, he then moved backwards from a Christian understanding of people and informed himself by such personality testing categories. This placed an even greater distance between himself and others. It placed a gulf between him and me. If this was a factor in the management of people at Carberry then it helped to explain the succession of wrong appointments over the years. Jock had told us that he had not discovered these new insights until he was in his forties. What he seemed not to be able to recognise was that many Christian people were blessed with more humanity and understanding of their fellow human beings without the necessity of personality testing theories. And given the nature of Jock Stein's conduct of Carberry, personality testing was the last thing that one would want to see institutionalised there.

I do not want to be categorised as an introvert or as a letter and number! This says nothing about my relationship with God in Jesus Christ. In claiming insight these systems multiply ignorance and let all manner of spiritual distortion enter working and personal relationships. They may also work against the way God communicates with His people. Whether you are a dog, an elephant or a deer, a dove, a swan or an eagle, a rose, a gladioli or a daisy, I do not particularly want to know. Neither do I think that the religion of North American Indians like the Hopi or Navajo will surpass what I have been given in Jesus Christ. I prefer to see the light of God in your eyes, the love of Christ in your heart and the Presence of the Holy Spirit in what you do. Power evangelicalism and oddball psychological categories are likely to make for trouble.

Yet if you go to any 'retreat centre' in Britain today, you may well find such personality-testing courses on offer. It is in my view a different matter for a human being freely to elect to attend such a course than it is for an employee to be 'expected' to attend one as part of their employment. Nevertheless, what has happened in church circles is that the hunger for self-knowledge is being addressed. Due to the paucity of real Christian understanding, human theories of personality are being substituted. This is simply the modern-day equivalent of the practice denouced in the Old Testament of turning to nature spirit worship in the absence of a living Word from the Lord. People turn in on themselves, becoming self-obsessed and narcissistic. 'New Age' theories abound in such ego-centred introversions. There can be no real Christian revival until these small false gods are thrown out. In Christ, our Maker has provided more than enough for our personal health and salvation. It is in being drawn out of ourselves into the life of God that we are healed. It is in denying ourselves that we find abundance of life. It is in dying that we are born to eternal life.

## 'Counselling'

I believe that many amateur 'counsellors' feed off the virtue, energy and strength of those they counsel. They are always in the superior posture and can very easily become mentors stripping individuals of their ability to solve their own problems and get on with their lives. Regrettably, I have also to say that I am deeply suspicious of the burgeoning 'counselling' industry. Many of the categories of explanation are purely humanistic and those which masquerade as 'spiritual' are often themselves wolves in sheep's clothing, false postulates dressed up in religious language. 'New Age' ideas are proliferating within church circles. Most retreat centres offer 'counselling' in some form or another. This is a large subject requiring more investigation. Nevertheless, I consider that the relationship with God in and through Jesus Christ is itself a healing and redeeming relationship. I believe that the ministry and saving sacraments of Reformed Christianity can and do provide all that is necessary for guidance and solutions to human problems. The more human beings analyse one another the further away they may get from true Christianity.

It is self-evident that some people need to talk about their problems to others. Spiritual seeking also requires conversation with those who have also been spiritual seekers. Few people however possess real understanding and true discernment. Some may substitute their own analyses of problems and these may be inaccurate and misleading. They can also be projections of themselves rather than disinterested evaluations of others. If they are dependent for a living on their counselling activity that fact may bring its own pressures. Yet it is those amateurs who are zealous of the role of 'counsellor' who may be more dangerous. Someone's views of the universe are behind each proposed counselling solution. It is clearly possible for Christians to counsel Christians using skills, techniques and theories which are not in themselves Christian. It is possible however that individuals without a depth or strength of Christian faith may be diminished or distracted by ill-advised 'counselling.' There are also cases which might be compared with a street-corner motor mechanic attempting to service a motor-car of sophistication where the counsellor is incapable of understanding the quality and complexity of the person they are trying to help. Damage then results. That much I know from personal experience.

I would never seek to discredit the scientifically based studies of the human mind, psychiatry and psychological medicine. To be sure these have not in the twentieth century made advances comparable with medicine or surgery. The dark recesses of the disturbed mind are less easy to heal than many diseases which afflict the human body. God is often left out of the proposed solution. That may be in some cases because 'God' is part of the individual's problem but it is also an affirmation of a too-materially based understanding of human life and destiny.

The false premises from which so-called 'counsellors' begin are chaotic if applied to Christian souls. Thankfully, I was possessed of the inner presence of the Holy Spirit and was able to withstand the brutality and the insidious hypocrisy of people who pretended to be 'concerned' when in fact they sought confirmation of their own mistaken analyses and conclusions and my own destruction.

## Holy Week Fast

I fasted during the last five days of Holy Week 1996. How good it was to have an empty stomach, especially in a place like Carberry which always had so much food available. On Palm Sunday I worshipped in Pencaitland Church and shared in the monthly Service of Healing there the same evening. I thought that the individual words of Grace which I communicated to those who came forward for healing indicated the Holy Spirit's continuing presence within. Some words were addressed to a very old and frail man. While in prayer I said to him that we are all children sharing the weakness of the flesh as a prelude to the joy of eternal life to come. To an elderly lady I said, "You are a character aren't you?" and she delighted everyone by responding "Yes." And I thanked God for the gift of personality and the gift of life. Now you may say that there is nothing special about such communications. But I did not manufacture them from my mind. They were given to me as appropriate to people whom I did not know. They were personal to them, these words, and meaningful in a way a human verbal contrivance could not have been. I shared in a number of Services of Healing at Pencaitland with the Minister, Colin Donaldson, with retired Minister Ray Sawers and with elders George McNeish and John Landon. Tina Landon organised the music on most occasions. Holy Communion was celebrated. I was always uplifted and sensitised by these services. I don't think we ministered long enough to compensate for our lack of giftedness in this specialised ministry, but there were cases of answered prayer and it was always a beautiful experience to be there in that lovely village church on a Sunday evening.

On the Monday of that week I journey to Ayrshire to attend the funeral of my mother's neighbour Bob Hall-Solomon. He had been such an excellent neighbour, doing so many items of house and garden do-it-yourself mending and repairing for my mother over the twenty years she had been living in Dundonald. Robert Mayes, the Minister took great care in preparing all his funeral services and fairly represented Bob's multitude of good deeds.

Then the glorious days of fasting! What was different this year was that on the Friday I felt deeply some of the pain of Jesus' last hours. This intensified towards mid-day and was quite acute from 2 00 to 3 00pm. But during that hour there was a sweetness in the spirit which countered the bitterness of the pain. This reminded me of the testimony of Teresa of Avila and of St John of the Cross. By 3 00pm I was possessed of a spiritual bliss rarely felt or experienced. It was as if I was being hugged by the Holy Spirit. I was filled with joy at what Jesus had achieved for us through His ghastly self-sacrifice and resurrection. I marvelled at our Maker's providence and could scarcely believe what I was permitted to know and share and receive. Then it was down to the staff room to break my fast with a cup of tea, a piece of cake and a laugh. Easter Sunday brought Holy Communion at Pencaitland Church and the kind of everlasting joy that it is impossible to describe. The burdens and struggles of recent months were lifted from me. I thought "Only God can do this - Christianity MUST be true!"

## Fund-Raising

I was given yet another 'review' in April. Guy Douglas handed me a list of duties to be accomplished by September. When I told people that I was being 'reviewed' again, they did not believe it. I gained the impression that Guy Douglas had been thinking that I might just swan around for the final months of my contract and do nothing. Thus the lack of understanding and diminishing of a committed Christian life continued. The Christian Right does not meet you on the level of realised faith and consequently brings lack of trust, suspicion and power-play into operation.

For most of the months of 1996 until I left Carberry on 30th September I was involved in the fund-raising effort. My remit on coming to Carberry had been very humble. I was an 'officer' not a 'director.' I was not expected or asked to mastermind a public appeal of and for £2,000,000. But the purchase on mortgage of the property increased the importance of money. Jock Stein still seemed to think that he only needed to ask the great and good and they would cough up the hundreds of thousands of pounds he wanted. I had never thought that this would happen. The first level of appeal used a colour leaflet which was distributed to the Friends of Carberry, to everyone with a connection with Carberry, through the Woman's Guild of the Church of Scotland, through agencies to the general public and by means of an insertion in the Church of Scotland magazine 'Life and Work.' Irony again! The old Kirk from which some of the Friends of Carberry had been viscerally keen for Carberry to depart was the main target to be touted for money to develop Carberry! The evangelical caucus was not too prominent in responding to the campaign for funds.

The second level of appeal was to charitable trusts and the business community. Included in this level were personal approaches to influential people. Iain Mulholland, a well-known professional Scottish fund-raiser who was employed on a part-time consultancy basis advised that only through personal contact would real results be obtained. Early in 1996 I advised Jock Stein to inject the Executive Fund-raising Committee with at least two high powered business people from the Edinburgh financial sector. He did not take this advice. What we had was another cosy group. When it transpired that the Friends of Carberry would receive monies from the public appeal, I advised the Friends of Carberry Committee in person to invite some distinguished public figures to join their Committee. Three members of this committee are single women whom the Steins have 'counselled.' This advice was ignored. Jock Stein had maintained since I had gone to Carberry that he had the connections which would bring in large sums of money. This did not happen. I was called a development officer. I was never a director of development nor a director of the Carberry Appeal. Since everyone knew that Carberry had for many years been a 'one man band' I felt relieved of any direct responsibility for the results of the Appeal.

Jock Stein confessed himself disappointed by what he called the "ho-hum attitude of the Scottish mafia" to his requests for large sums of money for Carberry. He had hoped that Brian Souter of Stagecoach would give at least £250,000. But the Souter Foundation, of which Professor Ewan Brown is a trustee, the same man who had torn the first version of the business plan apart, gave only a relatively modest donation. The Souter Foundation was reported in the national press to have given £400,000 to ARK2, the new Christian cable television enterprise. This seemed to me to set the tone of expectancy and bring the ridiculously optimistic sums which Jock Stein had been wont to pluck out of the air to a basis in reality. Some adopted a 'wait and see' response. Successful business people are so because they have made good decisions. Carberry was not wanted by the Church of Scotland. It did not pay its way without subsidy. The necessity was to put the business on a sound footing first and then seek investment. It made sense to me that people would not throw large sums of money at an enterprise which was failing. And when you added up the mortgage, and the necessary roof repairs and the development costs, this prohibited rather than encouraged large scale investment in Carberry. The reason then that Guy Douglas had given to the Friends of Carberry at their 1995 Annual General Meeting, namely that large sums of money were dependent on having title to the property had proved false.

It was interesting to learn about the relationship between business, trusts, charitable donations and the Establishment. Friends of friends of friends help each other, owe each other favours and pay each other off with decisions about the use of other's people's money. Jock Stein did not cultivate such people and I sometimes had to prime him simply to be polite to visitors who were successful in their fields of enterprise. To that extent Jock Stein had rejected the social side of Establishment mentality and perhaps his evangelicalism distanced him somewhat from the liberal circles where the good connections are made. In this world the magic word is 'Royalty.' If you can make any significant approach for advocacy to a member of the House of Windsor, you are in luck. Carberry, although with strong links to Queen Elizabeth, the Queen Mother whose sister was the last Lady Elphinstone, was not fortunate enough or otherwise to gain the patronage of any member of the Royal household. I realised too how all powerful is the Establishment. You can do little or nothing if you do not belong and if you do not belong and do not bow - you will not get far. I am not a royalist and I was glad that our connections were so vague that I was caused no issue of principle.

In my annual report of 29th August 1995 I had stated clearly that Carberry would struggle to raise funds. I also said why. This was the part of the report which had been supressed by the Steering Committee of the Friends of Carberry. The Annual Meeting of the Friends of Carberry was not allowed to see or to discuss my views. George Burnet had accused me at the time of having bad judgement. In January I had been told that the Board would not offer me a job. By August of 1996, I felt I had been vindicated in this and in other points I had made.

I myself got closer to pledges of large sums of money on Carberry's behalf than anyone, including Jock Stein. I was still being paid to do a job and I did the job conscientiously. I was not going to jeopardise or sabotage the Appeal. I would not make God's judgement for him. Robert (Bob) Kernohan, Chairman of the Carberry Appeal was fair, humorous, relaxed and committed and knew very little of what went on at Carberry. Perhaps as a member of the Board he should have but he did not seem interested in the points I sometimes tried to raise with him. I left a live file containing the potential for significant donations to Carberry over the next twelve months. I do not want to see any Christian enterprise fail. I would not like to see Carberry become a hotel or an old folks home. I thought God might still have a plan and a use for Carberry. I doubted whether the present management could take Carberry much further. Some aspects of the internal life of Carberry are questionable. These need to be sorted out if Carberry is to progress. People earn a living there. They are not, by and large, to blame for the way the place is run.

Every day throughout 1996 donations arrived from individuals in response to the Carberry Appeal. The groundswell of popular support was encouraging although Jock Stein and George Burnet seemed to look more for very large six figure sums from the trust and corporate world. My own 'bottom up' theory of how Carberry might progress, given in a letter to Guy Douglas in January of 1995 was a now a statement of fact. I and others were genuinely impressed by the generosity of so many people who wished Carberry well. I was concerned that their gifts should be properly used. Since I was silenced in 1995, it is right for them to know more now.

As I prepared to leave Carberry I thought of the contradiction of my going. On many issues I had given good advice. On three major issues my advice had been taken, namely, to retain the skilled female part-time domestic staff, to convert the Annexe to houses rather than rabbit-warren dormitories and to commission a buyer's valuation of the Carberry estate - which, when done, had saved £100,000 on the purchase price. I had given these advices independently of Jock Stein and in order to have them adopted I had opposed him in committees. It was for opposing him that I was not wanted and it was for that reason they had tried to force me to undertake 'counselling' and it was for that reason that I was leaving. And there were countless incidents within Carberry over my two years' stay when I had taken a different line from Jock Stein, not because I had personal problems but out of simple God-given common sense. And I thought how much Carberry needed a dimension of humanity. And I feared for the folks who lived and worked there when I had gone.

It is a miracle that Carberry has survived the years. Who knows what could be yet accomplished if Jesus Christ was genuinely first in everyone's priorities? If there was a correlation between Carberry's public claims and its internal organisation. If the staff participated in all decision-making processes. It is not Christian and not even good management to expect people to work hard and to be committed while they are effectively disenfranchised from the strategic planning and management of an enterprise. If you continually humiliate people, they will not and cannot give of their best. A demoralised work-force is the antithesis of Christian community. The answer is not to get rid of them time after time. Jesus took His disciples into His confidence. That was the only way the Kingdom and the Church could be established. Secretive, paranoic control of Carberry has simply led to introversion and the project falling in on itself. The very breathe of the Holy Spirit cannot flow freely. And the huge sums of money which were sought are still wanting.

On October 12th 1996, the Friends of Carberry at their Annual General Meeting were asked to participate in a tithing scheme to buy Carberry by the year 2,001. Devout people were being asked to pay. There were no 'up front' donations of significance to encourge them. And the wealthy who were present were not putting their hands in their pockets either, Jock Stein included. I was unhappy with this plan in view of what I perceived to have been previous wrong strategy and continuing suspect management.

My final report to the Friends of Carberry Chairman Guy Douglas was factual but at the end I recorded some issues for consideration such as Carberry's ambiguous image, fund-raising in a Christian context, decline in standards of service, justice towards members of staff and the need to review accounting procedures, development expenditure priorities and spiritual leadership. I noted that my pastoral care of the staff had not been welcomed by the Wardens and that my advice on other matters had been equally unwanted by Jock Stein in particular. I asked for the report to be circulated to all the Friends of Carberry but this was not done.

In broader terms I felt that my initial and continuing judgment had been vindicated. During the summer an articulate short-term volunteer had submitted a written list of complaints about the poor treatment of volunteers, specifying moral blackmail to overwork and lack of intellectual and spiritual stimulation. In August when building work began in the Annexe, five volunteers of mixed sexes and ages were to be accommodated in a small turret flat designed for one person until I suggested that they should not to accept such treatment. I advised another volunteer who sought my help not to continue with extensive 'counselling' sessions. Volunteers felt that the 'house groups' led by the Steins were being used by them to glean information about members of staff. Two years previously I had laughed with Albert Bogle. It was a joke then. It was not now.

## Sunny Dunny

Since coming to live in Edinburgh again in 1989, I have found East Lothian to be a most attractive place. It has been a refuge and a bolt-hole for me. Visiting the lovely unspoilt villages and travelling through the peaceful countryside has refreshed me time after time. Places like Garvald and Athelstaneford, Whitekirk and Gifford, Aberlady and Dirleton have been conserved, retaining both character and quality. I remember visiting the seaside town of Dunbar and stopping to watch people playing golf on the Winterfield Course. To my surprise I found out that this was a public course and that it was possible for myself to play there. It was a good investment to buy a yearly ticket for a relatively modest sum. I could telephone and book a time to play. In forty five minutes I could be standing on the first tee.

To get out of the car and smell the sea-salt air and to feel the sun beating down on your neck is wonderful. To look at the beautiful green parkland and links and then take in the broad sweep of Belhaven Bay, looking across to the John Muir Park, out to the great Bass Rock, over to North Berwick Law, across to Fife, out to the North sea and back into Dunbar itself, alongside red sandstone cliffs above black rocks - to drink deep of creation, to applaud the Creator, to exult in life and consciousness and to worship secretly in your inner heart is an unforgettable experience. And when I would reach the fourteenth hole, perched on a promontory, I would sit down on the grass, with the tide lapping beneath me, listen to the gulls crying and the distant putt-putt of an inshore fishing boat, watch the lines of yachts taking part in a local club race, feel the sun caressing my shoulders, bow my head and say "Lord, let me live and die here - in East Lothian." Yes - let me visit the west for its awesome and unsurpassed beauty - let my breath be taken away by Loch Awe, and Torridon, Loch Maree and the west of Harris - but let me live and die in East Lothian with its comforting and undemanding landscapes and Sunny Dunny as a *locus* of providence.

I loved playing golf on my own. If the course was not busy that was even better for me. Anonymity - the natural elements - a battle with myself and the course - the ever changing problems the game itself throws up - the disappointments and the joys of it - for someone whose inner life is intense in an immoderate way - this is occupational therapy which works. I quite often joined others to play. Norman MacKillop, a retired gentleman, invited me to accompany him one day and I played occasionally thereafter with him and some of his young friends from Dunbar. A great wit, Norman is good company. The seventh hole runs parallel to a road alongside which are houses. On one occasion as I addressed the ball, I took a moment longer than usual. "I'm slightly nervous about the road and the houses here," I said in mitigation. After a few more 'waggles' I had just begun the backswing when Norman quipped "You're not half as nervous as the people there are." Dissolution into laughter. "Did you hear about the chap who bought covers for his irons?" asked Norman one day. "No," said I. "After a week one of his friends asked him how he was getting on with his new iron covers." "They're great," said he, "But I seem to have lost a bit of distance." Then Norman himself would wheeze in delight at my schoolboy appreciation of such silliness. But being out there on Winterfield on my own of a summer's evening and the crimson sun setting slowly, turning round a hundred times to wave goodbye over the trees and fields and the Firth of Forth filled my soul with such a radiant happiness - and a decent drive into the bargain - I was as Max Magee had many years before described the life of my inner soul - like a puppy playing in the garden sun.

## Priestfield Church

In May and quite out of the blue Jock Stein asked me if I was interested in taking up a part-time locum at Priestfield Church in Edinburgh whose minister Tom Johnston was due to take four months off for sabbatical and annual leave. Tom needed a locum if he was to have his well earned break but the man he had telephoned to enquire about had himself been called to a charge and was not therefore available. Jock Stein always thinks 'money.' The two-day a week commitment would lessen my salary from Carberry, he thought. But in accepting the position, I decided to continue with my full-time job at Carberry and use the evenings for pastoral duties. It was not what I had in mind for the lovely summer evenings which I looked forward to and cherished and guarded jealously before the inevitable return of the Scottish winter.

But from the beginning of June to the end of September I found much joy and fulfilment in this humble and temporary role. To my great astonishment, the congregation responded to my sermons. I had never held Edinburgh congregations in high esteem. A '0-0' draw, I would say on most occasions whether I myself was preaching or simply attending as a worshipper. Civilities were always present but so were the skilled deflections and extrications of those who would always keep Christianity at arm's length. As Chaplain to Edinburgh University I had received few invitations to preach. Now I had a pulpit, albeit borrowed, for four months. It proved most enjoyable for me and at a deeper spiritual level a partial rehabilitation. I actually began to look forward to preaching Sunday by Sunday. When the congregation sung the concluding hymn, I could sense the conviction and sincerity of their worship of God. Marvellous!

The pastoral duties were not arduous and no burden attached to the position. I did require the occasional hour off to conduct funeral services but I compensated for that by working out of hours or counting the time against annual leave. Jim Turner the Director of Music is both committed and capable and I enjoyed our conversations. By the end of this most helpful interlude, it seemed that everyone had been blessed. Tom Johnston benefited from a deserved and profitable sabbatical. The congregation also had a sabbatical and I found a Christian community able to take the spice and humour of my anti-establishment preaching to themselves without offence. More seriously, we met at a deeper level of our spiritual understanding and communicated. And so the Name of Jesus Christ was honoured in everything.

## Walking on Water

Not in the blasphemous sense as fanatical supporters so idolise sportsmen! I am so far out on a limb now that I am supported only by my Faith. The water is deep and I cannot by my nature walk on it at all. I have no job and no home of my own. I am in temporary lodgings and will I ever be employed again? Like St Peter I cry, "Save me Lord or I will perish." Many have taken steps into the unknown for their beliefs. I have hitherto had the security of employment and a salary. What now?

This book is a casting upon the waters. The story is true but will anyone believe it? The risks are great in publishing. But the issues are greater. Many, many people experience God in their lives. Many Christians testify to knowing Jesus Christ. Some scientists, materialists, rationalists and humanists deny the possibility and reality of such specific spiritual experiences. My calling has been an open-minded experiment all the way. I know that I have been confirmed in times past and I await confirmation now. My personal preference would be to live a private life. But the issues of the truth of Christianity are greater than me by far. I cannot keep what God has revealed to me to myself. To do so would be to bury a God-given talent in the ground. To do so would be to betray my fellow Christians. To do so would to put myself before God's love of everyone in this world.

At the deeper level there is enmity between conflicting understandings and perceptions. Spiritual incompatability would be a neater descriptive phrase. I believe I have suffered for being a specially called servant of the living God in Jesus Christ and in not conforming to the herd mentalities of liberals and evangelicals. Why are such groups formed? Why do many join and stay? Some people like to be dependent. Others like to be led. If one or two people like others to depend upon them and to lead them, therein lies the trouble.

On leaving Carberry I prepared a booklet of two hundred of the witticisms and gaffes of the Carberry staff which I had collected over the year since my last similar production at Christmas 1995. For example, Rena - "She's lyin' there like a pun o' mince," "I think I'll ha'e some toast, ma back's sair." David - "I had a happy childhood, except for the occasional impression wi' a dug lead." Anne - "I had the Duchess of Argyll in the back of my van with all the junk." Agnes - "At coffee time you should keep your mouth shut and eat your roll." Adeline (the cook) - "Ach, Ah'll awa' an' dae ma melons." I called the booklet "Carberry XXX Files" and dedicated it "to the workers of Carberry for maintaining their humanity and their humour in stressful circumstances" and below this dedication I wrote the words of Isaiah 11:4, "He will not judge by appearance or hearsay. He will judge the poor fairly and defend the right of the helpless."

Does God have a purpose for Carberry? It keeps surviving. While I am grateful for having been there, the reasons I came were not just as Jock Stein's limited perceptions would admit. I consider some of the things that have gone on at Carberry, including the treatment of myself in November and December of 1995 to be a blight on Scottish Christianity. I shudder at the thought of years and years of the same mistakes and wrongs.

Within my soul burns a spiritual flame. Sometimes it wells up in a kindly manner. And I still may see from time to time the Holy City of the New Jerusalem. Occasionally there is a presence of angels. I cannot prove this to anyone. God exists. Jesus of Nazareth rose from the dead. Christianity is true. If, to someone as imperfect as me such *intimations of love divine* can be given, how much more is the history of Jesus true, and the life of our Maker, the living God the only reality. This book contains some of the empirical data of my personal history as I have understood it. It now falls like a seed to the ground to die or to become a new and more beautiful life.

# 12 : Two Hundred Years Of Wrong

## Many False Prophets

For more than two hundred years much European theology has misled people about the nature of Christianity and about the possibilities for a living relationship with God. Christianity was often limited to what seemed reasonable to the human mind. Reimarus (1694-1768) for example thought that Jesus intended to refine our moral character. Reimarus denied the supernatural dimension of the New Testament and held that the disciples stole Jesus' body, invented the story of His resurrection, circulated the promise of His return and preached for converts to this new false religion. Strauss (1808-1874) thought that Jesus was a disciple of John who proclaimed Himself to be the messiah, sought recognition at Jerusalem and was executed by the Romans. Bauer (1809-1882) developed literary criticism of the Bible. He dismissed any truthfulness on the part of the evangelists and decided that Jesus had never actually existed. Renan (1823-1892) thought that the Gospels were 'legendary biographies.' He wrote "For the historian, the life of Jesus finishes with his last sigh." (The Life of Jesus p.374) Albert Schweitzer (1875-1956) thought that Jesus was strong enough to think of himself as the spiritual ruler of mankind and try to bend history to his purpose. He tried to hasten the end-time but was betrayed and killed by the Jewish leaders. Kahler (1835-1912), Wrede (1859-1906) and Dibelius (1883-1947) also took a reductionistic view of Christianity, of Jesus and of the Gospels.

But the most influential of reductionistic or 'de-mythologising' Biblical scholars in the twentieth century was Rudolph Bultmann. (1884-1976) Bultmann thought that little or nothing could be known about the historical Jesus. He was not an atheist or even an agnostic. He wished however to separate faith in Christ from what he understood as the problems of the historical unreliability of the Gospels, as, for example in his books "Die Geschichte der synoptischen Tradition" (The History of the Synoptic Tradition,1921), "Jesus" (1929) and "Jesus And the Word." (1935) Bultmann and his precursors placed the rational human mind above the given revelation recorded in the Bible. What did not accord with contemporary understanding had to be wrong. Post-Enlightenment rationalistic humanism rejected the world-view portrayed in the Bible. The supernatural dimension was negated as fantasy. European academic man became the measure of all things religious, spiritual, supernatural and divine. Writers of books became their own messiahs. Others followed them.

These reductions of Christianity have continued in more recent years and with varying degrees in people like John A T Robinson ("Honest To God," 1963), Maurice Wiles and his cronies ("The Myth Of God Incarnate," 1973) and Don Cupitt ("Jesus and the Gospel of God," 1979) and ("Taking Leave of God," 1980). His "Sea of Faith" movement undermines Christianity. David Jenkins, the former Anglican Bishop of Durham and Daphne Hampson, the extreme feminist writer ("Theology And Feminism," 1990) have also expressed their doubts and disbeliefs about the reliability of Gospel accounts of the life of Jesus. They share a common trait of judging the New Testament by the standard of their own late twentieth century humanistic minds. They apply an assumed logic which they purport belongs to the scientific and technological age to Scripture, assuming and presuming that Scripture must be in error because it was written so long ago in what they would describe as a non-scientific age.

David Jenkins has written that he does not believe in miracles. (God, Miracle and the Church of England, 1987, p.5) In the same book he says that the birth of Jesus narratives are about obedience, not virginity (p.6) and that the resurrection is about encounters rather than the empty tomb. (p.6) For him the Gospels are not newspaper reports or scientific accounts (p.27) and he concludes that they are a mixture of historicity, myth, legend and embroidery which was just their way of doing things. (p.27)

Anthony Freeman's book "God In Us" (1993) is a recent description of personal rejection of Christianity. Freeman denies everything. He rejects the supernatural (p.7) and argues that religion is a purely human creation. (p 9) Feuerbach rides again! He is a disciple of Don Cuppitt's "Sea of Faith" movement and describes himself as a "Christian humanist."(p.58) His is a thoroughly negative and iconoclastic evaluation of the data of Christian history. He thinks that Christian revelation is only ever communicated by humans and therefore can only be a form of humanism. (p.22) He allows no corroborating testimony by countless Christians throughout the ages, no historical vindication of prophetic utterances and of just and good people in later time, no explanation for the originality and transcendence of the content of Christian revelation, no acknowledgement of the charismatic dimension of Christianity throughout its near 2,000 years and no possibility of the truth of the accounts of the reception of personal revelation in the Bible and in Christian literature throughout history since Jesus of Nazareth. Everyone but Anthony Freeman is a liar. Only he is honest!!

He rejects the facts and value of the life of Jesus, His ministry, death and resurrection. (p.37f) Sin is for Freeman a theological invention. He uses the secular existential ideas of 'lostness,' 'aimlessness' and 'lack of esteem' to describe what might be incomplete in human nature and conduct. (p. 30f) He allows no space for a positive and destructive force of evil, even within his humanism. Does he ever read the newspapers? For Freeman "the world is morally neutral" (p.66) - what an extraordinary suggestion! The world may well be morally neutral to him and his ideas, but the world has never been morally neutral to greater lives than his. The world was not morally neutral to Janani Luwum, Steve Biko, Martin Luther King, Mahatma Ghandi, nor indeed to Jesus of Nazareth. If Freeman means by 'world' the planet 'earth' then neither is it neutral for from time to time it wreaks destruction on the society of humans. The Biblical command to 'subdue' may be more relevant for millenia to come than Freeman thinks, extending to meteorogical forces and universes beyond our visible sight today.

Naturally for Freeman Jesus cannot be unique and so any offence to other religious claims is avoided. (p. 42f) But Muslims do not think that all religions are the same or that all religious claims are equal. So interesting from my own point of view is his assertion "..people receive great comfort and genuine healing at Christian 'homes of healing' but it is the devotion and skill of the staff and the positive attitude of all concerned which accounts for this." (p. 50) Indeed!

Freeman thinks that the Western world is afflicted by a sense of hopelessness today because the old 'pie in the sky when you die' Christianity no longer works for people. Could it not more realistically be because the Western world has abandoned and not rediscovered the essential truth of the existence of God in and through Jesus Christ? Could it not be that the supernatural, eternal dimension of human life must acknowledge its own fact and its Creator in order to be truly fulfilled? Might it not be that in turning away from Jesus Christ that other spiritual existences have taken His place in the collective consciousness of western society? 'New Age' testifies to the permanence of the supernatural in human understanding. Only - its object is perverted to human selves and to postulated intermediate supernatural beings. Is not false spirituality the result of apostasy rather than rationalistic and materialistic humanism? Has Freeman learned nothing from seventy years of atheistic communism in the former Soviet Union and its collapse? But then he wants some Christianity, even if it is not much. Enough to allow him to remain a priest in the Anglo-Catholic wing of the Church of England. And he is not pleased that he was thrown out while boasting that he felt like Martin Luther in making his personally liberating declaration. (p.11) Luther, of course rediscovered personal faith in God through Jesus Christ, while Freeman denies the existence of such a relationship. Freeman and I are at opposite ends of the ecclesiastical experience. I am mistrusted for being granted personal knowledge of God in an intensely and effective personal way by liberals and by right wing evangelicals. The former because they do not want to think that it can happen today. The latter because they do not want it to happen to anyone except them.

Some theologians like Paul Tillich and John Macquarrie have attempted to put the Christian Gospel into philosophical language in order to make it communicable to modern thinkers. The trouble with this method is that unless you understand the philosophy you cannot understand the elements of Christianity that are supposed to be communicated. Again, the assumption is that the language and description in the New Testament is itself flawed and wrong.

Not all theologians have negated or reduced Christianity to the confines of their own mental processes. Karl Barth, Tom Torrance and Karl Rahner have in fact done the opposite and attempted to substantiate Christianity for modern minds through argument from Revelation, using discursive encounter with scientific theory and expressing the faith of the community. In this, the historic tradition of Christian explanation and understanding has been continued.

There were also the dear ones, in whom thought and life were interlinked, who lived and learned rather than just thought, for example Blaise Pascal, Søren Kierkegaard and Scotland's own John McLeod Campbell. Each of these had a gentler understanding of Christianity and a personal vision which they articulated. Their individuality was a problem for their contemporaries and they suffered in some measure for the depth and sensitivity of their understanding. Their life circumstances reflected what they were trying to communicate. Later generations benefited more then they or those who lived alongside them ever did. They were seeds of witness dying in the ground, raised later to reputation and respect on earth and to some greater glory in heaven.

The general movement of Christian thinking in the twentieth century has been away from certainty to scepticism and away from devotion and faith to doubt and apostasy. The universities of Europe and North America have become temples of idolatry to the conceit of individual human minds. Published theories of the unreliability and untruthfulness of the New Testament have simply shown historic, personal, spiritual and actual ignorance on a grand scale.

What of the great intellectual enemies of Christianity? Karl Marx now consigned to history. Sigmund Freud proved wrong. Neitszche redivivus in today's pagan 'New Age' anti-Christianity. The terrible vacuum in European and north American society is filled by false gods, idolatry, idolisation, politics, power, entertainment, gambling, riches, self, self, self. Jesus of Nazareth was not wrong in what he taught about the meaning of life. The offence of the Son of God was to come to earth as a seemingly religious person. Yet the connection between the claims of religion and the mystery of human destiny can never be diminished. His resurrection was a non-religious happening. His life was not religious at all. Humans are meant to live in relationship to their Maker and not to become religious creatures. Therefore I myself have resisted all pressures and temptations to become religious. I do not regard prayer as religion. The meeting of the People of God is an expression of relationship. It has nothing to do with religion as such, or should not. However - if for some there is no content to their relationship with God - then indeed they must become religious and wear the right garments and perform rituals and say the right things at the right time. Jesus of Nazareth satirised those who, lacking true relationship with God, manufactured their piety to impress others. (Matthew 23)

The behavioural sciences, psychology and sociology in particular offer humano-centred explanations of human life and conduct. The general tenor of these disciplines excludes God as a factor in human consciousness, personality and conduct. If Christianity is true, if then God exists, if the highest relationship possible is with God, and if this is denied then all such theories are inadequate at best and false and dangerous at worst. If there is no place or space for a being as great and wonderful as must be our Maker in the petty and local theories of mind and of society which twentieth century pundits have peddled for money for generations then how poor and partial and limited and repressed and regressive and retentive are such theories and their proponents. But all society sets much store by these intellectual idols. Schools, businesses, caring agencies, the judicial system, and yes, churches, all pay due court to our human centred theories of mind and society. No wonder Christianity has become marginalised. Not by accident! And they simply cannot or will not draw any connections between the dreadful state of our living and the rejection and exclusion of Christianity from their self-centred learning. This is where a revolution is needed. To take the eternal dimension of human consciousness and life fully into psychology. To take the spiritual responsibility dimension of existence into sociology. Until this happens, our society will continue to decline in cohesion and indeed in the very humanity which is espoused but which is impossible for human beings without the redeeming relationship offered freely in Jesus Christ.

And what of the great ikons of philosophy Russell, Ayer, Wittgenstein? They tell us that within their own mental constructs there is little or no place for God. How childish! What little brats! Do they then define the sum of human awareness and intelligence according to the limits of their own horizons? Are we to think so little of ourselves that we can but agree with their views of the world? Is that what we are meant for? Surely not. My fellow countryman the philosopher David Hume (1711-1776) was mistaken all those years ago. He denied necessary connections between cause and effect and absolutely negated the possibility of miracle because he believed that natural law could not be breached. He said that the human personality is only "a bundle or collection of different perceptions, which succeed each other with inconceivable rapidity, and are in perpetual flux and movement." (An Enquiry p. 302) Unsurprisingly, Hume rejected Christianity. Yet Christianity continues to confound and contradict its detractors. What has happened to this writer is not supposed to happen. Never could have happened. Should never happen. These people have said so. So there. The theologians have said so too. And some bishops and ministers. How different is a real relationship with God from the cult of the church and the insidious corruptions of academia.

Among scientists such as Dawkins, Davies, Polkinghorne and Hawking there are mixtures of great arrogance and humility. Christianity has reacted badly to scientific discovery in the past. Remember Galileo, Newton, Darwin! Christianity today is supine before the empress Scientia. No contest. And yet many scientists do not claim for their theories the certainty that people like David Jenkins claim for their doubts. Some indeed say that the big questions of physics resolve into questions of theology. Why is there anything at all? Who caused the Big Bang? Who made the laws of physics which made the Big Bang work? Why is there conscious life on this particular portion of the immeasurable universe? There is a mystical dimension to science. We are more ignorant than knowledgeable about the universe. O for such humility among the theologians and Biblical scholars of Europe and north America!

But they are worshipping creatures too, just the same. They worship new gods, 'New Age' gods and goddesses. As do many who have abandoned Christianity and followed the devices of their own hearts forming their own religious systems. 'New Age' allows you to pick an idea here, a thought there, from the Sioux perhaps, or the Huron, or the lady astrologer in 'Yellow Pages' or this guru and quite often from that schizophrenic spiritualist medium. A polyglot fragmentation of conflicting claims and egos, of false messiahs and get-rich-quick hustlers. But anti-Christian, anti-Trinitarian and anti-Judaistic. And denying the One True God. Arrogating eternal life in perpetuity, high eschatological status and self-appointed divinity. And not the way of Jesus who redeemed the world through personal sacrifice - anathema. Becoming, self-development, actualisation - these are the buzz words. Disposable relationships, casuistic moral justifications, enclosed selfishness - these are the sacraments of the 'New Age.'

## Living Witnesses

There have been living witnesses to the actual discernible truth of God in Jesus Christ in every generation. But they have suffered a measure of what their Lord suffered. George Fox

(1624-91) was a hunted man, frequently imprisoned, beaten and despised. In that he was like St Paul. John Bunyan wrote his great book 'Pilgrim's Progress' as an allegory because he could not write otherwise. It was dangerous to be a radically thinking speaking Christian. John Wesley suffered abuse from time to time as an itinerant preacher. Quite often, these people were brutalised, not by atheists but by fellow Christians. It is with the persecuted that I find some sympathy and personal encouragement and an explanation of my own struggles. For all the enormous conceits of the present age and our obsession with human rights and personal freedoms it is still a very dangerous thing to be a radically thinking and speaking Christian. It is politically incorrect to be a confessing Christian today in Britain, in many schools, at work, in universities and, of course in the media. Joseph was the victim of fraternal jealousy. (Genesis 37ff) Jesus taught the Parable of the Tenants in the Vineyard (Luke 20:9-18) as a testimony against the same destructive and cancerous religious impulses of which he Himself became a victim.

Deep in the religious sub-conscious of each of us lie the seeds of spiritual enmity. Much it takes to change that from bad to good. A great and individual testing must take place. So many have not taken that path and do not know what is within them. And when they are tested, they are uncomfortable and what comes out is not truth and grace but deceit and wickedness. And if they have a public position they must defend their reputation and they do not care who suffers for that pretence to be maintained. Some form alliances, unholy indeed, not feeling confident enough to tackle a single person alone. Others use psychological categories to diminish and exclude the threat to their own artificially created personal empires.

The Christian Church has ever been a ground for internal persecution. Nothing has changed. Genteel society is as vicious as any other in any age. Poke it and see. Scratch the surface. Laugh at its transparent hypocrisies. Offer a better way. If Christ is real in your life in a way that is unexpected, which contradicts the dying conventions of the age then expect no little trouble. If you have a living Word to say - beware - you will find it hard to earn a salary on earth for such an enterprise. Jesus did not. And extraordinarily if your Lord has told you years and years ago that precisely these things will happen so that you are not at all surprised and you bear the amazing gift of special personal revelation in your most vulnerable and ordinary human life and body, then at least your sanity prevails and your being survives.

And everywhere there are hidden saints and believers. There is a commonwealth of the gentle ones, the gracious, the courageous, the honest, the triumphant. You recognise them. They, it seems, recognise you at least in part. They can live with you and tolerate you. For they are themselves redeemed and have nothing to fear. Nothing at all. Indeed - they can rejoice. And you are not alone at all, surrounded by a cloud of witnesses, above and on earth, invigorated by the communion of saints in heaven and in the Christian Church.

Wheat and tares (Matthew 13:24-30) exist in churches on earth side by side, good and bad, until the end-time when a final discrimen, a final discernment, a final judgement will be made. Some seem to be in the churches just to hinder the actual saving proclamation of the Christian Gospel. Church leadership is characterised by compromise and insincerity. No one needs be told of the atrocities committed in the Name of Jesus Christ throughout the ages. But we will never know all the good that has been done for it far outweighs the bad. And millions whose names are written only in heaven have lived as God intended that they should, not in perfection, but in faithfulness and under forgiving Grace. Those who presume to deny these have much to answer for.

Great is the religious ego dressed in drag, made high and wide, the centre of attraction - a little god. And then the mouth opens and out comes disappointment, unbelief, self-love, discouragement, prevarication, excuse, compromise, untruth. Is it no wonder that the churches are receding? The higher people go the less they believe. The more they are paid, the less they have to say. And they take to themselves position and ambition and status and power over others and the cause of Christ perishes in the ashes of their hearts. And in their hypocrisy they turn on those who actually do believe and live in relationship to and with God and mock them and vilify them and persecute them. Greater humility might say "I do not know everything: I do not know God all that well: what I say may not be true: I acknowledge the limits of my understanding." But - oh yes - they expect that of a true and called preacher. No certainties. No confidence. No prophesies. No truth.  Let me mouth my ignorance without contest. Do not you speak of the God revealed to you. Keep silent! (Compare Isaiah 30:10-11)

## Reform Christianity

I have found the Christianity articulated within the Reform tradition to be true, though I have not found the Reform tradition to articulate the whole of Christianity. God is different from human beings, existing independently of all of us. Relationship with God is possible in and through Jesus Christ. Jesus is different from human beings and exists independently from all of us. Relationship with Jesus Christ is possible with the help of the Bible and in the community of good Christians. The way is not that of equals. Neither is it the way of cruel obeisance, mediaeval patrimony or spiritual class distinction. All forms of Christian denomination are external to relationship with God in Jesus Christ. If these become ends in themselves, then they hinder and restrict the possibility of relationship with God in Jesus Christ. All forms of Christian ministry are helpful in nurturing relationship with God in Jesus Christ but if they place themselves between a human soul and our Maker, then they hinder and restrict such relationship with God in Jesus Christ.

Each living human being is offered in Jesus Christ a personal relationship with God. We have the capacity to respond to this offer, to keep it at arm's length or to reject it. We are dealing with Perfection and in consequence, we ourselves inevitably feel our human imperfection, inadequacy and sinfulness, the closer we get to God in Jesus Christ. The wonder is that what we feel about ourselves is not a barrier to God's offer of relationship with us. We cannot however spiritually justify ourselves or our conduct to God. Neither can we politically justify ourselves or our conduct to God though we may do so to our fellow human beings strategically and with seeming impunity.

We must rejoice in the moral distinction between ourselves and God in Jesus Christ. That is the guarantee that all life is based on good and not evil. That is the guarantee of a final justice and a restitution and recompense for those who have suffered innocently in this human life. If we are glad that God is good, we cannot then live as if there is no distinction between good and evil on earth, in the human community, in ourselves and in God. We should therefore embrace the repenting tradition as the way forward for all humanity in relationship to God in Jesus Christ. Liberal Christianity which does not take the repenting tradition seriously betrays human beings and betrays the life of Jesus. Right wing Christianity which complicates the simplicities of Christian calling with its agenda of power and money is guilty of coming between human beings and God in a hypocritical and pharasaical way.

Sacramental traditions make the fullest sense if they are consequences of relationship with God in Jesus Christ and not substitutions for such relationship. Systems of human ecclesiastical authority are deeply suspect. They allow professional clerical careers to develop. They breed defensiveness. They place false restrictions on Christian calling and service, excluding and including according to human criteria. Above all, in perpetuating themselves they become ends in themselves. They create classes of Christians. The apostles' lives were sacrificial. Church leaders' lives are generally self-indulgent, well remunerated and establishment integrated. Thus they gain much worldly status, comfort, position, prestige and wealth from the sacrifices of others of more noble and faithful calling. Much risk is involved in truly following Jesus Christ and living in relationship to God in and through Jesus Christ.

Each new born child may live in relationship to God in Jesus Christ freely throughout his or her life. Life on earth is not an end in itself. It is a preamble and a preparation for full and direct community with God in Jesus Christ in eternity. In the light of this prior Grace and given salvation, our human sojourn on earth finds its true base and purpose and meaning and direction. Christian morality is a part of our responsive relationship with God in Jesus Christ. It can only be in relationship to God in Jesus Christ that any perceived moral standards make sense. Moral standards are not ends in themselves. They are choices which those liberated by their relationship with God in Jesus Christ freely choose to make in order to respect this given relationship. Grace and forgiveness underpin all human moral choices.

There is a difference between right and wrong on earth and right and wrong in God's sight. But Christianity is primarily about the saving and redemption of what has gone wrong, what is lost and feels hopeless, what is manifestly abandoned and rejected. We enunciate Christian moral standards as good and advisable, likely to bring joy and happiness in earthly life and of value in themselves. But that is not Christianity. Christianity says to those who have utterly failed to keep Christian moral standards, "There is always a way back in Jesus Christ for you." And the mission and calling of Christianity is precisely to spread this good news and to be a vehicle and communicator of this reconciling good news. More - Christianity is in following Jesus Christ meant to be a practical means of helping those farthest away from reconciliation with God to find their way home. Christianity as a conservative, inactive and self-regarding group is a negation of the life of Jesus Christ.

Today, many Christians throughout the world live for and follow Jesus Christ. But - not everyone does. In Britain and in the western hemisphere it can be argued that fewer and fewer people are doing so. Why? Because of two hundred years and more of wrong. Because so many church leaders tell lies. Because of all the false teachings within the universities. Because of the arrogance of humanistic minds which raise themselves up against God's own life and self-disclosure in Jesus Christ. Because of the wayward tendencies of the human spirit to go our own way, experiment in our own religious ideas and wallow in such confusion which makes it impossible for us to join the repenting tradition and establish a relationship with God in Jesus Christ. Because as humans there is a percentage of built-in hatred for and rejection of God in our genes.

## Authority Of Scripture

The authority of the Bible has been basic to the existence and identity of Protestant Christianity. Vatican II opened up many lay Roman Catholics to the possibilities associated with Biblical teaching and preaching. Most strong Protestant evangelical traditions emphasise the importance of the Bible in the life of believers. Current liberal academic prejudice holds that the truth content of the Gospels, for example, is secondary to the propaganda motives of the writers. In April 1996, David Jenkins in his annual Holy Week negation of the historical accounts of the resurrection, once again stated his view that the empty tomb is but a symbol introduced into the Gospels after some decades of Christian experience. The Gospel stories, by the same token, illustrate 'faith-problems' rather than actual events. The Bible may have residual use for devotional purposes only. The notion that Christianity must be acceptable to the specific requirements of human reason governed as it is by knowledge and the lack of knowledge at any given moment in history has significantly undermined the inspirational, prophetic and charismatic voice of main-line European Protestantism. It has also dealt Scottish Christianity a mortal blow. Theology has become a matter of explaining the world to God and not of explaining God to the world. Theological education has become the application of doubt and scepticism rather than response to doubt and scepticism. The interior struggle towards an assurance of faith is too often rejected for a comfortable and well-dressed semi-agnosticism.

The conclusions of scholars who dispute the integrity of the first Christian witnesses and writers can be countered by the continuing *coincidence of faith* that exists between those whose lives provide the content of the New Testament and those who experience parallel living faith today. Of which I myself am such an one - a witness for the Living God in Jesus Christ. The Gospels do not occur in a vacuum but in the context of the community of Judaism. Today's Orthodox Jews have the same and continuing basis of faith as the heroes of the Old Testament. Such faith in God cannot be lightly dismissed or pronounced to be delusory or self-deceiving. Far less can it be held to be deliberate misleading of the community of gentiles. On the contrary - its purpose is to share the content of divine revelation within the Old Covenant with the rest of humanity. Contemporary faith continues to coincide with Biblical faith.

St Paul may be treated as an independent witness to the truths of the Gospels. He was well educated and an intellectual. He would have criticised any tendencies towards untruthfulness or even bad argument in the early Church. He would never have tolerated the proclamation of nonsense nor the ill-motivated intrusion of legend into something which he had found to be consummately true - that Jesus had risen from the dead and that God was in Christ reconciling the human community to Himself. St Paul corroborates the other New Testament writers, especially the evangelists. To attack St Paul himself as being deluded or intellectually promiscuous, insincere and misleading does not hold up either because his experience of faith is too close to that experience claimed and owned by so many throughout the ages of Christianity. The coincidence again outweighs the miserable scepticism of small minds.

It is astonishing that so much credence is given to scholars who destroy the reputation of the Bible as if they were somehow beyond questioning and as if they delivered their personal views with an eternal guarantee of perfection of motive in research and absolute reliability of conclusion. Many publish under pressure to say and to write something. To maintain their academic status. For money. Christianity's failures in human history and society are now recognised and it is politically correct to acknowledge them at the end of the twentieth century. But the devastation caused to the spiritual life of half the human populace by intellectual conceit and faithless rationalism is immeasurable. Except that the emptiness and disintegration of modern secular society, the addictions and false idols of current human consciousness show that something much deeper is wrong with and within the individualised and collectivised human spirit.

The continuing *coincidence of faith* is the life of Christianity. A more humble and honest approach to the sacred things of divine revelation might be based on the following maxim,

> "Do not dismiss these things to which
> the Bible bears witness which you
> have not found to be untrue."

This is a principle of open-minded rational, intellectual and academic enquiry. It leaves open possibilities and probabilities. It prevents the arrogant atomistic human mind from denying the life of God among us. The Holy Spirit may even get room to breathe - in theological colleges throughout the world! The intellectual search is best undertaken in parallel to a spiritual search for personal relationship to God in and through Jesus Christ. This is likely to be a life-long enterprise as it has been for many throughout Christian history. In saying "I have found this to be true" and "I have not found this to be untrue" human minds can find their appropriate status and function within the universe of knowledge still to be discovered.

## Other Claims

I have found that Christianity is true. It is true independently of my own life and consciousness. Anywhere. At any time. Christianity is as true today as it was on the day of the resurrection of Jesus. It will for ever be as true. Jesus is the way to relationship with God. The way of self-renunciation, of Grace, of forgiveness, of transparent confession of Jesus Christ and its meaning throughout the created universes is, in my view, of a differing quality from all other spiritual and religious claims. Jesus was inclusive. Only God has any final right to exclude. Those however who live in a fulfilled relationship with God in Jesus Christ are bound to distinguish Jesus Christ from other religious claimants. This will be politically incorrect and be the occasion of persecution. Christians who live in relationship with God in Jesus Christ will be treated as threats to human-made processes of social organisation intending forms of enforced political and religious unity. Thus all such will understand the gift of Jesus to the world, His words, His actions, His death, His resurrection, the giving of the Holy Spirit, the communion of saints and the gift of eternal life. For all these are of and belong to an order of creation which is greater than the life of the human community. Thus said Jesus to Pilate.

Men and women seek human greatness and power in this world to order the lives of others. Rivalries will be ever present on earth. Violence and strategic warfare will not cease in the centuries to come. Christians are called to live and witness to Jesus Christ's way of personal non-violence and to advocate as a human possibility strategic non-violence based upon acknowledgement of Jesus as the Prince of Peace and true means of relationship with God.

Unfortunately, the followers of alternative religious claims will react critically against the best as well as the worst of visible Christianity. There will be no subtle distinctions. Innocent suffering will occur. No-one wants to be proved mistaken in their religious understanding. That which is deepest in us matters most. In death Jesus redeemed us. In dying Christianity will be the seed-corn of the salvation of the world. In dying we ourselves are born to eternal life. We will not need to invite persecution. It will find us. It always has. Full of self-righteousness. Disguised as light. Deeply religious.

But are there not many people of differing religious insight, faith and creed who look towards their fellow humans beings with good will? Are there not many many on earth whose religion does not lead them to hatred and violence? Is there not a commonwealth of those who try to follow the highest teaching of their tradition with integrity and in peace? The same Jesus rejected by His own people must discern the hearts of those who live well by the light and truth given to them. The possibility of having a personal relationship with this same Jesus must be open to them without the necessity of religious institutionalism. In the quiet of their hearts - always.

## Gender

Jesus was a man, a male, masculine. Yet His life was not an affirmation of manhood, maleness or masculinity. Calvary, the naked crucifixion of an unmarried, childless, poverty ridden, powerless, friendless person was the negation of those characteristics and effects by which manhood is judged in human society. At Calvary all masculinity is judged and found wanting. It is God who is redeeming the world. It is politically correct today to consider the Old Testament to be a patriarchal document. At a social level of understanding this is a possible interpretation. But from the divine perspective all men throughout the Old Testament are under God's correction, discipline and judgement. There are occasional encouragements and heroics. The general trend, however is far from admirable. If the Old Testament is about men - it is not a flattering history. But the distinction between the human community and God is made clear throughout the Old Testament. So clear - that the Hebrew mind could not comprehend the Incarnation of God in Jesus Christ.

Any theology which seeks to justify a human gender must be but a human invention. A true theology will clarify the distinction between male and female human beings and God. If there is any attempt to divinise one gender as in some 'New Age' feminist writing, then that simply reflects the lack of divine revelation which underpins the self-justifying human invention. The cultural dishonesty which is evident in such writings can be refuted. Men have not started to justify themselves as men in theology. If and when they do, such a performance will be as hopeless as some feminist thought. For neither of these diversions will tell us anything about God. And it is God all of us want to know about - not one another. We see enough of each other, thank you. We cannot raise each other up. We are not the saviours of the other gender. Only God in Jesus Christ can redeem us, male and female, female and male by a way that was sacrificial, self-denying, gender obliterating, bloody, cruel but eternally victorious. The elevation of gender is a false path to the knowledge of God. Realistic assessment of gender in spiritual terms opens the possibility for the discovery of God.

## Left And Right

The basic tenets of Christianity are true. *Intimations of Love Divine* have substantiated the content of the New Testament and of the Apostles' Creed for me. If such specific corroboration of human faith and understanding can and is given, in time, in personal history, in circumstance, in context, in fact, and since such corroboration is consistent with the claims of Christians throughout the centuries and with the recorded claims of Jesus of Nazareth Himself then it is logical to believe in the original truths articulated. If modern human beings, puffed up with their own feeble learning, decide that in no way can these original truths be such, then they deny my own existence and that of so many witnesses to Jesus throughout the centuries. They testify to their own ignorance and lack of humility and not to any objective reality. The exercise of positive and unjust discrimination against someone to whom God has revealed Himself compounds the wilful blindness with which they articulate their chosen reductions and negations of Christianity.

There needs to be a new agenda. Atheism, agnosticism and false religions need to declare themselves for what they are. The Christianity-denying theologian or Biblical scholar, philosopher or literary pundit requires to be saying something like "God has never spoken to me: I cannot conclude that God does not exist or does not speak to some." For far too long we have been told "God does not speak to anyone. God never did. God never will because God is not there." Will all the false professors and lecturers in theological colleges and universities tender their resignations and give up their fat salaries and comfortable livings? Or - will they join us in the repenting tradition? There is a way back for them also! On God's terms revealed in Jesus Christ. Will they give the rest of their lives to redress the spiritual and intellectual devastation which they and their precursors have wreaked on earth for the last two hundred years and more?

The theological left has much to answer for and much to discover about God in Jesus Christ. The gravitational pulling away from incarnational Christology to mere human interpretations of Jesus is politically acceptable in the human community. It is wrong. The political exclusion of those who hold to the truest aspects of Christian understanding from positions of influence in churches and universities compounds the spiritual crime. The liberal establishment of the Church of Scotland, for example has presided over decades of decline. Will it now give way? Have they not sat there long enough?

The theological right must distinguish its desire for Christian orthodoxy from the unredeemed energies and forces which it trails along at the same time in Christ's own Name. A humbler and more wholesome and unifying vocabulary is required. The desire to act as if all knowledge and all revelation has been given to the right must be tempered with a real appraisal of the extent to which personal human will overtakes Christ in conduct, desire for money, business, attitudes to and treatment of other Christians and mission strategy. Voluntary faith is easily exposed for shallowness and hidden enmity with God. Organised certainty and the herd mentality are as likely to exclude improperly as liberalism's extravagant political manoeuvrings.

Anyone who has truly been the subject of God's personal and corroborating revelation is likely to show the paradoxical and seemingly diffident qualities of silence and space. But the loveliest things of God are hidden in this world. They are also hidden in the churches. They are not of the character of the world with its lords and fames, its riches and its presentations. There are no neon signs. No heralds. No pomp. No ceremony. God reveals Himself to those who will not use such precious gifts amiss. Not to build themselves up. Not to set up new churches or movements. Not to become the centre of a personality cult. Not to play power games. Not to bully. To be in fact the negation of all of these. Dependent on the same God in Jesus Christ to prove Himself true. A servant if required. And someone at least to be listened to.

Scotland is a safe place for such a person to live. The culture is not enthusiastic about its sons and daughters who succeed. No one is expected to get above himself. He or she will soon be brought down. Presbyterianism is a safe place for such a person to find context and community. No-one rules O.K. At least - no-one should rule. Spiritual egalitarianism is a blessed thing. Spiritual justice is precious. The possibility of being ignored is built in to Scottish Christianity. Being 'far ben' wi' God' will exclude rather than include.

Factions struggle for power and position and resources in the Church of Scotland and in all churches. Tearing the Church apart, they are in free fall themselves. Political spiritual viciousness transparently holds on to patronage, power and influence. Prayerful and committed evangelicalism struggles to keep up with the internecine machinations of the corrupt. Doctrinal uncertainty competes with doctrinal Faith. And on the Christian Right - there is the unjustified appropriation to the narrow group of claims to ultimate witness.

There is a way. It may be narrow. Not many may be walking on it. The way is that of rejoicing in the truth of God in Jesus Christ Incarnate and Eternal. The way is also a way of humility, of self-negation, within the repenting tradition, distinguishing human self will and God's will, serving others altruistically graced by the Love of Jesus Christ within. These at least are clues to the conditions in which God may make Himself known to us while here on earth. These are at least ways forward which may allow the original redemptive spiritual strength of Pentecost to visit the churches once again. However bad it may seem for the churches of western civilisation, there is hope. If Jesus rose from the dead, no matter how far we fall, there is always a way back. The testimony of my life is that if God can so speak to someone as imperfect as me - then has God not spoken to those whose names appear in the Holy Scriptures? And Has God not indeed visited earth in Jesus? And is there not that once-for all salvation accomplished into which you and I may enter with thanksgiving?

## Right At The Wrong Time

I cannot prove anything. I cannot submit myself to any scientific experiment to prove that God in Jesus Christ exists. God does not submit Himself to the material examination of the human mind. He did once. We murdered Him. There is overwhelming evidence that God in Jesus Christ communicates with, cares for, considers, helps and upholds those who in their lives on earth take their relationship with God seriously. Humorously too. Happily. Victoriously. Sacrificially. Like Jesus. The Lord.

The future belongs to the supernatural and the spiritual. To other worlds and to the life of God. Two hundred years and more of wrong have passed. Thousands of years are yet to come. The pathetic minds of those who deny the existence of God and who cannot accept the gift to the world of Jesus Christ have had their day. The age of the spiritual dwarf is over. Does it not make you glad to know that Jesus was God Incarnate and that by Him each life shall be welcomed or placed at distance from His company. So clear. So simple. So good. So true. It all makes sense.

## Theology Is Biography

We must depart for ever from the conceit that a human being can separate what he or she teaches and claims to be true or untrue from personal biography. This schizophrenic tendency has ruined much of western society. In relation to God no-one has the right to treat God as an object for prejudiced discussion. Everyone who does so is guilty of gossip at best and defamation at worst. And hypocrisy. And error. This most arrogant of human character traits is all too readily found in theological colleges the world over. If there is no living testimony then such people should cease to speak. What have they to say? Second-hand ideas, used concepts. Theological colleges are the charity shops of academia. Discarded doctrines, thrown away principles, unwanted theories. Giveaways. Buy them cheaply. No wonder that Christianity is in such decline. Strong is the hold of spiritual death upon the minds of generations of students. Great is the inhibition which ensures that the Holy Spirit will not sweep through the dying institutions of Christianity and revive them. Calculated are the strategies to enforce the political church upon all. And kill the Christ child within us at each new birth. Theologians and Biblical scholars shared in the responsibility for the murder of Jesus. They tried desperately to suffocate the emerging spiritual life of early Christianity. Their descendants have not changed. And every advocated false opinion reveals their nakedness. Not a pretty sight. Academic striptease. Theology is biography. Transparently so.

## The Falsest Prophets

And what of those who in their lives on earth have steadfastly maintained that there is no God? And what of those who have mocked and persecuted those who have believed? Those who have built great human edifices of stone or words, of empires or theories whose foundations deny God? Who introduce to and bequeath the world a tyranny of griefs. Who diminish spiritual consciousness without disproving it? Who appropriate to themselves a false authority? Who assume false religious messiahship and false divinity? Lenins, Hitlers, Pol Pots, Durkheims, Lawrences, Hawkings, Hubbards, Bagwans. How strange that Jesus should continue to remain above them all. He who was powerless in the world and lived in obscurity. Who was done to death by His enemies. Who was in the world's terms a nothing. Is eternally Everything. How right that He should be above all claimants, pre-eminent in lowliness, justice, truth, grace and self-sacrificial love.

And what of the multitude of scoffers and blasphemers. Those who take life and God for granted. Who care nothing for anyone or anything on earth. Of countless millions who never worshipped God though they had the chance. Who prefer their appetites to prayer and self-glorification to the honour of God. The deliberate agnostics who deep within themselves resist and deny the call of God. And teach their children the same. The utterly selfish. Godless. Drunken men. Good-time girls. Can any power redeem them? Yes. On earth?

> "Every eye shall now behold him,
> Robed in dreadful majesty,
> Those who set at naught and sold him,
> Pierced, and nailed him to the tree,
> Deeply wailing, deeply wailing, deeply wailing,
> Shall the true messiah see."
>
> (Charles Wesley)

## Saints, mystics, disciples, apostles, ministers, servants, martyrs

Let us commend those who have in their lives on earth followed Jesus of Nazareth to a logical conclusion. The heroes and heroines of Christian Mission who often singly carried

Christianity to peoples of the world who in turn voluntarily embraced the Lord. This was not always the pattern of Christian mission and much was associated with and compromised by forms of colonialism. But - among the morass of impure motives, there were genuine souls who believed and lived as if they truly did so, and served and were distinguished by the victims of political, military and economic expansionism. Who actually did some good somewhere. A light still shining. The first generations of apostles, the Celtic saints, pacifist European missionaries, workers of social reform, teachers, preachers, wives and mothers, husbands and fathers. Children - many, many children who in their infancy have known of Christ, who in their childhood did not forget and who in adulthood wrestled with the world and its evils and their own inherited human condition, faithful in humility. A million false media pundits are not the equal of one of these. They remained poor in the world's terms. Some chose this status willingly and with joy. Others sacrificed much voluntarily and involuntarily. Homeless and without work, beaten, imprisoned, tortured, killed. For nothing. For Christ. As He Himself was for us. Of whom the world was not worthy. Is not.

## The Quiet In The Land

The world has many lovely people. Gentle ones. Good neighbours. Kindly of disposition. Prayerful in faith. Anonymous in their millions. Not to God. The sparrow falls. Confessing Jesus Christ in life and with words. God has made His Covenant with them. They have not lived in vain. Heaven is vibrant with their laughter and their worship. And with purifying air. And rushing wind. And angels unnumbered. New bodies for old. Pain unremembered. Tears dried. Victims recompensed. Generously. Incredibly. Unexpectedly. As Jesus said they would be. For He is the corrective to all human aspiration, conduct and action. Who went about doing good, who healed the sick and had compassion, who demanded personal justice of all of us and beyond that self-renouncing love. Who died and rose again according to the Scriptures and is alive for evermore.

I wonder if I might belong with them. I have borne the cross of individuality. The greater cross of publicity awaits. The risks of writing and publishing are great. The seed that is the book falls to the ground. Perhaps in times to come it will bear a spiritual harvest.

It is written for the same reason as the writer of John's Gospel also wrote:

> **"But these have been written in order**
> **that you may believe that Jesus is**
> **the Christ, the Son of God, and that**
> **through your faith in Him you may**
> **have life."** (John 20: 31)

## Purpose

Spiritual biographies often become hagiographies. The intimations of God given to me were given at moments of crisis. They are inseperable from the circumstances in which they are eternally set. I have acted in faith on occasions and taken such risks as a self-interested person might not. But such a person might never follow Jesus of Nazareth. He taught that the Kingdom of God was hidden from those who held themselves to be clever in human society. Cleverness is not the way to God. Especially if it elevates the human spirit against its Maker and oppresses fellow human beings. The whole individual being is to be reconciled to God. Like children resisting innoculation, we fight against what is good for us.

We live public lives, all of us, to some extent. What is hidden will inevitably be revealed. I chose not to write a novel based on actual events but to record the events themselves. And to mention some of the actual people involved. Some will have to answer to God for the nature of their responses as I myself will for the truth of this book. I fear God. I know that God exists and I have discovered that the life of Jesus sets intelligible criteria for relating to this God both in our human existence and in the eternal life to follow. I therefore can have no reason to tell lies on earth since I myself am under the greatest discipline and judgement. Every day. *Coram Deo.* Before God.

The question is whether what has happened to me represents a qualitative contribution to human knowledge. I would contend that it does. Had I kept it all to myself for ever I would have done the human community a disservice. Although I have lived a life of individuality there has been a spiritual reason for this and there has come a time for sharing what, by necessity, I learned in secret. I have paid a social price for loving God more than myself and appearing to love God more than others. We live in such a godless age and for two hundred years and more our scholars and religious leaders have so misled us that it will be an earthquake of a shock to have to take what I have written seriously. Easier to dismiss, psychoanalyse, further persecute, sue, crush, kill.

The power of the Living God is the greatest power. Introduced to our world it creates havoc for human custom and contrived order. It is a whole new way of understanding. This is clearly demonstrated in Jesus Christ and in the disproportionate influence of His one apparently powerless and brief life on earth. I am a witness for Jesus. On earth. But once this most powerful of powers is introduced no-one can tell where the trauma will end. The first role should be in the strengthening of those who believe already in God in Jesus Christ. Thus renewal and revival of churches and congregations and groups of believers is a priority. That in turn will become a vehicle for reaching out in all places with the church as a ready made caring organisation to those outside the circle of faith who would like to believe but cannot do so because they have not found sufficient reason or evidence.

There are social ramifications. What kind of society do we want? Surely we want a society in which God in Jesus Christ can live among us in peace. Spiritual peace. This level of human reconciliation requires a much deeper level of understanding than mere humanistic reconciliation. We need to be reconciled so completely that the peace within us adds peace to the universe. This is a quantum leap in our understanding of how to bring peace to the human community. Only the human spirit reconciled completely to God in and through Jesus Christ will bring peace anywhere. This is a politically incorrect principle. But Jesus was the Prince of Peace. He eschewed military and political violence. Thus He stands above the best representatives of Judaism and Islam. Inasmuch as those of non-Christian religious views accept this distinction and themselves follow His example, then they contribute at least to peace between religions on earth. Let us not forget that millions of Jews went passively to their deaths during the Holocaust. And let us remember too that throughout much of Christian history violence has been visited upon the innocent in the name of this same Jesus. But not with His eternal approval. My understanding is that anyone who has so taken the Lord's Name in vain will have answered directly for such actions and their consequences.

But we must honour Jesus as the Prince of Peace. As God Incarnate. Throughout His world. His people. We may do this non-religiously as long as we do it in the depths of our heart. And in our conduct. Individually and collectively. And politically. For there are political consequences of Christian revelation in the human community. It was ever thus. And here is a can of worms. Of human posturing at leadership. Of lies and the justification of lies. Of huge egotisms and the manipulations of peoples to accommodate them. Of money, much money and the misuse of power. And the discovery of the vivifying effects of *dynamis*, what Henry Kissinger called the ultimate aphrodisiac. The force of energy that exalts and bloats the small human personality into a national and international and historical and even a cosmic entity. For good and ill together. Some only for ill. Few if any for only good.

And it is hard to decide on a fair political application of Christian revelation. It must be based on the concept of *neighbour*. It cannot be Marxism. It cannot be undiluted market philosophy. It must surely be as humane a mixture of already compromised ideas as is possible. There are iniquitous economic imbalances in the world. Always have been. They could be cancelled out. Greed and over-consumption rule so much and so many. Entire systems of government depend on them. They could be obliterated. There are individual geniuses who discover new products which bring linear advancement to human society. These are good. There is no reason not to produce them and sell them. Some industry and commerce seems good enough. Many service sectors likewise. Provision of life's necessities is within God's concern. Enjoyment of life was the original plan. But - living in relationship with God in fully reconciled peace is the means to true and lasting enjoyment. It is because we have not put God first so often that the forces of self-destruction have ruined human history. Christian revelation says that we can have our cake and eat it. We can be reconciled to God and we can enjoy our human life. That is why Jesus came to earth that the world might be saved, from itself, from us, from forces of enmity.

But what we do in life determines at the end of the day the state of our soul. And it does not seem likely that the human population will multilaterally disarm its violent intentions. Christianity will be preserved where individuals accept unilateral spiritual disarmament. If nations seek to follow Jesus politically and disarm then unless that is a total human response one group will simply take advantage with similar results to those of the Holocaust. And in the middle areas of the organisation of society with law and law enforcement, there will be confusion. And so the vision of peace remains as a possibility, an invitation from the Prince of Peace.

The new heaven and the new earth are here already in the souls of those who live in reconciliation to and with God in Jesus Christ. And eternal life is to follow. But as for world peace - that is a different matter. Most human beings desire to live in peace. And their collective good will can achieve much. But Jesus sacrificed His life to bring reconciliation for us and we must remember that great cost.

Is the earth worth it? Yes! Jesus died for it. That is how much it is worth. Every single human life is worth His sacrificial death. That is how our Maker values us. But because His Son died once for all does not mean that we can ignore the consequences of His example. Christianity will survive most effectively where this is recognised and implemented. In the unjust patterns of insitutionalised Christianity such as are too easily found, Christianity meets its death. Deservedly.

There is no pastoral or simple utopia on earth. And that is not the Kingdom of God. We deprive ourselves of the greatest powers of love and peace that exist in our Maker. Some were seen at the time of Pentecost, when the Holy Spirit was spread abroad. Our Maker offers and seeks to infuse our failing and unhappy existence with this transforming relationship of joy and wonder. There is a complete reconciliation within our souls, in human community, internationally, in the cosmos of spiritual powers above. New Agers take note! That is the glory of Christianity, it is the purpose of the Incarnation. The human community has not yet fully discovered the love of God. For us.

There are centuries to come and children yet unborn may know the love of God. Such Grace among us will attract its opposite. Adversaries. This has always been the case. It is unlikely that all human and social and political and cosmic evil will be extinguished. It could be but it is not likely that it will be. The range of unreconciled entities in the universe is large. On earth the same. Our own redeemed hearts are still impure. But let us understand what is on offer. And what might be done. Who knows if humans might not learn. Some. Enough to make a difference.

These thoughts will be to some a cause of wars to come. The Lord said as much Himself. I claim for Jesus Christ His unique place among us. He Himself could effect total peace on earth. But others have their own saviours and messiahs and systems and explanations. And since these are only shadows they will seek to exterminate the genuine One. Again. The prognosis is poor. Always was. Is now. Ever will be.

## The Spiritual Universe

We need to realise that in addition to Immanuel Kant's idea of the moral universe there is *the spiritual universe*. One represents a deeper level of perception and understanding than the other. It is a new testament to Kant's old testament. It is likewise a new testament to the tired philosophies of human beings, the individualistic world-views of authors and film script writers, poets and dramatists. In the spiritual universe there shine many who have found God and who have shared their knowledge with others. Chiefest is Jesus because he was sacrificed for the truth He sought to impart - the truth of His own divinity. And because He lives and is acknowledged by all other claimants and postulants in the spiritual universe to be who He said He was. He does not inhabit some grey intermediate world of spirits but belongs within the very existence of our Maker and Creator. Not alone. Accompanied by unnumbered of *the quiet in the land* and those who have suffered for His own Name and on behalf of goodness and right in this far from neutral world. Many unexpected according to the logic of human society. Considerable disappointments for others. Not limbo. Vibrant superior life. The heights of intelligence and speed and light and authenticity. Restitutions. Recompenses. Forgivenesses. Reunions. Blessed. Joy beyond measure. The opposite of human culture with its grubby systems of awards and tin-pot recognitions.

This is not the static Ptolemaic three-tier universe so mercilessly scorned by anti-fundamentalist pathology. Neither is it a rigid and enclosed system comparable with Newton's laws of gravity. It is not an associate to relativity and quantum mechanics either. It is the extremely subtle and pervading reality on which material forms are based. It is coincident with space and time, though these are human measurements. Unlike observable and controllable experiments, it is personal and relational in character. Thus it is distinguished from theories and plans of the human mind. The Spiritual Universe is the life of our Maker made intelligible and understandable. That someone should live, die and rise from physical death, maintaining the relationships fostered on earth is the scientific key to the possibilities of continuing dynamic relationships with God. It is the future present, here and now. Eternity is not a fixed concept but a relational reality. God is a person in relationship. Christianity has always said so. It is true. To attempt to 'prove' this by human logic and argument alone will not do. But it is no more casuistic a claim than those secular scientific absolutes which depend on their own internal logic and tautological language systems for their own 'proofs.' These - will be disproved by succeeding scientific theories of the same types. Resurrection will not succumb in this way. The Spiritual Universe is the key to humanity's future. Should not our Maker offer us a new vision, a new hope? Should not weary sodden western culture be offered the saving Life of God again, amid our prodigal abandonment of our Maker's love for us? And should not little Scotland, the trampled and exploited over the centuries, the Scotland of 'The Cheviot, the Stag and the Black Black Oil' share in such renewal? Whose Christian forms still hold that God and humans are different, even in Christ. A servant people. Pacifist. Egalitarian. Christ-centred. Neighbour-loving. Flooding the world with the life of God. Saving.

The supernatural exists in *the spiritual universe*. The supernatural exists in and around earth and human life on earth. There is a good supernatural and a bad supernatural. Human beings are not the controllers of these powers. We are vulnerable. Nearly all religion has been an attempt to gain some kind of remission from and control over the supernatural. The supernatural is not superstition, though superstition has often been used as a means of attempting to control the supernatural. Christianity redeems human lives from the fear and penultimate strength of the bad supernatural by bonding us with our Maker whose intelligent personal power is greater than that of the bad supernatural but which includes the good supernatural and more within its own care and love. The bad supernatural in our own culture is manifest for example in the prevalence of astrology and interest and experiment in the occult. Christianity is a saving personal relationship with a good Maker made known in Jesus Christ. The further significance of Jesus Christ is to be found in relation to the bad supernatural. The human community is infested with the bad supernatural. It is in everything, demeaning, injuring, devastating and destroying the best of creation, the best of human living and achievement and the innocence of children. Thus the Genesis story of 'The Fall' is repeated everywhere today in our own culture. For the knowledge that primeval men and women gained was indeed the knowledge of the supernatural. Their interest and curiosity in this powerful reality was harmful to them.

When Jesus of Nazareth walked on earth there were repeated occasional verbal ejaculations channelled through the subconscious of individual human persons from this bad supernatural reality. Christianity is founded on the transparent victory of Jesus of Nazareth over such cosmic supernatural powers including the agent of physical death in humans. The resurrection is therefore the most significant event to have happened on earth because it opens up the knowledge of the reality of our Maker's ultimate power over what we call evil as an objective force which intimidates human consciousness. All of this makes the Bible more understandable. It is not to be set simply against the mental constructs of materialistic and rationalistic human explanations, but against the much higher and more profound realities of *the spiritual universe* and the distinction between the good and the bad supernatural.

The agnostic or atheist lives without taking the reality of *the spiritual universe* into account. This can be a happy ignorance for some. But it misses entirely the point of our existence. Denying the reality of the supernatural is an inner defence mechanism which allows us to think that we are in control of our own destiny and elevates our own decisions and opinions, theories and explanations beyond their humble status. Thus we make gods and goddesses of ourselves and attempt to save ourselves by our own means. We, adrift and drowning in a cosmic ocean are our own lifebelts, rescue ships and rescuers!! Indeed 'The Fall.'

There are in *the spiritual universe* places of strife and quarrelling and recriminations, of arguments and posturing, of contrived authority and prestige and position like the leaders of human society and like so many church leaders. Lording it over their ghastly flocks. Godfathers all. Mother divas competing for every breath. Explaining why things are as they are for them - no better than they were on earth. Having all their reward. The emptiness of their own opinions. Nothing greater. The worst of hells. Masters of their own but no-one else's universe, spiritualistic mistresses with their miserable 'dead' devotees. The display of ego, blind even in eternity. Theatres of the absurd, the contrived, the pornographic.

And children who died of starvation transported past them to their Maker. And those ill-treated, misused, injured, murdered in spirit and in body. Who died anonymously every minute of creation's day. And the prayerful who bore burdens with silence and dignity and grace. Who kept secrets. Brave ones for others. Let no petty pharisaism in churches deny the greater character of heroes and heroines known only to God. Some to us.

And many who sacrificed much for the truth of Jesus Christ and suffered hardship, opposition, persecution and death - only for Christianity. And those who in history died unjustly at the hands of some claiming to be Christians who were not. For Jesus killed no-one and His Kingdom does not live by violence. And many who died for nothing. And those collectively sent to multiple deaths by inhuman regimes, the last ounces of their blood and life cruelly sucked from them by gloating overlords.

And some regarded as wrong-doers, some not all, whose hearts were larger than others and when tested found depths of sacrifice even they did not know existed within them. In fires. Spiritual gold remaining. And all the wrongs of earth put right as we would expect a just and good spiritual parent to do. For God is no-one's debtor. Nor are we brought into life only to be abused, to fail, to seek oblivion as an antidote to our circumstances. And die early. Accomplishing nothing. Not even a decent life.

And repentant hearts - from everywhere under the sun. For the Judaeo-Christian tradition highlights the spiritual fact that it is not human achievement or merit that receives God's affection but our apology for what we have made and not made of our condition. We all know we could have done better. And did not.

*The spiritual universe* is alive and dynamic with all the original powers of creation on view. Answers. Discussion about what humans discovered - the Mind above, behind, beneath, around it all. Quarks and bosons, quavers and minims, image and allegory, colour and contrast, prayer and supplication, healing and salvation. Laughter. Proof. Floating. Exstasis. Worship. Face to face. Friends. Purity. Perfection.

## Eternal Life

For this human life is not the end of anything and leads to something of immeasurable greatness in comparison. Exciting. Dynamic. Fulfilling. Wonderful indeed. Just as the life of Jesus was not simply a moment of human history but an eternal Person in continuing relationship. For that hope given to us in Him many have lived and some have died. Would not the certainty of meeting our Maker make us change our ways on earth? Would not the conditions and criteria taught to us by Jesus Christ of that last assize chasten us? And would that not be the means and the way to the discovery of the many and generous spiritual gifts which can elevate our poor human condition and our manufactured antidotes.

Some will have hard choices to make. Times of testing seem unavoidable for all. The world has not changed since the days of Jesus of Nazareth. Christians need not occupy the ghettoes of modern society - do not call it civilisation. Neither can they order the conduct of the world. We can witness to One who can and does and will. He can bring peace on earth and in the universe. Eternally.

# Index of Names